Gardner *and* Jewler's *Strategies for Success* Work . . .

This CONCISE Fourth Edition is a major breakthrough for enhanced student learning and retention!

Internationally acclaimed for their student success and retention strategies, **John N. Gardner** and **A. Jerome Jewler** make "a major advance" in this new concise fourth edition.

- Self-assessments at the beginning of every chapter and on a **new CD-ROM** customize the learning experience for students

- Research-based "Strategies for Success" throughout the book

- Hands-on instructor training workshops that help you integrate the best teaching strategies and approaches

- The most useful, state-of-the-art online, video, and print resources available today

- Custom publishing options that let you tailor the book to your students' needs

The
CONCISE
Media
Edition of

GARDNER | JEWLER

YOUR **COLLEGE** **4**TH EDITION

EXPERIENCE

SUCCESS

FREE
CD-ROM
INSIDE!

CONCISE
MEDIA
EDITION

Unmatched Expertise

John N. Gardner

A visionary educator, author, and leader of an international reform movement to improve the learning, success, and retention of first year college students, John Gardner is the founding director of the National Resource Center for the First-Year Experience and Students in Transition at the University of South Carolina.

He also served as executive director of the college success course, University 101, for 25 years. This internationally acclaimed program under Gardner's leadership has served as an inspiration for hundreds of similar courses at colleges and universities throughout the U.S. and internationally.

Distinguished Professor Emeritus of Library and Information Science and Senior Fellow for the National Resources Center, Gardner is now Executive Director of the Policy Center for the First Year of College, funded by the Pew Charitable Trusts and based in Brevard College in North Carolina. Gardner has received numerous local and national professional awards including USC's highest award for teaching excellence. He is the recipient of four honorary doctorate degrees recognizing him for contributions to higher education. He was recognized by the American Association for Higher Learning as one of 20 faculty in the U.S. who ". . .have made outstanding contributions to their institutions and/or American higher education." In a 1998 issue of *Change Magazine,* Gardner was included with approximately 80 people as the "past, present, and future leaders of higher education." The *Chronicle of Higher Education* described this same group as "the movers and shakers" and Gardner was included in a special category of 11 "agenda setters."

A. Jerome Jewler

A best-selling author, educator, and lecturer, A. Jerome Jewler has contributed his expertise and guidance to college success education and training since 1972.

During the six years he served as co-director for the University of South Carolina's University 101 freshman seminar program, he reshaped the course, which had focused on a first-year students' personal adjustment to college, to include more academic content and a new emphasis on writing.

In addition, he has conducted teaching workshops at many colleges, training participants to teach college experience courses. For 12 years he was a principal facilitator for the annual teaching institute at the University of Prince Edward Island, Charlottetown, PEI, Canada. He has also served as chair of his college tenure and promotion committee.

In 1996, he won the USC Outstanding Faculty Advisor of the Year award, and received the Mortar Board award for teaching excellence in 1993 and 1997. Now Distinguished Professor Emeritus of Journalism and Mass Communications, Jewler continues to contribute to the freshman year program as a workshop facilitator and author. A lover of theatre, he has dabbled in acting. In addition to *Your College Experience,* Jewler and co-author John N. Gardner have written *College Is Only the Beginning,* and *Step by Step to College Success.* Jewler is a strong believer in active learning and its ability to encourage creative thinking and analysis.

"Professors John Gardner and Jerry Jewler have the knowledge of what works and what doesn't that few can match. That knowledge is contained within the pages of this book. . . . I can't imagine a more comprehensive introduction to the college experience. . . . I have found that in my own institution, where I teach our version of the freshman seminar, their advice works!"

—VINCENT TINTO, author of *Leaving College;* student retention scholar; and Distinguished University Professor, Syracuse University

Our Goal:
To Help *you* Develop the Best Course for Your Students

College Success Workshops . . . your program's success begins here

Wadsworth offers both regional workshops and customized on-site workshops that prepare faculty to teach college success courses and help them design success programs geared for individual campus needs. Topics at these workshops include active learning strategies to engage first-year students, motivating students, using technology, working with peer leaders, and ways to promote critical thinking. Visit our Web site **www.success.wadsworth.com** for a list of upcoming events or call our toll-free consultation phone line for more information.

> **Toll-free telephone consultation services:**
> **1-800-400-7609**
> **for helpful advice and information**
> **about our products and services**

Teaching College Success:
The Complete Resource Guide

by **Constance Staley**

This all-inclusive package contains dynamic PowerPoint presentations combined with an extensive array of print resources—virtually everything you need to train your faculty to teach award-winning college success courses. *Teaching College Success* includes a blend of content information (the nature of the college success course, relevant theoretical approaches, and current national data) and experiential activities for trainers to try with training groups and later with students. Cost: $395.

Sampler package **ISBN: 0-534-53644-1.**

Full product **ISBN: 0-534-53640-9.**

Guiding Principles

Unique among college orientation books, **Your College Experience**—since its first edition—has been based on specific guiding principles presented throughout the book. The original 21 "Keys to Success" and additional "Keys" for minority and returning students have been renamed "Strategies for Success" and organized into five categories that help clarify the major concepts. A total of 32 specific research-proven strategies guide students throughout the text.

Based on the most reliable research into the foundations of success in college, these guiding principles are presented in Chapter One, printed for students' reference on the book's inside front cover, repeated in each part opener of the book, and included on the accompanying CD-ROM. As they are discussed and reinforced throughout the book, they drive home to students how new ways of behaving—often very different from those they practiced in high school—are necessary for their success in college and beyond.

A Book/CD-ROM Package That Actively Engages Students in the Areas They Need Most

- Guides students to the best practices in studying and learning including critical thinking and active learning
- Assists students in making personal choices that impact their success in college
- Synthesizes contributions of dozens of experts in a **NEW** unified voice
- Offers concise coverage that adapts even to zero credit and one-credit courses.

More Exercises

Your College Experience offers the most extensive and well-developed selection of activities ever offered in a first-year text. Types of exercises include:

- **Writing**
- **Journal Reflection**
- **Collaborative Learning**
- **Critical Thinking**
- **Resource Building**
- **Internet and Computer Technology**
- **Self-Assessment**
- **Presentation**
- **Goal Setting**
- **Class Discussion**

Chapter 1 College Makes the Difference 17

Exercise 1.4 The Many Reasons for College

For homework, compare the reasons for attending college in this chapter with your own reasons. How are they the same? How are they different? In a small group discuss the reasons in this chapter for attending college. Share with the group the ones that seem most relevant to you. Compile a group list of the most important reasons and discuss them with your instructor. What did you learn about yourself and your classmates?

Exercise 1.5 Set a Short-Term Goal

- Pick one problem that you can resolve as a short-term goal—one you can complete this week or next.
- Start by discussing this goal with a small group in your class.
- Identify how this short-term goal relates to your long-term goal of success in college.
- In group discussion and writing, complete the six steps for achieving a short-term goal listed in this chapter.
- Establish a date (a week or month from now) when you will determine whether you have achieved the goal. At that time set at least one new goal. Be sure your goal is something you genuinely want to achieve, written down in measurable terms, and achievable.

Also be certain to

- Identify and explore potential problems.
- Create a specific set of steps for achieving the goal.
- Set a schedule for the steps as well as a date for completion.

Your Personal Journal

Each chapter of this book will ask you to write your thoughts about the material you've just read. This is another way to remember the content of the chapter, so you might try it with your other classes as well. Choose one or more of the following questions or choose another topic related to this chapter and write about it.

1. Go back to the list of concerns on pages 8–9. Which of them are you feeling right now? How do you think you can begin overcoming them?
2. Of the five major strategies, which one will give you the greatest challenge? Which will be easiest? Why?
3. Of the many points under each strategy, which do you need to work on most? Suggest some ways to accomplish this.
4. Anything else on your mind this week? If you wish to share it with your instructor, add it to this journal entry.

Emphasis

An Impressive Revision
Built on an Effective Approach

An expanded chapter on critical thinking and writing. Expanding William T. Daly's four-phase approach to critical thinking into a broader context, Gardner and Jewler utilize motivational discussion and activities to show first-year students how to make critical thinking a key tool in their goals for success. This new chapter (5) also delves into the crucial role of writing as a development tool for critical thinking and an effective method for reinforcing learning. In addition, "Critical Thinking" boxes are featured throughout the text.

Memory is now greatly expanded upon, especially in Chapter 8, *Making the Grade: Tests, Memory, Presentations,* helping students become better equipped to master exams and retain important information.

An expanded Chapter 13 on Stress Management includes a streamlined discussion of money and now contains a valuable new section on campus safety (personal property safety, automobile safety, personal safety, and how to get help).

A new "Examining Values" feature integrates coverage of values and integrity throughout the text, giving students on-going guidance on how to approach both personal and academic decisions on campus.

A focus on binge drinking in the revised chapter on alcohol and drugs. Now recognized nationally as the single most troubling college public health problem, binge drinking is effectively addressed in Chapter 14, *Alcohol, Other Drugs, and Sexuality: Making Healthy Choices.* Without becoming preachy, this chapter addresses how students have the power to make choices and the consequences of those choices.

Chapter **13**

Stress
Management

Coping with Tension, Campus Safety, and Money Issues

IN THIS CHAPTER, YOU WILL LEARN

- That stress is natural, but some proven ways can control it
- That rest, exercise, and a healthy diet can help combat stress
- How to protect personal property
- How to move safely around campus
- How to talk yourself into a relaxed mood
- How to manage your money
- How to avoid the "perils of plastic"
- How to seek financial aid for your education

keep your head above water

A Greatly Expanded Activities Program Throughout . . .

SELF-ASSESSMENT: CRITICAL THINKING AND WRITING

Checkmark all items that apply to you. Then read the statement at the end of this exercise.

_____ I frequently allow my emotions to get in the way of making the right decision.

_____ I find it hard to appreciate the achievements of a person if I find that person irritating.

_____ I am quick to reject ideas that I come up with. As a result, I don't come up with many good ideas.

_____ Although it's easy for me to memorize facts, quizzes that require me to explain things are difficult.

_____ I have writer's block. I can stare at a blank page or screen forever before I get even the germ of an idea.

_____ If I didn't have to worry so much about spelling and grammar, I'd be a much better writer.

_____ The more you narrow a topic for a paper, the harder it is to come up with ideas for the paper.

_____ An answer is either right or it isn't.

NOTE: The more items you checked, the more you need to read this chapter to learn how to eliminate the behaviors described in this assessment.

Each chapter begins with a Self-Assessment activity, to spark self-reflection as students explore chapter content.

Exercise 1.4 The Many Reasons for College
For homework, compare the reasons for attending college in this chapter with your own reasons. How are they the same? How are they different? In a small group discuss the reasons in this chapter for attending college. Share with the group the ones that seem most relevant to you. Compile a group list of the most important reasons and discuss them with your instructor. What did you learn about yourself and your classmates?

Exercise 1.5 Set a Short-Term Goal
• Pick one problem that you can resolve as a short-term goal—one you can complete this week or next.
• Start by discussing this goal with a small group in your class.
• Identify how this short-term goal relates to your long-term goal of success in college.
• In group discussion and writing, complete the six steps for achieving a short-term goal listed in this chapter.
• Establish a date (a week or month from now) when you will determine whether you have achieved the goal. At that time set at least one new goal. Be sure your goal is something you genuinely want to achieve, written down in measurable terms, and achievable.

Exercises now located at the end of chapters. By reviewer request, this edition's greatly expanded selection of exercises and activities is now located at the end of chapters. This allows students the flexibility of reading the text without interruption—and gives instructors a clear picture of how the exercises build on one another

New attention to collaborative learning. Backed by the research of collaborative learning specialist Joe Cuseo (Marymount College), this edition shows students how studying in groups can lead to higher levels of retention, and, at the same time, help them develop their speaking and writing skills. New collaborative learning exercises at the end of every chapter give students practice in working within teams.

Internet activities . . . your students' gateway to an online world. Reviewers love these engaging, detailed activities found in every chapter, where students practice the multiple uses of the Internet, from email, to chat groups, to using the World Wide Web for personal and academic research.

New to This Edition

Enhancing the Learning Cycle

Designed to reinforce the content of the text, the cross-platform *Media Edition Student CD-ROM* adds a new level of interactivity to the book's features. Every chapter includes self-assessments that direct your students to the skills exercises, readings, and Internet resources that best meet their needs. In addition to the self-assessments, the CD-ROM's exercises, quizzes, journal writing opportunities, resources activities, and *InfoTrac® College Edition* exercises provide your students with an interactive way to hone their strategies for success.

Features on the CD-ROM

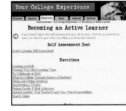

- **Self-Assessments** guide students to the material where they need more practice.
- **Quizzes** reinforce chapter content.
- **Crossword puzzles** are fun to work through.
- **Journal opportunities** allow students to reflect on who they are and where they want to be.
- **Goal Setting** exercises help students develop action plans for success.
- **Resources** activities help students build a reference list for future success.
- **Exercises** adapted from the book give lots of opportunity for practice.
- **Links to the Internet** provide more exercises and on-line resources.
- **Reinforcement of advice** offered in the text helps students master materials.
- *InfoTrac College Edition* exercises help students research more information on their success goals.
- *Franklin-Covey/Premiere Agenda's* mission statement builder exercise helps students discover who they are and what they want to be.

FranklinCovey.

Bonus! Franklin Covey Electronic Planner

In addition, every CD-ROM will contain a **FREE** semester-long trial version of Franklin Covey's electronic scheduler/planner. *Available for Windows only.* **Retail value $99.**

Incredible Online Resources

Four months of FREE access to InfoTrac® College Edition
an online database of hundreds of journals and periodicals

InfoTrac College Edition . . . available exclusively from Wadsworth

The student edition of the text is packaged with FREE access to this online virtual library that can be accessed from students' own computers rather than just at the campus library. *InfoTrac College Edition* opens the door to the full text of articles from hundreds of scholarly and popular journals and publications. **"Search Online" activities in every chapter link students to *InfoTrac College Edition*.** With the help of these great, search-based exercises, it's an easy transition from this book to the extensive *InfoTrac College Edition* database.

Thomson Learning Web Tutor® on WebCT and Blackboard

Take your course beyond the boundaries of the classroom!
Designed to complement Gardner and Jewler's new edition, this content-rich, Web-based teaching and learning tool helps students succeed by taking the course beyond classroom boundaries to an anywhere, anytime environment. *Web Tutor* is rich with study and mastery tools, communication tools, and course content. You can use *Web Tutor* to provide virtual office hours, post your syllabi, set up threaded discussions, track student progress with the quizzing material, and more. *Web Tutor* is preloaded with content specific to the Concise Media Edition and is ready to use as soon as your students log on.

For your students, *Web Tutor* offers real-time access to a full array of study tools, including flashcards (with audio), practice quizzes, online tutorials, and Web links.

ISBN for stand-alone WebCT version: 0-534-55058-4. ISBN for stand alone Blackboard version: 0-534-55060-6.

The Wadsworth College Success Resource Center
www.success.wadsworth.com

This new web service provides current and helpful professional resources including:

- **Training information** for instructors of new and established college success courses
- **Faculty Forum** for sharing ideas with your colleagues around the country
- **Course Tools** to easily create a Web site for your own course
- **Online Instructor's Manuals** and PowerPoint slides
- **The ability to create your own custom textbook online**, by selecting individual chapters or sections from Wadsworth texts and combining them with your own campus materials

ExamView™

ISBN: 0-534-55057-6

Create, deliver, and customize tests and study guides (both print and online) in minutes with this easy-to-use assessment and tutorial system. *ExamView* offers both Quick Test Wizard and an Online Test Wizard that guide you step-by-step through the process of creating tests, while its unique "WYSIWYG" capability allows you to see the test you are creating on the screen exactly as it will print or display online. You can build tests of up to 250 questions using up to 12 question types.

ExamView™ and ExamView Pro™ are trademarks of FSCreations, Inc.

Even More Tools to Enrich Your Course . . .

Annotated Instructor's Manual

ISBN: 0-534-55056-8

Contains the entire text three hole punched with teaching tips plus each of the following subtopics: background on the college success course; information on training faculty and working with peer leaders; ideas for getting the most out of collaborative learning; ideas for promoting more critical thinking; chapter by chapter teaching tips; list of questions students typically ask; ideas for in-class use of exercises; additional exercises, and chapter quizzes.

CNN Today: College Success Video Series

1999–2000 Edition: **ISBN: 0-534-53754-5**. 2000–2001 Edition: **ISBN: 0-534-53799-5**.

Now you can integrate the up-to-the-minute programming power of CNN and its affiliate networks right into your course. Updated yearly, CNN Today Videos are course specific to help you launch lectures and encourage discussion. Organized by topics covered in college success courses, these 45-minute videos are divided into many exciting clips.

College Success Link: Presentation Tool . . . the lecture enhancer

ISBN: 0-534-56409-7

This cross-platform CD-ROM contains charts, diagrams, checklists, and self assessments. Use this CD-ROM in conjunction with your own PowerPoint program for the additional flexibility of adding your own slides, making changes or deleting existing slides, or rearranging the slide order. Available free to qualified adopters.

Transparency Acetates for College Success

ISBN: 0-534-56408-9

A collection of 50 color transparencies focusing on important college success topics. Free to qualified adopters.

Videos for the classroom and independent study

Video Series: Your College Experience: Strategies for Success

This award-winning video series by the National Resource Center for the First-Year Experience and Students in Transition is comprised of twelve 5–7 minute programs. Topics include time management, learning styles, textbook reading, relationships, health issues, and more. **(Call 1-800-400-7609)**

Wadsworth Study Skills Video

Volume I: Improving Your Grades: **ISBN: 0-534-54983-7**

This video features students talking to students and involves viewers in the issues that contribute to their success. It is divided into five parts designed to help students get what they want out of college: *Choosing an Approach to Learning, Making Decisions About Your Time, Learning in Your Class, Making Sense of Textbooks,* and *Taking Tests.*

Wadsworth Study Skills Video

Volume II: Lectures for Notetaking Practice: **ISBN: 0-534-54984-5**

This video features a series of college lectures that provide students with the opportunity to practice their notetaking skills and gives instructors the opportunity to assess student skills.

A World of Diversity Videos

Volume I: **ISBN: 0-534-23229-9**. Volume II: **ISBN: 0-534-23230-2**.

A powerful two-video set on communication and conflict resolution between cultures. Reviewed by African American, Asian American, Latino American, and other multicultural scholars for language authenticity and content accuracy.

Wadsworth College Success Video Series

Qualified adopters may choose from this excellent collection of videos (from the *Films for Humanities and Sciences*) covering such topics as managing stress, improving grades, and maximizing mental performance. Ask your Wadsworth/Thomson Learning representative for a list of videos and policy by adoption size.

Bundle any of the following student resources with this book ... and your students save $!

College Success Factor Index Assessment Tool

Developed by **Edmond Halberg, Kaylene Halberg,** and **Loren Sauer**

Using 80 self-scoring statements, this self-assessment tool is designed to help students discover their strengths and weaknesses in eight important areas that can affect their success in college: responsibility vs. control, competition, task precision, expectations, wellness, time management, college involvement, and family involvement.

Franklin Covey/Premiere Agenda Planner

Wadsworth offers inexpensive planners designed specifically for college students by experts in time management—the Franklin Covey/Premiere Agenda team. Ask your Wadsworth representative for details on our latest calendar offerings.

Critical Thinking: Building the Basics

by **Donald E. P. Smith**, **Glenn Kundsvig** & **Timothy Walter**
One hundred pages of valuable guidance for improving learning through critical thinking. Helps students apply critical thinking strategies to their own textbooks. **Bundle ISBN: 0-534-75185-7**

Wadsworth College Success Internet at a Glance

A handy pocket guide, this tri-fold brochure contains URL addresses for Web sites related to college success such as study skills, learning styles, health, financial management, and career choice. Available FREE and only when bundled with Wadsworth college success texts.

Students Save!

11

Because Every College Experience Course is Different . . .

The **UNBOUND, THREE-HOLE-PUNCHED** *version of*

The CONCISE Media Edition of *Your College Experience: Strategies for Success,* Fourth Edition

This is the easiest way to customize Gardner and Jewler's *Your College Experience Concise* with your own campus-specific materials. Unbound, this version comes with a front and back cover and with all the pages conveniently three-hole-punched so students can create their own course-specific binders. The looseleaf edition comes packaged with *InfoTrac College Edition.*

Or, if you'd like a specially customized text . . .

You can select chapters from this and other Wadsworth college success titles to bind with your own materials (campus maps, syllabi, etc.) into a fully customized book. You can also build your customized book online at Success Online: **www.success.wadsworth.com.**

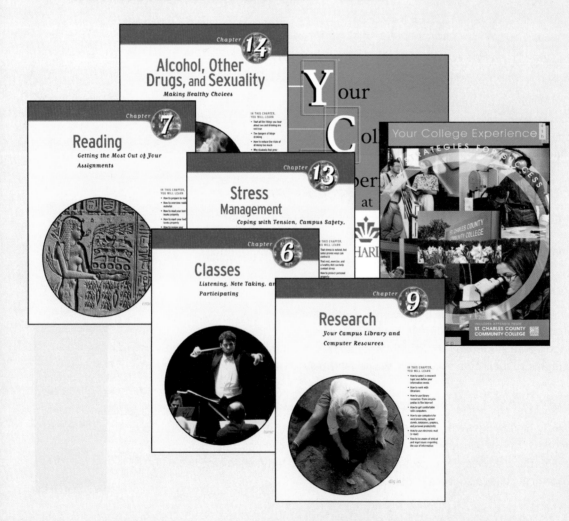

Customized Flexibility!

The Concise Media Edition of
Your College Experience: Strategies for Success, Fourth Edition
Ancillary Correlation Guide

Chapter 1

COLLEGE MAKES THE DIFFERENCE: STRATEGIES FOR SUCCESS

CD-ROM Exercises

Franklin Covey Mission Statement Builder

Self-Assessment

Solving a Problem

Your Reasons for Attending College

Assessing Your Basic Skills

Set a Short Term Goal

Internet Activity: Using the Digest of Education Statistics Online

Key Person Resources

Learning About Campus Resources

Search Online with InfoTrac College Edition

Quiz

Crossword Puzzle

Videos

CNN Today: College Success 2000, 0-534-53754-5
"Student Day"

Transparency Package

Transparency Masters from Annotated Instructor's Manual for *Your College Experience,*
0-534-55056-8
TM 1.1 "Earnings and Education of Males and Females"

PowerPoint Slides

Wadsworth College Success PowerPoint CD-ROM, 0-534-53357-4
PP 14-3 "Covey's Seven Habits of Highly Effective People"

Additional Exercises

Annotated Instructor's Manual for *Your College Experience,*
0-534-55056-8:
Peer Leadership Exercise
"Group Building"
"What I Like About My College"
"Role Playing"
"Interviewing Another Student"

Ancillary Correlation Guide

Ancillary Correlation Guide

Chapter 2

TIME MANAGEMENT: FOUNDATION FOR ACADEMIC SUCCESS

CD-ROM Exercises

Self-Assessment

Logging Your Time and Identifying Priorities

Setting Goals and Priorities

Goal Setting for Courses

Limiting Your Time Online

Your Monthly Plan/Timetable for the Term

Your Weekly Plan/Timetable

Your Daily Plan

Internet Activity: Procrastination

Resources Activity

Search Online with InfoTrac College Edition

Quiz

Crossword Puzzle

Videos

Wadsworth Study Skills Video, Volume 1: Improving Your Grades, 0-534-54983-7

"Time Management" Video from Films for the Humanities and Sciences, 18 minutes, #CAK7082

Video Series: *Your College Experience: Strategies for Success* (Call 1-800-400-7609)

Transparency Package

Wadsworth College Success Transparency Acetate Package, 0-534-56408-9

T 2-1 "Controlling Your Time"

T 2-2 "Task and Time Plan"

T 2-3 "Timetable"

T 2-4 "Scheduling"

Transparency Masters from Annotated Instructor's Manual for *Your College Experience,* 0-534-55056-8:

TM 4.1 "Timetable and Master Plan"

TM 4.2 "Guidelines for Scheduling"

PowerPoint Slides

Wadsworth College Success PowerPoint CD-ROM, 0-534-53357-4

PP 3-2 "Managing Time"

PP 3-3 "Elements of a Task and Time Plan"

PP 3-4 "The Weekly Plan: Questions to Ask Yourself"

PP 3- 6 a & b: "Forms of Procrastination"

PP 3-7 "How to Overcome Procrastination"

Additional Exercises

Annotated Instructor's Manual for *Your College Experience,* 0-534-55056-8

Peer Leadership Exercise

Chapter 3

ACTIVE LEARNING: THE STUDENT-TEACHER CONNECTION

CD-ROM Exercises

Self-Assessment

Learning Actively

Forming Your Ideal Learning Team

To Collaborate or Not?

What Do College Teachers Expect of Students?

Giving and Getting Feedback

Interviewing a Teacher

Finding Faculty E-Mail Addresses

Internet Activity: Your Teacher's—and Your Own—Responsibilities

Search Online with InfoTrac College Edition

Quiz

Crossword Puzzle

Videos

"Strategic Learning" Video from Films for the Humanities and Sciences, 9 minutes, # CAK7079

Transparency Package

Wadsworth College Success Transparency Acetate Package, 0-534-56408-9

T 5-1 "Serious About Learning"

T 5-2 "Participating in Class"

T 5-3 "Overcoming Distraction"

T 6-3 "Types of Collaborative Learning Teams"

T 6-8 "Concept Map of Lecture System"

Transparency Masters from Annotated Instructor's Manual for *Your College Experience,* 0-534-55056-8:

TM 5.2 "Teaching and Learning"

TM 2.1 "How to Show Teachers You Are Serious About Learning"

PowerPoint Slides

Wadsworth College Success PowerPoint CD-ROM, 0-534-53357-4

PP 2-4 "Participating in Class"

Additional Exercises

Annotated Instructor's Manual for *Your College Experience,* 0-534-55056-8

Peer Leadership Exercise

Ancillary Correlation Guide

Chapter 4

LEARNING STYLES: DISCOVERING HOW YOU LEARN BEST

CD-ROM Exercises

Self-Assessment
Your Learning Style: A Quick Indication
Assessing Your Courses and Instructors
Resources Activity
Internet Activity: Learning Style Inventory
Internet Activity:
The Keirsey Temperament Sorter
Search Online with InfoTrac College Edition
Quiz
Crossword Puzzle

Videos

Video Series: *Your College Experience: Strategies for Success* (Call 1-800-400-7609)

Transparency Package

Wadsworth College Success Transparency Acetate Package, 0-534-56408-9
T 4-1 "Myers Briggs Styles"
T 4-2 "Myers Briggs Scales"
T 4-3 "Teaching & Learning Styles"

Transparency Masters from Annotated Instructor's Manual for *Your College Experience,* 0-534-55056-8
TM 5.1 "Learning Styles"
TM 5.2 "Teaching and Learning"

PowerPoint Slides

Wadsworth College Success PowerPoint CD-ROM, 0-534-53357-4
PP 2-1 "Defining Learning Styles"
PP 2-2 "Scales for Myers-Briggs Type Indicator"

Additional Exercises

Annotated Instructor's Manual for *Your College Experience,* 0-534-55056-8
Peer Leadership Exercise
"Working with Other Learning Styles"
"Assessing Your Courses and Instructors"
"Instructor's Learning Style"
"Strategies for Developing Other Learning Styles"
"Learning Styles and Critical Thinking"

Chapter 5

CRITICAL THINKING & WRITING: DEVELOPING CORE TOOLS

CD-ROM Exercises

Self-Assessment

Reflecting on Arguments

Critical Thinking—Unnatural Acts?

Engage by Writing

Freewriting

The Power of Focused Observation

Polishing

Parallels

More and Less Productive Thinking

Resources Activity

Internet Activity: Reflect on Critical Thinking

Search Online with InfoTrac College Edition

Quiz

Crossword Puzzle

Videos

"On Writing" Video from Films for the Humanities and Sciences, 25 minutes, # CSW8661

"Unlocking Language" Video from Films for the Humanities and Sciences, 29 minutes, # CSW8594

Transparency Package

Wadsworth College Success Transparency Acetate Package, 0-534-56408-9
Critical Thinking:

T 7-1 "Characteristics of Critical Thinkers"

T 7-3 "Four Aspects of Critical Thinking"

T 7-5 "Brainstorming"

T 7-6 "Model of Efficient Information Processing"

T 7-7 "Gardner's Seven Areas of Cognitive Ability"

T 7-8 "Thinking Skills in Bloom's Taxonomy"

T 7-9 "The Lakota Medicine Wheel"

Writing:

T 11-1 "Habits of Effective Writers 1"

T 11-2 "Habits of Effective Writers 2"

T 11-3 "Three Steps"

T 11-4 "Writing Problems"

Transparency Masters from Annotated Instructor's Manual for Your College Experience, 0-534-55056-8

TM 3.2 "Three Steps to Better Writing"

TM 3.1 "Four Aspects of Critical Thinking"

PowerPoint Slides

Wadsworth College Success PowerPoint CD-ROM, 0-534-53357-4
Critical Thinking:

PP 2-6 "Brainstorming"

PP 6-5 "Seven Areas of Cognitive Ability"

PP 8-1 "Thinking Skills in Bloom's Taxonomy"

PP 8-2 a & b "Characteristics of Good Critical Thinkers"

PP 8-3 "The IDEAL Method"

PP 8-4 "Good Problem Solvers"

PP 8-5 "Improving Your Reasoning Skills"

PP 8-6 "Keys to Creativity"

PP 8-7 "The Medicine Wheel"

Writing:

PP 9-1 a & b "Habits of Effective Writers"

PP 9-2 "Tips for Saving Your Work"

PP 9-3 "Writing Problems"

Additional Exercises

Annotated Instructor's Manual for Your College Experience, 0-534-55056-8
Peer Leadership Exercise "Participating in Classroom Thinking"

Ancillary Correlation Guide

Chapter 6
CLASSES: LISTENING, NOTE TAKING, AND PARTICIPATING

CD-ROM Exercises

Self-Assessment / Using a Recall Column
Applying an Active Listening and Learning System
Looking Back on Your Notes
Resources Activity
Internet Activity: Study Skills Guides on the Internet
Search Online with InfoTrac College Edition
Quiz / Crossword Puzzle

Videos

CNN Today: College Success 2001, 0-534-53799-5
"Professional Note-Taking"
"Note-Taking" Video from Films for the Humanities and Sciences (featuring the Cornell note-taking system), 8 minutes, # CSW8661
Wadsworth Study Skills Video, Volume 2: Lectures for Note-Taking Practice, 0-534-54984-5
"Listening" Video from Films for the Humanities and Sciences, 15 minutes, # CSW6091

Transparency Package

Wadsworth College Success Transparency Acetate Package, 0-534-56408-9; T 5-4 "Note-Taking Formats"; T 5-5 "Cornell Method Looseleaf Page"; T 5-6 "Sample Lecture Notes"; T 5-7 "The Cornell Method"

Transparency Masters from Annotated Instructor's Manual for Your College Experience, 0-534-55056-8; TM 6.1 "Note-Taking"; TM 6.2 "Sample Lecture Notes"

PowerPoint Slides

Wadsworth College Success PowerPoint CD-ROM, 0-534-53357-4
PP 5-3 a & b "Note-Taking Strategies"
PP 5-4 "Note-Taking Format"
PP 5-6 "The Cornell Method"

Additional Exercises

Annotated Instructor's Manual for Your College Experience, 0-534-55056-8
Peer Leadership Exercise

Chapter 7
READING: GETTING THE MOST OUT OF YOUR ASSIGNMENTS

CD-ROM Exercises

Self-Assessment
Overviewing a Chapter
How to Read Fifteen Pages of a Textbook in an Hour or Less
Resources Activity
Internet Activity: Reading Web Pages Critically
Search Online with InfoTrac College Edition
Quiz / Crossword Puzzle

Videos

"Reading Improvement" Video by Films for the Humanities and Sciences, 11 minutes, # CAK7081

Video Series: *Your College Experience: Strategies for Success* (Call 1-800-400-7609)

Transparency Package

Wadsworth College Success Transparency Acetate Package, 0-534-56408-9; T 6-4 "Your Reading Plan"; T 6-5 "Sample Unmarked Page"; T 6-6 "Handling Different Types of Reading"

Transparency Masters from Annotated Instructor's Manual for Your College Experience, 0-534-55056-8; TM 7.1 "Sample Unmarked Page"; TM 7.2 "Handling Different Types of Reading"

PowerPoint Slides

Wadsworth College Success PowerPoint CD-ROM, 0-534-53357-4
PP 5-7 "Elements of Your Reading Plan"
PP 5-8 a & b "More Strategies to Improve Reading"

Additional Exercises

Annotated Instructor's Manual for Your College Experience, 0-534-55056-8
Peer Leadership Exercise
"Handling Different Types of Reading"

Chapter 8

MAKING THE GRADE: TESTS, MEMORY, AND PRESENTATIONS

CD-ROM Exercises

Self-Assessment
Designing an Exam Plan
Online Exam Schedules
Forming a Study Group
Writing a Summary
Key on Task Words
Introduce Yourself
Writing an Opening
Thoughts on Delivery
Motivation Lists
Study Resources on Campus
Speaking in Public
Memory and Online Tutorial Speaking
Search Online with InfoTrac College Edition
Quiz
Crossword Puzzle

Videos

"Expressing Yourself" Video from Films for the Humanities and Sciences, 20 minutes, #CSW1563

"Speaking" Video from Films for the Humanities and Sciences, 15 minutes, #CSW6092

Transparency Package

Wadsworth College Success Transparency Acetate Package, 0-534-56408-9
Memorizing:
T 6-9 "How To Memorize 1"
T 6-2 "How To Memorize 2"

Taking Exams:
T 8-1 & 2 "Long Term Strategies"
T 8-3 "Short Term Strategies"
T 8-4 "General Strategies"
T 8-5 "Sample Essay Questions"
T 8-6 "Sample Essay Outline"
T 8-7 "Cheating"
T 8-8, T 8-9 & T 8-10 "Cheating"

Transparency Masters from Annotated Instructor's Manual for Your College Experience, 0-534-55056-8
TM 8.2 "Sample Essay Questions"
TM 8.3 "Sample Essay Exam Outline"
TM 11.2 "Steps to Successful Speaking"
TM 11.3 "The GUIDE Checklist"

PowerPoint Slides

Wadsworth College Success PowerPoint CD-ROM, 0-534-53357-4
Memorizing:
6-3 a & b "How to Memorize"

Taking Exams:
PP 7-5 "General Test Taking Strategies"
PP 7-6 "Strategies for Multiple-Choice Questions"
PP 7-7 "Strategies for True/False Questions"
PP 7a & b "Strategies for Essay Questions"

Additional Exercises

Annotated Instructor's Manual for Your College Experience, 0-534-55056-8
Peer Leadership Exercise

Ancillary Correlation Guide

Chapter 9

RESEARCH: YOUR CAMPUS LIBRARY AND COMPUTER RESOURCES

CD-ROM Exercises

Self-Assessment
Some Possible Misconceptions
Key-Word and Subject Searching
Getting Oriented to Periodicals
Rating Your Computer Skills
Know Your Campus Computer Resources and Access
Preventing Disaster
Knowing What Can Be Done
Word Processing Assessment – Beginning and Advanced
Finding Information on the WWW and Learning to Use Email
Library Databases
Researching a Topic
User Support
Bookmarking Useful Sources on the World Wide Web
Search Online with InfoTrac College Edition
Quiz
Crossword Puzzle

Videos

Video Series: *Your College Experience: Strategies for Success* (Call 1-800-400-7609)

Transparency Package

Wadsworth College Success Transparency Acetate Package, 0-534-56408-9
T 6-1 "Refining Basic Academic Skills"
T 9-1 "Touring Questions One"
T 9-2 "Touring Questions Two"
T 9-3 "Sources of Information"

Transparency Masters from Annotated Instructor's Manual for *Your College Experience,* 0-534-55056-8
TM 9.1 "Sources of Information"
TM 10.1 "Ten Questions About Computers"

PowerPoint Slides

Wadsworth College Success PowerPoint CD-ROM, 0-534-53357-4
PP 4-2 "Touring the Library: Questions to Ask"
PP 4-3 "Overcoming Computer Fears"
PP 4-4 "Computer Tools for Academic Works"

Additional Exercises

Annotated Instructor's Manual for *Your College Experience,* 0-534-55056-8
Peer Leadership Exercise
"Using the Library Effectively"
"The Web Versus Usenet Newsgroups"
"Myths and Misconceptions About the Internet"

Chapter 10

COURSE AND CAREERS: UTILIZING ACADEMIC ADVISORS AND OTHER RESOURCES

CD-ROM Exercises

Self-Assessment / Who's Your Academic Advisor? / Advising Process and Schedules / Preparing to Meet with Your Advisor / Finding Some Key Dates / Scoping Out the Catalog / What Are Your Life Goals? / Personality Mosaic / The Holland Hexagon / Exploring New Fields / Writing a Resume and Cover Letter / Resources Activity / Internet Activity: Online Career Assistance / Search Online with InfoTrac College Edition / Quiz / Crossword Puzzle

Videos

CNN Today: College Success 2000, 0-534-53754-5, "College Careers," "Education for Jobs," "Black Engineering," "Girls & Science" **"The Exceptional Employee" Video from Films for the Humanities and Sciences,** # CSW8401 **"Interview Tips: What Employers Want" Video from Films for the Humanities and Sciences,** # CSW8006 **Video Series: Your College Experience: Strategies for Success** (Call 1-800-400-7609)

Transparency Package

Wadsworth College Success Transparency Acetate Package, 0-534-56408-9; T 13-1 "Getting the Right Course"; T 13-2 "Academic Advisors"; T 13-3 "Admissions Advisors"; T 13-4 "Current Resume" **Transparency Masters from Annotated Instructor's Manual for Your College Experience,** 0-534-55056-8; TM 13.1 "My Current Resume"; TM 13.2 "My Ideal Resume at Graduation"

PowerPoint Slides

Wadsworth College Success PowerPoint CD-ROM, 0-534-53357-4 PP 13-5 "Most Important Skills of a Job Candidate"

Additional Exercises

Annotated Instructor's Manual for Your College Experience, 0-534-55056-8 Peer Leadership Exercise "Choosing Courses" "Effective Advisors"

Chapter 11

RELATIONSHIPS: FRIENDS, FAMILY, AND CAMPUS INVOLVEMENT

CD-ROM Exercises

Self-Assessment / Balancing Relationships and College / Gripes / Five Over 30 / Roommate Roulette / Connecting with Campus Organizations / Resources Activity / Internet Activity: Relationships and the Web / Search Online with InfoTrac College Edition / Quiz / Crossword Puzzle

Videos

CNN Today: College Success 2000, 0-534-53754-5 "Americorps," **CNN Today: College Success 2001,** 0-534-53799-5 "Homeless Class" **Video Series: Your College Experience: Strategies for Success** (Call 1-800-400-7609)

Transparency Package

Wadsworth College Success Transparency Acetate Package, 0-534-56408-9: T 15-1 "Eight Keys to Successful Interpersonal Communication"; T 15-3 "Strategies for Keeping Relationships Positive"; T 15-4 "Nonverbal Cues"; T 15-5 "Barriers to Effective Verbal Communication"; T 15-6 "Ten Reasons to Join a Campus Organization"

PowerPoint Slides

Wadsworth College Success PowerPoint CD-ROM, 0-534-53357-4 PP 4-1 "Getting the Help You Need"

Additional Exercises

Annotated Instructor's Manual for Your College Experience, 0-534-55056-8: Peer Leadership Exercise "Learning Axioms of Relationships"

Ancillary Correlation Guide

Chapter 12

DIVERSITY: CELEBRATING DIFFERENCES IN CULTURE, AGE, GENDER, AND ABILITIES

CD-ROM Exercises

Self-Assessment

Sharing Your Background

Creating Common Ground

Combating Discrimination and Prejudice on Campus

Constructive Steps: Advocating for Pluralism

Is Hate Speech Permitted on Your Campus?

Resources Activity

Internet Activity: Questions About Homosexuality

Internet Activity: Diversity in the Population and on Campus

Search Online with InfoTrac College Edition

Quiz

Crossword Puzzle

Videos

CNN Today: College Success 2000, 0-534-53754-5, "Auburn Gays," "University Diversity," "Affirmative Admission," "Diversity Report Card"

CNN Today: College Success 2001, 0-534-53799-5, "Shepard Funeral"

"The Heart of Hatred," Video, featuring Bill Moyers, from Films for the Humanities and Sciences, 52 minutes, # CSW6797

"Understanding Prejudice" Video, from Films for the Humanities and Sciences, 50 minutes, # CSW8038

"Skin Heads, USA: The Pathology of Hate" Video from Films for the Humanities and Sciences, 54 minutes, # CSW6287

"Latin and African Americans: Friends or Foes" Video from Films for the Humanities and Sciences, 44 minutes, # CSW7988

"Without Pity: A Film About Abilities," narrated by Christopher Reeve, the film celebrates the efforts of disabled people to live full lives; Video from **Film for Humanities,** 56 min., # CSW6981

"World of Diversity Video, Volumes I & II," Wadsworth,
Volume 1: 0-534-23229-9,
Volume 2: 0-534-23230-2

Transparency Package

Wadsworth College Success Transparency Acetate Package, 0-534-56408-9
T 16-1 "Attitude Scale"
T 16-2 "Examples of Sexism"
T 16-3 "Improving Relations"

Transparency Masters from Annotated Instructor's Manual for *Your College Experience,*
0-534-55056-8
TM 16.1 "Diversity Attitude Scale"

PowerPoint Slides

Wadsworth College Success PowerPoint CD-ROM, 0-534-53357-4
PP 11-2 "Examples of Sexism"
PP 11-3 "Sexual Harassment"
PP 11-4 "Gender-Based Strategies for Self-Improvement for Women"
PP 11-5 "Gender Based Strategies for Self-Improvement for Men"
PP 11-6 a & b "Strategies for Improving Relations with Diverse Others"

Additional Exercises

Annotated Instructor's Manual for *Your College Experience,*
0-534-55056-8
Peer Leadership Exercise

"Finding Common Ground"

"Hot Topics"

"The New Majority"

"Cross-cultural Skits"

"Listening Actively"

"Expressing Feelings Appropriately"

"A Shared Living Contract"

Chapter 13

STRESS MANAGEMENT: COPING WITH TENSION, CAMPUS SAFETY, MONEY ISSUES

CD-ROM Exercises

Self-Assessment

Your Signs of Stress

Protection From Stress

Adding to and Using the Stress Reduction List

My Annual Budget

Timing Income and Expenses

My Monthly Budget

Applying Critical Thinking to the Money Management Process

Monitoring the Media

The College Readjustment Rating Scale

Self-Assessment

Tracking Stress

Financing Your Education

Internet Activity: Stress, Anxiety, and Relaxation

Internet Activity: Pell Grants

Internet Activity: Myths About Financial Aid

Search Online with InfoTrac College Edition

Quiz

Crossword Puzzle

Videos

CNN Today: College Success 2000, 0-534-53754-5, "College Tuition," "College Costs," "Student Jobs," "Summer Jobs"

CNN Today: College Success 2001, 0-534-53799-5, "Mindful Living," "AIDS 101," "Perfectionism," "College Students and Credit Cards," "Texas A&M Bonfire," "Seton Hall Fire," "College Financing," "College Gambling"

"Saving" (includes 128-page teachers' guide), Video from Films for the Humanities and Sciences, 35 minutes, # CSW8879

Video Series: *Your College Experience: Strategies for Success* (Call 1-800-400-7609)

Transparency Package

Wadsworth College Success Transparency Acetate Package, 0-534-56408-9

T 3-1 "Budgeting"

T 3-2 "Money Managing Process"

T 3-3 "Financial Aid"

T 17-1 "Lifestyle and Poor Health"

T 17-2 & 17-3 "Sleep Better"

Transparency Masters from Annotated Instructor's Manual for *Your College Experience*, 0-534-55056-8

TM 17.1 "Effective Methods for Managing Stress"

TM 20.1 "The Money Managing Process"

PowerPoint Slides

Wadsworth College Success PowerPoint CD-ROM, 0-534-53357-4

PP 3-8 "Budgeting"

Additional Exercises

Annotated Instructor's Manual for *Your College Experience*, 0-534-55056-8

Peer Leadership Exercise "Role Play"

Ancillary Correlation Guide

Chapter 14

ALCOHOL, DRUGS, AND SEXUALITY: MAKING HEALTHY CHOICES

CD-ROM Exercises

Self-Assessment

Personal Reflection on Sexuality

Which Birth Control Method is Best?

What's Your Decision About Safer Sex?

Why Students Binge

Alcohol Usage Questions

A Safe Stress Antidote

Advice to a Friend

Lower the Drinking Age?

Help for Sensible Decisions About Sex

Gathering Information about Alcohol and Other Drugs

Internet Activity: The Core Alcohol and Drug Survey

Internet Activity: Speak of the Devil

Search Online with InfoTrac College Edition

Quiz

Crossword Puzzle

Videos

CNN Today: College Success 2000, 0-534-53754-5, "Drunken Memory"

CNN Today: College Success 2001, 0-534-53799-5, "Binge Drinking," "Drug-Free Dorm," "Definition of Rape"

"The Gender Tango" Video from Films for the Humanities and Sciences, 47 minutes, # CSW7123

"Rape: An Act of Hate" Video from Films for the Humanities and Sciences, 30 minutes, # CSW1055

Video Series: *Your College Experience: Strategies for Success* (Call 1-800-400-7609)

Transparency Package

Wadsworth College Success Transparency Acetate Package, 0-534-56408-9
T 17-7 "Secondary Effects of Binge Drinking"
T 17-8 "Behaviors (Alcohol and Drugs)"
T 17-10 "Annual Consequences of Alcohol and Other Drug Use Among Students"

Transparency Masters from Annotated Instructor's Manual for *Your College Experience,* 0-534-55056-8
TM 18.1 "Risk-Reduction Strategies for Sexual Assault"
TM 19.1 "Annual Consequences of Alcohol and Other Drug Use Among All Students, All Drinkers, and All Bingers"
TM 19.2 "Correlation of Drinks Consumed Per Week and GPA"
TM 19.3 "Secondary Effects of Binge Drinking"

PowerPoint Slides

Wadsworth College Success PowerPoint CD-ROM, 0-534-53357-4
PP 12-4 "Reasons College Students May Increase Their Use of Drugs"
PP 12-5 "Protection Against STDs"
PP 12-6 "Contraceptive Choices"

Additional Exercises

Annotated Instructor's Manual for *Your College Experience,* 0-534-55056-8
Peer Leadership Exercise
"What's Your Decision"
"Social Barometer"
"Media Influences on Sex"
"Role Play"
"Quality of Life"

www.wadsworth.com

wadsworth.com is the World Wide Web site for Wadsworth Publishing Company and is your direct source to dozens of online resources.

At *wadsworth.com* you can find out about supplements, demonstration software, and student resources. You can also send e-mail to many of our authors and preview new publications and exciting new technologies.

wadsworth.com
Changing the way the world learns®

The Wadsworth College Success™ Series

FIRST-YEAR EXPERIENCE/ORIENTATION

Campbell: *The Power to Learn, 2nd Edition* (0-534-26352-6)

Corey/Corey/Corey: *Living and Learning* (0-534-50501-5)

Gardner/Jewler: *Your College Experience, 4th Concise Media Edition* (0-534-55053-3)

Gardner/Jewler: *Your College Experience, 4th Media Edition* (0-534-53415-5)

Gardner/Jewler: *Your College Experience, Expanded Reader Edition* (0-534-51898-2)

Gardner/Jewler: *Your College Experience, Expanded Workbook Edition* (0-534-51897-4)

Gordon/Minick: *Foundations: A Reader for College Students* (0-534-25422-5)

Harbin: *Your Transfer Planner: Strategic Tools and Guerilla Tactics* (0-534-24372-X)

Holkeboer/Walker: *Right From the Start, 3rd Edition* (0-534-56412-7)

Levey/Blanco/Jones: *How to Succeed in a Majority Campus* (0-534-50671-2)

Matte/Henderson: *Success, Your Style! Right and Left Brain Techniques for Learning* (0-534-24468-8)

Petrie/Denson: *A Student-Athlete's Guide to College Success* (0-534-54792-3)

Rowe: *College Survival Guide: Hints and References to Aid College Students, 4th edition* (0-534-35569-2)

Santrock/Halonen: *Your Guide to College Success* (0-534-53352-3)

Smith/Walter: *The Adult Learner's Guide to College Success* (0-534-23298-1)

Staley: *Teaching College Success* (sampler 0-534-53644-1)(full product 0-534-53640-9)

Steltenpohl/Shipton/Vilines: *Orientation to College—A Reader on Becoming an Educated Person* (0-534-26484-0)

Thornton/Wahlstrom/Williams: *The Urban Student* (0-534-52893-7)

Wahlstrom/Williams: *The Commuter Student* (0-534-53289-6)

Wahlstrom/Williams: *Learning Success, 2nd Edition* (0-534-53424-4)

Wahlstrom/Williams: *The Practical Student* (0-534-53406-6)

STUDY SKILLS/CRITICAL THINKING

Hettich: *Learning Skills for College and Career, 2nd edition* (0-534-34878-5)

Kurland: *I Know What It Says. What Does It Mean?* (0-534-24486-6)

Longman/Atkinson: *CLASS: College Learning and Study Skills, 5th Edition* (0-534-54972-1)

Longman/Atkinson: *SMART: Study Methods and Reading Techniques, 2nd Edition* (0-534-54981-0)

McKay: *Reasons, Explanations, and Decisions: Guidelines for Critical Thinking* (0-534-57411-4)

Smith/Knudsvig/Walter: *Critical Thinking: Building the Basics* (0-534-19284-X)

Sotiriou: *Integrating College Study Skills: Reasoning in Reading, Listening and Writing, 5th Edition* (0-534-54990)

Van Blerkom: *College Study Skills, 3rd* (0-534-56349-5)

Van Blerkom: *Orientation to College Learning, 2nd Edition* (0-534-52389-7)

Watson: *Strategies for Success in College and Life* (0-534-56161-6)

Your College Experience

Strategies for Success

FOURTH CONCISE MEDIA EDITION

JOHN N. GARDNER

Distinguished Professor Emeritus, Library and Information Science
Senior Fellow, National Resource Center for the First-Year Experience and
    Students in Transition
University of South Carolina, Columbia

Executive Director
Policy Center for the First Year of College
Distinguished Professor of Educational Leadership
Brevard College

A. JEROME JEWLER

Distinguished Professor Emeritus, College of Journalism and Mass Communication
University of South Carolina, Columbia

Wadsworth
Thomson Learning

AUSTRALIA • CANADA • MEXICO • SINGAPORE • SPAIN • UNITED KINGDOM • UNITED STATES

Executive Manager, College Success: Elana Dolberg
Development Editor: Sherry Symington
College Success Assistant: Sally Cobau
Print Buyer: Barbara Britton
Permissions Editor: Joohee Lee
Production Service: Cecile Joyner/
  The Cooper Company
Text Designer: Paul Uhl Associates
Photo Reseacher: Terri Wright
Copy Editor: Betty Duncan
Indexer: Kay Banning
Cover Designer: Stephen Rapley
Compositor: New England Typographic Service
Printer/Binder: Transcontinental

LB
2343.32
.G35
2001

Printed in Canada

1 2 3 4 5 6 7 04 03 02 01 00

For permission to use material from this
text, contact us by
  web: http://www.thomsonrights.com
  fax: 1-800-730-2215
  phone: 1-800-730-2214

**Library of Congress
Cataloging-in-Publication Data**
Gardner, John N.
  Your college experience: strategies for success/
John N. Gardner, A. Jerome Jewler—
4th concise ed.
    p. cm.
  In earlier editions of this work the chapters were
written by various authors; the text of this edition
was written by Gardner and Jewler.
  Includes bibliographical references and index.
  ISBN 0-534-55053-3
  1. College student orientation—United States.
  2. Study skills—United States. 3. Critical think
ing—United States. 4. Success—United States. I.
Jewler, A. Jerome. II. Title.

LB2343.32.Y68 2000
378.1'98—dc21   00-028331

This book is printed on
acid-free recycled paper

Photograph Credits
Page 3, PhotoDisc; **5,** Less Todd/Photo Courtesy of Duke
University; **7,** photo courtesy of Bill Denison; **21,** Oliver
Pinchart/The Image Bank; **25,** CORBIS; **37,** Tad
Yoshida/Photo Researchers; **42,** Dollarhide/Monkmeyer
Press Photo; **45,** Photo © David Weintraub/Photo
Researchers, Inc.; **51,** Tony Freeman/Photo Edit; **53,**
Jeffery Titcomb/Stock Connection/PNI; **53,** State
University of West Georgia; **65,** David Young Wolff/Photo
Edit; **69,** ©1992 Chuck Savage/Photo courtesy of Beloit
College; **71,** Photo by David Gonzales; **79,** Alvis
Upitis/The Image Bank; **82,** Photo by David Gonzales;
93, CORBIS; **98,** Pages adapted with permission from
James W. Kalat, *Introduction to Psychology,* 4th ed.,
Pacific Grove, CA (Brooks/Cole/1996); **100,** Tom
Jorgenson/Photo courtesy of the University of Iowa; **107,**
William Saliaz/CORBIS; **129,** Tim Wright/CORBIS; **132,**
Jon Riley/Tony Stone Images; **134,** Bob Kramer/Stock,
Boston; **138,** John Henley/The Stock Market; **142,** Photo
courtesy of University of Utah; **153,** Richard
Cummins/CORBIS; **156,** © Brian Smith/Stock, Boston;
159, © Rogers/Monkmeyer Press Photo; **173,** PhotoDisc;
178, Dollarhide/Monkmeyer; **187,** Mark Harwood/Tony
Stone Images; **192,** Courtesy of Earlham College; **192,**
Angela Mann; **194,** Michael Newman/Photo Edit; **195,**
Jonathan Nourok/PhotoEdit; **203,** Mark M. Lawrence/The
Stock Market; **207,** Rob Gage/PNI; **211,** Deborah
Davis/PhotoEdit; **215,** John Maher/PNI; **223,** Stephen
Frisch/Stock, Boston; **228,** Matthew McVay/Allstock/PNI;
232, A. Ramey/PhotoEdit; **238,** Heather Dutton.

For more information, contact
Wadsworth/Thomson Learning
10 Davis Drive
Belmont, CA 94002-3098
USA
http://www.wadsworth.com

International Headquarters
Thomson Learning
International Division
290 Harbor Drive, 2nd Floor
Stamford, CT 06902-7477
USA

UK/Europe/Middle East/South Africa
Thomson Learning
Berkshire House
168-173 High Holborn
London WC1V 7AA
United Kingdom

Asia
Thomson Learning
60 Albert Street, #15-01
Albert Complex
Singapore 189969

Canada
Nelson/Thomson Learning
1120 Birchmount Road
Scarborough, Ontario M1K 5G4
Canada

Brief Table of Contents

Part 1 Strategies for Success 1

Chapter 1 College Makes the Difference:
Strategies for Success 3

Part 2 Plan Ahead! 19

Chapter 2 Time Management:
Foundation of Academic Success 21

Part 3 Take Charge of Learning! 35

Chapter 3 Active Learning:
The Student-Teacher Connection 37

Chapter 4 Learning Styles:
Discovering How You Learn Best 51

Chapter 5 Critical Thinking and Writing:
Developing Core Tools 65

Part 4 Hone Your Skills! 77

Chapter 6 Classes:
Listening, Note Taking, and Participating 79

Chapter 7 Reading:
Getting the Most Out of Your Assignments 93

Chapter 8 Making the Grade:
Tests, Memory, and Presentations 107

Chapter 9 Research:
Your Campus Library and Computer Resources 129

Part 5 Get Connected! 151

Chapter 10 Courses and Careers:
Utilizing Academic Advisors and Other Resources 153

Chapter 11 Relationships:
Friends, Family, and Campus Involvement 173

Chapter 12 Diversity:
Celebrating Differences in Culture, Age, Gender, and Abilities 187

Part 6 Know Yourself! 201

Chapter 13 Stress Management:
Coping with Tension, Campus Safety, and Money Issues 203

Chapter 14 Alcohol, Other Drugs, and Sexuality:
Making Healthy Choices 223

Contents

Part 1   Strategies for Success   1

Chapter 1   College Makes the Difference: Strategies for Success   3

SELF-ASSESSMENT: Success   4

Five Key Strategies   5

Plan Ahead   5

Take Charge of Learning   6

Hone Your Skills   6

Get Connected   7

Know Yourself   8

Easing the Transition   8

CRITICAL THINKING: Successful Strategies   9

Defining Values   9

EXAMINING VALUES   10

Those Who Start and Those Who Finish   10

First-Year Questions of Freedom and Commitment   10

WHAT TODAY'S STUDENTS REALLY WANT ARE JOBS THAT PAY WELL   11

Education, Careers, and Income   12

Liberal Education and Quality of Life   12

Setting Goals for Success   13

WHERE TO GO FOR HELP   14

SEARCH ONLINE!   Welcome to InfoTrac College Edition   15

Exercises   15–17

SEARCH ONLINE!   **Internet Exercise 1.1:** Using the *Digest of Education Statistics* Online; **Internet Exercise 1.2:** Discovering More About the Value of College

ADDITIONAL EXERCISES   **Exercise 1.1:** Solving a Problem; **Exercise 1.2:** Focusing on Your Concerns; **Exercise 1.3:** Your Reasons for Attending College; **Exercise 1.4:** The Many Reasons for College; **Exercise 1.5:** Set a Short-Term Goal

Your Personal Journal   17

Resources   18

Part 2   Plan Ahead!   19

Chapter 2   Time Management: Foundation of Academic Success   21

SELF-ASSESSMENT: Time Management   22

Setting Priorities: Assessing Your Use of Time   23

Developing a Master Plan   23

Guidelines for Scheduling Week by Week   23

Organizing Your Day   25

Making Your Time Management Plan Work   26

EXAMINING VALUES   26

Reduce Distractions   26

Beat Procrastination   26

CRITICAL THINKING: Setting Goals and Priorities   27

Time and Critical Thinking 27

Exercises 28–33

SEARCH ONLINE! **Internet Exercise 2.1:** Limiting Your Time Online; **Internet Exercise 2.2:** Procrastination Resources; **Internet Exercise 2.3:** Discovering More About Time Management

ADDITIONAL EXERCISES **Exercise 2.1:** Logging Your Time and Identifying Priorities; **Exercise 2.2:** Goal Setting for Courses; **Exercise 2.3:** Your Weekly Plan/Timetable; **Exercise 2.4:** Your Daily Plan

Your Personal Journal 32

Resources 34

Part 3 Take Charge of Learning! 35

Chapter 3 Active Learning: The Student-Teacher Connection 37

The Big Difference Between High School and College 38

SELF-ASSESSMENT: Active Learning 38

Why You'll Learn Better as an Active Learner 38

Why Active Learners Can Learn More Than Passive Learners 39

EXAMINING VALUES 40

The 1-Minute Paper 41

The Value of Collaboration 41

Making Learning Teams Productive 41

THE MANY USES OF LEARNING TEAMS 42

Connecting with Your College Teachers 43

CRITICAL THINKING: What Do College Teachers Expect of Students? 43

Making the Most of a Student-Teacher Relationship 44

Learning Actively 44

From Certainty to Healthy Uncertainty 44

Academic Freedom in the Classroom 45

FINDING A MENTOR 45

When Things Go Wrong Between You and a Teacher 46

Exercises 47–49

SEARCH ONLINE! **Internet Exercise 3.1:** Your Teachers'–and Your Own–Responsibilities; **Internet Exercise 3.2:** Finding Faculty E-Mail Addresses; **Internet Exercise 3.3:** Discovering More About College Teachers and Learning

ADDITIONAL EXERCISES **Exercise 3.1:** Differences Between High School and College; **Exercise 3.2:** Learning Actively; **Exercise 3.3:** To Collaborate or Not?; **Exercise 3.4:** Forming Your Ideal Learning Team; **Exercise 3.5:** Interviewing a Teacher; **Exercise 3.6:** A Teaching Experience

Your Personal Journal 49

Resources 50

Chapter 4 Learning Styles: Discovering How You Learn Best 51

SELF-ASSESSMENT: Learning Preferences 52

An Informal Measure of Learning Style 53

Classroom Behavior and Learning Style 53

Personality Preferences and Learning Style 54

CRITICAL THINKING: Stick with Your Own Type or Seek Out Other Types? 55

Strengths and Weaknesses of the Types 55

EXAMINING VALUES 56

Using Knowledge of Your Learning Style 57

IMPROVING YOUR LESS DOMINANT LEARNING STYLES 57

Study Groups and Learning Styles 57

Dealing with Your Instructors' Teaching Styles 58

Clues to Instructors' Teaching Styles 58

Exam Preparation and Learning/Teaching Styles 58

Exercises 59–63

SEARCH ONLINE! **Internet Exercise 4.1:** Learning-Style Inventory; **Internet Exercise 4.2:** Discovering More About Learning-Style Theory

ADDITIONAL EXERCISES **Exercise 4.1:** Your Learning Style–A Quick Indication; **Exercise 4.2:** Assessing Your Learning Style; **Exercise 4.3:** Assessing Your Courses and Instructors

Your Personal Journal 63
Resources 64

Chapter 5   Critical Thinking and Writing: Developing Core Tools 65

SELF-ASSESSMENT: Critical Thinking and Writing 66
How College Encourages Critical Thinking 67
EXAMINING VALUES 67
Four Aspects of Critical Thinking 68
  1. Abstract Thinking: Discovering Larger Ideas from Details 68
  2. Creative Thinking: Finding New Possibilities 68
    CRITICAL THINKING: Unnatural Acts? 68
  3. Systematic Thinking: Organizing the Possibilities 69
  4. Precise Communication of Your Ideas to Others 69
Writing to Think and to Communicate 69
  Explore First and Explain Later 69
Three Steps to Better Writing 70
  Prewriting for Ideas 70
  Writing for Organization 71
  Rewriting to Polish 72
  Allocating Your Time for Writing 72
Some Good and Bad Habits in Thinking and Writing 72
Exercises 73–75

SEARCH ONLINE! **Internet Exercise 5.1:** Critical Thinking Resources; **Internet Exercise 5.2:** Discovering More About Critical Thinking and Writing

ADDITIONAL EXERCISES **Exercise 5.1:** Reflecting on Arguments; **Exercise 5.2:** The Challenge of Classroom Thinking; **Exercise 5.3:** Engage by Writing; **Exercise 5.4:** The Power of Focused Observation; **Exercise 5.5:** Parallels

Your Personal Journal 75
Resources 76

Part 4   Hone Your Skills!   77

Chapter 6   Classes: Listening, Note Taking, and Participating 79

SELF-ASSESSMENT: Listening, Note Taking, and Participating 80
Short-Term Memory: Listening and Forgetting 81
Before Class: Prepare to Remember 82
During Class: Listen Critically and Take Good Notes 83
  Listen for Information 83
  EXAMINING VALUES 83
  Take Effective Notes 84
  Note Taking in Nonlecture Courses 84
  Comparing Notes 85
  OTHER KINDS OF NOTES 85
  Class Notes and Homework Problems 86
  Computer Notes in Class? 86
After Class: Respond, Recite, and Review 86
  Remember and Respond 86
  Fill In the Recall Column, Recite, and Review 87
    CRITICAL THINKING: Determining Main Ideas and Major Details 87
Participating in Class: Speak Up! 88

Exercises   90–91

SEARCH ONLINE!   **Internet Exercise 6.1:** Study Skill Guides on the Internet; **Internet Exercise 6.2:** Discovering More About Listening and Learning

ADDITIONAL EXERCISES   **Exercise 6.1:** Listening and Memory; **Exercise 6.2:** Comparing Notes; **Exercise 6.3:** Memory–Using a Recall Column; **Exercise 6.4:** Applying an Active Listening and Learning System

Your Personal Journal   91

Resources   92

Chapter 7   Reading: Getting the Most Out of Your Assignments   93

Preparing to Read   94

Overviewing   94

SELF-ASSESSMENT: Evaluating Your Reading Strengths and Weaknesses   94

Mapping   95

Reading Your Textbook   96

Building Concentration and Understanding   96

CRITICAL THINKING: Reading to Question, Interpret, and Understand   96

Marking Your Textbook   97

Monitoring   97

EXAMINING VALUES   97

Recycle Your Reading   100

Reviewing   100

Adjusting Your Reading Style   100

Another Study Method: SQ3R   101

Developing Vocabulary   101

Exercises   102–104

SEARCH ONLINE!   **Internet Exercise 7.1:** Reading Web Pages Critically; **Internet Exercise 7.2:** Discovering More About Reading Texts

ADDITIONAL EXERCISES   **Exercise 7.1:** Overviewing and Creating a Visual Map; **Exercise 7.2:** Preparing to Read, Think, and Mark; **Exercise 7.3:** How to Read Fifteen Pages of a Textbook in 1 Hour or Less; **Exercise 7.4:** Expanding Your Vocabulary

Your Personal Journal   104

Resources   105

Chapter 8   Making the Grade: Tests, Memory, and Presentations   107

SELF-ASSESSMENT: Test Taking   108

Academic Honesty   109

Types of Misconduct   109

Reducing the Likelihood of Problems   110

DOES CHEATING HURT ANYONE?   110

EXAMINING VALUES   111

Exams: The Long View   111

Planning Your Approach   112

Physical Preparation   112

Mental Preparation   112

Find Out About the Test   112

Design an Exam Plan   113

Join a Study Group   113

Tutoring and Other Support   113

EMERGENCY? YOUR INSTRUCTOR NEEDS TO KNOW   113

Now It's Time to Study   114

Recall Sheets and Mind Maps   114

Summaries   114

Taking the Test   115

Essay Exams   115

CRITICAL THINKING: Key on Task Words   117

Multiple-Choice Exams   117

True/False Exams   118

Matching Exams   118
Aids to Memory   118
Succeeding at Presentations   120
Steps to a Successful Presentation   120
1. Clarify Your Objective   120
2. Analyze Your Audience   120
3. Collect and Organize Your Information   120
4. Choose Your Visual Aids   123
5. Prepare Your Notes   123
6. Practice Your Delivery   124
Using Your Voice and Body Language   124
A Final Word   124
Exercises   125–127
SEARCH ONLINE! **Internet Exercise 8.1:** Examining Institutional Values; **Internet Exercise 8.2:** More Memory Devices; **Internet Exercise 8.3:** Discovering More About Making the Grade
ADDITIONAL EXERCISES **Exercise 8.1:** Designing an Exam Plan; **Exercise 8.2:** Forming a Study Group; **Exercise 8.3:** Writing a Summary; **Exercise 8.4:** Writing an Opening
Your Personal Journal   127
Resources   128

Chapter 9   Research: Your Campus Library and Computer Resources   129
SELF-ASSESSMENT: Library and Computer Skills   130
Get a Grip on the Library   131
Selecting and Surveying a Topic   131
Defining Your Need for Information   131
Talking to Librarians   132
Finding Your Way   132
General Encyclopedias   132
Subject Encyclopedias   133
Catalogs   134
Indexes   134
Information Databases   135
Periodicals   135
World Wide Web Information Resources   135
Going Directly to a Website   136
Using a Subject Dictionary   136
Using a Search Engine   136
CRITICAL THINKING: Evaluating Sources   137
Computing for College Success   137
What You Need to Know   138
What if You Don't Feel Comfortable with Computers?   138
Computer Basics   139
Keyboarding   139
Accessing Computers   139
Finding the Right Kind of Help   139
EXAMINING VALUES   140
Preventing Disaster   140
Computer Applications   141
Word Processing (Writing)   141
Spreadsheets   141
Databases   141
Graphics and Presentation Software   142
Personal Productivity Software   142
Communication over the Internet   142
Electronic Mail–Some Basics   143
Ethical and Legal Issues   144
Exercises   144–148
SEARCH ONLINE! **Internet Exercise 9.1:** Finding Information on the World Wide Web; **Internet Exercise 9.2:** Learning to Use E-Mail; **Internet Exercise 9.3:** Discovering More About Libraries and Computers

ADDITIONAL EXERCISES **Exercise 9.1:** Key-Word and Subject Searching; **Exercise 9.2:** Getting
Oriented to Periodicals; **Exercise 9.3:** Rating Your Computer Skills; **Exercise 9.4:**
Preventing Disaster; **Exercise 9.5:** Word Processing; **Exercise 9.6:** Computer Ethics
Your Personal Journal   148
Resources   149

Part 5   Get Connected!   151

Chapter 10   Courses and Careers: Utilizing Academic Advisors and Other Resources   153

Learning from Your Academic Advisor/Counselor   154
SELF-ASSESSMENT: Majors and Careers   154
Preparing for Your Meeting   155
Is Your Advisor/Counselor Right for You?   155
WHAT ARE YOU LOOKING FOR IN YOUR ACADEMIC ADVISOR?   155
EXAMINING VALUES   156
Your College Catalog 156
What's in the Catalog?   156
Planning for Your Career   157
Majors = Careers? Not Always   157
CRITICAL THINKING: Courses and Careers   158
Factors in Your Career Planning   158
Time for Action   161
Building a Résumé   161
The Cover Letter   163
More Things You Can Do   163
Exercises   165–170
SEARCH ONLINE! **Internet Exercise 10.1:** Internet Career Resources; **Internet Exercise 10.2:**
Discovering More About Courses and Careers
ADDITIONAL EXERCISES **Exercise 10.1:** Your Academic Advisor/Counselor; **Exercise 10.2:**
Finding Your Catalog and Starting a File; **Exercise 10.3:** Recording Key Dates; **Exercise 10.4:**
What Are Your Life Goals?; **Exercise 10.5:** Personality Mosaic; **Exercise 10.6:** The Holland
Hexagon; **Exercise 10.7:** Writing a Résumé and Cover Letter
Your Personal Journal   171
Resources   172

Chapter 11   Relationships: Friends, Family, and Campus Involvement   173

Dating and Mating   174
Loving an Idealized Image   174
SELF-ASSESSMENT: Relationships   174
Sexual Orientation   175
Developing a Relationship   175
EXAMINING VALUES   176
Becoming Intimate   176
Getting Serious   177
Breaking Up   177
Married Life in College   178
You and Your Parents   178
Friends   179
Roommates   180
Campus Involvement   180
CRITICAL THINKING: Relationships   180
LEARNING THROUGH SERVICE   181
Exercises   182–185
SEARCH ONLINE! **Internet Exercise 11.1:** Relationships and the Web; **Internet Exercise 11.2:**
Discovering More About Relationships

ADDITIONAL EXERCISES **Exercise 11.1:** Balancing Relationships and College; **Exercise 11.2:** Gripes; **Exercise 11.3:** Five over Age 30; **Exercise 11.4:** Common Roommate Gripes; **Exercise 11.5:** Connecting with Campus Organizations

Your Personal Journal 185

Resources 186

Chapter 12 Diversity: Celebrating Differences in Culture, Age, Gender, and Abilities 187

SELF-ASSESSMENT: Diversity 188

Expanding Our View of Diversity 189

EXAMINING VALUES 190

Race, Ethnic Groups, and Culture 190

Cultural Pluralism: Replacing the Melting Pot with Vegetable Stew 191

A Diverse Campus Culture 192

"I KNOW I WILL ALWAYS HAVE A CAUSE I AM FIGHTING FOR" 193

THE NEW MAJORITY 194

CRITICAL THINKING: Diversity 195

Discrimination and Prejudice on College Campuses 195

Exercises 196–198

SEARCH ONLINE! **Internet Exercise 12.1:** Questions About Homosexuality; **Internet Exercise 12.2:** Diversity in the Population and on Campus; **Internet Exercise 12.3:** Discovering More About Diversity

ADDITIONAL EXERCISES **Exercise 12.1:** Sharing Your Background; **Exercise 12.2:** Creating Common Ground; **Exercise 12.3:** Getting the Diversity Facts on Your Campus; **Exercise 12.4:** Checking Your Understanding; **Exercise 12.5:** Combating Discrimination and Prejudice on Campus; **Exercise 12.6:** Is Hate Speech Permitted on Your Campus?

Your Personal Journal 199

Resources 200

Part 6 Know Yourself! *201*

Chapter 13 Stress Management: Coping with Tension, Campus Safety, and Money Issues 203

A Healthy Lifestyle 204

SELF-ASSESSMENT: Stress, Campus Safety, and Money Issues 204

When You Are Tense 205

Identifying Your Stress 205

START HEALTHY 206

A Stress-Relief Smorgasbord 207

Get Physical 207

ROAD WARRIOR 207

Get Mental 208

Get Spiritual 208

Use Mind and Body Together 208

Develop New Skills 209

A RELAXATION PROCESS 209

Stress and Campus Crime 210

Personal Property Safety 210

Automobile Safety 210

Personal Safety 210

EXAMINING VALUES 211

Alcohol and Crime 212

A Word About Victims 212

Stress and Money 212

Analysis 212

CRITICAL THINKING: Managing Money 214

Planning 214

Budgeting   215
THE PERILS OF PLASTIC   215
Increasing Resources   216
Financial Aid   216
Work Opportunities   217
Applying for Financial Aid   217
A Final Word   217
Exercises   218–220
SEARCH ONLINE!   **Internet Exercise 13.1:** Stress, Anxiety, and Relaxation; **Internet Exercise 13.2:** Pell Grants and Scholarships; **Internet Exercise 13.3:** Discovering More About Stress, Campus Safety, and Money Management
ADDITIONAL EXERCISES   **Exercise 13.1:** The College Readjustment Rating Scale; **Exercise 13.2:** Protection from Stress; **Exercise 13.3:** Setting Priorities; **Exercise 13.4:** Monitoring the Media
Your Personal Journal   221
Resources   222

Chapter 14   Alcohol, Other Drugs, and Sexuality: Making Healthy Choices   223

Alcohol Ups and Downs   224
SELF-ASSESSMENT: Alcohol, Other Drugs, and Sexuality   224
Why Do College Students Drink?   225
Truths, Not Perceptions   225
Binge Drinking   225
"THE POLICE GOT ME DRUNK. HONEST."   226
What Should *You* Do?   229
Other Drugs   230
Marijuana   230
Cocaine   231
Methamphetamine   231
Tobacco–The Other Legal Drug   231
Making Decisions and Finding Help   232
Sex and the College Student   232
EXAMINING VALUES   233
Birth Control   233
Sexually Transmitted Diseases (STDs)   235
Preventing Sexually Transmitted Diseases   237
CRITICAL THINKING: Alcohol, Drugs, and Sex   238
CONDOMS   239
Perilous Relationships   239
Abusive Relationships   239
Avoiding Sexual Assault   240
Relationships with Teachers   240
A Final Word   241
Exercises   241–243
SEARCH ONLINE!   **Internet Exercise 14.1:** The Core Alcohol and Drug Survey; **Internet Exercise 14.2:** Speak of the Devil; **Internet Exercise 14.3:** Discovering More About Alcohol, Drugs, and Sex
ADDITIONAL EXERCISES   **Exercise 14.1:** Why Students Binge; **Exercise 14.2:** A Safe Stress Antidote; **Exercise 14.3:** Advice to a Friend; **Exercise 14.4:** Which Birth Control Method Is Best?; **Exercise 14.5:** What's Your Decision?
Your Personal Journal   243
Resources   244

Suggestions for Further Reading   245

Index   251

Preface to Students and Their Instructors

Best wishes on this journey, one of life's most important. You can and will make it if you diligently practice the advice and skills within these covers. And when a task seems impossible, stop what you're doing, talk yourself into a relaxed state, and keep repeating, "If everyone else can do it, so can I."

And you can.

> —John N. Gardner and A. Jerome Jewler

Just as first-year students are forever learning new ways to succeed, we as textbook authors are forever discovering new ways to help. Both of us had shaky beginnings in college, yet by using common sense and the advice of others, we succeeded. Not once during those college years did we realize what impact our college experiences would have on the rest of our lives—or on the lives of thousands of other students.

As founders and dedicated supporters of the First-Year Experience movement, we have always kept two ideas foremost in our minds:

- All students should be able to succeed in their first year of college.
- As educators and scholars, it is our responsibility to provide dedicated support, customized to a variety of students' unique needs.

This new concise media edition of *Your College Experience* continues to focus on these vital goals. We have been greatly assisted in this revision by the input of instructors who have used this text over the years, reviewers, our Wadsworth editorial staff, survey respondents who have shared their insights and, of course, our own students.

Strategies for Success Enhanced

Research by scholars at the National Resource Center for the First-Year Experience and Students in Transition at the University of South Carolina and at other institutions continues to show that students are most likely to succeed if they follow the strategies featured in this text. These Strategies for Success (formerly called Keys to Success) inform all the chapters. They are introduced in Chapter 1, printed in a summary chart for students' reference on the inside front cover of the book, and included in the accompanying CD-ROM. In this new edition of *Your College Experience*, these 31 Strategies for Success have been grouped into five new categories that help clarify major concepts:

- **Plan Ahead!** Among the most important things students must learn in college is how to manage time so that they don't find themselves cramming for exams, getting too little sleep, or studying day and night with no fun breaks. Without planning, college can turn into a frightening maze of due dates that creep up too soon, missed classes, and sheer exhaustion.

- **Take Charge of Learning!** If a student doesn't take charge of his or her learning, no one else will. Students will discover there are good ways and bad ways to study, and the good ways aren't any harder than the bad ways. This text helps students uncover critical thinking skills they may never have used before, and assists them in communicating those thoughts in writing more clearly.
- **Hone Your Skills!** Students will find that active participation is one of the key talents for taking charge of learning and of life. When a student speaks up in class, learning is more exciting and productive, for both students and instructors.
- **Get Connected!** A critical factor in success at college is to develop and maintain connections. Students benefit from getting involved in campus life, studying with a group, arranging conferences with teachers, and choosing a good advisor or counselor. Such connections can lead to some wonderful friendships as well as success in classes.
- **Know Yourself!** This phrase may sound odd. Of course, don't we all know ourselves? But what about potential? What about doing things that keep one healthy? What about developing a set of personal values one can be proud to share with others? Those things are part of this book, too.

Other New Features of This Edition

Unified Voice

With this edition we have consolidated the contributions of dozens of experts from around the country into a shorter format and a completely unified voice. One great strength of *Your College Experience* has always been its reliance on a multitude of experts in their fields. With this new revision, we believe we have made that expertise more accessible to student readers.

Customized Learning with a CD-ROM Boost

Packaged with every book is a new CD-ROM to bridge students' needs with the exercises in the text. A self-assessment exercise at the beginning of each chapter on the CD allows students to better understand their strengths and weaknesses. The CD then guides students to specific resources and interactive exercises that will help them hone their skills. Completing the inventories also provides the reader with a guide to what he or she needs to focus on in that particular chapter.

All text exercises are available on the CD, along with hot links to Internet resources and *InfoTrac® College Edition*. Features on the CD-ROM include:

- Exercises adapted from the book.
- Quizzes that reinforce chapter content.
- Crossword puzzles that are fun to work through.
- Journal opportunities for students to reflect on who they are and where they want to be.
- Goal-setting exercises that help students develop action plans for success.
- Resource activities that will help students build a reference list for future success.
- Links to the Internet for more exercises and online resources.
- Reinforcement of advice offered in the text.
- *InfoTrac College Edition* exercises that help students research more information on their success goals.
- Franklin-Covey Bonus—A free 120-day trial version of their popular electronic planner, goal setting exercises, and the the Franklin-Covey "mission statement builder" exercise.

New Chapter on Critical Thinking and Writing

Prior editions integrated William T. Daly's four-phase approach to critical thinking in discussions and exercises throughout the chapters. In this edition, we add to that a full chapter on critical thinking and writing early in the text, to provide a broader context for Daly's approach and more discussion and activities to introduce critical thinking as a key objective for first-year students. We also make explicit the crucial role of writing as both a tool for critical thinking and an effective method to reinforce learning. In addition, each chapter contains at least one critical thinking exercise.

Enhanced Coverage of Memory

To better equip students to master exams and retain important information, the discussion of memory has been expanded in Chapter 8, Making the Grade: Tests, Memory, Presentations.

New Feature "Examining Values"

We believe that the values—their core beliefs about what is good, bad, desirable, undesirable, right wrong—that college students bring to college and those they develop during college, are the basis for behaviors that lead to success. The discussion of values in Chapter 1 is reinforced and enhanced throughout the text by a new boxed feature, "Examining Values." This gives students continuing guidance on how to approach both personal and academic decisions.

More on Collaborative Learning

Although individuals must be able to make it on their own, we're discovering more and more about the value of working together. One sees collaboration in business as well as in colleges and universities. Perhaps life has become too complex, perhaps the flood of information at our fingertips has become overwhelming. Whatever the reason, studying with one other person or with a small group seems to benefit everyone who participates. Backed by the research of collaborative learning specialist Joe Cuseo of Marymount College, this edition provides new exercises and tips throughout to encourage students to study and learn together.

Increased Internet Connections

Each chapter contains Internet exercises, one of which uses the *InfoTrac College Edition* that may have come with this text. Chapter 9, Research: Your Campus Library and Computer Resources gives new, updated information on how to conduct a search as well as how to evaluate the quality of material found on the Internet.

More on Alcohol Abuse

In the completely rewritten chapter on alcohol and drugs, more attention is paid to the single most troubling college health problem, binge drinking. Without being preachy, this chapter addresses how students have the power to make choices and the consequences of those choices.

Expanded Activities Program

A new self-assessment feature kicks off each chapter and allows students to understand what aspects of the chapter to focus on.

In response to feedback from instructors who have used this text and by reviewer request, this edition's expanded selection of exercises and activities is now located at the **end** of chapters. This allows students the flexibility of reading the text without interruption, and gives instructors a clearer picture of how the exercises build on one another.

Teaching Aids for Instructors

A complete resources package for instructors accompanies this text. For advice and information about products and services that will help you teach your course, call the Toll-Free Consultation Service: 1-800-400-7609.

Instructor Resources

Custom Publishing Options. Faculty can select chapters from this and other Wadsworth College Success titles to bind with your own materials (campus maps, syllabi, etc.) into a fully customized book. For more information visit our website at *http://www.success.wadsworth.com.*

Instructor's Edition contains the entire text in full color, with chapter-at-a-glance reference tool to correlate the complete supplements package with each chapter of the text. (0-534-55054-1)

Unique Annotated Instructor's Manual. Contains the entire text with teaching tips (annotations) in the margins, plus each of the following subtopics: Background on the college success course; information on training faculty and working with peer leaders; ideas for getting the most out of collaborative learning; ideas for promoting more critical thinking; chapter by chapter teaching tips; list of questions students typically ask; ideas for in-class use of exercises; additional exercises, and chapter quizzes. (0-534-55056-8)

ExamView Testing and Tutorial System. Allows you to create, deliver, and customize tests and study guides (both print and online). The clear step-by-step process allows you to see what you are creating on the screen exactly as it will print or display online. (0-534-55057-6)

Workshops and Training

College Success Workshops. We offer a variety of faculty development workshops regionally and on campuses nationwide throughout the year. Visit our website for dates and places: *http://www.success.wadsworth.com.* Topics at these workshops include active learning strategies to engage first-year students, motivating students, using technology, working with peer leaders, and ways to promote critical thinking. Call 1-800-400-7609 for more information.

Teaching College Success: The Complete Resource Guide. Designed as a stand-alone resource or as a reference, this training package by Constance Staley focuses on faculty development. It includes PowerPoint slides and print resources, along with experiential activities. (Sampler package: 0-534-53644-1. Full product: 0-534-53640-9.)

Internet Resources

InfoTrac College Edition: A free 4-month subscription to this extensive online library is enclosed with every book. Designed to help your students make the most of the Internet, *InfoTrac College Edition* is an online database featuring access to the full text of articles from more than 900 scholarly and popular publications, updated daily. It is ideal for launching lectures, igniting discussions, and opening whole new worlds of information and research for students. Exclusive to Wadsworth-Thomson Learning. Journals subject to change.

Success Online: http://www.success.wadsworth.com This website offers lecture tips and professional resources, including training information, a faculty forum, online instructor's manual and PowerPoint slides, and the option of creating your own custom textbook online.

Thomson Learning Web Tutor: Use the online learning aids and communication tools of Web Tutor to help your students master your course. Students have access to study tools that correspond chapter by chapter and topic by topic with the book, including flashcards (with audio), practice quizzes, and online tutorials. You can post your syllabi and office hours, set up threaded discussions, track student progress with the quizzing material, and more. There is also a calendar built into Web Tutor that allows you to post, and change, important dates as needed. There is an integrated e-mail system and a "real time" chat option, as well. In addition, you can customize your Web Tutor website easily to meet your course needs. (Web CT stand-alone 0-534-55058-4; Web CT bundle 0-534-71293-2; Blackboard stand-alone 0-534-53431-7; Blackboard bundle 0-534-71137-5)

Presentation Tools

College Success Link: Presentation Tool: This cross-platform CD-ROM contains text and images to illustrate important concepts in the college success course. (0-534-56409-7)

Transparency Acetates for College Success: A collection of 50 color transparencies focusing on important college success topics. (0-534-56408-9)

Videos

CNN Today: College Success Video Series: Updated yearly, *CNN Today Videos* are course-specific to help launch lectures and encourage discussion. The 45-minute videos include a collection of recent 1- to 4-minute CNN news features on a wide range of relevant topics. (1999/2000 edition 0-534-53754-5; 2000/2001 edition 0-534-53799-5)

Video Series: Your College Experience: Strategies for Success: This award-winning video series produced at the University of South Carolina by the National Resource Center for the First-Year Experience and Students in Transition is comprised of twelve 5- to 7-minute programs. Topics include time management, learning styles, textbook reading, academic advising, relationships, using the library, career planning, and health issues. (Call 1-800-400-7609)

Wadsworth Study Skills Video: Volume I, Improving Your Grades: Designed for independent study in the media library or classroom, this video assists students in studying and test-taking. (0-534-54983-7)

Wadsworth Study Skills Video: Volume II, Notetaking: Featuring a series of college lectures and the opportunity for students to practice their note-taking skills, this video is designed for independent study in the media library or classroom. (0-534-54984-5)

A World of Diversity Videos: A two-video set on communication and conflict resolution between cultures. Reviewed by African American, Asian American, Latino American, and other multicultural scholars for language authenticity and content accuracy. (Volume 1: 0-534-23229-9. Volume II: 0-534-23230-2)

Wadsworth College Success Video Series: A collection of videos from the Films for Humanities and Sciences covering such topics as managing stress, improving grades, and maximizing mental performance. (Find a film you like at *http://www.films.com* and call us for ordering information.)

Student Resources

CD-ROM: All text exercises are available on the CD-ROM, along with hot links to Internet resources and *InfoTrac College Edition.* An electronic planner, goal-setting exercises, and a Mission Statement Builder exercise from Franklin-Covey are added bonuses. Features on the CD-ROM include: interactive self-assessments, quizzes, crossword puzzles, journal writing opportunities, resource activities, links to the Internet, and *InfoTrac College Edition* exercises. (CD-ROM stand-alone 0-534-55059-2)

Three-Hole Punch Version of the Text: This is the easiest way to customize Gardner and Jewler's *Your College Experience* with your own campus-specific materials. Unbound, this version of the book comes with a front and back cover and with all the pages conveniently three-hole punched so students can create their own course-specific binders.(0-534-55055-X)

College Success Factors Index Assessment Tool, developed by Edmond Hallberg, Kaylene Hallberg, and Loren Sauer: Using 80 self-scoring statements, this self-assessment tool is designed to help students discover their strengths and weaknesses in eight important areas that can affect their success in college: responsibility vs. control, competition, task precision, expectations, wellness, time management, college involvement, and family involvement. It will give you a starting point for discussion and provide your students direction to those areas of the text that need to be emphasized. Students can access this assessment in a password-protected site on the Wadsworth website.

Franklin-Covey/Premiere Agenda Planners: Wadsworth offers inexpensive planners designed specifically for college students by experts in time management—the Franklin-Covey/Premiere Agenda team. Ask your Wadsworth representative for details on our latest calendar offerings, or call our toll-free consultant hotline 1-800-400-7609.

Critical Thinking: Building the Basics: This 100-page publication by Donald E. P. Smith, Glenn Knudsvig, and Timothy Walter helps students apply critical thinking strategies to their own textbooks. (Bundle 0-534-70804-8)

Wadsworth College Success Internet-at-a-Glance: A handy pocket guide, this trifold brochure contains URL addresses for websites related to college success such as study skills, learning styles, health, financial management, and career choice. (Bundle 0-534-71818-3)

Acknowledgments

Although this text speaks through the voices of its two editors, it represents major contributions from many others. We gratefully acknowledge those contributions and thank these individuals whose special expertise has made it possible to introduce new college students to "their college experience" through the holistic approach we deeply believe in.

Preface. Vince Tinto, Syracuse University, for his pioneering research on leaving college.

Chapter 1. Richard L. Morrill, University of Richmond, for his discussion of values. Thorne Compton, University of South Carolina, for his thoughts on a liberal education.

Chapter 2. Johanna Dvorak, University of Wisconsin–Milwaukee, for her suggestions on time management.

Chapter 3. Joseph Cuseo, Marymount College, for his thoughts on collaborative learning, as well as for his authorship of the instructor's manual for this text.

Chapter 4. Steven Blume, Marietta College, for his detailed explanation of learning styles.

Chapter 5. William T. Daly, The Richard Stockton College of New Jersey, for developing a clear formula for critical thinking.

Chapter 6. Donald Jugenheimer, Southern Illinois University at Carbondale, for stressing the importance of listening and note taking in the classroom.

Chapters 7 and 8. Mary Walz-Chojnacki and Johanna Dvorak, University of Wisconsin–Milwaukee, for providing a sound approach for reading textbooks and studying for exams.

Chapter 9. Marilee Birchfield, University of South Carolina, for demystifying the campus library for new college students. Kenneth C. Greene, Claremont Graduate School, and Steven W. Gilbert, American Association for Higher Education, for underscoring the significance of the computer in higher education.

Chapter 10. Linda Salane, Columbia College, and Viki Fecas, University of South Carolina, for their advice on career planning. Mary Stuart Hunter, University of South Carolina, for information on catalogs and advising.

Chapter 11. Tom Carskadon and Nancy McCarley, Mississippi State University, for their extensive look at relationships. David Janes, The International Partnership for Service Learning, for urging students to be involved in service learning.

Chapter 12. Joan A. Rasool, Westfield State College, for new perspectives on diversity. Monita Johnson for her stirring article on being a minority on campus.

Chapter 13. Kevin W. King, counseling psychologist, for his advice on reducing stress. Danny Baker, University of South Carolina, for explaining how to avoid becoming a victim of campus crime. Ray Edwards, former college financial aid officer, on managing your money.

Chapter 14. James Turner, M.D., University of Virginia, for straightforward advice on alcohol and drugs. Michelle Sutherlin for "The Police Got Me Drunk." Lisa Ann Mohn, Mind/Body Medical Institute, for her discussion of sexual decisions. Tricia Phaup, University of South Carolina, for her advice on sexual assault.

We would also like to thank Daniel J. Kurland for providing Internet exercises throughout the text that are both useful and imaginative. We appreciate, as well, his work in creating the *Wadsworth College Success Internet-at-a-Glance* pocket guide.

Special thanks also to reviewers and survey respondents whose wisdom and suggestions guided the creation of this text:

Reviewers

Jeffrey Ballom, Temple College; Sharon Cordell, Roane State Community College; Barbara Lyman, Southwest Texas State University; Alison Murray, Indiana University; Karen Patterson, Central Missouri State University; Wayne C. Smith, Spokane Falls Community College

Survey Respondents

Susan E. Allen, Whittier College; Matt Aschenbrener, Ottawa University; Todd Benatouch, University of Texas–Arlington; Elizabeth Biggert, Cosumnes River College; Marilee Birchfield, University of South Carolina; Rosemarie Bogal-Allbritten, Murray State University; C. B. Bright, Jackson State Community College; Doyce M. Butts, John Brown University; Lori Campbell, Walters State Community College; Leslie Chilton, Arizona State University; Charlotte Cone, University of Central Arkansas; Dr. Mary Webber Coplen, Hutchinson Community College; Lynda Coupe, Pace University; Edward

Dadez, Chowan College; Joan Del Gaudio, Canada College; Daisy Duncan Foster, Wilberforce University; Howard Hayward, Lewis University; Glynes Hill-Chandler, Northern Virginia Community College; Damon Hof, Eastern Wyoming College; Sonja Hutchins, Central Piedmont Community College; Vernon Keith Jones, Montgomery College; Jeanette A. Karjala, Winona State University; Elizabeth Kennedy, Florida Atlantic University; Sandra Kuchynka, Northern Illinois University; Alice Lanning, University of Oklahoma; Barbara Luby, Raritan Valley Community College; Dee Ludwig, Eastern Wyoming College; Tara L. Lydy, Wilmington College; Krista Maddox, University of Cincinnati; Mary McNerney, Cottey College; Janet McReynolds, Southern Illinois University; Miki Mikolajczak, Saddleback College; Sister Nancy Miller, Holy Cross College; Julie Montgomery, University of Cincinnati; Stephen Morgan, Concordia University; Alicia Ortez, University of Michigan; Marjean D. Puriton, Texas Tech University; Karen Renfroe, University of Oklahoma; Dr. M. M. Richardson, Valdosta State University; Kevin C. Robbins, Indiana University; Debra Roberts, Delaware Technical and Community College–Terry Campus; Denise L. Rode, Northern Illinois University; Scott E. Rodwell, Howard Payne University; Rosann Rookey, Middle Georgia College; Bonnie Rosen, Rockland Community College; Reginald Ross, Bloomfield College; Tom Rossi, Broome Community College; Jane A. Rysberg, California State University; Kari Sayers, Marymount College; Carolyn Schnell, North Dakota State University; Mike Schoenecke, Texas Technical University; Miya Simpson, Virginia Polytechnic Institute; Mary Silva, Modesto Junior College; Barbara Stanley, Valdosta State University; Jo Stejskal, Winona State University; Frank Torre, College of Staten Island; Louis Vangieri, Delaware Technical and Community College; David Volckmann, Whittier College; Libby Wagner, Peninsula College; Jan Wencel, Curry College; Elizabeth White, University of South Carolina–Sumter; Michael Wilson, University of Missouri–Kansas City; Frankie Yockey, University of Idaho

Finally, all this could not have happened without the Wadsworth team that supported our text, guided us through the writing and production, and worked at least as hard as we did to make *Your College Experience* one of the most popular texts in its field. Our special thanks to Susan Badger, President; Sean Wakely, Vice President and Editorial Director; Elana Dolberg, Executive Manager of College Success; Sherry Symington, Senior Development Editor; Sally Cobau, Editorial and Marketing Assistant; Debby Kramer, Editorial Production Supervisor; Stephen Rapley, Creative Director; Cecile Joyner/The Cooper Company, Production; Paul Uhl, Designer; Betty Duncan, Copy Editor; Barbara Britton, Manufacturing Supervisor; and Joohee Lee, Permissions.

We also want to thank Cynthia Sanner, Director of Technology Product Development; Vince Tang, Technology Project Manager; Becky Stovall, Executive Producer; Kate Crowley, Media Assistant; Carolyn Kuhn/Software Mart, Inc.; Tom Thackrey/Willow Glen Productions; Deborah Thackrey/Willow Glen Productions; Nan Fritz/nSight; Margaret Parks, Director of Advertising; Bryan Vann, Advertising Project Manager; Jean Thompson/Jean Thompson Marketing; Joy Westberg/Lightning Mountain Communications; Constance Staley, Workshop Facilitator; and Ilana Sims, Workshop Coordinator and College Success Consultant.

John N. Gardner

A. Jerome Jewler

Foreword to the Instructor

By Vincent Tinto
DISTINGUISHED UNIVERSITY PROFESSOR
SYRACUSE UNIVERSITY

I have been involved as a researcher and consultant in studies of student retention and retention programs for nearly 30 years. In that time, I have come to learn four important lessons about the character of successful retention strategies.

First, retention is the result of successful education. Students who learn, stay.

Second, becoming a successful learner takes time and skills, both academic and social. It is not easy, but it is doable.

Third, environment matters. Students who are involved, both academically and socially, are not only more likely to stay, but are more likely to learn while staying.

Fourth, the first year of college is a critical period for student learning and persistence. It is a period of transition and adjustment, both academically and socially, during which students acquire important skills that furnish the foundation for subsequent learning. It is a period when involvement matters most, and when learning is most readily shaped by educational programs designed to provide students with learning experiences that are motivating, challenging, and involving.

In this regard, I have also discovered that few individuals are more qualified to speak to the needs of new students and the first-year experience than Professors John Gardner and Jerry Jewler. They have been working with new students and with faculty who teach those students for nearly 30 years. In that time, they have acquired knowledge that few can match of what works and what doesn't.

That knowledge is contained within the pages of this book and in the programs their work has inspired. The first section, **Strategies for Success,** introduces students to the goal-setting process and the value of a liberal education, and provides them with a set of "strategies for success" that are developed subsequently throughout the book.

The next section, **Plan Ahead!,** focuses on time management, one of the most critical skills for college success. This is followed by **Take Charge of Learning!** which points out the benefits of active participation and becoming familiar with how you learn best.

In **Hone Your Skills!** you'll discover how to bring your study skills up to college level. Critical thinking, writing, taking notes, reading textbooks, preparing for exams, team learning, and conducting research are all covered within the chapters of this section.

Next, **Get Connected!** looks at the more personal side of college success. You'll explore courses and careers, academic advisors or counselors, relationships with friends and family, and the value of getting involved on campus. You'll also learn how becoming actively involved with students of diverse backgrounds can be an education in itself.

Finally, in **Know Yourself!** you'll read about managing stress, campus safety, money issues, sexuality, and alcohol and other drugs.

Each chapter opens with a self-assessment tool and includes both a values and a critical thinking feature. At the end of each chapter are Internet exercises (Search Online!), including one calling for the use of *InfoTrac® College Edition,* plus additional exercises based on active and collaborative learning strategies that instructors may assign at will. Annotations in the Annotated Instructor's Edition suggest other activities for classroom use and the Instructor's Resource Manual provides additional ideas for teaching each chapter of the book.

I can't imagine a more comprehensive, yet concise, introduction to the college experience. So, as I would recommend to students, let me also recommend that you take Gardner and Jewler's advice seriously and use it as a guide to your own thinking about the education of new students on your campus. As I have found in my own institution, where I teach our version of the first-year seminar, their advice works.

Part 1

Strategies for Success

PLAN AHEAD!

- Show up for class
- Have work done on time
- Set up a daily schedule
- If full-time, limit work week to 20 hours. Work on campus if possible
- If stressed, enroll part time

TAKE CHARGE OF LEARNING!

- Choose instructors who favor active learning
- Assess how you learn best
- Improve your reading, note-taking, and study habits
- Develop critical thinking skills
- Improve your writing

HONE YOUR SKILLS!

- Participate in class
- Practice giving presentations
- Learn how to remember more from every class
- Learn from criticism
- Take workshops on how to study
- Get to know your campus library and other information sources
- Embrace new technologies

GET CONNECTED!

- Study with a group
- Get to know one person on campus who cares about you
- Get involved in campus activities
- Learn about campus helping resources
- Meet with your instructors
- Find a great academic advisor or counselor
- Visit your campus career center
- Take advantage of minority support services
- Enlist support of your spouse, partner, or family

KNOW YOURSELF!

- Take your health seriously
- Have realistic expectations
- Learn how to be assertive yet tactful
- Be proud of your heritage

College
Makes the Difference

Strategies for Success

**IN THIS CHAPTER,
YOU WILL LEARN**

- Five major strategies for college success

- The meaning and importance of values

- Why some students graduate and others don't

- The impact of college on your future earnings

- The advantages of a liberal education

- How to set your own goals for success

find your way

"I just stood in line for two hours and spent over a hundred dollars for two books. And I realized I have three exams during the same week in October. First week of college and I'm already stressing out. At least I've met a few interesting people. Wish I had time to talk to them!"

Welcome to college! And congratulations. The fact that you're here means that you meet the admissions standards for your campus and that you should have no trouble passing your classes and earning your degree. But if that's so, why do so many entering students drop out? And why do so many drop out during their first year? Usually, it does not have to do with their capacity for thinking and learning, or they wouldn't have been admitted in the first place.

What then? That's what this book is about. It's a game plan for succeeding in college. A package of strategies that, if followed, can help you achieve beyond your wildest dreams. And since you're going to be exercising your memory constantly in college, especially around exam time, take a moment to memorize these five key strategies. One way to do so is to focus on the key words *plan, charge, skills, connected,* and *yourself.* Try it. Read the list three times, close the book, and recite these five strategies:

Plan Ahead

Take Charge of Learning

Hone Your Skills

Get Connected

Know Yourself

Many of the following strategies may strike you as common sense, and many of them are. Nonetheless, you will benefit from a careful reading of them. Researchers have confirmed that they can pave your way to success.

SELF-ASSESSMENT: SUCCESS

With a pencil, place a check mark in front of every strategy listed on the next four pages that you think will be challenging for you. Later in this course, as you determine you have mastered them, come back and convert the check marks to Xs. Throughout this book, you will learn how to master these strategies.

Five Key Strategies

Plan Ahead

☐ **Show up for class.** Be there daily. When you're not there, you're missing something. You're also sending your instructor a message that you don't care. If you know you are going to miss class because of an appointment, sickness, or an emergency, contact your instructor as soon as possible and certainly before the next class meeting.

☐ **Have work done on time.** Not only may you face a grade penalty if you don't, you will most certainly irritate some of your teachers if you are perpetually late with assignments. Some instructors may have a policy of not accepting late work. Ask if you are uncertain. If your work is late because of illness or an emergency, let your instructor know. It can help things.

☐ **Set up a daily schedule.** And stick to it. Learning how to manage your time can make the difference between success and frustration. Get a portable appointment calendar from your campus bookstore this week and always keep it handy.

☐ **If you are a full-time student, limit your work week to 20 hours.** Most students begin a downhill slide after that. Need more money? Consult a financial aid officer. If you must work, look for a job on campus. Students who do have a higher graduation rate than those who work off campus.

☐ **If stressed, enroll part time.** Adjust the number of courses you're taking to reduce your stress. You'll more than likely do better in all classes.

Take Charge of Learning

☐ **Choose instructors who favor active learning.** The more you're asked to participate in class, the more you'll enjoy learning. Ask upper-class students who these instructors are.

☐ **Assess how you learn best.** Discover learning style theory, which suggests that we are all individuals with differing approaches to the world around us, the information we receive, the decisions we make, and the way we choose to live. Perhaps you'll understand why you hate math and love English, whereas your best friend is just the other way around, and you'll learn how to accommodate for your weaker learning preferences.

☐ **Improve your reading, note-taking, and study habits.** Starting with a time management plan, make every minute of every day count. Master the most effective methods for reading textbooks, listening and taking notes in class, studying for exams, and using information sources on campus. If your campus has an academic skills center, visit it whenever you need help with your studies.

☐ **Develop critical thinking skills.** Challenge and ask why. Seek dependable information to prove your point. Look for unusual solutions to ordinary problems. Never accept something as fact simply because you found it on the Internet or someone tells you it's true. And don't be swayed by your emotions when your logical thinking powers are at work.

☐ **Improve your writing.** Instructors—and employers—want people who can think *and* write. Learn to rehearse your thoughts, put them on paper, and revise them till they sing! Remember, the more you write, the better you'll write.

Hone Your Skills

☐ **Participate in class.** Research indicates that students who involve themselves in class discussions usually remember more about the discussion than students who don't. As a result, they usually enjoy the class more and earn higher grades.

☐ **Practice giving presentations.** This is another way to stay active in class and is a skill most of you will be using for the rest of your lives. There *is* a way to overcome stage fright! Some actors do it every performance.

☐ **Learn how to remember more from every class.** Effective listening not only results in better notes but also helps you improve memory techniques. This is important as exams approach.

☐ **Learn from criticism.** Criticism should be healthy and helpful; it's how we all learn. If you get a low grade, ask to meet with your instructor to discuss what you should do to improve your work.

☐ **Take workshops on how to study,** especially if you've been out of school for awhile. After reviewing the study skills in this book, you may decide to take a comprehensive study skills course. You also may need to review basic math or writing skills. Fortunately, relearning is much easier than learning new material.

☐ **Get to know your campus library and other information sources.** This means not only knowing how to do a conventional library search but also getting comfortable with databases and the World Wide Web. For much of your research, all you may need is a computer terminal anywhere on campus.

☐ **Embrace new technologies.** If you don't already know, ask how to use word processors, do a computerized library search, access journals online, and send and receive e-mail. The computer skills you develop in college will prove valuable in later employment.

Get Connected

☐ **Study with a group.** Research shows that students who collaborate in study groups often earn the highest grades and survive college with fewer academic problems.

☐ **Get to know at least one person on campus who cares about you.** He or she might be the teacher of this course, some other instructor, your academic advisor, someone at the counseling or career center, an advisor to a student organization, or an older student. You may have to take the initiative to establish this relationship, but it will be worth it.

☐ **Get involved in campus activities.** Visit the student activities office. Work for the campus newspaper or radio station. Join a club or support group. Play intramural sports. Most campus organizations crave newcomers—you're their lifeblood.

☐ **Learn about campus helping resources.** Find out where they are. Academic and personal support services are usually free and confidential. Successful students use them.

☐ **Meet with your instructors.** Students who do tend to stay in college longer. Your instructors are required to have office hours; they expect you to visit.

☐ **Find a great academic advisor or counselor.** Be sure he or she is someone you can turn to for both academic and personal guidance and support.

☐ **Visit your campus career center.** A career counselor can help you learn more about your academic major or find another major that suits you better. If you can't decide on a major immediately, remember that many first-year students are in the same boat. Instead, talk about your options.

☐ **Take advantage of minority support services.** If you are a minority student, find out if your campus has centers for minority students. Pay a visit and introduce yourself. Take advantage of mentoring programs that a center might offer.

☐ **Enlist support of your spouse, partner, or family.** If you are a returning student, you may need to adjust household routines and duties. Let others know when you need extra time to study. A supportive partner is a great ally, but a nonsupportive partner can threaten your success in college. If your partner feels threatened and tries to undermine what you are doing, sit down and talk it over or seek counseling.

Know Yourself

☐ **Take your health seriously.** How much sleep you get, what you eat, whether you exercise, and what decisions you make about drugs, alcohol, and sex all affect your well-being and how well you will do in classes. Find healthful ways to deal with stress, too. Your counseling center can help.

☐ **Have realistic expectations.** At first you may be disappointed in the grades you make but remember that college is a new experience and things can, and probably will, improve. Remember, you are not alone. Thousands of other students have faced the same uncertainties you may be facing. Hang on to that positive attitude. It makes a difference.

☐ **Learn how to be assertive yet tactful.** If you don't, others may take advantage of you. If it's difficult for you to stand up for yourself, take assertiveness training. Your counseling center probably offers workshops that can teach you to stand up for your rights in a way that respects the rights of others.

☐ **Be proud of your heritage.** No matter what your heritage is, you may hear ugly remarks and witness or be the target of bigotry caused by ignorance or fear. Stand tall. Be proud. Refuse to tolerate disrespect. Remember that most of the college population embraces tolerance.

Challenge yourself to learn all five major strategies. Here's how: Take one group at a time and learn it well, using the "key word" idea we mentioned earlier. Then proceed to the next group and do the same. When you know the second group, repeat the first and the second and then continue with the rest. You may be amazed at how easy it is to remember information!

Easing the Transition

It used to be that college teachers and administrators made some big assumptions about new students. Among other things, they assumed that by the time students got to college they would know how to manage their time, how to handle stress, how to do research, and how to choose a major. In many cases, they were wrong.

We know because we were the new students then, and we didn't know how to do *any* of these things. Eventually, we learned them the hard way and often too late.

In the 1970s, things changed for new students with the introduction of the first contemporary "college success" course, which was designed to eliminate as many of the barriers to success as possible. At most campuses that offer this course, the dropout rate has declined.

If you're a new or returning college student, we suspect you're having some of the following thoughts:

- This is the first time someone has not been there to tell me I had to do something. Will I be able to handle all this freedom? Or will I just waste time?
- I've never been away from home before, and I don't know anybody. How am I going to make friends?

Critical Thinking

Successful Strategies

Go back over the list of strategies and choose a handful of them that mean the most to you. In an essay, explain why they mean the most to you, what influences or events in your life caused these strategies to be important to you, and how far along you believe you are in mastering each strategy you have chosen.

- I have responsibilities at home. Can I get through college and still manage to take care of my family? What will my family think about all the time I'll have to spend in classes and studying?
- As a minority on a primarily White campus, will I be in for some unpleasant surprises?
- Maybe college will be too difficult for me. I hear college teachers are more demanding than high school teachers.
- Not only do I miss being at home, but I hope I won't disappoint the people I care about and who expect so much of me.
- What if my children or spouse complains about all the time I spend studying?
- In high school, I got by without working too hard. Now I'll really have to study. Will I be tempted to cut corners, maybe even cheat?
- Will I like my roommate? What if (he, she) is from a different culture?
- What if I don't pick the right major? What if I don't know which major is right for me?
- Can I afford this? Can my parents afford this? I wouldn't want them to spend this much and then have me fail.
- Maybe I'm the only one who's feeling like this. Maybe everyone else is just smarter than I, and they know it.
- Looking around class makes me feel so old! Will I be able to keep up at my age?
- Will some teachers be biased toward students of my age and culture?

This book will help you find the answers to such questions. Each chapter will take you one step closer to your goal of making it through college. But first, think about why you wanted to go to college in the first place. Was it because everyone else was going? Or was it to make enough money to support a family or to start a new midlife career?

No matter your reason, it resulted from your own life experiences and your personal values system, a system that may be about to undergo major changes.

Defining Values

One of the most important concepts to understand in college is that of values. Social scientists define *values* as the beliefs that people have which serve as the basis for their decision making. Those beliefs generally come from our life experiences, and since those experiences differ from person to person, so do their values.

A value commits us to take action, to do something. For instance, we might watch a television program showing starving people and feel sympathy but take no action whatsoever. But if our feelings move us to action to help those who are suffering, those feelings qualify as values.

Examining Values

Most students find that college life challenges their existing personal and moral values. First-year students are often startled at the diversity of personal moralities found on campus. For instance, you may have been taught that it is wrong to drink alcohol, yet you find that friends you respect and care about see nothing wrong with drinking, often to great excess. Students from more liberal backgrounds may be astonished to discover themselves forming friendships with classmates whose personal values are very conservative. So far, how has college life made you think about what you value strongly as compared with the values of others?

We can also define values as beliefs that we accept by choice, with a sense of responsibility and ownership. Much of what we think is what others have taught us, but only when we fully embrace them ourselves can those thoughts and feelings become values.

Finally, we should be proud of our values and want others to know it. We should also be ready to sacrifice for them and to establish our priorities around them. In summary, our values are those important attitudes or beliefs that we

- Accept by choice
- Affirm with pride
- Express in action

We will mention values frequently throughout this book because research tells us that a central key to success in college is the appropriateness of decisions that students make, and the values held by college students form the basis for such decisions.

Those Who Start and Those Who Finish

In 1900 fewer than 2 percent of Americans of traditional college age attended college. As we enter the new millennium, new technologies and the information explosion are changing the workplace so drastically that few people can support themselves and their families adequately without some education beyond high school.

Today more than 60 percent of high school graduates go on to college, with over 3800 colleges serving more than 14 million students. More than half of those enrolling in college begin in 2-year institutions. Adult students are also enrolling in record numbers. As the new millennium begins, over one-third of college students are over age 25.

SEE SEARCH ONLINE!
INTERNET EXERCISE 1.1

Half a century ago, most college students were White males. Today, women outnumber men, minorities are making steady gains in numbers, and college has become financially possible for nearly everyone, regardless of income.

That's the bright side. The not-so-good side is that 40 percent of students who start in 4-year programs never finish their degrees. In 2-year colleges, half or more of the entering class will drop out by the end of the first year.

First-Year Questions of Freedom and Commitment

Your first year—that's when the highest dropout rate occurs. Yet of those who leave, the majority are in good academic standing. What is it, then, that causes so many students to drop out of college?

What Today's Students Really Want Are Jobs That Pay Well

Claudia Smith Brinson
Associate Editor, *The State*, Columbia, South Carolina

The parking lots are full, the elevators are full, the dorms are full, and so are the classes. The college students are back, and a pragmatic bunch they are. They're attending college so they can get a good job and make more money. They want to end up authorities in their fields; they want to end up well off financially.

That's what this year's sophomores thought last year, according to data culled from 275,811 students at 469 institutions, adjusted by the Higher Education Research Institute at UCLA's Graduate School of Education & Information Studies to be statistically representative.

The students were interviewed in 1998 as they entered four-year colleges as first-time freshmen. They were asked about their attitudes on college, their objectives, their beliefs.

And they sound so grounded they must be barefoot.

A third attend the only college they applied to; another third applied to just one or two others. Three-fourths attend their first choice. Almost half say they chose their school because it has a good academic reputation and/or its graduates get good jobs.

Although these are students who want a college education, they sound downright disengaged when it comes to school. Education seems a means to an end—getting a job. A record high, 38 percent, said they were bored in class. A record high, 60 percent, came late to class. A record low, 33 percent, studied or did homework six or more hours a week.

The culture of the Web is far more interesting than the culture of school. Just 18 percent report checking a book out of the school library. Only 21 percent stayed after class to ask advice of a teacher. Only 21 percent voted in a student election. Yet 83 percent used the Internet for research or homework, 80 percent played computer games, 66 percent communicated by e-mail, 54 percent participated in chat rooms and 73 percent used the Internet in some other way.

The Internet is "a way of life for the majority of students," says Linda J. Sax, who directed the survey. "What remains to be seen, however, is whether proficiency on the Internet enhances student learning during college."

The summer between my freshman and sophomore year in college, my parents lived in Louisiana, just across Lake Ponchartrain from New Orleans. I had a very low-paying job as a waitress and took on baby-sitting jobs to add to the money I was saving for the next semester. One night, a couple didn't leave the house for almost half an hour because they were so busy lecturing me about college: "Have fun! These are the best years of your life! It'll never be so good again! Enjoy!"

They sounded almost desperate about it. Alas, I was working my way through college, and fun was a distant third after classes and work. Anyway, I nobly promised I would do my best.

What I say to my own college student is entirely different: "You have to graduate from college to even make it out of poverty! Mediocre grades will yield a mediocre job! This is a world that demands a decent education! Your job is to study and do well in school! What do you mean, you got a C?"

Maybe that's why the most frequently chosen objectives of the surveyed students went like this: being very well-off financially, 74 percent; raising a family, 73 percent; becoming an authority in my field, 60 percent; helping others who are in difficulty, 60 percent; obtaining recognition from my colleagues for contributions to my special field, 50 percent.

I suspect a lot of teens get the same lecture I give because parents fear the world has become harsher. It takes two wage earners to make a middle-class lifestyle nowadays. And it takes four years of college, not two, to earn more than a subsistence income. There is more to life than paying off a mortgage, though. These students don't seem to dream about such things: Only one in 10 wants to write original works or create artistic works, only one in five wants to clean up the environment or participate in community action, only one in four cites developing a meaningful philosophy of life; only one in four (a record low) keeps up with politics; only one in three wants to influence social values.

They manage a rather interesting trick, recording a record low in interest in politics and a record high in volunteerism. So they are engaged, just in their own particular way.

Nonetheless, they're probably heading toward major mid-life crises. I'd like to warn them: Yes, you have to eat, but you also have to dream.

Courtesy *The State*, Columbia, South Carolina, September 4, 1999

TABLE 1.1   MEDIAN ANNUAL EARNINGS OF COLLEGE AND HIGH SCHOOL GRADUATES, 1996

EDUCATION LEVEL	MEDIAN EARNINGS	PREMIUM OVER HIGH SCHOOL GRADUATES	PREMIUM OVER HIGH SCHOOL GRADUATES
Professional degree	$71,868	208%	$48,551
PhD	$60,827	161%	$37,510
Master's	$46,269	98%	$22,952
Bachelor's	$36,155	55%	$12,838
High school	$23,317		

SOURCE: U.S. DEPARTMENT OF LABOR, 1998

For those fresh out of high school, the overriding problem involves newfound freedom. No more will teachers tell you exactly what, how, or when to study. No more can parents wake you in the morning, see that you eat properly and get enough sleep, monitor whether or how well you do your homework, or remind you to allow enough time to get to school. In almost every aspect of your life, it suddenly *all* depends on you.

For returning students, the opposite is true: a daunting lack of freedom. Working, caring for a family, and meeting other adult commitments and responsibilities compete for the time and attention it takes to do your best or even simply to persist in college. The easiest thing to do is quit.

SEE EXERCISE 1.1

SEE EXERCISE 1.2

Whichever problem you are facing, what will motivate you to persist? What about the enormous investment of time and money that getting a college degree requires? Are you convinced that those investments will pay off?

Education, Careers, and Income

Facing a job market that places a high premium on education and technology, men and women with only a high school education will make less than their contemporaries who earn college degrees.

The gap in earnings from high school to college is widening (Table 1.1). In 1996 men with college degrees were earning an average of one-and-a-half times the salary of high school graduates; in 1970 the difference was only one-and-a-quarter times as much. In 1996 women with college degrees were earning nearly twice as much as women with high school diplomas. One probable reason for the growing disparity is the sudden spurt of jobs in technology and information. Whatever the reason, it becomes more evident each year that a college education is truly worth its cost.

SEE EXERCISE 1.3

In the past several decades, college-educated women's wages have increased more quickly than the wages of college-educated men. However, much of that gain has come from working longer hours. Regrettably, college-educated men still earn substantially more than college-educated women. But these are averages, of course, and many women with college degrees have earnings equal to or higher than those of many men.

In addition to higher earnings, according to the Carnegie Commission on Higher Education, as a college graduate you will have a less erratic job history, will earn more promotions, and will likely be happier with your work. You will be less likely than a nongraduate to become unemployed. As the saying goes, "If you think education is expensive, try ignorance."

Liberal Education and Quality of Life

Of course, college will affect you in other ways. No matter what your major, you will emerge from college with a liberal education. Liberal, as in "liberate" or "free," signifies that a well-rounded college education will expand life's possibilities for you by steeping you in the richness of how our world, our nation, our society and its people came to be.

Liberal education is about learning to learn, discovering how to think for yourself, on your own and in collaboration with others. The result is that you will understand how to accumulate knowledge. You will encounter and learn more about how to appreciate the cultural, artistic, and spiritual dimensions of life. You will be more likely to seek appropriate information before making a decision. Such information also will help you realize how our lives are shaped by global as well as local political, social, psychological, economic, environmental, and physical forces. You will grow intellectually through interaction with cultures, languages, ethnic groups, religions, nationalities, and social classes other than your own.

The evidence from many studies suggests that as a liberally educated college graduate, you will

- Know more, have more intellectual interests, be more tolerant of others, and continue to learn throughout life.
- Have greater self-esteem and self-confidence, which helps you realize how you might make a difference in the world.
- Be more flexible in your views, more future oriented, more willing to appreciate differences of opinion, more interested in political and public affairs, and less prone to criminal activity.
- Tend to delay getting married and having children, have fewer children and share child-care and household responsibilities with your partner, and devote more energy to child rearing.
- Have a slightly lower divorce rate than those who did not graduate from college.
- Have children with greater learning abilities who will achieve more in life.
- Be an efficient consumer, save more money, make better investments, and spend more on home, intellectual, and cultural interests, as well as on your children.
- Be able to deal with bureaucracies, the legal system, tax laws, and advertising claims.
- Spend less time and money on television and movies for leisure and more on continuing education, hobbies, community and civic affairs, and vacations.
- Be more concerned with wellness and preventive health care and consequently—through diet, exercise, stress management, a positive attitude, and other factors—live longer and suffer fewer disabilities.

SEE EXERCISE 1.4

Setting Goals for Success

SEE SEARCH ONLINE!
INTERNET EXERCISE 1.2

Now that you've read the strategies for success, what should you be doing to accomplish them? One method is to set specific goals for yourself, beginning now, that will help you maximize your potential in college.

We know from years of working with new college students that many hold a number of negative self-fulfilling prophecies. A self-fulfilling prophecy is something you predict is going to happen, and by thinking that's how things will turn out, you greatly increase the chances that they will. This book is designed to help you rid yourself of your negative prophecies, replace them with positive ones, and learn how to fulfill them. Look back at the list of comments and questions on pages 8–9. If some of these sound familiar, take comfort; most other entering students share the same fears.

College is an ideal time to begin setting and fulfilling short- and long-term goals. A short-term goal might be to set aside three hours this week to study chemistry, whereas a long-term goal might be to devise a strategy for passing chemistry with an A. It's okay if you don't yet know what you want to do with the rest of your life. It's

Where to Go for Help

To find the college support services you need, ask your academic advisor or counselor; consult your college catalog, phone book, and home page on the Internet. Or call or visit student services (or student affairs). Most of these services are free.

Academic Advisement Center Help in choosing courses, information on degree requirements

Academic Skills Center Tutoring, help on study and memory skills, help on studying for exams

Adult Reentry Center Programs for returning students, supportive contacts with other adult students, information about services such as child care

Career Planning and Placement Career library, interest assessments, counseling, help in finding a major, job and internship listings, co-op listings, interviews with prospective employers, help with résumés and interview skills

Chaplains Worship services, fellowship, personal counseling

Commuter Services Off-campus housing list, roommate lists, orientation to community, maps, information on public transportation, babysitting, and so forth

Computer Center Minicourses, handouts on campus and other computer resources

Counseling Center Confidential counseling on personal concerns, stress management programs

Disabled Student Services Assistance in overcoming physical barriers or learning disabilities

Financial Aid and Scholarship Office Information on financial aid programs, scholarships, grants

Health Center Help on personal nutrition, weight control, exercise, sexuality; information on substance-abuse programs and other health issues; often includes a pharmacy

Housing Office Help in locating on- or off-campus housing

Legal Services Legal aid for students; if you have a law school, it may offer assistance by senior students

Math Center Help with math skills

Physical Education Center Facilities and equipment for exercise and recreational sports

Writing Center Help with writing assignments

even okay if you don't know what to major in. More than 60 percent of college students change majors at least once. Using the strategies to success as a starting point, practice the following process by setting some short-term goals now.*

1. **Select a goal.** State it in measurable terms. Be specific about what you want to achieve and when (for example, not "improve my study skills" but "master and use the recall column system of note taking by the end of October").
2. **Be sure that the goal is achievable.** Have you allowed enough time to pursue it? Do you have the necessary skills, strengths, and resources? If not, modify the goal to make it achievable.
3. **Be certain you genuinely want to achieve the goal.** Don't set out to work toward something only because you feel you should or because others tell you it's the thing to do. Be sure your goal will not have a negative impact on yourself or others and that it is consistent with your most important values.
4. **Know why the goal matters.** Be sure it has the potential to give you a sense of accomplishment.
5. **Identify and plan for difficulties you might encounter.** Find ways to overcome them.
SEE EXERCISE 1.5
6. **Devise strategies for achieving the goal.** How will you begin? What comes next? What should you avoid? Create steps for achieving your goal and set a timeline for the steps.

*Adapted from *Human Potential Seminars,* by James D. McHolland and Roy W. Trueblood, Evanston, Illinois, 1972. Used by permission of the authors.

Search Online!   《●》

Welcome to *InfoTrac College Edition* A Powerful Research Database

InfoTrac College Edition is a powerful information database that includes numerous encyclopedias and other reference works, as well as articles from many academic journals and magazines. You may find a comprehensive version of *InfoTrac* available on your campus.

Your Direct Access to InfoTrac College Edition

If your instructor arranged for your purchase of this textbook to include a subscription, you can also access *InfoTrac College Edition* on the Internet using your own computer. To set up your four-month *InfoTrac College Edition* account, go to *http://www.infotrac-college.com/ wadsworth* and submit the account number issued on the *InfoTrac College Edition* insert that accompanied this book. The program will lead you through the enrollment process.

The *InfoTrac College Edition* includes more than 600 current magazines and journals and is growing. You'll find it easy to search for information using key words or by using the extensive Subject Guide. Many entries include the complete text of an article, which you can download to your computer. Each entry starts with an abstract to give you an idea of whether the article is likely to meet your needs.

In each chapter of this book, you'll find key words and subject-guide phrases for the topic of that chapter, plus specific articles you might want to read.

Make *InfoTrac College Edition* a regular part of your college-success work. Use it to find information for writing papers and for broadening your learning in other courses, too.

Internet Exercise 1.1 Using the *Digest of Education Statistics* Online

The Internet is particularly useful as a source of government statistics and information. The *Digest of Education Statistics* provides extensive data on postsecondary education in the United States. Figure 15 in Chapter 3 of the 1997 edition, the most recent version currently available on the Web, at *http://nces.ed.gov/pubs/digest97/d970003.html*, presents a graph, "Enrollment in institutions of higher education, by age: fall 1978 to fall 2007." (*Note:* Web addresses change. Go to *http://success.wadsworth.com* for the most up-to-date uniform resource locators, or URLs.) Visit the website and answer the following questions:

Which age group has the highest percentage of individuals enrolled?   _____

Which age group has the smallest percentage of individuals enrolled?   _____

For the years 1970 to 1995, which age group increased the most?   _____

For the years 1970 to 1995, which age group increased the least?   _____

What do these trends say about how the profile of college students will change in the coming years?

What explanation can you offer for these changes?

Note: A key-word search is not always the best way to find information on the Web. When searching for statistical data, you may have better luck starting from resource menus such as the University of Michigan Documents Center—*http://www.lib.umich.edu/libhome/ Documents.center/*—a central reference and referral point for government information; Uncle Sam—Statistical Resources of the U.S. at *http://www.lib.memphis.edu/gpo/statis1.htm*; Argus Clearinghouse, formerly known as the Clearinghouse for Subject-Oriented Internet Resource Guides, at *http://www.clearinghouse.net*.

Search Online!   《 ● 》

Internet Exercise 1.2 Discovering More About the Value of College

Using *InfoTrac College Edition,* try these phrases and others for key-word and subject-guide searches: "college success," "liberal arts," "personal values," "goal setting," "college," and "universities and colleges."

ALSO LOOK UP:

Adult enrollment and educational attainment. Jerry A. Jacobs, Scott Stoner-Eby. *Annals of the American Academy of Political and Social Science* Sept 1998 v559 p91(18)

Not to worry: the college mold doesn't hold. (effects of college on student values) Philip G. Altbach, Lionel S. Lewis. *Esquire* Mar 1999 v131 i3 p86(1)

First encounters of the bureaucratic kind: early freshman experiences with a campus bureaucracy. Glen J. Godwin, William T. Markham. *Journal of Higher Education* Nov-Dec 1996 v67 p660(32)

The values of student environmentalists. Glenn D. Shean, Tamara Shei. *Journal of Psychology* Sept 1995 p559(6)

Age and gender differences in value orientation among American adolescents. Kimberly Badger, Rebecca Simpson Craft, Larry Jensen. *Adolescence* Fall 1998 v33 i131 p591(6)

Additional Exercises

These exercises will help you sharpen what we believe are the critical skills for college success: writing, critical thinking, learning in groups, planning, reflecting, and taking action. Also, check out the CD-ROM that came with your book—you will find these exercises and more.

Exercise 1.1 Solving a Problem

What has been your biggest unresolved problem to date in college? What steps have you attempted to solve it? Write a letter or memo to your instructor about these two questions. Read your instructor's response and see if it's of any help to you. If you still have questions, ask to meet with your instructor.

Exercise 1.2 Focusing on Your Concerns

Browse the table of contents of this book. Find one or more chapters that address your most important concerns. Take a brief look at each chapter you have chosen. If a chapter appears to be helpful, read it before your instructor assigns it and try to follow its advice.

Exercise 1.3 Your Reasons for Attending College

List three reasons you chose to go to college:

1. _____

2. _____

3. _____

Which one of these was the most important? Why?

_____

_____

_____

_____

Exercise 1.4 **The Many Reasons for College**

For homework, compare the reasons for attending college in this chapter with your own reasons. How are they the same? How are they different? In a small group discuss the reasons in this chapter for attending college. Share with the group the ones that seem most relevant to you. Compile a group list of the most important reasons and discuss them with your instructor. What did you learn about yourself and your classmates?

Exercise 1.5 **Set a Short-Term Goal**

- Pick one problem that you can resolve as a short-term goal—one you can complete this week or next.
- Start by discussing this goal with a small group in your class.
- Identify how this short-term goal relates to your long-term goal of success in college.
- In group discussion and writing, complete the six steps for achieving a short-term goal listed in this chapter.
- Establish a date (a week or month from now) when you will determine whether you have achieved the goal. At that time set at least one new goal. Be sure your goal is something you genuinely want to achieve, written down in measurable terms, and achievable.

Also be certain to

- Identify and explore potential problems.
- Create a specific set of steps for achieving the goal.
- Set a schedule for the steps as well as a date for completion.

Your Personal Journal

Each chapter of this book will ask you to write your thoughts about the material you've just read. This is another way to remember the content of the chapter, so you might try it with your other classes as well. Choose one or more of the following questions or choose another topic related to this chapter and write about it.

1. Go back to the list of concerns on pages 8–9. Which of them are you feeling right now? How do you think you can begin overcoming them?
2. Of the five major strategies, which one will give you the greatest challenge? Which will be easiest? Why?
3. Of the many points under each strategy, which do you need to work on most? Suggest some ways to accomplish this.
4. Anything else on your mind this week? If you wish to share it with your instructor, add it to this journal entry.

Resources

This book can be a continuing resource for you throughout your college career. Many of the activities and topics covered in this book will be important throughout your life. The resource page at the end of each chapter is for you to fill with names, phone numbers, addresses, e-mail addresses, and other helpful information. When you're done, you'll have a valuable personal resource file for college success.

Your Personal Information

Your name ....

School name ....

Your local address ....

Permanent address ....

Social Security number .... School ID number ....

Driver's license—state and number ....

(Marking or engraving your belongings with your Social Security and driver's license numbers can help you recover them if they are stolen.)

Key Personal Resources

List several names, phone numbers, and addresses for the following. Choose people who are supportive of your college goals, good listeners when you need to talk, and fun to hang out with.

FAMILY

....

....

....

....

FRIENDS

....

....

....

....

EXTRACURRICULAR GROUPS

....

....

....

....

FACULTY

....

....

....

....

Part 2

Plan Ahead!

Strategies for Success

PLAN AHEAD!	TAKE CHARGE OF LEARNING!	HONE YOUR SKILLS!	GET CONNECTED!	KNOW YOURSELF!
• Show up for class • Have work done on time • Set up a daily schedule • If full-time, limit work week to 20 hours. Work on campus if possible • If stressed, enroll part time	• Choose instructors who favor active learning • Assess how you learn best • Improve your reading, note-taking, and study habits • Develop critical thinking skills • Improve your writing	• Participate in class • Practice giving presentations • Learn how to remember more from every class • Learn from criticism • Take workshops on how to study • Get to know your campus library and other information sources • Embrace new technologies	• Study with a group • Get to know one person on campus who cares about you • Get involved in campus activities • Learn about campus helping resources • Meet with your instructors • Find a great academic advisor or counselor • Visit your campus career center • Take advantage of minority support services • Enlist support of your spouse, partner, or family	• Take your health seriously • Have realistic expectations • Learn how to be assertive yet tactful • Be proud of your heritage

Time Management

Foundation of Academic Success

IN THIS CHAPTER,
YOU WILL LEARN

- How to set up a daily schedule
- How to complete your work on time
- How to set priorities for work and play
- How to develop your master time plan
- How to schedule your week for work and play
- How to make all of this work
- How to use critical thinking to manage time

don't miss the train

"*B*ig test tomorrow! Gonna be a late night tonight. I was going to study, but something happened and the time just sort of disappeared. Now I have to pull it all together. Let's see, now. Did I read all those chapters? Did I read any of them? Do I remember what I read if I did?"

How do you approach time? Because people have different personalities and come from different cultures, they may also view time in different ways.

Some of these differences may have to do with your preferred style of learning. For example, if you're a detail-oriented individual (called a "senser"), you may spend an inordinate amount of time on those details, whereas conceptual thinkers ("intuitors") often have to redo tasks because they neglected important details or jumped to conclusions. If you're a natural time manager ("judger"), you're probably the first one in class who enters on a calendar all due dates for assignments, exams, and quizzes as soon as you receive the syllabus. Your opposites, the "perceivers," can become so engaged with assignments that they don't want to wrap up things until it's absolutely necessary, which too often is after the deadline has passed. Such a student may actually tell a teacher, "I need three more days because it isn't quite the way I want it yet." Complete the self-assessment inventory below to see what kind of a time manager you are.

SELF-ASSESSMENT: TIME MANAGEMENT

Take a few moments to reflect on yourself and your past experiences with time. Then write a few paragraphs on how you use time, using these questions as guidelines:

- What are my personal views on time? How conscious am I of time passing? Do I wear a watch? How important is time in my life?

- How have my views on time been influenced by my family, culture, lifestyle, gender, age, and other factors?

- Am I punctual or am I a procrastinator? Can I concentrate or am I easily distracted? Do I try to control time, or does it seem to control me?

- Am I early, prompt, or late to class, appointments, or meetings? Do I often skip class or miss appointments?

- Do I complete my assignments early, on time, or late?

- How much time do I spend on social activities? How important are these uses of time to me?

- How is my use of time affecting my stress level? How is my anxiety about not getting work done on time affecting my performance?

- What are some specific things I can do to manage my time? How do I balance work, study, and socializing?

Setting Priorities: Assessing Your Use of Time

Time management involves

- Knowing what your goals are
- Knowing in advance where you must be
- Deciding where your priorities lie
- Anticipating future needs and possible changes
- Placing yourself in control of your time
- Carrying out your plans

To make optimum use of your time, you'll need a schedule. Instead of simply dividing the day into blocks of time, it's important to prioritize. In college, as in your future professional life, work often comes before pleasure. So begin with the essentials: sleep, food, showering, dressing, attending classes, studying. Leave time for fun things (socializing, watching TV, going out for the evening, and so forth); you deserve them. But finish what *needs* to be done before you move from work to pleasure. Exercise 2.1 will help you structure your time. Complete it and promise yourself you'll try to stick with the schedule that you create for at least 2 weeks. If it doesn't work, make sensible adjustments. **SEE EXERCISE 2.1**

Developing a Master Plan

In college as in life, you will quickly learn that managing time is an important key not only to success but also to survival. One way to put your goals in order is to make a term assignment preview of your long-term assignments (Figure 2.1), a timetable of your weekly schedule (Figure 2.2), and a daily plan (Figure 2.3).

A good way to start is to look at the big picture. Use the term assignment preview (Figure 2.1) to give yourself an idea of what's in store for you. You should complete your term assignment preview by the beginning of the second week of class so that you can continue to use your time effectively. Then purchase a week-at-a-glance organizer for the current year, enter the notes from your preview sheets, and continue to enter all due dates as soon as you know them. Write in meeting times, scheduled social events, study time for each class you're taking, and so forth. Always carry your planner with you in a convenient place.

Get into the habit of checking your notes daily for the current week and the coming week. Choose a specific time of day to do this, perhaps just before you begin studying in the evening or at a set time on weekends. But check it daily. It takes just a moment to be certain you aren't forgetting something important.

Guidelines for Scheduling Week by Week

- **Examine your toughest weeks**. If paper deadlines and test dates fall during the same week, find time to finish some assignments early, to free up study time for tests. Note this in your organizer. **SEE EXERCISE 2.2**
- **Break large assignments such as term papers into smaller steps** (choosing a topic, doing research, writing an outline, writing a first draft, and so on). Add deadlines in your schedule for each of the smaller portions of the project.
- **All assignments are not equal**. Estimate how much time you'll need for each one and begin your work early. A good student time manager frequently finishes assignments before actual due dates to allow for emergencies.

	Sunday	Monday	Tuesday	Wednesday	Thursday	Friday	Saturday
Week # _____							
Week # _____							
Week # _____							
Week # _____							

	Sunday	Monday	Tuesday	Wednesday	Thursday	Friday	Saturday
Week # _____							
Week # _____							
Week # _____							
Week # _____							

FIGURE 2.1 Term Assignment Preview
(1) Make two copies of this page and number the weeks to reflect one full term.
(2) To see the big picture of your workload for this term, gather your syllabi and list all tests, reports, papers, and other projects.

Time management is a lifelong skill. The better the job you have after college the more likely that you'll be managing your own and possibly other people's time.

- **Set aside time for research and other preparatory tasks**. Instructors may expect you to be computer literate, and they usually don't have time to explain how to use a word processor, spreadsheet, or statistical computer program. Most campuses offer tutoring, walk-in assistance, or workshops to assist you with computer programs, e-mail, or the Internet at a student support center or computer center. Your library may offer sessions on how to search for information using computer databases. Such services will save you time and usually are free.

Using your term assignment preview, develop a weekly plan for one week of the term, following the directions in Exercise 2.3.

SEE EXERCISE 2.3

Organizing Your Day

Time management consultant Alan Lakein, comparing the efficient time manager with one who takes more time because of poor planning, advises you to "work smarter, not harder." Lakein's words ring true for college students who have to juggle many deadline pressures. Once you've set the framework of the term and weekly schedules, make a daily plan to set priorities.

Being a good student does not necessarily mean grinding away at studies and doing little else. Keep the following points in mind as you write out your daily schedule:

SEE EXERCISE 2.4

- Set aside time to read and review notes to help prepare for class.
- Prevent forgetting by allowing time to review as soon as possible after class.
- It's hard to study on a full stomach. Schedule time right after lunch for leisure activities.
- Always build in a short break in the middle of a study session to keep yourself alert.
- Program an exercise session daily. It will help you study better.
- Schedule free time to keep you refreshed and relaxed for more study.
- Break extended study sessions into a variety of activities, each with a specific objective.
- Restrict repetitive tasks (such as checking your e-mail) to a certain time, not every hour.

SEE SEARCH ONLINE! INTERNET EXERCISE 2.1

Making Your Time Management Plan Work

With the best intentions of making their time management plans work, some students allow themselves to become overcommitted. If there's not enough time to carry your course load and meet your commitments, drop any courses before the drop date so that you won't have a low grade on your permanent record. Or learn to say no to commitments that you can afford to drop. If you are on financial aid, keep in mind that you must be registered for a certain number of hours (usually twelve per term) to be considered a full-time student.

If you're a commuter student, you may prefer block scheduling, which runs classes together without breaks. Although block scheduling allows you to cut travel time by attending school 1 or 2 days a week, there's little time to process information between classes. If you become ill on a class day, you could fall behind in all your classes. You may become fatigued sitting in class after class. Finally, you might become stressed when exams are held in several classes on the same day. Block scheduling may work better if you can attend lectures at an alternative time in case you are absent, if you alternate classes with free periods, and if you seek out instructors who allow you flexibility to complete assignments.

Examining Values

The opening sentence in this chapter asks, "How do you approach time?" It might also have read, "How do you *value* time and the way you choose to spend it?" Make a list starting with the things you enjoy doing most and ending with the things you enjoy doing least. From that list, generate another list beginning with the things you know you must do first and ending with those you can save for later or omit. Then make a third list that balances your "musts" with your "wants." What does this say about your own personal values system as it relates to managing time?

Reduce Distractions

Where should you study? Not at places associated with leisure—such as the kitchen table, the living room, or in front of the TV—because they lend themselves to interruptions by others. Your association with social activities in these locations can distract you even when others aren't there. The solution is to find quiet places, both on campus and at home, where you can concentrate and develop a study mind-set each time you sit down to do your work.

Try to stick to a routine as you study. The more firmly you have established a specific time and a quiet place to study, the more effective you will be in keeping up with your schedule. To review or catch up on major projects, take advantage of large blocks of time that may be available on the weekend. If you break down large tasks and take one thing at a time, you'll make more progress toward your ultimate goal—high grades.

Beat Procrastination

Procrastination may be your single greatest enemy. Getting started when it's time to start takes self-discipline and self-control. Here are some ways to beat procrastination:

- Say to yourself, "A mature person is capable, responsible, and a self-starter. I'm that kind of person if I start now." Then start!

Critical Thinking

Setting Goals and Priorities

Time management involves planning, judgment, anticipation, flexibility, and commitment. You must first determine what your goals are for college and beyond. Thinking about the big picture, ask yourself some serious questions and try to answer them in essay form:

Why did I choose to go to college? What are my goals for my first year of college? What are my long-term goals regarding where I want to be after college? (These goals no doubt will change as you move closer to graduation.)

- On a 3 x 5 note card write a list of everything you need to do. Check off items as you get them done. Use the list to focus on the items that aren't getting done. Move them to the top of your next day's list and make up your mind to do them. Working from a list will give you a feeling of accomplishment and lead you to do more.
- Break down big jobs into smaller steps. Tackle short, easy-to-accomplish tasks first.
- Apply the goal-setting technique described in Chapter 1 to whatever you are putting off.
- Promise yourself a suitable reward (an apple, a phone call, a walk) whenever you finish something difficult.
- Take control of your study environment. Eliminate distractions—including the ones you love! Say no to friends who want your attention. Agree to meet them at a specific time later. Let them be your reward for doing what you must do now. Don't make or take phone calls during planned study sessions. Close your door. (See Internet Exercise 2.2 for more help.)

SEE SEARCH ONLINE!
INTERNET EXERCISE 2.2

Time and Critical Thinking

You may be tempted to think that most college assignments can and should be done quickly and that instructors simply have to mark them right or wrong. However, most questions worthy of study in college do not have clear and immediate yes or no answers; if they did, no one would be paying scholars to spend years doing research.

Good critical thinkers have a high tolerance for uncertainty. Confronted by a difficult question, they begin by saying, "I don't know." They suspend judgment until they can gather information and take the time it requires to find and verify an answer.

Thus, effective time management doesn't always mean making decisions or finishing projects quickly. Effective critical thinkers resist finalizing their thoughts on important questions until they feel they have developed the best answers possible. This is not an argument in favor of ignoring deadlines, but it does suggest the value of beginning your research, reading, and even the writing phases of a project early so that you will have time to change direction if necessary as you gather new insights.

SEE SEARCH ONLINE!
INTERNET EXERCISE 2.3

Give your thoughts time to incubate. Allow time to visit the library more than once. Sometimes insights come unexpectedly, when you're not consciously thinking about a problem. So, begin reviewing as early as you can, take a break from your studies, and then return to the topic. If you're successful, you'll be well ahead of the game when it's time for class, quizzes, or that final exam.

Internet Exercise 2.1 Limiting Your Time Online

Anyone who has surfed the Web has realized its addictive nature. The Web can be a veritable black hole for your time. It is thus essential that you limit your time online.

As with any addiction, the first step is to realize that you have a problem. Make a log of how you spend your time at each of the following activities in one week. Then create a target time for each area.

ACTIVITY	ACTUAL TIME	TARGET TIME
Reading and writing academic e-mail	_____	_____
Reading and writing personal e-mail	_____	_____
Surfing casually for academic topics	_____	_____
Surfing casually for personal interest	_____	_____
Searching rigorously for academic materials	_____	_____
Searching rigorously for personal information	_____	_____
Number of times a day you check your e-mail	_____	_____

How might you limit the time you spend on each activity?

_____

_____

_____

Internet Exercise 2.2 Procrastination Resources

The Procrastination Research Group at Carleton University in Ottawa, at *http://superior.carleton.ca/~tpychy/*, offers access and information and research on procrastination from all over the world. (Go to *http://success.wadsworth.com* for the most up-to-date URLs.)

What is the earliest reference they cite for the use of the term procrastination?

_____

What strategies do they offer for reducing procrastination?

_____

List three organizations for which links are offered for further study.

_____

Internet Exercise 2.3 Discovering More About Time Management

Using *InfoTrac College Edition,* try these phrases and others for key-word and subject-guide searches: "time management," "procrastination," and "goal setting."

ALSO LOOK UP:

What to do when being overworked leads to procrastination. (Workforce Extra) Linda R. Dominguez. *Workforce* Jan 1999 v78 i1 pE6(2)

Scheduling snafu: I thought a web calendar might bring order to my messy life—but it just confused me more. (personal time/your technology) (Brief Article) Anita Hamilton. *Time* May 10, 1999 v153 i18 p96(1)

Got a moment? (time management) (Interview) Margo Vanover Porter. *Association Management* Mar 1999 v51 i3 p41(3)

Additional Exercises

These exercises will help you sharpen what we believe are the critical skills for college success: writing, critical thinking, learning in groups, planning, reflecting, and taking action. Also, check out the CD-ROM that came with your book—you will find these exercises and more.

Exercise 2.1 Logging Your Time and Identifying Priorities

The following shows how typical residential first-year students allocate their time on a weekday.*

ACTIVITY	HOURS PER DAY
Class time	3
Studying	3
Employment	$1/4$
Idle leisure	3
Social	$2\,1/4$
Travel between classes	1
Eating	$1\,1/2$
Grooming	1
Resting	$6\,1/2$
Recreation	$1\,1/2$
Other	1

Make a daily log of how you spend your time for 1 week, using the chart in this exercise. Each evening jot down the amount of time you spent on different activities that day. At the end of the week, add up the time you spent and enter it in the different categories in the chart. Next record the amount of time you would like to spend on each category. Remember, there are only 168 hours in a week! Your plan should help you reach both your personal and academic goals. Notice that new students who live on campus devote almost 7 hours each day to socializing, recreation, and leisure pursuits. A commuter may spend much of this time on travel, work, and other responsibilities.

CATEGORIES	ACTUAL HOURS PER DAY	TARGETED HOURS PER DAY
Class time	_____	_____
Studying	_____	_____
Work	_____	_____
Travel	_____	_____
Home to college	_____	_____
Between classes	_____	_____
College to work	_____	_____
Work to home	_____	_____
Other	_____	_____
Total travel	_____	_____
Home responsibilities		
Shopping	_____	_____
Meals	_____	_____
Housecleaning	_____	_____
Laundry	_____	_____
Other	_____	_____
Total home	_____	_____

*Data adapted from David W. Desmond and David S. Glenwick, "Time-Budgeting Practices of College Students: A Developmental Analysis of Activity Patterns," *Journal of College Student Personnel 28*, 4 (1987): 318–323.

CATEGORIES	ACTUAL HOURS PER DAY	TARGETED HOURS PER DAY
Family responsibilities		
General time	_____	_____
Child care	_____	_____
Care for elderly or disabled	_____	_____
Other	_____	_____
Total family	_____	_____
Civic responsibilities		
Volunteer work	_____	_____
Other	_____	_____
Total civic	_____	_____
Personal		
Grooming/dressing	_____	_____
Reading for pleasure	_____	_____
Hobbies, entertainment	_____	_____
TV and music	_____	_____
Talking with or writing to friends	_____	_____
Exercising	_____	_____
Resting	_____	_____
Other	_____	_____
Total personal	_____	_____
Other	_____	_____
Total time for all responsibilities	_____	_____

Exercise 2.2 Goal Setting for Courses

A List each course you are taking this term, list the grade you hope to earn, and estimate the time you think you will need each week to achieve your goal. When deciding how much time to study for a course, consider this rule of thumb: Study 1 hour for every hour in class for a C, 2 hours for a B, and 3 hours for an A. Then consider the difficulty of the course as you complete the following chart.

COURSE	GRADE	ESTIMATED TIME PER WEEK
_____	_____	_____
_____	_____	_____
_____	_____	_____
_____	_____	_____
_____	_____	_____

B Now list additional steps you will need to achieve your goal. Some examples might be attending tutoring sessions each week, joining a study group, studying with a friend, learning a computer program, and learning to access a database in the library.

Exercise 2.3 Your Weekly Plan/Timetable

Refer first to your term assignment preview that gives you the big picture for the term; then develop a weekly plan for 1 week of the semester, using the form in Figure 2.2.

	Sunday	Monday	Tuesday	Wednesday	Thursday	Friday	Saturday
6:00							
7:00							
8:00							
9:00							
10:00							
11:00							
12:00							
1:00							
2:00							
3:00							
4:00							
5:00							
6:00							
7:00							
8:00							
9:00							
10:00							
11:00							

FIGURE 2.2 Weekly Timetable
(1) List all class meeting times and other fixed obligations (work, scheduled family responsibilities, and so forth).
(2) Try to reserve 1 or 2 hours of daytime study for each class hour. Reserve time for meals, exercise, and free time.
(3) Try to plan a minimum of 1-hour additional study in evenings or on weekends for each class.

A   Using the timetable in Figure 2.2, block out your time commitments. Start by filling in all your classes and any other regularly scheduled activities. Then look up that week on your term assignment preview and reread the syllabi for your courses. Most instructors use a syllabus to map out the entire semester. What are your tests, assignments, and readings for that week? What long-term assignments should you start this week? When should you plan your weekly reviews for each course?

B   Fill in your total study time for the week in 1-hour blocks at appropriate times. Remember that the best times to review course materials are directly before and after that class. It is best to schedule your hardest subjects earliest in the day when you feel fresh.

C   Follow your timetable for a week. Keep a record of the major obstacles you encountered during the week. Brainstorm strategies to overcome these obstacles in a small group and then share them with the class.

Exercise 2.4 **Your Daily Plan**

Using 1 day from this week's schedule, make a daily plan by filling in the Daily Planner in Figure 2.3. Circle the day of the week. List the day's appointments on the page with hours of the day. On the opposite page, list your "To Do" activities. Using a simple ABC priority system, label them with A, B, or C, with A's deserving the most attention. By tackling these first, you may not finish your list, but you probably will be more satisfied with your accomplishments.

Check out the different calendar and personal planner formats at your bookstore and get one that works for you. Make a commitment to use it. You may want to put your schedule on your computer, using personal information management (PIM) software or a spreadsheet program. Writing and revising the schedule, however, should not become a goal in itself. The important thing is not how you write the schedule, but how easily you can understand and use it.

Your Personal Journal

Here are several things to write about. Choose one or more or choose another topic related to time management.

1. Before you completed the exercises in this chapter, how successful were you at managing your time?
2. If you have completed the exercises, what difference—if any—have they made in the way you think about time?
3. How can you modify the ideas in this chapter to fit your own biological clock?
4. Which plan worked best for you—the term assignment plan, the weekly plan, or the daily plan? Why do you think this was so?
5. What else is going on with you this week? If you wish to share something with your instructor, add it to this journal entry.

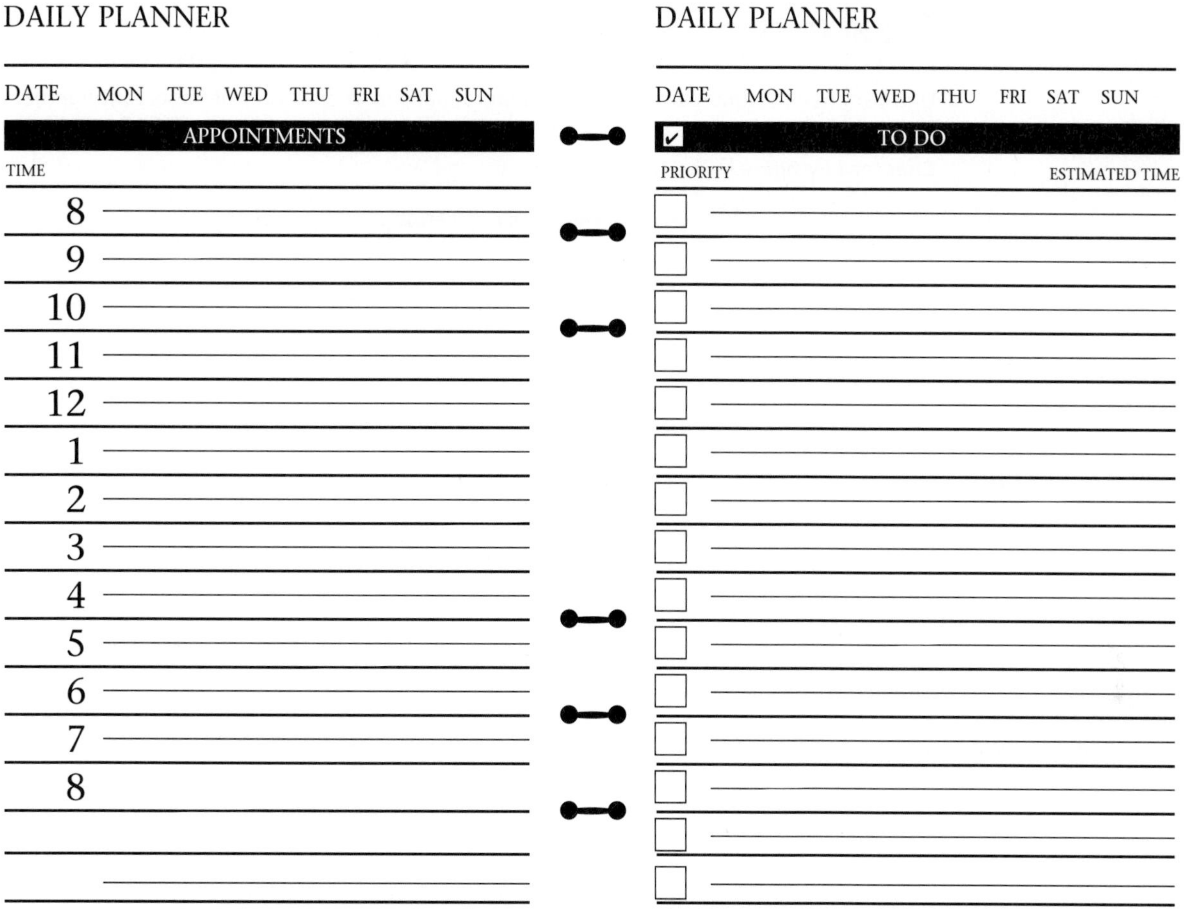

DAILY PLANNER

DATE   MON   TUE   WED   THU   FRI   SAT   SUN

APPOINTMENTS

TIME

8

9

10

11

12

1

2

3

4

5

6

7

8

DAILY PLANNER

DATE   MON   TUE   WED   THU   FRI   SAT   SUN

✔   TO DO

PRIORITY   ESTIMATED TIME

FIGURE 2.3 Sample Daily Planner
(1) Circle the day of the week and list the day's appointments next to the appropriate times.
(2) On the opposite page, list your "To Do" activities. Decide which are the most urgent and fill in the priority boxes with A for most important, B for next important, and so on.

Resources

One very helpful time-saver is your own personal phone directory of important numbers and addresses. Keep it handy. Continue the list you began on the "Resources" page in Chapter 1 by filling in the following:

FRIENDS | **Name** | **Phone number/address** | **e-mail**

_____ | _____ | _____

_____ | _____ | _____

_____ | _____ | _____

_____ | _____ | _____

FAMILY | **Name** | **Phone number/address** | **e-mail**

_____ | _____ | _____

_____ | _____ | _____

_____ | _____ | _____

_____ | _____ | _____

INSTRUCTORS | **Name** | **Phone number/address** | **e-mail**

_____ | _____ | _____

_____ | _____ | _____

_____ | _____ | _____

_____ | _____ | _____

Academic advisor _____

Campus security/local police _____

Campus health center/hospital _____

Doctor/dentist _____

Campus counseling center _____

Dean of students _____

Campus legal services _____

Child-care centers _____

Emergency road service/mechanic _____

Landlord (home and work) _____

Employer (home and work) _____

Tutorial/learning center _____

Commuter student service center _____

Neighbors _____

Taxi service _____

Campus and public libraries _____

Campus fax numbers _____

Campus home page _____

Part 3

Take Charge of Learning!

Strategies for Success

PLAN AHEAD!

- Show up for class
- Have work done on time
- Set up a daily schedule
- If full-time, limit work week to 20 hours. Work on campus if possible
- If stressed, enroll part time

TAKE CHARGE OF LEARNING!

- Choose instructors who favor active learning
- Assess how you learn best
- Improve your reading, note-taking, and study habits
- Develop critical thinking skills
- Improve your writing

HONE YOUR SKILLS!

- Participate in class
- Practice giving presentations
- Learn how to remember more from every class
- Learn from criticism
- Take workshops on how to study
- Get to know your campus library and other information sources
- Embrace new technologies

GET CONNECTED!

- Study with a group
- Get to know one person on campus who cares about you
- Get involved in campus activities
- Learn about campus helping resources
- Meet with your instructors
- Find a great academic advisor or counselor
- Visit your campus career center
- Take advantage of minority support services
- Enlist support of your spouse, partner, or family

KNOW YOURSELF!

- Take your health seriously
- Have realistic expectations
- Learn how to be assertive yet tactful
- Be proud of your heritage

Chapter 3

Active Learning

The Student-Teacher Connection

IN THIS CHAPTER, YOU WILL LEARN

- The big difference between high school and college

- What active learning means and why it can help you learn

- The value of collaborating with other students when you study

- How to choose the best college teachers and be comfortable with them

keep paddling

*"**M**y college teachers aren't like my teachers in high school. They don't seem as easy to approach. They don't even seem to notice me very much. I wonder when they're going to come out and say exactly what they mean? What exactly am I supposed to be learning?"*

The Big Difference Between High School and College

What is it that makes college such a totally different experience than high school for most new or returning students? For some, it may simply be that this is the first time they've been so far from home; or the entirely new experience of meeting others from across the country and around the world; or having time off from classes in the middle of the day and wondering what to do with it; or having class in the evenings after work; or having some days with no classes at all.

Other things change, too: Read three chapters of history by Wednesday; finish a biology lab experiment by Friday; keep up with a self-paced course in which you must set your own schedule to complete the requirements on time.

Above all, what we believe makes college so different, so challenging, and so rewarding—once you become accustomed to it—is that college offers you the chance to move from a pattern of being *taught passively* to one of *learning actively*.

SELF-ASSESSMENT: ACTIVE LEARNING

Checkmark those statements that are true. Leave the others blank. After reading this chapter, come back to this inventory and place an X beside those items you plan to work on this term.

_____ I'm usually comfortable asking a question in class.

_____ I'm also comfortable making a comment in class.

_____ Whether the class has 15 students or 150, it's okay to say something.

_____ I have participated in learning teams.

_____ I go to the library with classmates so that we can help one another with our research.

_____ I try to sit as close to the front as possible in every class so that I can focus on the topic.

_____ If I can't tolerate an instructor, I try to get out of that class as soon as possible. If I can, I try to register for another section of the same class.

SEE EXERCISE 3.1

Why You'll Learn Better as an Active Learner

Active learning involves participating in and out of class instead of passively recording notes and studying silently. Students who embrace active learning not only learn better but also enjoy learning more. Active learners become involved in learning rather than simply being an audience. They try new ideas and learn by exploring the world around them instead of just memorizing facts. Here are some things you can do to promote active learning:

- Ask other students which teachers will actively engage you in learning.
- Even in a class of 200 students, never hesitate to raise your hand if you don't understand something. Chances are, the other 199 didn't understand it either.
- Put learning into your own words instead of just memorizing the book or the lecture.
- Study with other students. Talking about assignments and getting other points of view will help you learn the material faster and more thoroughly. (More on this later.)
- Follow suggestions in this book or others about managing your time, optimizing your learning style, taking class notes, reading texts, and studying for exams.
- Politely question authority. When you don't agree, state your opinion. Good teachers will listen and may still disagree, but they may think more of you for showing that you can think.
- Stay in touch with teachers, other students, and your academic advisor. One great way is through e-mail, or you can call and leave a voice mail if the teacher is out. You'll get a reply.

What if you have an instructor who lectures for an entire period and leaves little or no time for questions? If the lectures are well organized and delivered, you may still be learning, but you might learn more through participation. One way to do this is to form a study group so that you can benefit from what other students have learned. Another way is to ask the teacher for an appointment so that you can discuss material from the lecture that isn't clear.

Why Active Learners Can Learn More Than Passive Learners

Active learning puts you in charge of your own learning. Indeed, it is the philosophy on which this book is based and why we include so many active exercises. Although you may acquire knowledge listening to a lecture, you probably won't be motivated to think much about that knowledge. Through active learning, you will learn not only content but also a number of processes to help you

SEE EXERCISE 3.2

- work with others
- improve your critical thinking, listening, writing, and speaking skills
- be able to function independently and learn to teach yourself
- manage your time
- gain sensitivity to cultural differences by working with students from diverse backgrounds.

With all its benefits, some students still resist active learning. One student described an active learning class as "scary" and a more traditional class as "safe." The traditional class was safe because the "teacher did not make students sit in a semi-circle, and he used a textbook and lectures to support his cases. On the other hand, discussions were scary. The process, the uncertainty, and the openness made them scary."*

True, the larger the class, the greater is the risk to speak out. As one student explains, "If I give the wrong answer in a class of 150, 149 students will see me as a dunce." Yet when your instructor creates an atmosphere where such participation is comfortable and makes it clear that "wrong" answers are better than no answers at all, you'll probably participate more often and thereby learn more.

*Adapted from Russell A. Warren, "Engaging Students in Active Learning," *About Campus*, March–April 1997.

FIGURE 3.1
Aspects of
Student Development

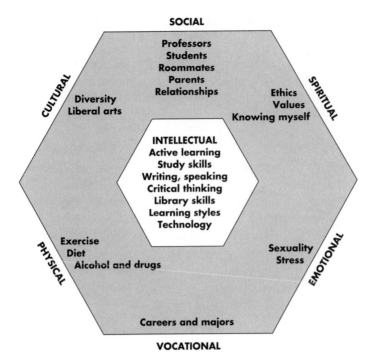

Active learning requires preparation before every class, not just before exams. It might include browsing in the library, making appointments to talk to faculty members, making outlines from your class notes, going to performances, working on a committee, asking someone to read something you've written to see if it's clear, or having a serious discussion with students whose personal values are different from yours.

According to student development theory, an active approach to learning and living has the potential to produce individuals who are well rounded in all aspects of life. The hexagon in Figure 3.1 depicts seven aspects of development, with intellectual development at its center. Optimal personal development depends on one area supporting every other area. For example, with good active learning skills, you will likely feel more comfortable socially, gain a greater appreciation for diversity and the liberal arts, and be better able to clarify your college major and future career. Staying physically active can reduce stress and keep your mind alert while studying. Developing a sense of values can help you choose your friends more carefully and decide how you choose to manage your time.

Many college teachers try new ideas in the classroom in hopes of discovering better, more exciting ways to help students learn. As a student, you can do the same. Instead of blending in with your peers—as many students do—ask the questions in class everyone else wants to ask but doesn't. Try to do something innovative with every paper and project. Sure, you'll make some mistakes, but your instructor may

Examining Values

What criteria do you employ in choosing friends? Try making a list of what you value most in a friendship. Then think of some friends you have at college and check your list against each person. If the list is a true representation of your values, which friends seem to be your closest ones? Which acquaintances probably will never be close friends because they lack some of the values you hold dear? Now ask friends to make their own lists. How similar are their lists to yours? What did you learn by comparing lists?

appreciate your inventiveness, reward you for it, and be more willing to help you improve your work. As one teacher said, "If your paper is mediocre, I can't push you forward. But if, by being innovative, it goes beyond what the assignment called for, I may be able to coax you back."

The 1-Minute Paper

One way to practice active learning and critical thinking daily is through a process called the 1-minute paper. At the end of each class, write what you think was the main issue of that class and what your unanswered questions are for the next class.

Even if your instructors don't require it, try writing your 1-minute paper each day at the end of class. Use it to think about the main issues discussed that day and save it so that you can ask good questions at the next class meeting. Some colleges offer "supplemental instruction" to groups who then practice this learning strategy along with others. Students who voluntarily participate usually earn higher grades and are less likely to drop out.

The Value of Collaboration

Collaborative learning is any learning situation requiring input from more than one learner. In a sense, you might even say that if you have a conference with your instructor about a writing project in draft stage, you're engaged in collaborative learning. But usually, the term refers to groups of students working together for the good of all.

How does collaboration improve learning? Joseph Cuseo of Marymount College, an expert on collaborative learning, points to these factors:

- Learners learn from one another as well as from the instructor.
- Collaborative learning is by its very nature active learning and so tends to increase learning by involving you more actively.
- "Two heads are better than one." Collaboration can lead to more ideas, alternative approaches, new perspectives, and better solutions.
- Learners who might not speak out in larger classes tend to be more comfortable speaking in smaller groups, resulting in better communication and better ideas.
- Students develop stronger bonds with other students in the class, which may increase their interest in attending. SEE EXERCISE 3.3
- An environment of positive competition among groups is developed when several groups are asked to solve the same problem—as long as the instructor clarifies that the purpose is for the good of all.
- Students in groups tend to develop leadership skills.
- Students learn to work with others, a fact of life in the world of work.

When students work effectively in a supportive group, the experience can be a very powerful way to improve academic achievement. Interviews with college students at Harvard University revealed that nearly every senior who had been part of a study group considered this experience to be crucial to his or her academic success.

Making Learning Teams Productive

You will be able to apply the teamwork skills you build in this course to future courses. SEE EXERCISE 3.4 But remember, not all learning groups are equally effective. Here are some ways to maximize the power of peer collaboration:

1. **In forming teams, look for students who are motivated.** Choose students who attend class regularly, are attentive, participate actively, and complete

A good study group shares a common goal of success for all its members. It also asks each member to contribute according to his or her own special perspective and style.

assignments. Include teammates from different ethnic, racial, or cultural backgrounds; different age groups; and different learning styles. Include males and females. Choosing only your friends may result in a learning group that is more likely to get off the track and not progress with the learning task.

2. **Keep the group small (three to six students).** Smaller groups allow for more face-to-face interaction and eye contact and less opportunity for any one individual to shirk responsibility. Also, it's easier for small groups to meet outside class. Consider choosing an even number of teammates (four or six) so that you can work in pairs in case the team decides to divide its work.

The Many Uses of Learning Teams

1. **Note-taking teams**   Team up with other students immediately after class to share and compare notes. One of your teammates may have picked up something you missed or vice versa. By meeting immediately after class, your group may still have a chance to consult with the instructor about any missing or confusing information.

2. **Reading teams**   After completing reading assignments, team up with other students to compare your highlighting and margin notes. See if all agree on what the author's major points were and what information you should study for exams.

3. **Library research teams**   Studies show that many first-year students are unfamiliar with library research, often due to anxiety. Forming library research teams is an effective way to develop a support group for reducing this fear and for locating and sharing sources of information. (*Note:* Locating and sharing sources of information isn't cheating or plagiarizing

as long as you cite your sources and the final product you turn in represents your own work.)

4. **Team/instructor conferences**   Have your learning team visit the instructor during office hours, to seek additional assistance in studying or completing work. If you are shy, you will probably find it easier to see an instructor in the company of other students. The feedback from your instructor is also received by your teammates so that useful information is less likely to be forgotten. Your team visit also tells your instructor that you are serious about learning.

5. **Team test-results review**   After receiving test results, the members of a learning team can review their individual tests together, to help one another identify the sources of their mistakes and to identify any answers that received high scores. This provides each team member with a clearer idea of what the instructor expects. You can use this information for subsequent tests and assignments.

3. **Remember that learning teams are more than study groups.** Many students think that collaborative learning simply involves study groups that meet the night before major exams. Effective student learning teams collaborate regularly for other academic tasks besides test review sessions. See the box on page 42 for other uses of learning teams.

4. **Hold individual team members personally accountable for their own learning and for contributing to the learning of their teammates.** One way to ensure accountability is to have each member come to group meetings prepared to share specific information with teammates and to ask for help on questions or points of confusion. Another way is to have individual members take on different roles or responsibilities for mastering a particular topic, section, or skill to be taught to others.

Connecting with Your College Teachers

Your college teachers want you involved! They want you to develop new ways of thinking about things, to realize there is often more than one possibility, to question existing knowledge, to take issue with something they say, to ask questions in class, and to offer possible solutions to problems. You may be surprised to find that most teachers do not fit the stereotype of the ivory tower scholar. Though the present generation of college instructors still must spend time doing scholarship and performing service, most of them admit they love teaching best of all because they get a "high" from motivating students to do their best.

Your college teachers may do things your high school teachers never did, such as

- Supplementing textbook assignments with other information
- Giving exams covering both assigned readings and lectures
- Disagreeing with something in your textbook or in other books or articles
- Accepting several different student opinions on a question
- Never checking to see if you are taking notes
- Demanding more reading from you in a shorter period of time
- Giving fewer quizzes or many more quizzes
- Being sympathetic to difficulties you may have while holding firm to high standards of grading. You may be on friendly terms with your instructor and find you have received a low grade because you missed too many classes, you did not complete all required work, or your work was average or less.

Critical Thinking

What Do College Teachers Expect of Students?

Look back over the differences between high school and college teachers. Then list five to ten qualities and behaviors you believe college teachers want in their students. Compare your response with those of several classmates. Consider asking one of your teachers to comment as well.

Making the Most of a Student-Teacher Relationship

1. **Make it a point to attend class regularly and on time.** Participate in the discussion; you'll learn more if you do. If you miss a class, copying another student's notes isn't the same as being present during class. Learning is easier when you're there every day, so save your cuts for emergencies. When you know you will be absent, let your instructor know in advance. It could make a big difference in your teacher's attitude toward you, and if the class is really large, it's one way of introducing yourself.

2. **Sit near the front.** Studies indicate that students who do so tend to earn better grades.

3. **Speak up.** Ask when you don't understand or need clarification and voice your opinion when you disagree. Your teacher will respond favorably as long as your comments are relevant.

SEE SEARCH ONLINE!
INTERNET EXERCISE 3.1

4. **See your instructor outside of class when you need help.** You may be surprised at how much your instructor is willing to meet with you. Make an appointment by phone, e-mail, or at the end of class. (See Internet Exercise 3.1.)

5. **Share one or more 1-minute papers,** either in writing or through e-mail, with your instructor. It could be the start of an interesting dialog.

Learning Actively

One teacher who believes that interaction in the classroom is still the best way to learn says,

My students learn best when they participate, so I make it my business to see that they do ... through discussion, presentations, group work, and constant feedback. You know, we now have the ability to "teach" students anywhere on two-way closed-circuit TV. We have computers in the classrooms, but we often fool ourselves into believing that the more we upgrade the software, the better a student will learn. Sometimes we get so wrapped up in technology that we tend to forget that good teaching consists of making a connection, building a relationship, inspiring a learner.

Seek out such teachers who encourage collaboration over competition, where each student turns in an original piece of work but is free to seek advice and criticism from another student. That's the way you probably will be working after college.

Good teachers set deadlines for work and stick to them to instill in you the importance of effective time management, another skill you'll be using all your life.

Good teachers keep lines of communication open. They not only grade your work but also ask you for comments on how you're learning, what you're learning, and how well you believe they are teaching. Those comments may provoke open discussion in and out of the classroom. In fact, some of the best active learning may take place not in the classroom but one on one in the instructor's office. Research shows that students who have such meetings stand a greater chance of returning to college for their second year.

SEE SEARCH ONLINE!
INTERNET EXERCISE 3.2

From Certainty to Healthy Uncertainty

If you have just completed high school, you may experience an awakening in college. In high school you may have been conditioned to believe that things are either right or wrong. If your high school teacher asked, "What are the three branches of the U.S. government?" you would answer, "legislative, judicial, and executive." A college instructor might ask instead, "What conflicts might arise among the three branches of government, and what does this reveal about the democratic process?"

Certainly, there is no simple—or single—answer. Most likely, your instructor is SEE EXERCISE 3.5 attempting to engage you in a process of critical thinking, which is thinking of a much higher order than simple memorization. You'll learn more about critical thinking in Chapter 5.

Academic Freedom in the Classroom

College instructors believe in the freedom to speak their thoughts, whether it be in a classroom discussion about economic policy, at a public rally on abortion or gay rights, or in the subject matter they choose to research for publication. What matters more than what instructors believe is their right to proclaim their values to others without fear. Colleges and universities have promoted the advancement of knowledge by granting scholars virtually unlimited freedom of inquiry, as long as human lives, rights, and privacy are not violated. Your campus should have a published statement on academic freedom. Get a copy and read it.

Some teachers may speak sarcastically about a politician you admire. Although you need not accept such ideas, you must learn to evaluate them for yourself, instead of basing your judgments on what others have always told you is right.

Academic freedom also extends to college students. This means you will have more freedom than in high school to select certain research topics or to pursue controversial issues. You will also have the right to disagree with the instructor if you feel differently about an issue, but be certain you can support your argument with reliable published or personal evidence. Above all, discuss—don't argue. Cite something you read or heard and ask what the instructor thinks about your reactions. Such discussions can be an enriching experience for the entire class.

Finding a Mentor

In his story of the aging process in men, the late Yale psychiatrist Daniel J. Levinson discovered several things about those who tended to be successful in life:

- They had developed a dream in adolescence, an idealized conception of what they wanted to become.
- They went on to find a mentor—an older, successful individual—who personified that dream.
- They also enjoyed relations with a few other people who encouraged, nurtured, and supported them in their pursuit of their dream.

A mentor is a person who, in some respect, is now what you hope to be in the future. What mentors have you had? What specific qualities have you tried to emulate? What are you seeking in a college mentor? If you have a mentor now, what might you do to make more use of this person? If you don't have a mentor, consider whether you might find one during your first year of college.

How do you find a mentor? Look for the person who takes a special interest in you, who encourages you to challenge yourself, who willingly listens to you when you have questions or problems, who offers to meet with you to discuss your work in class. A mentor may be an academic advisor, instructor, department chair, older student, or anyone else who appears to offer interest, wisdom, and support. Most important, find a person who you can trust, who will deal with you confidentially, and who is genuinely interested in your well-being but asks little or nothing in return.

SOURCE: D. J. Levinson et. al., *The Seasons of a Man's Life* (New York: Ballantine, 1978).

When Things Go Wrong Between You and a Teacher

What if you can't tolerate your instructor? Arrange a meeting to try to work things out. Getting to know the teacher as a person may help you cope with the way he or she teaches the course. If that fails, check the "drop-add" date, which usually falls at the end of the first week of classes. You may have to drop the course and pick up a different one. If it's too late to add classes, you may still decide to drop by the "drop date" later in the term to avoid a grade penalty. See your academic advisor or counselor for help.

If you can't get satisfaction from the instructor and need to stay in the class, see the head of the department. If you are still dissatisfied, move up the administrative ladder until you get a definite answer. Never allow a bad instructor to sour you on college. Even the worst course will be over eventually.

What if you're not satisfied with your grade? Make an appointment to see the instructor and discuss the assignment. Your teacher may give you a second chance because you took the time to ask for help. If you get a low grade on an exam, you might ask the instructor to review certain answers with you. Keep in mind that your teacher has the final word on what your grade will be, not a department head, a dean, or even the chancellor or president.

What about sexual harassment and sexism? Sexual harassment is a serious offense and a cause for grievance. See your department chair if an instructor makes inappropriate or threatening remarks of a sexual nature to you. No instructor should ask to date his or her student or otherwise pressure students to become involved in personal relationships because the implied threat is that if you refuse, you may fail the course. Your campus has specific procedures to follow if you believe you are being harassed sexually. Take advantage of them.

Sexism—as opposed to sexual harassment—refers to statements or behaviors that demonstrate a belief in the greater general worth of one gender over the other. Comments such as "I don't know why women take chemistry" or "Women are generally better writers than men" are not only insulting but also may cause you to lose confidence in your ability. The same rules apply to defamatory remarks about an ethnic group.

SEE SEARCH ONLINE!
INTERNET EXERCISE 3.3

"Great teachers know their subjects well. But they also know their students well," says Dr. Eliot Engel of North Carolina State University. "In fact," he continues, "great teaching fundamentally consists of constructing a bridge from the subject taught to the student learning it. Both sides of that bridge must be surveyed with equal care if the subject matter of the teacher is to connect with the gray matter of the student. But great teachers transcend simply knowing their subjects and students well. They also admire both deeply."*

SEE EXERCISE 3.6

As an active learner, you'll also find it easier to admire both your teacher and your subject deeply, just as your teacher will come to admire you.

*From a column in the *Dickens Dispatch,* the newsletter of the North Carolina Dickens Club, January 1989.

Search Online!

Internet Exercise 3.1 Your Teachers'–and Your Own–Responsibilities

Like everyone else, teachers must juggle many responsibilities. Indicate what percentage of their working time you think faculty spend in each of the following activities:

Teaching	_____
Research/scholarship	_____
Administration	_____
Outside consulting	_____
Service/nonteaching activities	_____

Check your answers against the data in 1997 *Digest of Educational Stastistics* at *http://nces.ed.gov/pubs/digest97/d97t228.html*. (Go to *http://success.wadsworth.com* for the most up-to-date URLs.)

Remember that these percentages are averages for all faculty at all schools surveyed. The particular percentages at any school or for any particular faculty member may vary considerably.

Survey several of your professors to find out how they spend their working time. Compare the results with the Internet figures.

Internet Exercise 3.2 Finding Faculty E-Mail Addresses

Although e-mail is often a poor substitute for an office visit, it is useful for specific questions, to explain why you missed class, or other short messages. If you can't reach your teacher by phone, you might e-mail to request an appointment by including your phone number in your message.

To send e-mail, just as with regular mail, you must know someone's address. Find the e-mail addresses of your instructors on the campus network or ask them for their e-mail addresses on the first day of class. You may also find their addresses in the course syllabus.

Internet Exercise 3.3 Discovering More About College Teachers and Learning

Using *InfoTrac College Edition,* try these phrases and others for key-word and subject-guide searches: "active learning," "good teaching," "collaborative learning," and "college teachers."

ALSO LOOK UP:

A new approach to collaborative learning. Brad Barrett. *Technological Horizons in Education* May 1999 v26, I10, p16

The Ten Commandments of good teaching. (Review). Eric Ries. *Techniques* May 1999 v74 I5 p66(1)

Collaborative learning through high-level verbal interaction: from theory to practice. Alexander Chizhik. *The Clearing House* Sept-Oct 1998 v72 n1 p58(4)

Innovative teaching: teaching at its best (teacher assessment). James Poon Teng Fatt. *Education* Summer 1998 v118 n4 p616(10)

Additional Exercises

These exercises will help you sharpen what we believe are the critical skills for college success: writing, critical thinking, learning in groups, planning, reflecting, and taking action. Also check out the CD-ROM that came with your book—you will find these exercises and more.

Exercise 3.1 Differences Between High School and College

This chapter lists just a few of the differences between high school and college that you may encounter. With a small group of other students, brainstorm other differences. Appoint one person in the group to list which differences seem beneficial and which do not. Explain your choices to the rest of the class.

Returning students may wish to form their own group and discuss the differences in their lives prior to college and now, or they may prefer to join a group of recent high school graduates to hear and provide a different point of view.

Exercise 3.2 Learning Actively

List the courses you are taking this term and then make a list of the active learning techniques taking place in each course. Observe each course at least twice. What did you do to promote active learning? What did your instructor do? What did other students do? If no active learning took place in a class, how did you feel about that?

Exercise 3.3 To Collaborate or Not?

Some people may prefer to work alone. This chapter has already listed many benefits of working together. What are some of the benefits of working by yourself? What might influence your decision to work alone as opposed to collaborating? What might influence you to prefer collaboration?

Exercise 3.4 Forming Your Ideal Learning Team

If you were to form a group with two or three other students in this class, who would you choose and for what characteristics? Write a paper describing your group. Don't reveal their names. Instead, name your collaborators "A," "B," and so forth. If you had to choose one more person, who would that be, and why? In what ways do members of this group complement one another's strengths and weaknesses, including yours?

Exercise 3.5 Interviewing a Teacher

Choose a teacher to interview—perhaps your favorite instructor or one you'd like to know more about. You might even choose an instructor whose course is giving you problems, in hopes that you can find out how to resolve those problems in the course of the interview. Make an appointment for the interview and prepare your questions before you arrive, but also be ready to go with the flow of your conversation. Then write a paper about what you learned and what surprised you the most. (*Note:* Arrive on time and dress comfortably but nicely to make the best impression; it may result in a better interview.) Here are some questions you might want to ask:

1. What was your first year of college like?
2. At what point in your life did you decide to teach? Why?
3. What steps did you take to become a teacher in your field?
4. What do you like most about teaching? Least? Why is that?
5. What are some of the things that keep you busiest outside the classroom?
6. What do you expect from students? What should they expect from you?
7. Where did you go to college? Why did you go there?
8. What advice can you offer to new college students?

Exercise 3.6 A Teaching Experience

Prepare a 5- to 10-minute presentation on some aspect of college success. You'll find plenty of information in this book. You might also do some digging in the library and ask a reference librarian how to use databases and the electronic card catalog. Organize your presentation, prepare brief notes that also remind you to use at least one active learning technique, and teach your topic to the class.

Your Personal Journal

Here are several things to write about. Choose one or more or choose another topic related to this chapter.

1. We've stated that college teachers are different than high school teachers. Can you give an example or two of those differences, based on one of your high school teachers and one of your current college teachers? Whose style are/were you more comfortable with? Why? In which class do you believe you'll learn more? Why?

2. If you've tried collaborative learning, write about how that went. If you haven't tried it yet, write about why you haven't and whether you plan to do so in the near future.

3. An important part of active learning is student participation. What if some students are reticent about speaking in class (their learning styles may indicate they are introverted). Should the teacher be flexible about this? If so, how? If not, what should she or he do?

4. What behaviors are you thinking about changing after reading this chapter? How will you go about changing them?

5. What else is on your mind this week? If you wish to share it with your instructor, add it to this journal entry.

Resources

You can learn a lot about your instructors both from the information they give you and from the information the school can give you. Connecting with your instructors inside and outside of class can make your college experience much more meaningful and successful. Fill in the following information about your instructors this semester. *(Copy this page before you fill it out if you have more than five instructors.)*

Instructor's name ....   Course name ....

Other courses he or she teaches ....

(You may want to take another class with him or her. Hint: Look in your course catalog.)

Office hours ....   Office location ....   Phone ....

Home phone number ....   E-mail address ....

Is it okay to call this instructor at home? ....   To send e-mail? ....

....

Instructor's name ....   Course name ....

Other courses he or she teaches ....

Office hours ....   Office location ....   Phone ....

Home phone number ....   E-mail address ....

Is it okay to call this instructor at home? ....   To send e-mail? ....

....

Instructor's name ....   Course name ....

Other courses he or she teaches ....

Office hours ....   Office location ....   Phone ....

Home phone number ....   E-mail address ....

Is it okay to call this instructor at home? ....   To send e-mail? ....

....

Instructor's name ....   Course name ....

Other courses he or she teaches ....

Office hours ....   Office location ....   Phone ....

Home phone number ....   E-mail address ....

Is it okay to call this instructor at home? ....   To send e-mail? ....

....

Instructor's name ....   Course name ....

Other courses he or she teaches ....

Office hours ....   Office location ....   Phone ....

Home phone number ....   E-mail address ....

Is it okay to call this instructor at home? ....   To send e-mail? ....

....

Learning Styles

Discovering How
You Learn Best

**IN THIS CHAPTER,
YOU WILL LEARN**

- How to determine your learning preferences
- How learning styles affect classroom behavior
- How personality preferences affect your learning style
- How learning styles can enhance study groups
- How to deal with your instructors' teaching styles

figure yourself out

"*Bill has a ball when he's around people. I like some time to myself. Janine can remember every date in a history lecture. I don't remember any, but I do pick up on the big ideas better than she does. Fred argues about issues based on how he feels, not on the facts themselves. I do just the opposite. What makes my friends so different, and why is it that, despite those differences, I like them all?*"

In high school, perhaps you found history easier than mathematics or biology easier than English. Part of the explanation for this has to do with what is called your learning style—that is, the way you acquire knowledge.

Learning style affects not only how you process material as you study but also how you absorb it. Some students learn more effectively through visual means, others by listening to lectures, and still others through class discussion, hands-on experience, memorization, or various combinations of these. An auditory learner learns best by listening, a visual learner does best with visual aids, and a kinesthetic or hands-on learner acquires knowledge through some physical activity such as building a model, designing a project, or drawing a schematic. Some learn better by studying alone, whereas others prefer study groups.

Although no one learning style is inherently better than another, you will need to be flexible no matter what style is required in a given course. An awareness of your learning style can be helpful in emphasizing your strengths and helping you compensate for your weaknesses.

SELF-ASSESSMENT: LEARNING PREFERENCES

Checkmark the items that apply to you. After you finish, review the checked items. What are you comfortable with? Look at the unchecked items. What things are you uncomfortable with? What do you think all this has to do with the way you prefer to learn?

_____ I like when people tell me I'm imaginative.

_____ I like when people tell me I get the facts straight.

_____ I enjoy spending some of my time alone with my thoughts.

_____ It's important for me to be with people as often as I can.

_____ I like to stick to tried and proven ways of getting things done.

_____ It's fun to experiment with new ways to get things done.

_____ I absolutely must set a schedule for myself and stick to it.

_____ I don't bother with schedules. Most times, things get done.

_____ I enjoy meeting new people. The more, the merrier.

_____ I value having just a few close friends. That's enough.

You will find a more comprehensive learning-style inventory later in this chapter.

One student's analytical style may thrive on the complexities of history. Another's satisfaction at mastering facts and understanding how they are related may lead her into science.

An Informal Measure of Learning Style

Think about three or four of your favorite courses from high school or college. What do they have in common? Did they tend to be hands-on courses or more abstract? Did they focus more on mastering facts or on broader interpretations? Was there a lot of discussion, or did the teacher mainly lecture? Then think about your least favorite courses. How did they tend to differ from the courses you liked?

If you prefer attending lectures, taking notes, and reading your notes aloud to yourself, you have a more auditory learning style. You might even read your notes into a tape recorder and play them back when you study for an exam. If you prefer instructors who outline their lectures on the chalkboard or who make liberal use of the board by illustrating the important points they are making, you have a more visual learning style. You probably find that copying and recopying your notes helps you learn the material. If you learn best by a hands-on approach, you may prefer a kinesthetic or physical learning style.

Being aware of your personal learning-style preferences can help you exploit your strengths as you prepare for classes and exams. It can also help you understand why you're having difficulty with some of your courses and what you can do to improve.

Classroom Behavior and Learning Style

A number of instruments can help you determine what your preferred learning styles are. One approach is based on the ways in which students behave in the classroom. Psychologists Tony Grasha and Sheryl Riechmann have put together the Grasha–Riechmann instrument. This tool assesses six learning styles based on classroom behavior: (1) competitive, (2) collaborative, (3) participant, (4) avoidant, (5) dependent, and (6) independent.

To understand the classroom learning style with which you are most comfortable, you need to answer certain questions. For example, do you find study questions or review questions helpful? Do you enjoy and find helpful studying with and learning from other students in your class? Do you like it when the instructor engages the class in discussion? If so, then you probably have a more collaborative, participant, and dependent learning style and will work best with an instructor who has a corresponding teaching style. On the other hand, you may prefer an instructor who lectures in class with minimal class participation. You may feel that straightforward study of your lecture notes and textbook is the most effective means of study. If so, your learning style is more competitive, independent, and avoidant.

SEE SEARCH ONLINE!
INTERNET EXERCISE 4.1

Personality Preferences and Learning Style

SEE EXERCISE 4.1
Another approach explores basic personality preferences that make people interested in different things and draw them to different fields and lifestyles. An example, the Myers–Briggs Type Indicator, based on Carl Jung's theory of psychological types, uses four scales:

- **E/I (Extroversion/Introversion)** This scale describes two opposite preferences depending on whether you would rather focus your attention on the outer or the inner world. Extroverted persons are attuned to the culture, people, and things around them. The extrovert is outgoing, socially free, and interested in variety and in working with people. The extrovert may become impatient with long, slow tasks and does not mind being interrupted by people.

    Persons more introverted than extroverted tend to make decisions somewhat independently of culture, people, or things around them. They are quiet, diligent at working alone, and socially reserved. They may dislike being interrupted while working and may tend to forget names and faces.

- **S/N (Sensing/Intuitive)** This scale describes opposite ways you acquire information. Sensers tend to take facts as they are and remember the details, whereas intuitors are more likely to absorb a number of facts, look for relationships among them, and emerge with broad concepts. The sensing type prefers the concrete, factual, tangible here and now, becoming impatient with theory and the abstract and mistrusting intuition. The sensing type thinks in detail, remembering real facts but possibly missing a conception of the overall.

    In contrast, the intuitive person prefers possibilities, theories, invention, and the new and becomes bored with nitty-gritty details and facts unrelated to concepts. The intuitive person thinks and discusses in spontaneous leaps of intuition that may neglect details. Problem solving comes easily for this individual, although there may be a tendency to make errors of fact.

- **T/F (Thinking/Feeling)** This scale describes how you make decisions, whether by analyzing and weighing evidence or by analyzing and weighing feelings. The thinker makes judgments based on logic, analysis, and evidence, avoiding decisions based on feelings and values. As a result, the thinker is more interested in verifiable conclusions than in empathy or values. The thinker may step on others' feelings and needs without realizing it, neglecting to take into consideration the values and feelings of others.

    The feeler makes judgments based on empathy, warmth, and personal values. As a consequence, feelers are more interested in people and feelings than in impersonal logic, analysis, and things and in achieving harmony more than in being on top or achieving impersonal goals. The feeler gets along well with people in general.

- **J/P (Judging/Perceiving)** This scale describes the way you relate to the outer world, whether in a planned, orderly way or in a flexible, spontaneous way. The judger is decisive, firm, and sure, setting goals and sticking to them. The judger wants to make decisions and get on to the next project. When a project does not yet have closure, judgers will leave it behind and go on to new tasks.

    The perceiver is a gatherer, always wanting to know more before deciding, holding off decisions and judgments. As a consequence, the perceiver is open, flexible, adaptive, nonjudgmental, able to see and appreciate all sides of issues, and always welcoming new perspectives. However, perceivers are also difficult to pin down and may become involved in many tasks that do not reach closure, so they may become frustrated at times. Even when they finish tasks, perceivers will tend to look back at them and wonder whether they could have been done another way. The perceiver wishes to roll with life rather than change it.

Critical Thinking

Stick with Your Own Type or Seek Out Other Types?

Some would say that this question is contradictory. If you feel most comfortable around friends and teachers who share your preferences, why bother making it a point to be around those with contradictory preferences? What is the big idea here? What might be some situations where it would be better to seek out a contradictory learning type? Review your decisions and come up with an answer that is logically sound. Share it with someone and get his or her reaction.

You will often feel most comfortable around people who share your preferences, and you will probably be most comfortable in a classroom where the instructor's preferences for perceiving and processing information are most like yours. But the Myers–Briggs instrument also emphasizes our ability to cultivate in ourselves all processes on each scale.

Just as no person's fingerprints are right or wrong, so no one's personality preference is right or wrong. The purpose of this inventory is to give you a picture of your preferences. Keep in mind that your preferences have nothing to do with intelligence.

The four pairs of dimensions are present to some degree in all people. It is the extremes that are described here. The strength of a dimension is indicated by the score for that dimension on an inventory such as the one in Exercise 4.2. The score determines how closely the strengths and weaknesses described fit an individual's learning preferences.

SEE SEARCH ONLINE!
INTERNET EXERCISE 4.2

SEE EXERCISE 4.2

Strengths and Weaknesses of the Types

Each person has strengths and weaknesses as a result of these dimensions. Committees and organizations with a preponderance of one type will have the same strengths and weaknesses.

	POSSIBLE STRENGTHS	POSSIBLE WEAKNESSES
Extrovert	Interacts with others	Does not work well without people
	Is open	Needs change, variety
	Acts, does	Is impulsive
	Is well understood	Is impatient with routine
Introvert	Is independent	Avoids others
	Works alone	Is secretive
	Reflects	Loses opportunities to act
	Works with ideas	Is misunderstood by others
	Avoids generalizations	Dislikes being interrupted
	Is careful before acting	

	POSSIBLE STRENGTHS	POSSIBLE WEAKNESSES
Senser	Attends to detail	Does not see possibilities
	Is practical	Loses the overall in details
	Has memory for detail, fact	Mistrusts intuition
	Is patient	Is frustrated with the complicated
	Is systematic	Prefers not to imagine future
Intuitor	Sees possibilities	Is inattentive to detail, precision
	Works out new ideas	Is inattentive to the actual and practical
	Works with the complicated	Is impatient with the tedious
	Solves novel problems	Loses sight of the here and now
		Jumps to conclusions
Thinker	Is logical, analytical	May not notice people's feelings
	Is objective	Misunderstands others' values
	Is organized	Is uninterested in conciliation
	Has critical ability	Does not show feelings
	Is just	Shows less compassion
	Stands firm	
Feeler	Considers others' feelings	Is not guided by logic
	Understands needs, values	Is not objective
	Is interested in conciliation	Is less organized
	Demonstrates feelings	Is overly accepting
	Persuades, arouses	
Judger	Decides	Is stubborn
	Plans	Is inflexible
	Orders	Decides with insufficient data
	Makes quick decisions	Is controlled by task or plans
	Remains with a task	Wishes not to interrupt work
Perceiver	Compromises	Is indecisive
	Sees all sides of issues	Does not plan
	Is flexible	Does not control circumstances
	Decides based on all data	Is easily distracted from tasks
	Is not judgmental	Does not finish projects

Examining Values

Can learning preferences have an influence on your values system? Certainly, those who value time and organization may do so because of their J-learning preference. Conversely, those who value the freedom to set their own schedules may do so as a result of their P-learning preference. After you have completed Exercise 4.2, review the characteristics of your learning preferences and write a paper in which you speculate on how those preferences may in part determine what you value most and least.

As you reflect on the results of Exercise 4.2 at the end of this chapter, keep in mind that your score merely *suggests* your preferences; it does not stereotype or pigeonhole you. Remember, too, that no one learning style is inherently preferable to another and that everyone knows and uses a range of styles. The fact that many of us exhibit behaviors that seem to contradict our preferences shows that we each embrace a wide range of possibilities.

Using Knowledge of Your Learning Style

Discovering your own strengths empowers you to recognize what you already do well. Discovering your weaknesses is also useful because it is to your advantage to cultivate your less dominant learning styles. Although certain disciplines and certain instructors may take approaches that favor certain styles, no course is going to be entirely sensing or entirely intuitive, entirely thinking or entirely feeling, just as you are not entirely one thing or another. You can also use your learning-style data to determine how to study more effectively. Diagram? Study aloud? Annotate texts in margins? Focus on details or concepts?

Improving Your Less Dominant Learning Styles

The key ingredient in developing your less dominant learning style is awareness. Try to develop one thing at a time.

RAISING YOUR SENSING (S) LEARNING STYLE
- Whenever you walk, try to notice and jot down specific details of the scenery—shapes of leaves; size, color, and types of rocks; and so on.
- Three or four times daily, pay careful attention to and then describe to a friend what someone else is wearing.
- Do a jigsaw puzzle.
- Break down an activity into its component parts.
- Describe in detail something you just saw, such as a picture, a room, or the like.

RAISING YOUR INTUITIVE (N) LEARNING STYLE
- Imagine a situation in a new light by asking, What if? For example, what if the Pilgrims had landed in California—how would their lifestyle have changed? What if you had attended a bigger (smaller) school? What if X were your roommate instead of Y?

- Read a novel and imagine yourself as one of the characters. What would happen to you following the novel's conclusion?

RAISING YOUR FEELING (F) LEARNING STYLE
- Write a feeling statement about your class, your day, your job, or your emotions and make sure you use a simile. For example, "I feel like a puppy that's just been scolded." If you use the word *think* in your statement, it's not a feeling statement. Write five feeling statements daily.

RAISING YOUR THINKING (T) LEARNING STYLE
- Have someone write a problem that's bothering him or her or a situation related to college. Then answer questions that explain who, what, where, when, and why and provide the details that back up each response. Do this daily for 15 or 20 minutes so that you'll learn to be objective.

Study Groups and Learning Style

Knowing your own learning-style preference can help you study more effectively with other students. When you form a study group, seek out students with some opposite learning preferences, but be sure, too, that you have some preferences in common. The best teamwork seems to come from people who differ on one or two preferences. If you prefer intuitive fact gathering, you might benefit from the details brought forth by a sensing type.

Dealing with Your Instructors' Teaching Styles

Just as your learning style affects how you study, perform, and react to various courses and disciplines, your instructors' learning styles also affect what and how they teach.

Clues to Instructors' Teaching Styles

The best clue to your instructor's teaching style is the language he or she uses. If your learning style is more visual, you can sense those clues more easily from printed material such as the syllabus or course handouts. If your learning style is more auditory, pay attention to the language your instructor uses when lecturing, asking discussion questions, or phrasing oral-test questions.

For example, earlier we discussed two ways of receiving and processing information: (1) sensing (factual and informational) and (2) intuitive (analytical and conceptual). An instructor who uses words such as *define, diagram, label, list, outline,* and *summarize* will tend to have a more sensing teaching style. He or she will want you to be extremely specific and provide primarily factual information. Words such as these really ask for very restricted answers.

On the other hand, an instructor whose syllabus or lecture is sprinkled with words such as *concept, theme, idea, theory,* and *interpretation* will tend to have a much more intuitive and analytical learning style and expect similar kinds of responses from students. On exams or on assignments, he or she may use terms such as *describe, compare, contrast, criticize, discuss, evaluate, explain, interpret, justify,* or *relate.* You may notice that instead of asking you to provide factual data or information, these words ask you to act on that information—that is, to use it in relation to other pieces of information, to evaluate it, or to examine it in terms of your own experience. An instructor who uses these words has a much more intuitive teaching style and will expect more analytical, imaginative, and conceptual responses. He or she will expect you to see that information in a new context rather than simply restate the facts as they have been given to you or as they appear in the textbook.

Exam Preparation and Learning/Teaching Styles

Understanding learning styles can help you to perceive more clearly the expectations of an instructor whose teaching style is incompatible with your learning style and thus allow you to prepare more effectively for his or her exams.

When Steven Blume, the main contributor to this chapter, was learning about the Myers–Briggs Type Indicator, he attended a workshop for college instructors. Those attending the workshop were divided into two groups—sensing and intuitive. Each group was given a five-page essay about the effects of divorce on young children and was asked to construct a short exam based on the reading. The sensing group was then asked to take the exam constructed by the intuitive group, and the intuitive group was asked to take the exam constructed by the sensing group.

In dealing with the questions, they could not believe that both groups had read and discussed the same essay. Those in the intuitive group had been asked to construct lists of details and respond to much factual data that they had regarded as less essential than the more analytical and conceptual themes of the essay. And those in the sensing group were taken aback by the very broad thematic questions the intuitive group had asked about the implications of divorce on the children and the larger questions about the children's future.

If your instructor's teaching style is compatible with your learning style, then you should be able to perform well simply by keeping up with your work. If your instructor's style is incompatible with yours, you might consider either mastering more factual material or interpreting or analyzing that material in order to be better prepared for exams or papers. In any case, a greater awareness of both your learning style and your instructor's teaching style can be of real benefit.

A variety of additional tests can help you learn more about your learning style. These are generally available through your career planning or learning center. A guidance counselor will both administer the test and help you interpret the results.   SEE EXERCISE 4.3 Ask about the following:

- The Myers–Briggs Type Indicator
- The complete Hogan/Champagne Personal Style Inventory
- The Keirsey Temperament Sorter on the Web at *http://www.keirsey.com.*
- Kolb Learning Style Inventory

And above all, remember: There are no good or bad learning styles, only different ones. And isn't that fortunate! What a dull and uncreative world this would be if each of us analyzed information in exactly the same manner!

Search Online!   《●》

Internet Exercise 4.1   Learning-Style Inventory

Which of the following best describes your most efficient learning style?

Visual learner—rely on visual cues, on things you see   _____

Auditory learner—rely on auditory stimuli, on things you hear   _____

Tactile learner—rely on touch, on working with your hands   _____

Your learning style: _____

Go to *http://www.hcc.hawaii.edu/intranet/committees/FacDevCom/guidebk/teachtip/ learnstyl.htm* and take the twenty-four-question Learning Style Inventory. Which type of learner are you? (Go to *http://success.wadsworth.com* for the most up-to-date URLs.)

Visual Preference Score   _____

Auditory Preference Score   _____

Tactile Preference Score   _____

What do your scores suggest about how you might adjust your study habits to optimize your learning?

Internet Exercise 4.2   Discovering More About Learning-Style Theory

Using *InfoTrac College Edition,* try these phrases and others for key-word and subject-guide searches: "learning style," "Howard Gardner," "Keirsey," and "Myers-Briggs."

ALSO LOOK UP:

An interview with Rita Dunn about learning styles. Michael F. Shaughnessy. *Clearing House* Jan-Feb 1998 v71 n3 p141(5)

Identifying how we think: The Myers-Briggs Type Indicator and the Hermann Brain Dominance Instrument. *Harvard Business Review* July-Aug 1997 v75 n4 p114(2)

Can we generalize about the learning style characteristics of high academic achievers? Deborah E. Burns, Scott E. Johnson, Robert K. Gable. *Roeper Review* May-June 1998 v20 n4 p276(6)

Problems in statistics: Learning style, age, and part-time students. (teacher assessment). James A. Bell. *Education* Summer 1998 v118 n4 p526(3)

Additional Exercises

These exercises will help you sharpen what we believe are the critical skills for college success: writing, critical thinking, learning in groups, planning, reflecting, and taking action. Also, check out the CD-ROM that came with your book—you will find these exercises and more.

Exercise 4.1 Your Learning Style—A Quick Indication

A List three or four of your favorite courses from high school or college:

1. _____

2. _____

3. _____

4. _____

What did these courses have in common? Did they tend to be hands-on courses? Lecture courses? Discussion courses? What were the exams like? Do you see a pattern from one course to the next? For example, did your favorite courses tend to use information-oriented tests such as multiple choice or true/false? Or did they often include broader essay exams? Did the tests cover small units of material or facts, or did they draw on larger chunks of material?

Now list your least favorite courses from high school or college:

1. _____

2. _____

3. _____

4. _____

What did these courses and their exams have in common? How did they tend to differ from the courses you liked?

B After doing part A, form a small group with two or three other members of the class. Brainstorm about what courses you are taking that seem to require factual learning styles, analytical learning styles, or a combination of both. Prepare an oral group presentation to the class about your conclusions and the reasons for them. What is the best way to prepare for an exam in these classes, and why? (Read this entire chapter before you give your presentation.)

Exercise 4.2 Assessing Your Learning Style

The following items are arranged in pairs (a and b), and each member of the pair represents a preference you may or may not hold. Rate your preference for each item by giving it a score of 0 to 5 (0 meaning you really feel negative about it or strongly about the other member of the pair; 5 meaning you strongly prefer it or do not prefer the other member of the pair). The scores for a and b must add up to 5 (0 and 5, 1 and 4, or 2 and 3). Do not use fractions such as $2\frac{1}{2}$.

I prefer:

____ 1a. making decisions after finding out what others think.   ____ 1b. making decisions without consulting anyone.

____ 2a. being called imaginative or intuitive.   ____ 2b. being called factual or accurate.

_____ 3a. making decisions about people based on available data and systematic analysis.

_____ 3b. making decisions about people based on empathy, feelings, and understanding of their needs and values.

_____ 4a. allowing commitments to occur if others want to make them.

_____ 4b. pushing for definite commitments to ensure they are made.

_____ 5a. quiet, thoughtful time alone.

_____ 5b. active, energetic time with people.

_____ 6a. using methods I know well that can get the job done.

_____ 6b. thinking of new ways to do tasks when confronted with them.

_____ 7a. drawing conclusions based on logic and careful analysis.

_____ 7b. drawing conclusions based on what I feel and believe about life and people from past experiences.

_____ 8a. avoiding making deadlines.

_____ 8b. setting a schedule and sticking to it.

_____ 9a. inner thoughts and feelings others cannot see.

_____ 9b. activities and occurrences in which others join.

_____ 10a. the abstract or theoretical.

_____ 10b. the concrete or real.

_____ 11a. helping others explore their feelings.

_____ 11b. helping others make logical decisions.

_____ 12a. communicating little of my inner thoughts and feelings.

_____ 12b. communicating freely my inner thoughts and feelings.

_____ 13a. planning ahead based on projections.

_____ 13b. planning as needs arise, just before carrying out the plans.

_____ 14a. meeting new people.

_____ 14b. being alone or with one person I know well.

_____ 15a. ideas.

_____ 15b. facts.

_____ 16a. convictions.

_____ 16b. verifiable conclusions.

_____ 17a. keeping appointments and notes written down as much as possible.

_____ 17b. using appointment and notebooks as little as possible (although I may use them).

_____ 18a. carrying out carefully laid, detailed plans with precision.

_____ 18b. designing plans and structures without necessarily carrying them out.

_____ 19a. being free to do things on the spur of the moment.

_____ 19b. knowing well in advance what I am expected to do.

_____ 20a. experiencing emotional situations, discussions, movies.

_____ 20b. using my ability to analyze situations.

Personal Style Inventory Scoring

Instructions: Transfer your scores for each item of each pair to the appropriate blanks. Be careful to check the a and b letters to be sure you are recording scores in the proper spaces. Then total the scores for each dimension.

Dimension		**Dimension**	
I	E	N	S
1b. _____	1a. _____	2a. _____	2b. _____
5a. _____	5b. _____	6b. _____	6a. _____
9a. _____	9b. _____	10a. _____	10b. _____

| 12a. _____ | 12b. _____ | 15a. _____ | 15b. _____ |
| 14b. _____ | 14a. _____ | 18b. _____ | 18a. _____ |

Totals:

| I _____ | E _____ | N _____ | S _____ |

Dimension		**Dimension**	
T	F	P	J
3a. _____	3b. _____	4a. _____	4b. _____
7a. _____	7b. _____	8a. _____	8b. _____
11b. _____	11a. _____	13b. _____	13a. _____
16b. _____	16a. _____	17b. _____	17a. _____
20b. _____	20a. _____	19a. _____	19b. _____

Totals:

| T_____ | F _____ | P _____ | J _____ |

Personal Style Inventory Interpretation

Letters on the score sheet stand for:

I—Introversion	*E*—Extroversion
N—i*N*tuition	*S*—Sensing
T—Thinking	*F*—Feeling
P—Perceiving	*J*—Judging

If your score is:	The likely interpretation is:
12–13	Balance in the strengths of the dimensions.
14–15	Some strength in the dimension; some weakness in the other member of the pair.
16–19	Definite strength in the dimension; definite weakness in the other member of the pair.
20–25	Considerable strength in the dimension; considerable weakness in the other member of the pair.

Your typology is those four dimensions for which you had scores of 14 or more, although the relative strengths of all dimensions actually constitute your typology. Scores of 12 or 13 show relative balance in a pair so that either member could be part of the typology.

Note: This exercise is an abridgment of the *Personal Style Inventory* by Dr. R. Craig Hogan and Dr. David W. Champagne, adapted and reproduced with permission from Organization Design and Development, Inc., 2002 Renaissance Blvd., Suite 100, King of Prussia, PA, 19406. For information on using the complete instrument, write to the above address.

Exercise 4.3 Assessing Your Courses and Instructors

Take some time over the next few days to think about the courses you are taking now. How well does your preferred learning style fit the style reflected in the syllabus, handouts, lectures, and study questions in at least two of your courses? Ask several of your instructors how they teach and learn best.

Do any of the key sensing words mentioned previously (*define, diagram,* and so on) or some close approximation of them appear? If so, list them and place a check mark next to them each time the word appears. Do any of the key intuition words (*describe, compare,* and so on) or similar words appear? List them also and note their frequency. Listen carefully in class. What key words do you hear? Write these down also. Which type of word do you hear most frequently? That will begin to give you some idea of each instructor's learning/teaching style.

Instructor/Course _____

Sensing Words   Intuition Words

_____   _____

_____   _____

_____   _____

_____   _____

_____   _____

_____   _____

Instructor's preferred style: Sensing _____ Intuitive _____

Other teaching style observations: _____

_____

_____

_____

How does your learning style as measured in Exercise 4.2 fit with the learning/teaching style of each instructor? Which courses will require some adjustment on your part? Discuss these problems with other students in class. Are there things your instructors do to help you take advantage of your strengths and learn more efficiently? In class discuss what these ideas are and how you might convey them to the appropriate instructor.

Your Personal Journal

Here are several things to write about. Choose one or more, or choose another topic related to learning styles.

1. The authors of this book discovered that understanding their learning styles helped them in many ways. It improved their relationships with people. It made them feel better about some things that had bothered them before. It showed them how to cope with what had been difficult situations. How has knowledge of your learning style helped you?

2. Think of one or more of your teachers whose methods you find uncomfortable. Try to describe the four dimensions of his or her learning style, as you see them. Tell how this might help you do better in this class.

3. Have a chat with one or two classmates about your learning style and theirs. Then write about the discussion.

4. Is there anything else on your mind this week that you'd like to share with your instructor? If so, add it to your journal entry.

Resources

Read the following descriptions of the sixteen different Myers–Briggs types. Put your name in the box that best describes your type. Where do the other significant people in your life fit? Put their names in the boxes that best describe their type preferences.

	SENSING TYPES		INTUITIVES	
	WITH THINKING	WITH FEELING	WITH FEELING	WITH THINKING

INTROVERTS

JUDGING

ISTJ
Serious, quiet, earn success by concentration and thoroughness. Practical, orderly, matter-of-fact, logical, realistic and dependable. See to it that everything is well organized. Take responsibility. Make up their own minds as to what should be accomplished and work toward it steadily, regardless of protests or distractions.

ISFJ
Quiet, friendly, responsible and conscientious. Work devotedly to meet their obligations and serve their friends and school. Thorough, painstaking, accurate. May need time to master technical subjects, as their interests are not often technical. Patient with detail and routine. Loyal, considerate, concerned with how other people feel.

INFJ
Succeed by perseverance, originality and desire to do whatever is needed or wanted. Put their best efforts into the work. Quietly forceful, conscientious, concerned for others. Respected for their firm principles. Likely to be honored and followed for their clear convictions as to how best to serve the common good.

INTJ
Have original minds and great drive which they use only for their own purposes. In fields that appeal to them they have a fine power to organize a job and carry it through with or without help. Skeptical, critical, independent, determined, often stubborn. Must learn to yield less important points in order to win the most important.

JUDGING

INTROVERTS

PERCEPTIVE

ISTP
Cool onlookers, quiet, reserved, observing and analyzing life with detached curiosity and unexpected flashes of original humor. Usually interested in impersonal principles, cause and effect, or how and why mechanical things work. Exert themselves no more than they think necessary, because any waste of energy would be inefficient.

ISFP
Retiring, quietly friendly, sensitive, modest about their abilities. Shun disagreements, do not force their opinions or values on others. Usually do not care to lead but are often loyal followers. May be rather relaxed about assignments or getting things done, because they enjoy the present moment and do not want to spoil it by undue haste or exertion.

INFP
Full of enthusiasms and loyalties, but seldom talk of these until they know you well. Care about learning ideas, language, and independent projects of their own. Apt to be on yearbook staff, perhaps as editor. Tend to undertake too much, then somehow get it done. Friendly, but often too absorbed in what they are doing to be sociable or notice much.

INTP
Quiet, reserved, brilliant in exams, especially in theoretical or scientific subjects. Logical to the point of hair-splitting. Interested mainly in ideas, with little liking for parties or small talk. Tend to have very sharply defined interests. Need to choose careers where some strong interest of theirs can be used and useful.

PERCEPTIVE

EXTRAVERTS

PERCEPTIVE

ESTP
Matter-of-fact, do not worry or hurry, enjoy whatever comes along. Tend to like mechanical things and sports, with friends on the side. May be a bit blunt or insensitive. Can do math or science when they see the need. Dislike long explanations. Are best with real things that can be worked, handled, taken apart or put back together.

ESFP
Outgoing, easygoing, acceptive, friendly, fond of a good time. Like sports and making things. Know what's going on and join in eagerly. Find remembering facts easier than mastering theories. Are best in situations that need sound common sense and practical ability with people as well as with things.

ENFP
Warmly enthusiastic, high-spirited, ingenious, imaginative. Able to do almost anything that interests them. Quick with a solution for any difficulty and ready to help anyone with a problem. Often rely on their ability to improvise instead of preparing in advance. Can always find compelling reasons for whatever they want.

ENTP
Quick, ingenious, good at many things. Stimulating company, alert and outspoken, argue for fun on either side of a question. Resourceful in solving new and challenging problems, but may neglect routine assignments. Turn to one new interest after another. Can always find logical reasons for whatever they want.

PERCEPTIVE

EXTRAVERTS

JUDGING

ESTJ
Practical realists, matter-of-fact, with a natural head for business or mechanics. Not interested in subjects they see no use for, but can apply themselves when necessary. Like to organize and run activities. Tend to run things well, especially if they remember to consider other people's feelings and points of view when making their decisions.

ESFJ
Warm-hearted, talkative, popular, conscientious, born cooperators, active committee members. Always doing something nice for someone. Work best with plenty of encouragement and praise. Little interest in abstract thinking or technical subjects. Main interest is in things that directly and visibly affect people's lives.

ENFJ
Responsive and responsible. Feel real concern for what others think and want, and try to handle things with due regard for other people's feelings. Can present a proposal or lead a group discussion with ease and tact. Sociable, popular, active in school affairs, but put time enough on their studies to do good work.

ENTJ
Hearty, frank, able in studies, leaders in activities. Usually good in anything that requires reasoning and intelligent talk, such as public speaking. Are well-informed and keep adding to their fund of knowledge. May sometimes be more positive and confident than their experience in an area warrants.

JUDGING

"Effects of the Combinations of All Four Preferences in Young People," pp. A-7, A-8, *People Types and Tiger Stripes: A Practical Guide to Learning Styles* by Gordon Lawrence, published by Center for the Application of Psychological Type, Inc. Gainesville, Florida, 1982.

Critical
Thinking and Writing

Developing Core Tools

**IN THIS CHAPTER,
YOU WILL LEARN**

- How college encourages critical thinking
- The four aspects of critical thinking
- Writing as a way to think and to communicate
- Three steps to improve your writing
- Good and bad habits in thinking and writing

go figure

"On my history quiz, my instructor asked us to analyze the causes of the American Civil War and to cite evidence showing which causes were the most important. I could've told him the dates of the war. I could've told him about most of the military decisions. But this! This really made me think! Maybe if I'd done some writing about the topic last night instead of just poring over my notes, I would've answered the question better."

Employers hiring college graduates often say they want an individual who can find information, analyze it, organize it, draw conclusions from it, and present it convincingly to others. One executive said she looked for superior communication skills "because they are in such short supply these days." These skills are also the basic ingredients of critical thinking. In essence, critical thinking is the ability to manage and interpret information in a logical and reliable way. It is the ability to examine existing ideas and to develop new ones. In critical thinking, the term *argument* refers not to an emotional confrontation but to reasons and information brought together in logical support of some idea. Critical thinking is the ability to recognize reliable evidence and form well-reasoned arguments.

When thinking about an argument, a good critical thinker considers questions like the following:

- Are the assumptions (the pieces of information given in support of the argument) true?
- Do the assumptions really support the conclusion?
- Do I need to withhold judgment until better evidence is available?
- Is the argument really based on good reasoning, or does it appeal mainly to my emotions?

SELF-ASSESSMENT: CRITICAL THINKING AND WRITING

Checkmark all items that apply to you. Then read the statement at the end of this exercise.

_____ I frequently allow my emotions to get in the way of making the right decision.

_____ I find it hard to appreciate the achievements of a person if I find that person irritating.

_____ I am quick to reject ideas that I come up with. As a result, I don't come up with many good ideas.

_____ Although it's easy for me to memorize facts, quizzes that require me to explain things are difficult.

_____ I have writer's block. I can stare at a blank page or screen forever before I get even the germ of an idea.

_____ If I didn't have to worry so much about spelling and grammar, I'd be a much better writer.

_____ The more you narrow a topic for a paper, the harder it is to come up with ideas for the paper.

_____ An answer is either right or it isn't.

NOTE: The more items you checked, the more you need to read this chapter to learn how to eliminate the behaviors described in this assessment.

- Based on the available evidence, are other conclusions equally likely (or even more likely)? Is there more than one right or possible answer?
- What more must I do to reach a good conclusion?

Good critical thinking also involves thinking creatively and imaginatively about what assumptions may be left out or what alternative conclusion may not have been considered. When communicating an argument or idea to others, a good critical thinker knows how to organize it in an understandable, convincing way in speech or in writing.

SEE EXERCISE 5.1

How College Encourages Critical Thinking

Many college students believe that their teachers will have all the answers and that all they need to do is gather and remember information. Unfortunately, most important questions do not have simple answers, and you may find numerous ways to look at important issues. It is important to be willing to challenge assumptions and conclusions, even those presented by the experts.

Critical thinking depends on your ability to evaluate different perspectives and challenge assumptions made by you or others. To challenge how you think, a good college teacher may insist that how you solve a problem is as important as the solution. Because critical thinking depends on discovering and testing connections between ideas, your instructor may ask open-ended questions that have no clear-cut answers, questions of "Why?" "How?" or "What if?" For example, an instructor might ask, "In these essays we have two conflicting ideas about whether bilingual education is effective at helping children learn English. What now?"

Your instructor may ask you to break a larger question into smaller ones: "Let's take the first point. What evidence does the author offer for his idea that language immersion programs get better results?"

She or he may insist that there is more than one valid point of view: "So, for some types of students, you agree that bilingual education might be best? What different types of students should we consider?"

Your instructor may require you to explain concretely the reason for any point you reject: "You think this essay is wrong. Well, what are your reasons?" He or she may challenge the authority of experts: "Dr. Fleming's theory sounds impressive. But here are some facts he doesn't account for . . ."

You may discover that often your instructor reinforces the legitimacy of your personal views and experiences: "So something like this happened to you once, and you felt exactly the same way. Can you tell us why?" And, most likely, an instructor will let you know that you can change your mind.

It is natural for entering college students to find this mode of thinking difficult and to discover that answers are seldom entirely wrong or right but more often somewhere in-between. Yet the questions that lack simple answers are the most worthy of study.

Examining Values

You have just read that critical thinking involves making informed decisions based on reliable evidence. But suppose you uncover evidence that conflicts with your values? For example, what if you value your independence so much that you have decided to take your time finding a long-term mate. Then you read a study that suggests that people with mates tend to live longer and enjoy life more fully than singles and that the happiest couples make it a point to spend some time away from each other. How would you use critical thinking to reconcile this apparent disparity between your values and what you have read?

Four Aspects of Critical Thinking

Good critical thinking cannot be learned overnight nor always accomplished in a neat set of steps. Yet as interpreted by William Daly, professor of political science at The Richard Stockton College of New Jersey, the critical thinking process divides neatly into four basic steps. Because these four aspects are so important, we've woven them into discussions and exercises throughout this book. Practicing these basic ideas can help you become a more effective thinker.

1. Abstract Thinking: Discovering Larger Ideas from Details

From large amounts of facts, seek the bigger ideas or the abstractions behind the facts. What are the key ideas? Even fields like medicine, which involve countless facts, culminate in general ideas such as the principles of circulation or the basic pattern of cell biology.

Ask yourself what larger concepts the details suggest. For example, you read an article that describes how many people are using the Internet now, how much consumer information it provides, what kinds of goods you can buy cheaply over the Internet, and that many low-income homes are still without computers. Thinking carefully about these facts, you might arrive at several different important generalizations. One might be that as the Internet becomes more important for shopping, the lack of computers in low-income households will put poor families at an even greater disadvantage. Or your general idea might be that because the Internet is becoming important for selling things, companies will probably find a way to put a computer in every home.

2. Creative Thinking: Finding New Possibilities

Use the general idea you have found to see what further ideas it suggests. This phase can lead in many directions. It might involve searching for ways to make the Internet more available to low-income households. Or it might involve searching out more detailed information on how much interest big companies really have in marketing various goods to low-income families. In essence, the creative thinking stage involves extending the general idea—finding new ways it might apply or further ideas it might suggest. The important thing at this stage is not to reject ideas out of hand but to explore wherever your general idea may take you.

Critical Thinking: Unnatural Acts?

A Professor Daly proposes that the four critical thinking skills he names are "unnatural acts"— not things that people do easily or without training. Do you agree? In what way has your previous education or other experiences prepared you to form abstractions? To generate new ideas or foresee new possibilities? To question the logic of what other people write and say? To examine the logic or evidence behind your own written or spoken arguments?

B Ask one or more of your instructors for their views on critical thinking and its importance to a college education. Ask what they do in their classes to stimulate critical thinking among students and how successful their methods are. What is their favorite or most successful method? Describe the interview in a paper and share it with your class.

A good class becomes a critical thinking experience. As you listen to the professor, try to predict where the lecture is heading and why. When other students raise issues, ask yourself whether they have enough information to justify what they have said. And when you raise *your* hand to participate, remember that asking a sensible question may be more important than trying to find the elusive "right" answer.

3. Systematic Thinking: Organizing the Possibilities

Systematic thinking involves looking at the outcome of the second phase in a more demanding, critical way. If you are looking for solutions to a problem, which ones really seem most promising? Do some conflict with others? Which ones can be achieved? If you have found new evidence to refine or further test your generalization, what does that new evidence show? Does your original generalization still hold up? Does it need to be modified? What further conclusions do good reasoning and evidence support? Which notions should be abandoned? This is where you narrow that list from step 2.

SEE EXERCISE 5.2

4. Precise Communication of Your Ideas to Others

Great conclusions aren't very useful if you cannot communicate them to others. Consider what your audience will need to know to follow your reasoning and be persuaded. Because written communication is so important in school and in the workplace, we expand on writing in the following section.

SEE SEARCH ONLINE!
INTERNET EXERCISE 5.1

Writing to Think and to Communicate

William Zinsser, the author of several widely respected books on writing, reminds us that writing is not merely something that professional writers do but a basic skill for life. He claims that far too many Americans are prevented from doing useful work because they never learned to express themselves. Being able to write clearly and logically will help you in college and help you land a great job after college.

Explore First and Explain Later

Writing serves two general purposes. Exploratory writing helps you discover what you want to say. Explanatory writing transmits information to others. It is "published" writing in the sense that it is ready for others to read. Although exploratory writing should be private, it serves as the basis for your explanatory writing.

Carolyn Matalene, an award-winning teacher at the University of South Carolina, says that writing forces you to know what you don't know and enables you to see relationships. It also requires you to structure information so that you can remember

SEE EXERCISE 5.3

it. Writing, she adds, allows and inspires creativity. Writing requires you to address an audience—first yourself and then your reader. Writing smoothes the way to a higher level of literacy.

Three Steps to Better Writing

Most writing teachers agree that the writing process consists of three steps:

- Prewriting or rehearsing (including preparing to write by gathering information through assigned work and other research)
- Writing or drafting
- Rewriting or revising

They also agree that the reason many students turn in poorly written papers is that they skip the first and last steps and make do with the middle one.

Prewriting for Ideas

One way to start writing is simply to pick up a pen and begin to write your thoughts in response to some idea or topic. This is the basic idea of freewriting, an important prewriting technique. The goal is not to write something that anyone else can read, or even necessarily to stick with the topic, but simply to keep writing to explore your reactions to and ideas about some general area, to discover what interests you about it, what you know and don't know, where your thoughts are centered. In freewriting you don't worry about spelling, grammar, or punctuation. Even if you feel you have nothing to say, you keep writing about where your thoughts are going.

What happens is that, without forcing things, you will begin to make connections between the initial topic and some of your freewriting. The most important thing at this point is finding you have something to say and capturing those rough ideas in writing for later use.

Freewriting is a good starting point for critical and creative writing assignments. It is also one way to deal with writer's block—the feeling that you have something to say but just can't seem to get it down.

Many writing experts, such as Donald Murray, believe that, of all the steps, prewriting should take the longest. This is where you explore what you want to say about something, write down all you think you need to know about a topic, and then go digging for the answers.

Prewriting can involve a lot of thinking time, whether or not any words appear on paper. It's a time to compare ideas and question things that seem illogical, to think about what others have said or written, and to ask yourself how your own views and information compare with theirs.

SEE SEARCH ONLINE!
INTERNET EXERCISE 5.2

Finding a Topic

Sometimes your teacher will assign you a specific topic to write about. If not, finding a topic can be the main task of prewriting. When is a topic appropriate? When is it neither too broad nor too narrow? The answers will depend on several things including the assignment length, how much you know or have time to find out, and how narrow or broad a topic the assignment requires. Think of the topic in terms of a question you will try to answer. Is the question big enough to reflect your learning? Is it narrow enough that you can answer with specific ideas, well supported by evidence? Once you think you have a suitable topic, test it by completing the following sentence: "The purpose of this paper is to convince my instructor that …" If the completed sentence is clear and the task is doable, the topic is probably right.

In many ways, the personal computer has revolutionized the act of writing. Above all, it has made the process of revising a number of drafts easier. Random thoughts can be easily grouped and related into a coherent discussion. When you make minor changes, you do not have to retype the complete manuscript; you simply insert the corrections and print. And you can disseminate your thoughts to a worldwide audience in seconds via an Internet discussion group.

In *Zen and the Art of Motorcycle Maintenance,* a classic of the 1970s, Robert Pirsig writes about teaching English composition. Each week the assignment was to turn in a 500-word essay. One week, a student failed to submit her paper about the town where the college was located, explaining that she had "thought and thought, but couldn't think of anything to write." Pirsig gave her an additional weekend to complete the assignment. As he did so, an idea flashed through his mind. "I want you to write a 500-word paper about Main Street, not the whole town," he said. She stared at him angrily. How was she to narrow her thinking to just one street when she couldn't think of anything to write about the entire town?

Monday she arrived in tears. "I thought and thought, and I think you're not being fair. I'll never learn to write." Pirsig's answer: "Write a paper about one building on Main Street. The opera house. And start with the first brick on the lower left side. I want it next class."

Her eyes opened wide. Something was happening. Indeed, she walked into class the next time with a 5000-word paper on the opera house.

"I don't know what happened," she exclaimed. "I sat across the street and wrote about the first brick, then the second, and all of a sudden I couldn't stop. Hope it's not too long."

What had Pirsig done for this student? He had helped her find a focus, a place to begin. And getting started is what blocks most students from approaching writing properly. Had she continued to write about bricks? Of course not. She probably began to see, for the first time, the beauty of the opera house and went on to describe it, to find out more about it in the library, to ask others about it, and to comment on its setting among the other buildings on the block.

SEE EXERCISE 5.4

Writing for Organization

Once you have explored your information and ideas through prewriting, it's time to move to the writing stage. Now you begin to write in larger chunks, building your paper around the topic and, as much as possible, putting things in a suitable order. At this point you begin to pay attention to the flow of ideas from one sentence and from one paragraph to the next. For some kinds of papers, you might add headings. When you have completed this stage, you will have the first draft of your paper in hand.

Put it away for a day or so and then read it. Does it say what you want to say? Are the ideas well organized? What changes may you need to make?

Rewriting to Polish

Are you finished? Not by a long shot. Now, in the third stage of writing, you take a good piece of writing and make it great. The essence of good writing is rewriting. You read again. You correct. You add smoother transitions. You slash through wordy sentences or paragraphs that add nothing. You substitute strong words for weak ones. You double-check spelling and grammar. You continue to revise until you're satisfied. And then you "publish."

Allocating Your Time for Writing

When Murray was asked how long a writer should spend on each of the three stages, he offered this breakdown: prewriting, 85 percent (including research and rumination); writing, 1 percent (the first draft); rewriting, 14 percent (revising until it's right).

Do the figures surprise you? If they do, consider the writer who was assigned to create a brochure. He had other jobs to do and kept avoiding that one. But the other work he was doing had direct bearing on the brochure he was told to write. So as he was putting this assignment off, he was also researching material for it.

After nearly 3 months, he could stand it no longer. So he sat at his computer and dashed off the words in just under 30 minutes. He felt a rush of ideas, he used words and phrases he'd never used before, and he was afraid to stop for fear of forgetting something. Then he did some revising, sent it around the office, and took other suggestions; eventually, the brochure was published.

He had spent a long time prewriting (working with related information without trying to write the brochure). He went through the writing stage quickly because his mind was primed for the task. As a result, he had time to polish his work before deciding the job was done.

So how should you approach writing? To become a better writer and thinker, start writing the day you get an assignment, even if it's only for 10 or 15 minutes. That way, you won't be confronting a blank paper later in the week.

Write something every day. The more you write, the better you'll write. Read good writing and begin to imitate the kinds of writing you admire. Above all, know that the hard work of becoming a better thinker and writer will pay off—in college and beyond.

SEE EXERCISE 5.5

Some Good and Bad Habits in Thinking and Writing

Certain errors often creep in when people try to construct or examine arguments. Several of these logical fallacies are mentioned in the following list, along with more positive advice for developing good habits.

- **Try to answer important questions.** Perhaps our greatest accomplishment as human beings is how very much we have managed to discover about the natural world, our history, and ourselves.
- **Expect the truth to be complicated and sometimes painful.** It is no small feat to understand the true cause of an important event. The obvious cause may not be the true one.
- **Be willing to say, "I don't know."** Suspend judgment or reconsider. Don't draw conclusions in haste. Good questions take time and patience to answer.

- **The fact that there is no evidence against an idea does not mean that the idea is true.** Until there is good evidence for the idea, it is still just an idea.
- **Don't substitute sincerity for real knowledge.** Sincere belief that aliens built the pyramids is no substitute for knowledge. Test your opinions in the light of the evidence and be willing to change your mind.
- **Get used to clarifying what you mean and asking others to do so.** Unproductive arguments are often the result of misunderstandings about definitions, especially of words like *freedom* or *fair*.
- **Question facts.** Do they come from a reliable source, from someone who is really an authority on the subject? Is there some way to check that they are really true?
- **Trust your own experience.** In the end, there is no higher authority for truth. At the same time, recognize its limits. There is nothing wrong with relying on experts when your own information is limited.
- **Judge an argument on its merits, not on the basis of who said it.** It is never appropriate to reject an argument simply because it comes from someone you dislike or disagree with on other matters.
- **Don't get trapped into thinking that you must win every argument.** That's just a way to make yourself lonely. The truth is more important.

A great way to better understand many of these principles is to take good courses in logic, writing, and critical thinking beyond what your school may require. Different departments offer such courses, but the best course for you in logic and thinking is probably taught by the philosophy department. Find out from other students who have taken such a course how valuable it was.

Search Online!

Internet Exercise 5.1 Critical Thinking Resources

The Center for Critical Thinking, at *www.criticalthinking.org/University/univlibrary/library.nclk*, offers resources and discussion of the fundamentals of critical thinking. Their site includes discussion of "Three Categories of Questions: Crucial Distinctions." Look up this site and compare that discussion with the one in this chapter. (Go to *http://success.wadsworth.com* for the most up-to-date URLs.) Using your critical thinking skills, write a paper comparing the similarities and differences. Share your ideas with other members of the class.

Internet Exercise 5.2 Discovering More About Critical Thinking and Writing

Using *InfoTrac College Edition,* try these phrases and others for key-word and subject-guide searches: "critical thinking," "creative thinking," "composition," "writing," "grammar," "English language," and "debate."

ALSO LOOK UP:

Critical thinking is totally inadequate. (can you teach your people to think smarter?) (Cover Story) Edward deBono. *Across the Board* Mar 1996 v33 n3 p25(2)

Obstacles to open discussion and critical thinking: The Grinnell College study. (includes related article on the Grinnell College study) Carol Trosset. *Change* Sept-Oct 1998 v30 n5 p44(6)

The logic of creative and critical thinking. Richard W. Paul. *American Behavioral Scientist* Sept-Oct 1993 v37 n1 p21(19)

The clay that makes the pot. Shelby A. Wolf, Kathryn A. H. Davinroy. *Written Communications* Oct 1998 v15 i4 p419(1)

The writing process goes to San Quentin. Jane Juska. *Phi Delta Kappan* June 1999 v80 i10 p759

Additional Exercises

These exercises will help you sharpen what we believe are the critical skills for college success: writing, critical thinking, learning in groups, planning, reflecting, and taking action. Also, check out the CD-ROM that came with your book—you will find these exercises and more.

Exercise 5.1 **Reflecting on Arguments**

Review the list of bulleted questions on pages 66 and 67. Are they the kinds of questions that you tend to ask when you read, listen to, or take part in discussions? Each evening for the next week, reread the list and think about whether you have asked such questions that day. Also ask yourself whether you have been noticing that day whether people are stating their assumptions or conclusions.

Exercise 5.2 **The Challenge of Classroom Thinking**

Think about your experiences in each of your classes up to now this term and the kinds of bulleted questions on pages 66 and 67.

- Have your instructors pointed out any conflicts or contradictions in the ideas they have presented?
- Have they been asking questions for which they sometimes don't seem to have the answers?
- Have they challenged you or other members of the class to explain yourselves more fully?
- Have they challenged the arguments of other experts? Have they called on students in the class to question or challenge certain ideas?

How have you reacted to their words? Do your responses reflect an attitude of active learning? Write down your thoughts for possible discussion in class. Consider sharing them with your instructors.

Exercise 5.3 **Engage by Writing**

Sit down with a reading assignment you have recently completed in one of your courses. Write a summary of what you read. Write down any questions that the reading raised for you. Write about why you think you were asked to read the material and what reading it accomplished for you. Finally, write down any additional personal responses you may have had to the material. This is private writing, so you don't have to share it with others, but your instructor may ask how going through this process has helped you with the material. Be prepared to answer.

Exercise 5.4 **The Power of Focused Observation**

Remember the student Pirsig wrote about, the one who began with the first brick of the opera house and went on to write a 5000-word paper? Find a favorite spot of yours on campus where you can sit comfortably. Take a good look at the entire area. Now look again, this time noticing specific parts of the area. Choose something; it may be a statue, building, tree, fence, and so on. Now look carefully at just one portion of that part and start writing about it. See where the writing takes you and write about that experience.

Exercise 5.5 Parallels

In what ways are the critical thinking and writing processes similar?

_____

_____

_____

In what ways are they different?

_____

_____

_____

Your Personal Journal

Here are several things to write about. Choose one or more or choose another topic related to this chapter.

1. Based on the definition in this chapter, do you think you already are a critical thinker? If so, tell why. If not, tell how you plan to become more of one.
2. Some students have complained that "the teacher should have all the answers" and have resented a teacher saying, "I'm not sure. What do you think about that, Mary?" How would you characterize their thinking?
3. If you find the writing process in this chapter helpful, explain how it is. If you don't, describe how you write and why this works better for you.
4. How would you rate your writing on a scale of 1 to 5, with 5 being excellent? If you rate it high, tell why. If you rate it low, explain what steps you will take to improve.
5. Anything else on your mind this week? If you wish to share it with your instructor, add it to this journal entry.

Resources

One way to improve your critical thinking and writing skills is to explore certain topics and issues you normally would not pay attention to. You might, for example, watch a PBS special on the Middle East instead of a major league baseball game. Or read a book about mood-triggering chemicals in the brain instead of reading the latest spy thriller. Or see a film based on a classic novel instead of the new sci-fi flick. Start making a list here.

	The Usual Choices	Something Different
Movies		
TV		
Books		
Magazines		
Live Entertainment		

Compare lists with friends. You might even find a way to exchange preferences in order to complete this table.

Do a library or Internet search to come up with a list of articles about critical thinking. List the ones that seem the most interesting.

....

....

....

....

....

....

Now choose one or two, read them, and reflect on what you have learned in writing.

Part 4

Hone Your Skills!

Strategies for Success

PLAN AHEAD!

- Show up for class
- Have work done on time
- Set up a daily schedule
- If full-time, limit work week to 20 hours. Work on campus if possible
- If stressed, enroll part time

TAKE CHARGE OF LEARNING!

- Choose instructors who favor active learning
- Assess how you learn best
- Improve your reading, note-taking, and study habits
- Develop critical thinking skills
- Improve your writing

HONE YOUR SKILLS!

- Participate in class
- Practice giving presentations
- Learn how to remember more from every class
- Learn from criticism
- Take workshops on how to study
- Get to know your campus library and other information sources
- Embrace new technologies

GET CONNECTED!

- Study with a group
- Get to know one person on campus who cares about you
- Get involved in campus activities
- Learn about campus helping resources
- Meet with your instructors
- Find a great academic advisor or counselor
- Visit your campus career center
- Take advantage of minority support services
- Enlist support of your spouse, partner, or family

KNOW YOURSELF!

- Take your health seriously
- Have realistic expectations
- Learn how to be assertive yet tactful
- Be proud of your heritage

Classes

Listening, Note Taking, and Participating

tune in

IN THIS CHAPTER, YOU WILL LEARN

- How to determine your "note-taking IQ" and how to improve it

- Why it's important to review your notes as soon as possible after class

- How to prepare to remember before class

- How to listen critically and take good notes in class

- Why you should speak up in class

- How to review class and textbook materials after class

*B*ummer. Bad grade on my first history test, and I thought I took good notes every day. I read all the assigned chapters in the text, too, and underlined the important points. Maybe I just wasn't listening hard enough in class. Guess I'll have to write faster and take down everything the instructor says, or I'll never pass this course."

In virtually every college class you take, you'll need to master two skills to earn high grades: listening and note taking. Taking an active role in your classes—asking questions, contributing to discussions, or providing answers—will help you listen better and take more meaningful notes, and that in turn will enhance your ability to formulate concepts, find new possibilities, organize your ideas, and remember the material after class.

SELF-ASSESSMENT: LISTENING, NOTE TAKING, AND PARTICIPATING

Checkmark each of the following statements that come close to describing you:

_____ 1. If I can't tell what's important in a lecture, I write down everything the instructor says.

_____ 2. If an instructor moves through the material very fast, it might be a good idea to tape-record the lecture and not worry about paying attention in class.

_____ 3. If the instructor puts an outline on the board, I usually copy it right away.

_____ 4. Listening in a class that is mainly discussion is better than trying to take notes.

_____ 5. Once class is over, I usually don't look at my notes again until the next class—or later.

_____ 6. When the instructor says something I don't understand, I figure I'll get it from a friend later.

_____ 7. I like when the instructor is late for class; it gives me time to talk to my friends.

_____ 8. Just before a quiz, I rarely or never compare my notes with those of another student.

_____ 9. Whatever I miss in class, I'll catch up on in the textbook.

_____ 10. It's better to sit and take notes than to raise my hand and ask a question.

Listening and note taking are critical to your academic success because (1) your college instructors are likely to introduce new material in class that your texts don't cover and (2) chances are that much of this material will resurface on quizzes and exams. By the way, none of the statements in the self-assessment inventory is considered good practice for the classroom. So, pay attention to the suggestions in this chapter, practice them regularly, and watch your grades improve.

Here are some comments on the self-assessment. Try to remember them.

1. Writing down everything the instructor says won't help. Instead, raise your hand and ask questions that will help you capture the main points, get help from your study skills center, or compare your notes with a friend's.

2. Recording a lecture means you must sit through it at least twice in order to understand it. Instead, ask the instructor to speak more slowly or to repeat points that you missed.

3. Copying an outline immediately may not allow enough room for filling in the finer details. A good instructor will cover each point in sequence. Write down the first point and listen. Take notes. When the next point is covered, do the same, and so forth.

4. Discussion can be deceiving. Your instructors may be taking notes on what is said and could use them on exams. You should be taking notes as well, in addition to participating.

5. As you soon will learn, it's helpful to review notes after class as soon as possible.

6. Better yet, ask the instructor in class or after class. Your friend may not have "gotten it" either or may have misunderstood the point the instructor was making.

7. As you'll learn in this chapter, you'd be wasting valuable review time.

8. In team learning, reviewing notes with one or two other students can be beneficial to all.

9. Whoa! What the instructor says in class may not always be in the textbook and vice versa.

10. Learning is a participatory sport. Speak up!

Short-Term Memory: Listening and Forgetting

Ever notice how easy it is to learn the words of a song? We remember songs and poetry more easily in part because they follow a rhythm and a beat. We remember prose less easily, and we can hardly remember nonsense words at all (Figure 6.1).

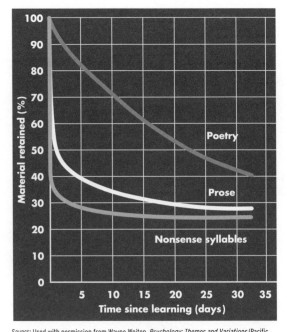

SOURCE: Used with permission from Wayne Weiten, *Psychology: Themes and Variations* (Pacific Grove, CA: Brooks/Cole, 1989, p. 254. Based on data from D. van Guilford, Van Nostrand, 1939).

FIGURE 6.1
Learning and Forgetting
Psychologists have studied human forgetting in many laboratory experiments. Here are the forgetting curves for three kinds of material: poetry, prose, and nonsense syllables. The shallower curves for prose and poetry indicate that meaningful material is forgotten more slowly than non-meaningful information. Because poetry contains internal cues such as rhyme and rhythm, it is forgotten less quickly than prose.

Most forgetting takes place within the first 24 hours after you see or hear something. That's why a good study habit is to review as soon after class as possible. Forgetting can be a serious problem when you are expected to remember a mass of facts, figures, concepts, and relationships. Once you improve your ability to remember, you will retain information more easily.

Many instructors draw the bulk of their test items from their lectures; remembering what is presented in class is crucial to doing well on exams. The following system will help you remember and understand material better and relate certain information to things you already know. It consists of three major parts: preparing to listen before class, listening and taking notes during class, and reviewing and recalling information after class.

SEE SEARCH ONLINE!
INTERNET EXERCISE 6.1

Before Class: Prepare to Remember

Even if lectures don't allow for active participation, you can take a number of active learning steps to make your listening and note taking more efficient. Because many lectures can be demanding intellectual encounters, you need to be intellectually prepared before class begins. You would never walk in cold to give a speech, interview for a job, plead a case in court, or compete in sports. For the same reasons, you should begin active listening, learning, and remembering before the lecture.

1. **Do the assigned reading.** You may blame lecturers for seeming disorganized and confusing when in fact you may not have done the assigned reading. Some instructors refer to assigned readings for each class session; others may hand out a syllabus and assume you are keeping up with the readings. Completing the assigned readings on time will help you listen better in class.
2. **Warm up for class.** Take good notes on what you've read. Then warm up by referring to the underlined sections in your text and your classroom notes.
3. **Keep an open mind.** Don't assume that you already know this topic and what is going to be said. Every situation holds the promise of discovering new information and uncovering different perspectives.

You'll get more out of a lecture if you prepare ahead of time. Stay abreast of the readings. Get your own ideas flowing by reviewing notes from the previous lecture. What questions were left unanswered? Where should today's session begin?

During Class: Listen Critically and Take Good Notes

Listening in class is not like listening to a TV program, a friend, or even a speaker at a meeting. Knowing how to listen in class can help you understand the lecture or discussion and save you time.

Listen for Information

1. **Listen to the main concepts and central ideas, not just to fragmented facts and figures.** Although facts are important, they will be easier to remember and make more sense when you can place them in a context.
2. **Listen for new ideas.** Even if you are an expert on the topic, you can still learn something new. When you listen, try to match what you are hearing with what you already know. Take an active role in deciding how best to recall what you are learning.
3. **Really hear what is said.** Listening involves hearing what the speaker wants you to understand. Don't give in to distractions, such as daydreaming or looking at other students. And try not to pass quick judgment on what is being said because this will distract you. As a true critical thinker, note questions that arise in your mind as you listen but save the judgments for later.
4. **Repeat mentally.** Words can go in one ear and out the other unless you make an effort to retain them. Think about what you hear and make an active effort to retain it by repeating it silently to yourself.
5. **Decide whether what you have heard is not important, somewhat important, or very important.** If it's really not important, let it go. If it's very important, make it a major point in your notes by underscoring it or using it as a major topic in your outline. If it's somewhat important, try to relate it to a very important topic by writing it down as a subset of that topic.
6. **Ask questions.** If you did not hear or understand what was said, raise your hand. Now is the time to clarify things. If you can't hear another student's question, ask that the question be repeated.
7. **Listen to the entire message.** Try to avoid agreeing or disagreeing with the speaker, based only on the opening of the lecture.
8. **Respect your ideas.** You already know a lot of things. Your own thoughts and ideas are valuable, and you need not throw them out just because someone else's views conflict with your own. At the same time, you should not reject the ideas of others too casually.

Examining Values

A student is overheard saying, "Boy, these lectures are boring. I just sit there and doodle to make the time pass." Another student says, "You know, I read the assignment two days ago, but all this stuff he's talking about doesn't connect to the book." A third student says, "Well, this isn't the most exciting material on Earth, but I want to get a good grade, so I've practiced focusing on the lecture and asking questions when I don't understand something." How would you characterize the values of each student? Or, said another way, what things does each student value most? Least?

Take Effective Notes

You can make class time more productive by using your listening skills to take effective notes. Here's how:

1. **Identify the main ideas.** Good lectures always contain certain key points. The first principle of effective note taking is to identify and write down the most important ideas (usually four or five) around which the lecture is built. Although supporting details are important as well, focus your note taking on the main ideas. These main ideas may be buried in details, statistics, anecdotes, or problems, but you need to locate and record them for further study.

   Instructors sometimes announce the purpose of a lecture or offer an outline, thus providing you with the skeleton of main ideas, followed by the details. Some lecturers change their tone of voice or repeat themselves at each key idea. Some ask questions or promote discussion. These are all clues to what is important. If a lecturer repeats something, it is probably essential information. Ask yourself, What does my instructor want me to know at the end of today's session?

   Don't try to write down everything. Because of insecurity or inexperience, some first-year students stop being thinkers and become stenographers. Learn to avoid that trap. If you're an active listener, you will have shorter but more useful notes.

   As you take notes, leave spaces so that you can fill in additional details later that you might have missed during class. But remember to do it as soon after SEE EXERCISE 6.1 class as possible; remember the forgetting curve!

2. **Don't be thrown by a disorganized lecturer.** When a lecture is disorganized, you need to try to organize what is said into general and specific frameworks. When this order is not apparent, you'll need to take notes on where the gaps lie in the lecturer's structure. After the lecture, you may need to consult your reading material or classmates to fill in these gaps.

   You might also consult your instructor. Most instructors have regular office hours for student appointments, yet it is amazing how few students use these opportunities for one-on-one instruction. You can also raise questions in class. Asking such questions may help your instructor discover which parts of his or her presentation need more attention and clarification.

3. **Leave space for a recall column.** This is a critical part of effective note taking. In addition to helping you listen well, your notes become an important study device for tests and examinations.

   Here's how to create a recall column. Using one side of the paper only, draw a vertical line to divide the page into two columns. The column on the left, about 2 to 3 inches wide, is the recall column and remains blank while you take notes during class in the wider column on the right. The recall column is essentially the place where you highlight the main ideas and important details for tests and examinations as you sift through your notes after class.

   Completing the blank recall column as soon after class as possible (and perhaps with a small group of your classmates) is a powerful study device that reduces forgetting, helps you warm up for class, and promotes understanding in class.

Note Taking in Nonlecture Courses

Always be ready to adapt your note-taking methods to match the situation. In fact, group discussion is becoming a popular way to teach in college because it involves active learning. How do you keep a record of what's happening in such classes?

Assume you are taking notes in a problem-solving group assignment. You would begin your notes by asking yourself, What is the problem? and writing down the answer. As the discussion progresses, you would list the solutions offered. These would be your main ideas. The important details might include the positive and negative aspects of each view or solution.

The important thing to remember when taking notes in nonlecture courses is that you need to record the information presented by your classmates, as well as from the instructor, and to consider all reasonable ideas, even though they may differ from your own.

When a course has separate lecture and discussion sessions, you will need to understand how the discussion sessions augment and correlate with the lectures. If different material is covered in the lecture than is covered in the discussion, you may need to ask for guidance in organizing your notes. If similar topics are covered, combine your notes so that you have comprehensive, unified coverage of each topic.

How to organize the notes you take in a class discussion depends on the purpose or form of the discussion. But it usually makes good sense to begin with a list of issues or topics that the discussion leader announces. Another approach is to list the questions that the participants raise for discussion. If the discussion is exploring reasons for and against a particular argument, it makes sense to divide your notes into columns or sections for pros and cons. Even if you do not agree with others, you need to understand their views and rationales, and your teacher may ask you to defend your own opinions in light of the others.

Comparing Notes

You may be able to improve your notes by comparing notes with another student. When you know that you are going to compare notes, you will tend to take better notes. Knowing that your notes will be seen by someone else will prompt you to make your notes well organized, clear, and accurate. See whether your notes are as clear and concise as the other person's and whether you agree on the important points. Share how you take and organize your notes with each other. If you used the recall column in your notes, share notes after class and take turns reciting to each other what you have learned.

SEE EXERCISE 6.2

Incidentally, comparing notes is not the same as copying somebody else's notes. You simply cannot get the course material from someone else's notes, no matter how good they are, if you have not attended class.

Other Kinds of Notes

- **Outline notes are widely used.** If you use this approach, try to determine the instructor's outline and re-create it in your notes. Add details, definitions, examples, applications, and explanations. Be careful not to confuse the supporting information with the main points.
- **Definitional notes work in some courses.** Using this method, you would enter the major terms on the left edge of the page and then place all material for that term—definitions, explanations, examples, and supporting evidence—beside it.
- **Paragraph notes work in some situations.** Write detailed paragraphs, with each containing a summary of a topic. This may work better for summarizing what you

have read rather than for class notes because it may be difficult to summarize the topic until your teacher has covered it completely, by which time it may be too late to recall critical information.

- **Fact notes include only the critical points from the lecture or discussion.** The major problem with this method is trying to organize the facts into meaningful groups. Too often they wind up as a collection of terms with little organization or rationale.

Keep in mind that it can help to go back through your course notes, reorganize them, highlight the essential items, and have new notes that let you connect with the material one more time and are better than the originals.

Class Notes and Homework Problems

Good class notes can help you complete homework assignments. Follow these steps:

1. **Take 10 minutes to review your notes.** Try to place the material in context: What has been going on in the course for the last few weeks? How does today's class fit in?
2. **Warm up for your homework.** Look through your notes again. Use a separate sheet of paper to rework examples, problems, or exercises. If there is related assigned material in the textbook, review it.
3. **Do any assigned problems and answer any assigned questions.** Now you are actually starting your homework. As you read each question or problem, ask: What am I supposed to find out? What is essential and what is extraneous? The last sentence may be where you will find the essential question or answer. Read the problem several times and state it in your own words.
4. **Persevere.** Don't give up too soon. When you encounter a problem or question that you cannot readily handle, move on only after a reasonable effort. After you have completed the entire assignment, come back to those items that stumped you. Try once more, then take a break. You may need to mull over a particularly difficult problem for several days. Give your unconscious mind a chance. Inspiration may come when you are waiting for a stoplight or just before you fall asleep.
5. **Complete your work.** When you finish an assignment, talk to yourself about what you learned from this particular assignment. Generalize about how the problems and questions were different from one another, which strategies were successful, and what form the answers took.

You may be thinking, That all sounds good, but who has the time to do all that extra work? In reality, this approach does work and actually can save you time. Try it for a few weeks. You will find that you can diminish the frustration that comes when you tackle your homework cold.

Computer Notes in Class?

Laptops are often poor tools for taking notes. Computer screens are not conducive to making marginal notes, circling important items, or copying diagrams. And, although most students can scribble coherently without watching their hands, few are really good keyboarders. Finally, notes on a computer are often harder to access or scan when it's time to review. Entering notes on a computer after class for review purposes may be helpful. On the other hand, if you enter everything the lecturer says during class, you may be wasting time that could be spent more productively.

After Class: Respond, Recite, and Review

Remember and Respond

Using your powers of memory, make a conscious effort to remember. One way is to repeat important data to yourself every few minutes. Another approach is to tie one idea to another idea, concept, or name so that thinking of one will prompt recall of the other.

Often, the best way to learn something is to teach it to someone else. You will understand something better and remember it longer if you try to explain it. This helps you discover your own reactions and uncover gaps in your comprehension of the material. (Asking and answering questions in class also provides you with the feedback you need to make certain your understanding is accurate.)

Before the next class, get ready to listen again. You have already learned how to prepare yourself to listen well. Maintain that readiness so that you are prepared to listen daily.

Fill In the Recall Column, Recite, and Review

Don't let the forgetting curve take its toll on you! Replace it with the memory curve. As soon after class as possible, review your notes and fill in the details you still remember, but missed writing down, in those spaces you left in the right-hand column. Then go through these three important steps for remembering the key points in the lecture:

1. **Write the main ideas in the recall column.** For 5 or 10 minutes, quickly review your notes and select key words or phrases that will act as labels or tags for main ideas and key information in the notes. Highlight the main ideas and write them in the recall column next to the material they represent.

2. **Use the recall column to recite your ideas.** Cover the notes on the right and use the prompts from the recall column to help you recite out loud a brief version of what you understand from the class in which you have just participated. If you don't have a few minutes after class to review your notes, find some other time during that same day to review what you have written. You might also want to ask your teacher to check your recall column for accuracy.

3. **Review the previous day's notes just before the next class session.** As you sit in class the next day waiting for the lecture to begin, use the time to quickly review the notes from the previous day. This will put you in tune with the lecture that is about to begin and will prompt you to ask questions about material from the previous lecture that may not have been clear to you.

These three engagements with the material will pay off later, when you begin to study for your examinations.

SEE EXERCISE 6.3

What if you have three classes in a row and no time for recall columns or recitations between them? Recall and recite as soon after class as possible. Review the most recent class first. Never delay recall and recitation longer than one day; reviewing, making a recall column, and reciting will then take you longer. With practice, you can complete your recall column quickly, perhaps between classes, during lunch, or while riding a bus.

SEE EXERCISE 6.4

Critical Thinking

Determining Main Ideas and Major Details

Divide a piece of looseleaf paper as shown in Figure 6.2. In one of your classes other than your first-year seminar, take notes on the right side of the paper, leaving the recall column and the last few lines on the page blank. As soon after class as possible, use the critical thinking process to abstract the main ideas and write them in the recall column. Use the blank lines at the bottom to write a summary sentence or two for that page of notes. Use the recall column to jot down any thoughts or possibilities that occur to you. For example, your possibilities may include, "I wonder what I can attach this information to so that I can recall it later?" or "Maybe if I break my American lit notes into small chunks, I'll recall them easier."

Sept 21 How to take notes

| Problems with lectures | Lecture _not_ best way to teach.
Problems: Short attention span (may be only 15 minutes!). Teacher dominates. Most info is forgotten. "Stenographer" role interferes with thinking, understanding, learning. |
| Forgetting curves | Forgetting curves critical period: over ½ of lecture forgotten in 24 hours. |
| Solution: Active listening | Answer: Active listening, really understanding during lecture. Aims—
(1) immediate understanding
(2) longer attention
(3) better retention
(4) notes for study later |
| Before: Read Warm up | BEFORE: Always prepare.
Read: Readings parallel lectures & make them meaningful.
Warm up: Review last lecture notes & readings right before class. |
| During: main ideas | DURING: Write main ideas & some detail. No steno. What clues does prof. give about what's most important? Ask. Ask other questions.
Leave blank column about 2½" on left of page. Use only front side of paper. |
| After: Review Recall Recite | AFTER: Left column for key recall words, "tags." Cover right side & recite what tags mean. Review / Recall / Recite |

FIGURE 6.2 Sample Lecture Notes

Participating in Class: Speak Up!

Learning is not a spectator sport. You won't learn much just by sitting in classes listening to teachers, memorizing readings and notes, and regurgitating answers on exams. To really learn, you must talk about what you are learning, write about it, relate it to past experiences, and make what you learn part of yourself.

One of the authors of this book still remembers his fears about speaking in class. Whenever the teacher asked a question about the lesson and let his eyes pan across the room, the author bent his head down so as not to be seen. He sat as far back in the room as he could. When he _was_ called on, he was so nervous he couldn't think or get the words formed properly.

Then he began graduate school, where he had a teacher who would ask a question and wait for an answer, an answer from anybody. He never called on anyone, but the silence during the wait for an answer would drive the author crazy. It forced him to blurt out an answer, and the more he did so, the more he learned. In fact, he got much satisfaction from speaking up and looked forward to class each day.

Participation is the heart of active learning. We know that when we say something in class we are more likely to remember it than when someone else does. So when a teacher tosses a question your way or when you have a question to ask, you're actually making it easier to remember the day's lesson.

Naturally, you will be more likely to participate in a class where the teacher emphasizes discussion, calls on students by name, shows students signs of approval and interest, and avoids shooting you down for an incorrect answer. Often, answers that are not quite correct can lead to new perspectives on a topic.

Unfortunately, many classes, especially large ones of 100 or more, force instructors to use the lecture method. Large classes can be intimidating. If you speak up in a class of 100 and feel you've made a fool of yourself, 99 people will know that. Of course, that's somewhat unrealistic, since you've probably asked a question that they were too timid to ask and they'll silently thank you for doing so. If you're lucky, you might even find that the instructor of such a class takes time out to ask or answer questions. To take full advantage of these opportunities in all classes, you should:

1. **Take a seat as close to the front as possible.** If you're seated by name and your name is Zoch, plead bad eyesight or hearing—anything to get moved up front.
2. **Keep your eyes trained on the teacher.** Sitting up front will make this easier for you to do.
3. **Raise your hand when you don't understand something.** The instructor may answer you immediately, ask you to wait until later in the class, or throw your question to the rest of the class. In each case, you benefit. The instructor gets to know you, other students get to know you, and you learn from both the instructor and your classmates.
4. **Don't feel that you're asking a "stupid" question.** There is no such thing. If you don't understand something, you have a right to ask for an explanation.
5. **When the instructor calls on you to answer a question, don't bluff.** If you know the answer, give it. If you're not certain, begin with, "I think … but I'm not sure I have it all correct." If you plain don't know, just say, "I'm sorry, but I don't know the answer."
6. **If you've recently read a book or article that is relevant to the class topic, bring it in and use it to either ask questions about the piece or provide information from it that was not covered in class.** Of course, you'll want to do this in a way that doesn't suggest your instructor has forgotten something important!

Next time you have the opportunity, speak up. Class will go by faster, you and your fellow students will get to know one another, your instructor will get to know each of you, and he or she will in all likelihood be grateful to have such a highly participatory class.

SEE SEARCH ONLINE! INTERNET EXERCISE 6.2

Search Online!   《●》

Internet Exercise 6.1 Study Skill Guides on the Internet

The Internet can be a major source of study skill and self-help materials. Handouts prepared by many college learning centers are available online. Check out the following:

- The CalREN Project, a series of tips and exercises to help develop better study strategies and habits: *http://128.32.89.153/CalRENHP.html.*
- Dartmouth Study Skills Guide Menu *http://www.dartmouth.edu/admin/acskills/index.html.*
- Study Tips—A collection of some of the handouts used in the University of Texas at Austin Learning Skills Center: *http://www.utexas.edu/student/lsc/handouts/stutips.html.*
- Virginia Polytechnic Institute Study Skills Self-Help Information: *http://www.ucc.vt.edu/stdysk/stdyhlp.html.*

What information did you find that you will be able to use? (Go to *http://success.wadsworth.com* for the most up-to-date URLs.)

Internet Exercise 6.2 Discovering More About Listening and Learning

Using *InfoTrac College Edition,* try these phrases and others for key-word and subject-guide searches: "study skills," "note taking," and "recalling information."

ALSO LOOK UP:

Visual note taking: drawing on my doodling past. Andrew John Katz. *School Arts* Sept 1997 v97 n1 p33(3)

Teaching study skills through classroom activities. John M. Kras, Brad N. Strand, Julie Abendroth-Smith, Peter Mathesius. *JOPERD–Journal of Physical Education, Recreation & Dance* Jan 1999 v70 i1 p40(5)

Note-taking strategies that work. Lois Laase. *Instructor* (1990) May-June 1997 v107 n8 p58(1)

Additional Exercises

These exercises will help you sharpen what we believe are the critical skills for college success: writing, critical thinking, learning in groups, planning, reflecting, and taking action. Also, check out the CD-ROM that came with your book—you will find these exercises and more.

Exercise 6.1 Listening and Memory

Form groups of five and chat about the importance of listening, how well students listen in class, and what they should do to improve their listening. Each student who speaks after the first speaker must use at least one word from the *last* sentence spoken by the last speaker. The first speaker should do the same after the last student has spoken. How did this affect the quality of your listening? How can you apply it to the classroom?

Exercise 6.2 Comparing Notes

Pair up with another student and compare your class notes for this course. Are your notes clear? Do you agree on what is important? Take a few minutes to explain to each other your note-taking systems. Agree to use a recall column during the next class meeting. Afterward, share your notes again and check on how each of you used the recall column. Again, compare your notes and what each of you deemed important.

Exercise 6.3 **Memory—Using a Recall Column**

Suppose the information in this chapter had been presented to you as a lecture rather than a reading. Using the system described previously, your lecture notes might look like those in Figure 6.2. Cover the right-hand column. Using the recall column, try reciting in your own words the main ideas from this chapter. Uncover the right-hand column when you need to refer to it. If you can phrase the main ideas from the recall column in your own words, you are well on your way to mastering this note-taking system for dealing with lectures. Does this system seem to work? If not, why not?

Exercise 6.4 **Applying an Active Listening and Learning System**

Write down your study schedule for this week or the coming week. Before you begin, answer the following questions:

1. Where should you build in time for using the recall column?

   _____

   _____

   _____

2. What problems might you have in performing review-recall-recite as soon after class as possible?

   _____

   _____

   _____

3. How might you address and solve these problems?

   _____

   _____

   _____

Share your answers with other students in a small group.

Your Personal Journal

Here are several things to write about. Choose one or more, or choose another topic related to this chapter.

1. Think of one of your courses in which you're having trouble taking useful notes. That must be frustrating! Now write down some ideas from this chapter that may help you improve your note taking in that course.
2. How might a study group help you improve your note taking and other study habits? Is there a possibility that you might join one? Jot down the names of students in your classes whom you admire for their academic achievements. Ask one of them if he or she is interested in forming a group. If that person already belongs to a group, ask if you might join.
3. What behaviors are you willing to change after reading this chapter? How might you go about changing them?
4. What else is on your mind this week? If you wish to share it with your instructor, add it to your journal entry.

Resources

Throughout this book, we mention the helpfulness of study groups for success in college. Use this Resources page to list names, phone and e-mail numbers and meeting times for the study groups you are in. Keep the list handy, especially close to test time. If you are not in a study group, list potential study group members and contact them.

Study group .... **meets** ....

Name .... **Phone number** .... **E-mail** ....

....

....

....

....

....

Study group .... **meets** ....

Name .... **Phone number** .... **E-mail** ....

....

....

....

....

....

Study group .... **meets** ....

Name .... **Phone number** .... **E-mail** ....

....

....

....

....

....

Libraries

Library	Regular hours	Hours during finals	Phone number	Web address

Reading

Getting the Most Out of Your Assignments

**IN THIS CHAPTER,
YOU WILL LEARN**

- How to prepare to read
- How to overview reading material
- How to read your text-books properly
- How to mark your text-books properly
- How to review your reading
- How to adjust your reading style to the material
- How to use the SQ3R method
- How to develop a larger vocabulary

crack the code

"I've read this paragraph five times, and I still don't understand it. How am I supposed to be ready to discuss this tomorrow when I can't even get through the first page? Can't someone just drill a hole in my head and pour it in?"

Preparing to Read

Reading college textbooks is more challenging than reading high school texts or reading for pleasure. College texts are loaded with concepts, terms, and complex information that you are expected to learn on your own in a short period of time. To do this, you will need to learn and use a study-reading method such as the one presented in this chapter.

The following plan for study reading will increase your focus and concentration, promote greater understanding of what you read, and prepare you to study for tests and exams. This system is based on four steps: overviewing, reading, marking, and reviewing.

Overviewing

Begin by reading the title of the chapter. Ask yourself, What do I already know about this subject? Next, quickly read through the introductory paragraphs; then turn to the end of the chapter and read the summary (if one is there). Finally, take a few minutes to page through the chapter headings and subheadings.

Note any study exercises at the end of the chapter. As part of your overview, note how many pages the chapter contains. It's a good idea to decide in advance how

SELF-ASSESSMENT: EVALUATING YOUR READING STRENGTHS AND WEAKNESSES

Before you read further, it's a good idea to consider your study-reading strengths and weaknesses. Answer yes or no to the following statements:

1. I skim or overview a chapter before I begin to read. _____

2. I lose concentration while reading a text. _____

3. I wait to highlight or mark the text after I read a page or more. _____

4. I take notes after I read. _____

5. I pause at the end of each section or page to review what I have read. _____

6. After reading I recount key ideas to myself or with a partner. _____

7. I review everything I have read for a class at least once a week. _____

A yes to any question except 2 indicates a strength. A no indicates a weakness.

Wheel Map

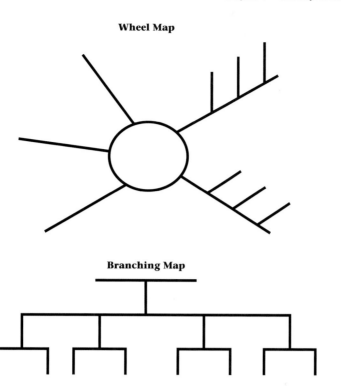

Branching Map

FIGURE 7.1
Wheel and Branching Maps

many pages you will try to cover in your first 50-minute study period. This can help build your concentration as you work toward your goal of reading a specific number of pages.

Mapping

Mapping the chapter as you overview it provides a visual guide of how different chapter ideas fit together. Because about 75 percent of students identify themselves as visual learners, visual mapping is an excellent learning tool that will be useful for test preparation as well as active reading.

How do you map a chapter? While you are overviewing, use either a wheel or branching mapping structure (Figure 7.1). In the wheel structure, place the central idea of the chapter in the circle, place secondary ideas on the spokes emanating from the circle, and place offshoots of those ideas on the lines attached to the spokes. In the branching map, the main idea goes at the top, followed by supporting ideas on the second tier, and so forth. Fill in the title first. Then as you skim through the rest of the chapter, use the headings and subheadings to fill in the key ideas.

SEE EXERCISE 7.1

This active learning step may require more time up front, but it will save you time later because you have created an excellent review tool for quizzes and tests. You will be using your visual learning skills as you create "advance organizers" to help you associate details of the chapter with the larger ideas. Such associations will be essential later.

As you overview the text material, look for connections between the text and the related lecture material. Call to mind the related terms and concepts that you recorded in the lecture. Use these strategies to warm up. Ask yourself, Why am I reading this? and What do I want to know?

Reading Your Textbook

After completing your overview, you are ready to read the text actively. With your skeleton map or outline, you should be able to read more quickly and with greater comprehension. To avoid overmarking or marking the wrong information, read first without using your pencil or highlighter. When you have reached the end of a section, stop and ask yourself, What are the key ideas in this section? and What do I think I'll see on the test? Then, and only then, decide what to mark.

Building Concentration and Understanding

Two common problems students have with textbooks are having trouble concentrating and not understanding the content. Many factors may affect your ability to concentrate and understand texts: the time of day, your energy level, your interest in the material, and your study location.

Consider these suggestions and decide which would help you improve your reading ability:

- Find a study location, preferably in the library if you are on campus, that is removed from traffic and distracting noises.
- Read in 50-minute blocks of time, with short breaks in-between. By reading for 50 minutes more frequently during the day instead of cramming all your reading in at the end of the day, you should be able to process material more easily.
- Set goals for your study period, such as, "I will read twenty pages of my psychology text in the next 50 minutes." Reward yourself with a 10-minute break after each 50-minute study period.
- If you are having trouble concentrating or staying awake, take a quick walk around the library or down the hall. Take some deep breaths and think positively about your study goals. Then go back and resume studying.

Critical Thinking

Reading to Question, Interpret, and Understand

Turn one statement in this chapter into a question. One might come from the very first sentence in the chapter: "Why is reading college textbooks a more challenging activity than reading general interest books?" Then use the critical thinking process to arrive at some understanding. In this case, you might abstract this thought: "This is really a matter of reading for pleasure and reading because you need to learn something. We usually enjoy play more than work." Moving to stage 2 of the critical thinking process, you might write, "I wonder if I can make reading a textbook entertaining. Then it won't be so difficult to read." Then brainstorm ways to make reading this text more entertaining. Finally, sift through your ideas and choose one or more that seem to work. Explain why to other students and your instructor. Here are others to choose from:

- Why should I take the time to read the title of the chapter and ask myself what I already know about the subject?
- Why should I spend extra time creating a map of this chapter? Isn't there some better way to learn it?
- Does a relationship exist between lack of concentration and inability to understand material? If so, what is the relationship, and how can understanding it help me overcome my difficulties with concentrating and understanding? If there is no relationship, which should I work on first, and why?
- What is the difference between "reading before you mark" and "thinking before you mark"? Why isn't it just as useful to mark as you read?
- (Any other question that you can construct from this chapter.)

- Jot study questions in the margin, take notes, or recite key ideas. Reread confusing parts of the text and make a note to ask your instructor for clarification.
- Experiment with your reading rate. Try to move your eyes more quickly over the material by focusing on phrases, not individual words.
- Focus on the high-yield portions of the text: Pay attention to the first and last sentences of paragraphs and to words in italics or bold print.
- Use the glossary in the text to define unfamiliar terms.

Marking Your Textbook

Think a moment about your goals for marking your texts. Some students report that marking is an active reading strategy that helps them focus and concentrate on the material as they read. In addition, most students expect to use their text notations when studying for tests. To meet these goals, some students like to underline, some prefer to highlight, and others use margin notes. Look at Figure 7.2 for examples of different methods of marking. You can also combine methods. No matter what method you prefer, remember these two important guidelines:

1. **Read before you mark.** Finish reading a section before you decide which are the most important ideas and concepts. Mark only those ideas, using your preferred methods (highlighting, underlining, circling key terms, making margin notes).
2. **Think before you mark.** When you read a text for the first time, everything may seem important. Only after you have completed a section and reflected on it will you be ready to identify the key ideas. Ask yourself, What are the most important ideas? and What will I see on the test? This can help you avoid marking too much material. An overzealous use of highlighting can convert a text to pages of Day-Glo color, in which nothing stands out as important.

SEE EXERCISE 7.2

One caution: If you just mark pages, you are committing yourself to at least one more viewing of all the pages that you have already read—all 400 pages of your anatomy or art history textbook! Better to also use margin notes or create a visual map or outline as you read.

Although these study-reading methods take more time initially, they can save you time in the long run: Active reading not only promotes concentration as you read but also makes it easy to review, so you probably won't have to pull an all-nighter before an exam.

Monitoring

An important step in a study-reading method is to monitor your comprehension. As you read ask yourself, Do I understand this? If not, stop and reread the material. Look up words that are not clear. Try to clarify the main points and how they relate to one another.

Examining Values

After reading this chapter, one of your classmates tells you, "I don't have the time to go over my assigned readings like this. I work every night from six to midnight." Another classmate tells you, "Well, I'll try this in a few weeks, but my calendar is busy right now with meetings, football games, and other things." As they walk away, you start thinking about the choices they just made. What's your reaction to them?

7. *Some students who read a chapter slowly get very good grades; others get poor grades. Why?*

8. *Most actors and public speakers who have to memorize lengthy passages spend little time simply repeating the words and more time thinking about them. Why? (Check your answers on page 288.)*

People need to monitor their understanding of a text to decide whether to keep studying or whether they already understand it well enough. Most readers have trouble making that judgment correctly.

SELF-MONITORING OF UNDERSTANDING

Whenever you are studying a text, you periodically have to decide, "Should I keep on studying this section, or do I already understand it well enough?" Most students have trouble monitoring their own understanding. In one study, psychology instructors asked their students before each test to guess whether they would do better or worse on that test than they usually do. Students also guessed after each test whether they had done better or worse than usual. Most students' guesses were no more accurate than chance (Sjostrom & Marks, 1994). Such inaccuracy represents a problem: Students who do not know how well they understand the material will make bad judgments about when to keep on studying and when to quit.

Even when you are reading a single sentence, you have to decide whether you understand the sentence or whether you should stop and reread it. Here is a sentence once published in the student newspaper at North Carolina State University:

He said Harris told him she and Brothers told French that grades had been changed.

Ordinarily, when good readers come to such a confusing sentence, they notice their own confusion and reread the sentence or, if necessary, the whole paragraph. Poor readers tend to read at their same speed for both easy and difficult materials; they are less likely than good readers to slow down when they come to difficult sentences.

Although monitoring one's own understanding is difficult and often inaccurate, it is not impossible. For example, suppose I tell you that you are to read three chapters dealing with, say, thermodynamics, the history of volleyball, and the Japanese stock market.

Later you will take tests on each chapter. Before you start reading, predict your approximate scores on the three tests. Most people make a guess based on how much they already know about the three topics. If we let them read the three chapters and again make a guess about their test performances, they do in fact make more accurate predictions than they did before reading (Maki & Serra, 1992). That improvement indicates some ability to monitor one's own understanding of a text.

A systematic way to monitor your own understanding of a text is the SPAR method: Survey, Process meaningfully, Ask questions, and Review and test yourself. Start with an overview of what a passage is about, read it carefully, and then see whether you can answer questions about the passage or explain it to others. If not, go back and reread.

why

How

SPAR
Survey
Process
Ask
Review

Also decide about larger units?

THE TIMING OF STUDY

Other things being equal, people tend to remember recent experiences better than earlier experiences. For example, suppose someone reads you a list of 20 words and asks you to recall as many of them as possible. The list is far too long for you to recite from your phonological loop; however, you should be able to remember at least a few. Typically, people remember items at the beginning and end of the list better than they remember those in the middle.

That tendency, known as the **serial-order effect,** includes two aspects: The primacy effect is the tendency to remember the first items; the recency effect refers to the tendency to remember the last items. One explanation for the primacy effect is that the listener gets to rehearse the first few items for a few moments alone with no interference from the others. One explanation for the recency effect is that the last items are still in

Cause of primacy effect

FIGURE 7.2 Sample Marked Pages

the listener's phonological loop at the time of the test.

Cause of recency effect

The phonological loop cannot be the whole explanation for the recency effect, however. In one study, British rugby players were asked to name the teams they had played against in the current season. Players were most likely to remember the last couple of teams they had played against, thus showing a clear recency effect even though they were recalling events that occurred weeks apart (Baddeley & Hitch, 1977). (The phonological loop holds information only for a matter of seconds.)

So, studying material—or, rather, *reviewing* material—shortly before a test is likely to improve recall. Now let's consider the opposite: Suppose you studied something years ago and have not reviewed it since then. For example, suppose you studied a foreign language in high school several years ago. Now you are considering taking a college course in the language, but you are hesitant because you are sure you have forgotten it all. Have you?

Harry Bahrick (1984) tested people who had studied Spanish in school 1 to 50 years previously. Nearly all agreed that they had rarely used Spanish and had not refreshed their memories at all since their school days. (That is a disturbing comment, but beside the point.) Their retention of Spanish dropped noticeably in the first 3 to 6 years, but remained fairly stable from then on (Fig-

ure 7.18). In other words, we do not completely forget even very old memories that we seldom use.

In a later study, Bahrick and members of his family studied foreign-language vocabulary either on a moderately frequent basis (practicing once every 2 weeks) or on a less frequent basis (as seldom as once every 8 weeks), and tested their knowledge years later. The result: More frequent study led to faster learning; however, less frequent study led to better long-term retention, measured years later (Bahrick, Bahrick, Bahrick, & Bahrick, 1993).

The principle here is far more general than just the study of foreign languages. *If you want to remember something well for a test,* your best strategy is to study it as close as possible to the time of the test, in order to take advantage of the recency effect and decrease the effects of retroactive interference. Obviously, I do not mean that you should wait until the night before the test to start studying, but you might rely on an extensive review at that time. You should also, ideally, study under conditions similar to the conditions of the test. For example, you might study in the same room where the test will be given, or at the same time of day.

However, *if you want to remember something long after the test is over,* then the advice I have just given you is all wrong. To be able to remember something whenever you want, wherever you are, and whatever you are doing, you should study it under as varied circumstances as possible. Study and review at various times and places with long, irregular intervals between study sessions. Studying under such inconsistent conditions will slow down your original learning, but it will improve your ability to recall it long afterwards (Schmidt & Bjork, 1992).

Studying for Test vs. studying for long term

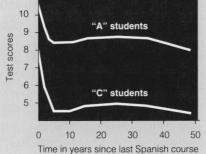

FIGURE 7.18
(Left) Spanish vocabulary as measured by a recognition test shows a rapid decline in the first few years but then long-term stability. (From Bahrick, 1984.) (Right) Within a few years after taking your last foreign-language course, you may think you have forgotten it all. You have not, and even the part you have forgotten will come back (through relearning) if you visit a country where you can practice the language.

CHAPTER 7
MEMORY
———
284

FIGURE 7.2 *(continued)*

Source: Pages adapted with permission from James W. Kalat, *Introduction to Psychology*, 4th ed. (Pacific Grove, CA: Brooks/Cole, 1996).

Write as you read. Taking notes on your reading helps you focus on the key ideas and summarize as you go. You take in and digest the material rather than skim it.

Another way to check comprehension is to try to recite the material aloud to yourself or your study partner. Using a study group to monitor your comprehension gives you immediate feedback and is highly motivating. One way that group members can work together is to divide up a chapter for prereading and studying and get together later to teach the material to one another.

Recycle Your Reading

After you have read and marked key ideas from the first section of the text, proceed to each subsequent section until you have finished the chapter. After you have completed each section, again ask, What are the key ideas? or What will I see on the test? before you move on to the next section. At the end of each section, try to guess what information the author will present in the next section. Good reading should lead you from one section to the next, with each new section adding to your understanding.

SEE SEARCH ONLINE!
INTERNET EXERCISE 7.1

Reviewing

The final step in a study-reading method is reviewing. Many students expect the improbable—that they will read through their text material one time and be able to remember the ideas 4, 6, or even 12 weeks later at test time. More realistically, you will need to include regular reviews in your study process. Here is where your margin notes, study questions, and visual maps or outlines will be most useful. Your study goal is to review the material from each chapter every week.

SEE EXERCISE 7.3

Adjusting Your Reading Style

With effort, you can improve your reading dramatically, but remember to be flexible. How you read should depend on the material. Assess the relative importance and difficulty of the assigned readings and adjust your reading style accordingly. Connect one important idea to another by asking yourself, Why am I reading this, and where does this fit in? When the textbook material is virtually identical to the lecture material, you can save time by concentrating mainly on one or the other. It takes a planned approach to read textbook materials and other assigned readings with good understanding and recall.

Another Study Method: SQ3R

Developed in 1941, SQ3R has proven its worth as a study method many times over. If other methods don't seem to be working, try this one:

S = Survey   Survey the material you are going to read. Get a good idea of what you'll be learning by reading the introductory paragraphs, the summary at the beginning or end, and the major and minor headings.

Q = Question   As you survey, write some questions to ask yourself later. For example, if you saw the heading above—"Another Study Method: SQ3R"—you might write "What is SQ3R, and how does it help one study?"

R = Read   Now you're ready to read in earnest. Read a paragraph and think about what it says. Pay attention to the picture and tables. Look up words you don't know. Continue until you have finished the reading.

R = Recite   Ask yourself the questions you jotted down. Answer them in your own words instead of trying to memorize the author's exact words. If you can't answer a question, look for the answer and write it down. Look for connections between this material and what you already know about the subject.

R = Review   Now go back and review the entire reading, perhaps with your study group. Be certain you understand the major points. Keep reviewing until the material becomes familiar. Do another review just before the exam, using your questions and answers as a guide.

SEE SEARCH ONLINE! INTERNET EXERCISE 7.2

Developing Vocabulary

Textbooks are full of new terminology. In fact, one could argue that learning chemistry is largely a matter of learning the language of chemists and that mastering philosophy or history or sociology requires a mastery of the terminology of each particular discipline. Because words are such a basic and essential component of our knowledge, what is the best way to learn them? Follow these basic vocabulary strategies:

- During your overview of the chapter, notice unfamiliar terms.
- For challenging words that you encounter, consider the context. See if you can predict the meaning of the unfamiliar term, using the surrounding words.
- If context by itself is not enough, try analyzing the term to discover the root or other meaningful parts of the word. For example, *emissary* has the root "to emit" or "to send forth," so we can guess that an emissary is someone sent forth with a message.

SEE EXERCISE 7.4

- Use the glossary of the text, a dictionary, or *www.dictionary.com* on the Internet to locate the definition. Note any multiple definitions and search for the meaning that fits this usage.
- Take every opportunity to use these new terms in your writing and speaking. If you use a new term, then you'll know it! In addition, studying new terms on flash cards or study sheets can be handy at exam time.

Internet Exercise 7.1 Reading Web Pages Critically

Since anyone can publish on the Internet, you should read material on the Internet with a critical eye. Examine the "Checklist for an Informational Web Page" offered by the Widener
University Wolfgram Memorial Library, at *http://www.science.widener.edu/~withers
/inform.htm*. This page offers questions to ask about an informational Web page. (Go to
http://success.wadsworth.com for the most up-to-date URLs.)

Evaluate that Web page using its own five criteria:

1. What evidence is there to indicate how authoritative the site is?

   _____

   _____

   _____

2. What confirms that the information is accurate?

   _____

   _____

   _____

3. What leads you to believe the site is objective? Biased?

   _____

   _____

   _____

4. How current is the information on the site?

   _____

   _____

   _____

5. How complete is the coverage of the topic as cited in the page title?

   _____

   _____

   _____

See also "Evaluating World Wide Web Information" presented by the Libraries of Purdue
University: *http://thorplus.lib.purdue.edu/library_info/instruction/gs175/3gs175/evaluation
.html*, which includes an Internet evaluator checklist, and "Thinking Critically About World Wide
Web Resources" at *http://www.library.ucla.edu/libraries/college/instruct/web/critical.htm*.

Internet Exercise 7.2 Discovering More About Reading Texts

Using *InfoTrac College Edition,* try these phrases and others for key-word and subject-guide
searches: "reading" and "college reading."

ALSO LOOK UP:

Their eight secrets of success. (how to make a better student)(Cover Story) Claudia Wallis. *Time* Oct 19, 1998 v152 n16 p79(8)

College reading instruction as reflected by current textbooks. Nancy V. Wood. *Journal of College Reading and Learning* Spring 1997
    v27 n3 p79(17)

Students' study tips help others in economics. Munir Quddus, Marie Bussing-Burks. *College Teaching* Spring 1998
    v46 n2 p57(1)

Additional Exercises

These exercises will help you sharpen what we believe are the critical skills for college success: writing, critical thinking, learning in groups, planning, reflecting, and taking action. Also, check out the CD-ROM that came with your book—you will find these exercises and more.

Exercise 7.1 Overviewing and Creating a Visual Map

Overview this chapter and create a visual map, noting the following information: title, key points from the introduction, any graphics (maps, charts, tables, diagrams), study questions or exercises built into or at the end of the chapter, and introduction and summary paragraphs. Create either a wheel or a branching map as shown in Figure 7.1. Add spokes or tiers as necessary. In a small group, compare your work.

Exercise 7.2 Preparing to Read, Think, and Mark

Choose a reading assignment for one of your classes. After overviewing the material as described earlier in this chapter, begin reading until you reach a major heading or until you have read at least a page or two. Now stop and write down what you remember from the material:

_____

_____

_____

_____

Now go back to the same material and skim it. As you do so, mark what you believe are the main ideas. Don't fall into the trap of marking too much. Now list four of the main ideas from the reading:

1. _____

2. _____

3. _____

4. _____

Exercise 7.3 How to Read Fifteen Pages of a Textbook in 1 Hour or Less

It takes practice—but it can be done! Find a chapter in one of your textbooks that is at least fifteen pages long. Plan to read the first fifteen pages only. Then, with a watch or clock nearby, complete the following process:

Chapter overview		4 minutes
Pages 1–3:	Read and mark	10 minutes
	Review and recite	2 minutes
Pages 4–7:	Read and mark	10 minutes
	Review and recite	2 minutes
Pages 8–12:	Read and mark	10 minutes
	Review and recite	2 minutes
Pages 13–15:	Read and mark	10 minutes
	Review and recite	2 minutes

Review and recite for all fifteen pages. Answer aloud the questions: What did I learn? How does it relate to the course?   8 minutes

                                        Total   60 minutes

Done. Take a break—you've earned it!

Exercise 7.4 Expanding Your Vocabulary

Use this space to write down at least six terms encountered in your reading that are new to you.

_____   _____

_____   _____

_____   _____

Consult a dictionary for the meanings of these terms. Write down the meanings and make a conscious effort to use at least one term once each day for a week. On the second day of the week, add another term, and so forth. Within a few weeks, you will have learned six new terms and can begin the process again.

Your Personal Journal

Here are several things to write about. Choose one or more, or choose another topic related to this chapter.

1. How can you use the suggestions in this chapter with those in Chapter 6 on taking notes in class to improve your study skills? What should you do first?
2. The chapter makes a number of suggestions for reading textbooks. Which ones strike you as the most important? Explain.
3. Try following some of the suggestions in this chapter the next time you are reading a homework assignment. Then write about how it felt to use them.
4. What behaviors are you willing to change after reading this chapter? How might you go about changing them?
5. What else is on your mind this week? If you wish to share it with your instructor, add it to this journal entry.

Resources

The only way to improve your study reading is to read more. The more reading you do on your own, for pleasure, unrelated to school or study, the more you will begin to absorb information about writing, presentation, and vocabulary, in addition to whatever the material is about. Reading anything (almost) can contribute to your success in college—as long as you keep up with your study reading as well. Use this Resources page to brainstorm a list of extracurricular reading materials. Use the second half of the page to list 10-minute rewards that you can give yourself when you finish a 50-minute study-reading session.

Things I would enjoy reading for pleasure. Need ideas? Wander through the library or a good bookstore. (Try spending at least 1 hour a week reading something just for you.)

FICTION BOOKS	NONFICTION BOOKS	MAGAZINES	NEWSPAPERS	INTERNET PAGES

Make a list of 10-minute rewards that you can give yourself after a 50-minute study reading session. Include a few bigger rewards for a week of successful studying.

10-minute rewards:

....

....

....

....

....

End-of-the-week rewards:

....

....

....

....

....

Making the Grade

Tests, Memory, and Presentations

**IN THIS CHAPTER,
YOU WILL LEARN**

- How cheating hurts you, your friends, and your campus
- How to prepare for taking an exam
- How study groups can help you prepare for an exam
- How to devise a plan for studying for an exam
- What to do when you're actually taking the exam
- Some memory techniques to help you study
- How to prepare for and deliver a class presentation

reach the top

" **T**hree tests in the next two days! I am never going to live through this week. I studied hard and I never gave a thought to cheating. Now here I am walking into class, and my mind is a total blank. Help!"*

Now that you've learned how to listen and take notes in class and how to read and review your notes and assigned readings, you're ready to use those skills to do your best on exams. Just as there are a number of right and wrong ways to take notes and read texts, there also are certain study methods that work better than others.

Regardless of the study method you use, your goal always will be to seek the truth. Many students entering college assume that education is a process in which unquestioned authorities pour truth into their open ears. They may believe that every problem has a single right answer and the instructor or the textbook is always a source of truth. Yet most college instructors don't believe this because they are seeking as many valid interpretations of the information as possible. So they continually ask for reasons, for arguments, for the assumptions on which a given position is based, and for the evidence that confirms or discounts it.

SELF-ASSESSMENT: TEST TAKING

Place a check mark in front of the sentence in each pair that best describes you. Then write a paragraph about yourself as a test taker, based on your answers to this inventory and your general feelings about taking tests.

_____ 1a. I always study for essay tests by developing questions and outlines.

_____ 1b. I rarely study for essay tests by developing questions and outlines.

_____ 2a. I always begin studying for an exam at least a week in advance.

_____ 2b. I rarely begin studying for an exam a week in advance.

_____ 3a. I usually study for an exam with at least one other person.

_____ 3b. I rarely study for an exam with another person.

_____ 4a. I usually know what to expect on a test before I take the exam.

_____ 4b. I rarely know what to expect on a test before I take the exam.

_____ 5a. I usually finish an exam early or on time.

_____ 5b. I sometimes do not have enough time to finish an exam.

_____ 6a. I usually know that I have done well on an exam when I finish.

_____ 6b. I rarely know whether I have done well on an exam when I finish.

_____ 7a. I usually perform better on essay tests than on objective tests.

_____ 7b. I usually perform better on objective tests than on essay tests.

This means that, on essay exams particularly, your instructor is as interested in *how* you think as in how detailed your answer is. You can cough up a list of details from lecture notes or readings, but unless you can make sense of them, you probably won't get much credit.

In preparing for an exam, you can choose any number of approaches:

APPROACH	ATTITUDE	DECISION	OUTCOME
The easy way out	I don't know why I had to take this course. I learned nothing. *(I skipped a few classes and didn't take notes or read the assignments.)*	So I'll get the answers from someone who took the test the day before and memorize them.	I still didn't learn anything, but at least I'll know I'll pass. *(And the guys who studied so hard will probably hate me.)*
The defeatist approach	This course has been rough. I've been getting so-so grades. I can't seem to understand what's being taught. *(I never joined a study group or asked my teacher for guidance.)*	So I'll cram the night before and hope for the best.	Blew the exam, too. Barely passed the course. Didn't learn much. *(Only have myself to blame. Oh well. There's always next time.)*
The logical approach	I'm here to learn all I can. Who knows what I'll need to get a job? Besides, it's expensive to go to college.	So I've set up a schedule that allows me to study longer for my toughest classes. Since I've been reviewing my notes all term, I think I'll do okay on the exam.	Got a B+. More important, going through the study process and writing the exam helped me understand the material even better.

Later in this chapter we'll discuss the third—and most successful—approach. But before that, you need to consider an even more important topic: how cheating harms you, your classmates, and your college.

Academic Honesty

Imagine where our society would be if researchers reported fraudulent results that were then used to develop new machines or medical treatments. Integrity is a cornerstone of higher education, and activities that compromise that integrity damage everyone: your country, your community, your college, your classmates, and yourself.

Colleges and universities have academic integrity policies or honor codes that clearly define cheating, lying, plagiarism, and other forms of dishonest conduct, but it is often difficult to know how those rules apply to specific situations. Is it really lying to tell an instructor you missed class because you were "not feeling well" (whatever "well" means) or because you were experiencing vague "car trouble" (some people think car trouble includes anything from a flat tire to difficulty finding a parking spot!)?

Types of Misconduct

Institutions vary widely in how they define broad terms such as *lying* or *cheating*. For instance, one campus defines cheating as "intentionally using or attempting to use unauthorized materials, information, notes, study aids or other devices . . . [including] unauthorized communication of information during an academic exercise." This would apply to looking over a classmate's shoulder for an answer, using a calculator when it is not authorized, procuring or discussing an exam without permission, copying lab notes, and duplicating computer files.

Plagiarism, or taking another person's ideas or work and presenting them as your own, is especially intolerable in academic culture. Just as taking someone else's property constitutes physical theft, taking credit for someone else's ideas constitutes intellectual theft.

On tests you do not have to credit specific individuals. On written reports and papers, however, you must give credit any time you use (1) another person's actual words; (2) another person's ideas or theories, even if you don't quote them directly; and (3) any other information not considered common knowledge.

Many schools prohibit other activities besides lying, cheating, and plagiarism. For instance, one prohibits intentionally inventing information or results; another outlaws earning credit more than once for the same piece of academic work, without permission; another rules out giving your work or exam answer to another student to copy during the actual exam or before the exam is given to another section; and another prohibits bribing in exchange for any kind of academic advantage. Most schools also outlaw helping or attempting to help another student commit a dishonest act.

SEE SEARCH ONLINE!
INTERNET EXERCISE 8.1

Reducing the Likelihood of Problems

To avoid becoming intentionally or unintentionally involved in academic misconduct, consider the reasons it could happen.

- **Ignorance**   In a survey at the University of South Carolina, 20 percent of students incorrectly thought that buying a term paper wasn't cheating. Forty percent thought using a test file (a collection of actual tests from previous terms) was fair behavior. Sixty percent thought it was all right to get answers from someone who had taken an exam earlier in the same or in a prior semester. What do you think?
- **Cultural and campus differences**   In other countries and on some U.S. campuses, students are encouraged to review past exams as practice exercises. Some campuses permit sharing answers and information for homework and other assignments with friends.

Does Cheating Hurt Anyone?

It Hurts Individuals

- **Cheating sabotages academic growth.** Because the grade and the instructor's comments apply to someone else's work, cheating makes accurate feedback impossible.
- **Cheating sabotages personal growth.** Educational accomplishments inspire pride and confidence. What confidence will students have when their work is not their own?
- **Cheating can have long-term effects.** Taking the easy way out in college may spill over into graduate school, jobs, and relationships. Would you want a doctor, lawyer, or accountant who had cheated on exams handling your affairs?

It Hurts the Community

- **Cheating jeopardizes the basic fairness of the grading process.** Widespread cheating causes honest students to become cynical and resentful, especially if grades are curved and the cheating directly affects other students.
- **Widespread cheating devalues a college degree.** Alumni, potential students, graduate students, and employers learn to distrust degrees from schools where cheating is widespread.

Examining Values

Review the box "Does Cheating Hurt Anyone?" on page 110. Imagine what the world would be like if the majority of college students decided to cheat. How would this affect (1) your values as a college student? (2) Your values about society in general? (3) Your values with regard to friends or someone you love very much? (4) Your perceptions of the relative importance of honesty and truth?

- **Different policies among instructors**   Because there is no universal code that dictates such behaviors, ask your instructors for clarification. When a student is caught violating the academic code of a particular school or teacher, pleading ignorance of the rules is a weak defense.

- **A belief that grades—not learning—are everything, when actually the reverse is true**   This may reflect our society's competitive atmosphere. It also may be the result of pressure from parents, peers, or teachers. In truth, grades are nothing if one has cheated to earn them.

- **Lack of preparation or inability to manage time and activities**   Before you consider cheating, ask an instructor to extend a deadline so that a project can be done well.

Here are some steps you can take to reduce the likelihood of problems:

1. **Know the rules.** Learn the academic code for your school. If a teacher does not clarify his or her standards and expectations, ask exactly what they are.
2. **Set clear boundaries.** Refuse to "help" others who ask you to help them cheat. In test settings, keep your answers covered and your eyes down and put all extraneous materials away.
3. **Improve time management.** Be well prepared for all quizzes, exams, projects, and papers. This may mean unlearning habits such as procrastination.
4. **Seek help.** Find out where you can obtain assistance with study skills, time management, and test taking. If your methods are in good shape but the content of the course is too difficult, see your instructor.
5. **Withdraw from the course.** Your school has a policy about dropping courses and a last day to drop without penalty (drop date). Some students may choose to withdraw from all classes and take some time off before returning to school if they find themselves in over their heads or if a long illness, a family crisis, or some other unexpected occurrence has caused them to fall behind. See your advisor or counselor.
6. **Reexamine goals.** Stick to your own realistic goals instead of giving in to pressure from family or friends to achieve impossibly high standards. You may also feel pressure to enter a particular career or profession of little or no interest to you. If so, meet with professionals in your career and counseling centers or your academic advisor and counselor and explore alternatives.

Exams: The Long View

You actually began preparing for a test on the first day of the term. All your lecture notes, assigned text pages, and homework problems were part of that preparation. As the test day nears, you should know how much additional time you will need to review, what material the test will cover, and what format the test will take.

Three things will help you study well: good communication with your instructor, effective time management, and organization of materials:

- **Ask your instructor**. Have you learned from your instructor the purpose, conditions, and content of the exam? Talked with your instructor to clarify any misunderstandings you may have about the content of the course?
- **Manage your time wisely.** Have you laid out a schedule that will give you time to review effectively for the exam, without waiting until the night before?
- **Sharpen your study habits.** Have you created a body of material from which you can effectively review what is likely to be on the exam? Collaborated with other students in a study group or as study partners to share information?

Planning Your Approach

Physical Preparation

1. **Maintain your regular sleep routine.** Don't cut back on your sleep in order to cram in additional study hours. Remember that most tests will require you to apply the concepts that you have studied, and to do that effectively, you must have all your brain power available.
2. **Maintain your regular exercise program.** Walking, jogging, swimming, or other aerobic activities are effective stress reducers and provide positive—and needed—breaks from studying.
3. **Eat right.** Avoid drinking more than one or two caffeinated drinks a day or eating foods that are high in sugar. Eat fruits, vegetables, and foods that are high in complex carbohydrates so that you won't experience highs and lows in your energy level.

Mental Preparation

1. **Know your material.** If you have given yourself adequate time to review, you will enter the classroom confident that you are in control.
2. **Practice relaxing.** Some students experience upset stomachs, sweaty palms, racing hearts, or other unpleasant physical symptoms before an exam. See your counseling center about relaxation techniques.
3. **Use positive self-talk.** Instead of telling yourself, "I never do well on math tests" or "I'll never be able to learn all the information for my history essay exam," make positive statements such as "I have attended all the lectures, done my homework, and passed the quizzes. Now I'm ready to pass the test!"

Find Out About the Test

Ask your instructor whether it will be essay, multiple choice, true/false, or another kind of test. Ask how long the test will last and how it will be graded. Some instructors may let you see copies of old exams, so you can see the types of questions they use. Never miss the last class before an exam because your instructor may summarize valuable information.

Design an Exam Plan

Use the information about the test as you design a plan for preparing. Build that preparation into a schedule of review dates. Develop a "To Do" list of the major steps you need to take in order to be ready, such as joining a study group. The week before the exam, set aside a schedule of 1-hour blocks for review, along with notes on what you specifically plan to accomplish during each hour.

SEE EXERCISE 8.1

Join a Study Group

Study groups help students develop better study techniques. In addition, students benefit from different views of instructors' goals, objectives, and emphasis; have partners to quiz on facts and concepts; and gain the enthusiasm and friendship of others to help sustain their motivation.

Ask your instructor, advisor, or tutoring center to help you identify interested students and decide on guidelines for the group. Study groups can meet all semester, or they can review for midterms or final exams. Group members should complete their assignments before the group meets and prepare study questions or points of discussion ahead of time. If your study group decides to meet just before exams, allow enough time to share notes and ideas. Together, devise a list of potential questions for review. Then spend time studying separately to develop answers, outlines, and mind maps. The group should then reconvene shortly before the test to share answers and to review.

SEE EXERCISE 8.2

Tutoring and Other Support

If you think tutoring is just for failing students, you're wrong! Excellent students often seek tutorial assistance to ensure their A's. In the typical large lecture classes for first-year students, you have limited opportunity to question instructors. Tutors know the highlights and pitfalls of the course.

Many tutoring services are free. Ask your academic advisor/counselor or campus learning center. Most academic support centers or learning centers have computer labs that can provide assistance for course work. Some offer walk-in assistance for help in using word processing, spreadsheet, or statistical computer programs. Often, computer tutorials are available to help you refresh basic skills. Math and English grammar programs may also be available, as well as access to the Internet.

Emergency? Your Instructor Needs to Know

Things happen. Even if your instructor has warned you that there is no excuse for missing a quiz or turning in a late paper, he or she may bend the rules in a true emergency. Even if you missed an important quiz or deadline for dubious reasons, it's better to admit you overslept, forgot a paper was due, or left an essay at home. Your instructor may be willing to help. In a real emergency, however, here's what you can do:

1. **Let your instructor know about a recurring medical condition that may occasionally keep you out of class.** Make it clear you are not asking for relief from required work but for some allowance for turning in work late if necessary.

2. **Get phone numbers and/or e-mail addresses in advance.** Leave a number where you can be reached or the number of a friend or relative who can contact you. Some colleges may distribute a memo to your instructors to inform them of your situation, especially if you'll be out for a week or more. Find out whom to contact for this service.

3. **When you know in advance you can't make class, tell the instructor as soon as possible.** In any event, contact your instructor to explain why you're absent. This thoughtful action may result in your instructor's allowing you to turn in work early or make up work when you return.

Now It's Time to Study

Through the steady use of proven study techniques, you already will have processed and learned most of what you need to know. Now you can focus your study efforts on the most challenging concepts, practice recalling information, and familiarize yourself with details.

Recall Sheets and Mind Maps

To prepare for an exam covering large amounts of material, you need to condense the volume of notes and text pages into manageable study units. Review your materials with these questions in mind: Is this one of the key ideas in the chapter or unit? Will I see this on the test? Some students like to highlight the most important ideas; others like to create lists or visual maps containing only the key ideas.

Sheets summarizing main ideas can be organized chapter by chapter or according to the major themes in the course. Look for relationships between ideas. Try to condense your recall sheets to one page of essential information. Key words on this page can bring to mind blocks of information.

A mind map is essentially a recall sheet with a visual element. Its word and visual patterns provide you with highly charged clues to jog your memory. Because they are visual, mind maps help many students recall information more easily.

Figure 8.1 shows what a mind map might look like for a chapter on listening and learning in the classroom. See if you can reconstruct the ideas in the chapter by following the connections in the map. Then make a visual mind map for this chapter and see how much more you can remember after studying it a number of times.

Summaries

SEE EXERCISE 8.3

A written summary is especially helpful when preparing for essay and short-answer exams. By condensing the main ideas into a concise written summary, you store information in your long-term memory so that it can be retrieved to answer an essay question. Here's how:

1. **Predict a test question from your lecture notes or other resources.**
2. **Read the chapter, article, notes, or other resources.** Underline or mark main ideas as you go or make notations on a separate sheet.
3. **Analyze and abstract.** What is the purpose of the material? Does it compare, define a concept, or prove an idea? What are the main ideas?
4. **Make connections between main points and key supporting details.** Reread to identify each main point and supporting evidence. Analyze the author's argument for bias or insufficient details.
5. **Select, condense, and order.** Review underlined material and begin putting the ideas into your own words. Number what you underlined in a logical order.
6. **Write your ideas precisely in a draft.** In the first sentence, state the purpose of your summary. Follow with each main point and its supporting ideas.
7. **Rewrite.** Read it over, adding missing transitions or insufficient information. Check the logic of your summary. Annotate with the material you used, for later reference.
8. **Make a brief outline of key ideas from your summary.** Create questions and answer them. Number each main point. Associate supporting evidence with each main idea. Use flash cards for your outline. Memorize your outline to help you recall the information.

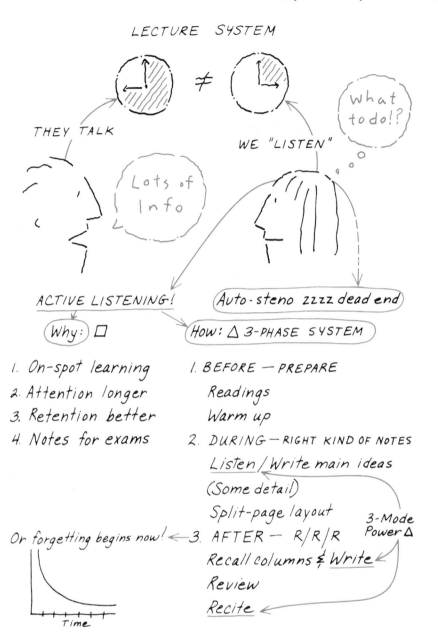

FIGURE 8.1
Sample Mind Map on Listening and Learning in the Classroom

Taking the Test

1. **Analyze, ask, and stay calm.** Read all the directions so that you understand what to do. Ask for clarification if you don't understand something. Be confident. Don't panic! Answer one question at a time.
2. **Make the best use of your time.** Quickly survey the entire test and decide how much time you will spend on each section.
3. **Answer the easy questions first.** Expect that you'll be puzzled by some questions. Make a note to come back to them later.
4. **If you finish early, don't leave.** Stay and check your work for errors.

Essay Exams

Although you will take objective (multiple choice, matching, and true/false) exams in college, most college teachers, including the writers of this book, have a strong preference for the essay exam for a simple reason: It promotes higher-order critical thinking, whereas other types of exams tend to be exercises in memorization. Some instructors use objective tests in large classes. Grading over 100 essay exams might take days, whereas objective exams can be machine scored and returned quickly. Generally, the closer you are to graduation, the more essay exams you'll take.

1. **Budget your exam time.** Quickly survey the entire exam and note the questions that are the easiest for you, along with their point values. Take a moment to weigh their values, estimate the approximate time you should allot to each question, and write the time beside each number. Start with the questions that are easiest for you. Remember, it can be a costly error to write profusely on easy questions of low value that take up precious time you may need on more important questions. Wear a watch so that you can monitor your time, including time at the end for a quick review.

2. **Write focused, organized answers.** In your quick survey of the test, did you find questions that you were prepared to answer? If so, quickly jot down your memorized outline for such questions. Many well-prepared students write fine answers to questions that may not have been asked because they did not read a question carefully. Others hastily write down everything they know on a topic. Answers that are vague and tend to ramble will be downgraded by instructors.

3. **Know the key task words in essay questions.** Being familiar with the key word in an essay question will help you answer it more specifically. The following key task words are most frequently asked on essay tests. Take time to learn them so that you can answer essay questions more accurately and precisely.

Analyze   To divide something into its parts in order to understand it better, to show how the parts work together to produce the overall pattern.

Compare   To look at the characteristics or qualities of several things and identify their similarities or differences.

Contrast   To identify the differences between things.

Criticize/critique   To analyze and judge something. Criticism can be either positive or negative; a criticism should generally contain your own judgments (supported by evidence) and those of other authorities who can support your point.

Define   To give the meaning of a word or expression. Giving an example of something sometimes helps clarify a definition, but giving an example is not in itself a definition.

Describe   To give a general verbal sketch of something, in narrative or other form.

Discuss   To examine or analyze something in a broad and detailed way. Discussion often includes identifying the important questions related to an issue and attempting to answer these questions. A good discussion explores all relevant evidence and information.

Evaluate   To discuss the strengths and weaknesses of something. Evaluation is similar to criticism, but the word *evaluate* places more stress on the idea of how well something meets a certain standard or fulfills some specific purpose.

Explain   To clarify something. Explanations generally focus on why or how something has come about.

Interpret   To explain the meaning of something. In science you might explain what an experiment shows and what conclusions can be drawn from it. In a literature course you might explain—or interpret—what a poem means beyond the literal meaning of the words.

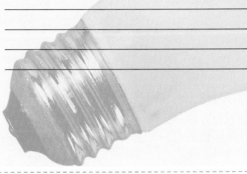

Critical Thinking

Key on Task Words

Essay questions may require quite different responses, depending on their key task words. Discuss the following in class. In your discussion, include what each task word is asking you to do and how it differs from the other two listed here.

1. **How would you *define* the purposes of this chapter?**

_____

_____

_____

_____

2. **How would you *evaluate* the purposes of this chapter?**

_____

_____

_____

_____

3. **How would you *justify* the purposes of this chapter?**

_____

_____

_____

_____

Justify To argue in support of some decision or conclusion by showing sufficient evidence or reason in its favor. Try to support your argument with both logic and concrete examples.

Narrate To relate a series of events in the order in which they occurred. Generally, you will also be asked to explain something about the events you are narrating.

Outline To present a series of main points in appropriate order.

Prove To give a convincing logical argument and evidence in support of some statement.

Review To summarize and comment on the main parts of a problem or a series of statements. A review question usually also asks you to evaluate or criticize.

Summarize To give information in brief form, omitting examples and details. A summary is short yet covers all important points.

Trace To narrate a course of events. Where possible, you should show connections from one event to the next.

Multiple-Choice Exams

Preparing for multiple-choice tests requires you to actively review all material covered in the course. Reciting from flash cards, summary sheets, or mind maps is a good way to review these large amounts of material.

Take advantage of the many cues that multiple-choice questions contain. Careful reading of each item may uncover the correct answer. Always question choices that use absolute words such as *always, never,* and *only.* These choices are often incorrect. Also, read carefully for terms such as *not, except,* and *but* that are introduced before the choices. Be sure to choose the answer that is the most inclusive.

True/False Exams

Remember, for the question to be true, every detail of the question must be true. Questions containing words such as *always, never,* and *only* are usually false, whereas less definite terms such as *often* and *frequently* suggest the statement may be true. Read through the entire exam to see if information in one question will help you answer another.

Matching Exams

The matching question is the hardest to answer by guessing. In one column you will find the term, in the other the description of it. Before answering any question, review all terms or descriptions. Match those terms you are sure of first. As you do so, cross out both the term and its description.

Aids to Memory

Forty years after he had heard a song, a man thought about it one day, hummed the tune, and began singing the lyric. He had no idea what had triggered this memory and was astounded when he found he knew all the words. Of course, this was a rather unusual song. Music and rhymes are known aids to memory, but the lyrics of this rather daffy song offered another aid: They were based on the alphabet: "A, you're adorable; B, you're so beautiful; C, you're a cutie full of charms …"

Rhymes, music, and lyrics pegged to letters—all made it easier to remember the song. But you aren't trying to remember a song. What you are trying to remember are thoughts, concepts, reasons, and ideas.

Anecdotal evidence suggests that elephants, which possess the largest brain of any land animal, are intelligent creatures with impressive memories. The animals can learn up to 100 commands. After mastering tricks, circus elephants seem able to recall them indefinitely. Other animals, including the domesticated dog, have the capacity to associate human words with actions. When you say, "Gracie, sit!" Gracie usually sits.*

Cal Fussman tells of discovering a simple way to remember things:

My eureka came at the library when I stumbled onto a book called Total Recall *by Joan Minninger. I fixed on a phrase on the jacket that read, "How to Remember 20 Things in Less Than Two Minutes."*

The book suggests associating the first ten things you want to remember with body parts, starting at the top of your head and going down to your forehead, nose, mouth, throat, chest, belly button, hips, thighs, and feet.

I was determined to memorize a list of twelve white wines, going roughly from lightest to weightiest. I tapped the top of my head. That would be the two lightest whites, Soave and Orvieto. Then my forehead—that'd be Riesling. Nose: muscadet. Mouth: champagne. Throat: Chenin blanc … I tapped each corresponding body part, saying the name of the wine aloud. By the fifth time, without even trying, crazy associations began to invade my mind. As I tapped the top of my head, I thought, Start Out, and the S made me think of Soave and the O of Orvieto. I touched my forehead, thought, ReeeememberS, and the reeee brought Riesling off my tongue. I tapped my nose and smelled musk cologne, which triggered muscadet, then tapped my lips and blew a kiss as if I'd just tasted Dom Perignon champagne … Took me less than three minutes—and it solved my problems.†

*Who you calling dumbo? (memory in elephants) Steve Nadis. *Omni* June 1993 v15 n8 p20(1)

†Cal Fussman, "Thanks for the Memory," *Esquire* (Feb. 1999): 142.

Another way to "peg" words goes like this: As you're driving to campus, choose some landmarks along the way. The next day you pass those landmarks, relate them to something from your class notes or readings. The white picket fence might remind you of "work 20 hours or less a week," while the tall oak tree on the next block reminds you to "work on campus if at all possible."

Remember How You Remember Best Have you ever had to memorize a speech or lines from a play? One actor records her lines as well as the lines of others on a cassette and listens to them in her car to and from work each day. Another actor records only others' lines and leaves blank time on the tape so that he can recite his lines at the proper moments. Another remembers lines by visualizing where they appear in the script: left-hand page, top; right-hand page, middle; and so forth. And another simply reads and rereads the script over and over until it becomes branded on her brain.

Can you apply similar approaches to remembering material for exams? To some degree, perhaps. But though knowing certain words will help, remembering concepts and ideas may be much more important. To embed such ideas in your mind, ask yourself as you review your notes and textbooks:

1. What is the essence or main point of the idea?
2. Why does this idea make sense? (What is the logic behind the idea?)
3. What arguments against the idea could there be?
4. How does this idea connect to other ideas in the material?

SEE SEARCH ONLINE!
INTERNET EXERCISE 8.2

More Aids to Memory The human mind has discovered ingenious ways to remember information. Here are some additional methods that may be useful to you when you're nailing down the causes of the Civil War, trying to remember the steps in a physics problem, or absorbing a mathematical formula.

1. **Overlearn.** Even after you know the material, go over it again to make sure you'll retain it for a long time.
2. **Categorize.** If the information seems to lack an inherent organization, impose one. Most information can be organized in some way, even if only by the look or sound of the words.

    To remember limited amounts of specific details, try one or more of these methods, reminding yourself that they are more likely to help you remember lists of facts rather than relationships between facts:
3. **Use mnemonics.** Create rhymes, jingles, sayings, or nonsense phrases that repeat or codify information. "Homes" is a mnemonic for remembering the five Great Lakes: Huron, Ontario, Michigan, Erie, and Superior. "Spring forward, fall back" reminds many Americans how to set their clocks. Setting a rhyme to music is one of the most powerful ways to make words memorable.
4. **Associate.** Relate the idea to something you already know. Make the association as personal as possible. If you're reading a chapter on laws regarding free speech, pretend that your right to speak out on a subject that's important to you may be affected by those laws. In remembering the spelling difference between *through* and *threw,* think of walking through something "rough" and that "threw" comes from "throw."
5. **Visualize.** Make yourself see the things that you've associated with important concepts. Concentrate on the images so that they'll become firmly planted in your memory.
6. **Use flash cards.** Write the word or information to be learned on one side and the definition or explanation on the other. Review the cards often. Prepare them early and spend more time on the hard ones.

SEE SEARCH ONLINE!
INTERNET EXERCISE 8.3

Succeeding at Presentations

Speaking in front of others may be one of our most prevalent fears, but it doesn't have to be. For example:

- **Once you begin speaking, your anxiety is likely to decrease.** Anxiety is highest right before or during the first 2 minutes of a presentation.
- **Your listeners generally will be unaware of your anxiety.** Although your heart sounds as if it were pounding audibly or your knees feel as if they were knocking visibly, rarely is this the case.
- **Some anxiety is beneficial.** Anxiety indicates that your presentation is important to you. Channel your nervousness into energy and harness it to propel you enthusiastically through your talk.
- **Practice is the best preventive.** The best way to reduce your fears is to prepare and rehearse thoroughly. World-famous violinist Isaac Stern is rumored to have once said, "I practice eight hours a day for forty years, and they call me a genius?!"

Steps to a Successful Presentation

If you're assigned a speaking task in class, how should you proceed?

1. Clarify Your Objective

Identify what you want to accomplish. To persuade your listeners that your campus needs additional student parking? To inform your listeners about student government's accomplishments? What do you want your listeners to know, believe, or do when you are finished?

2. Analyze Your Audience

You need to understand the people to whom you'll be talking. Ask yourself what they already know about your topic. If you're going to give a presentation on the health risks of fast food, find out how much your listeners already know about fast food so that you don't risk boring them.

You should also determine how much interest your classmates have in nutrition. Would they be more interested in some other aspect of college life? What about their attitudes toward you, your ideas, and your topic?

3. Collect and Organize Your Information

Now comes the critical process of building your presentation by selecting and arranging blocks of information. One useful analogy is to think of yourself as guiding your listeners through the ideas they already have to the new knowledge, attitudes, and beliefs you would like them to have. Imagine you've been selected as a guide for next year's prospective first-year students and their parents visiting campus. You want to get their attention and keep it in order to achieve your objective: raising their interest in your school. Let's be more specific by discussing the GUIDE checklist in Figure 8.2.

THE GUIDE CHECKLIST

G Get your audience's attention

U "You"– don't forget yourself

I Ideas, ideas, ideas!

D Develop an organizational structure

E Exit gracefully and memorably

FIGURE 8.2
The GUIDE Checklist

[G] Get Your Audience's Attention To do so, you can relate the topic to your listeners:

> "Let me tell you what to expect during your college years here—at the best school in the state."

Or you can state the significance of the topic:

> "Deciding on which college to attend is one of the most important decisions you'll ever make."

Or you can arouse their curiosity:

> "Do you know the three most important factors students and their families consider when choosing a college?"

SEE EXERCISE 8.4

You can also quote a famous person, tell a joke, startle the audience, question them, tell a story, or ask a rhetorical question. Remember that a well-designed introduction must not only gain the attention of the audience but also develop rapport with them, motivate them to continue listening, and preview what you are going to say during the rest of your speech.

[U] "You"–Don't Forget Yourself In preparing any speech, don't exclude the most important source of your presentation—you. Even in a formal presentation, you will be most successful if you develop a comfortable style that's easy to listen to. Don't play a role. Let your wit and personality shine through.

[I] Ideas, Ideas, Ideas! Create a list of all the possible points you might want to make. Then write them out as conclusions you want your listeners to accept. For example, imagine that in your campus tour for prospective new students and their parents you want to make the following points:

- Tuition is reasonable.
- The faculty is composed of good teachers.
- The school is committed to student success.
- College can prepare you to get a good job.
- Student life is a blast.
- The library has adequate resources.
- The campus is attractive.
- The campus is safe.
- Faculty members conduct prestigious research.
- Our college is the best choice.

For the typical presentation, about five main points are the most that listeners can process. After considering your list for some time, you decide that the following five points are critical:

- Tuition is reasonable.
- The faculty is composed of good teachers.
- The school is committed to student success.
- The campus is attractive.
- The campus is safe.

Try to generate more ideas than you think you'll need so that you can select the best ones. Don't judge them at first (use your critical thinking). Then, from the many ideas you come up with, decide which meet your objectives.

Ideas rarely stand on their own merit. To ensure that your main ideas work, use a variety of supporting materials such as examples, statistics, and testimony.

- **Examples**   These include stories and illustrations, hypothetical events, and specific cases. They can be powerful, compelling ways to dramatize and clarify main ideas, but make sure they're relevant, representative, and reasonable.
- **Statistics**   These are widely used as evidence in speeches. Of course, numbers can be manipulated, and unscrupulous speakers sometimes lie with statistics. Make sure any statistics you use are clear, concise, accurate, and comprehensible to your listeners.
- **Testimony**   This includes quoting outside experts, paraphrasing reliable sources, and generally demonstrating the quality of individuals who agree with your main points. Make sure such testimony is accurate, qualified, and unbiased.

Because each person in your audience is unique, you are most likely to add interest, clarity, and credibility to your presentation by varying the types of support you provide.

[D] Develop an Organizational Structure Now you must decide how to arrange your ideas. You may decide to use a chronological narrative approach by discussing the history of the college from its early years to the present. Or you might wish to use a problem–solution format in which you describe a problem (such as choosing a school), present the pros and cons of several solutions (or other schools), and finally identify your school as the best solution.

Begin with your most important ideas. List each main point and subpoint separately on a 3 x 5 or 4 x 6 note card. Spread the cards out on a large surface (such as the floor) and arrange, rearrange, add, and delete cards until you find the most effective arrangement. Then simply number the cards, pick them up, and use them to prepare your final outline.

As you organize your presentation, remember that your overall purpose is to guide your listeners. That means you must not neglect connectors between your main points. For example:

Now that we've looked at the library . . .

The first half of my presentation has identified our recreational facilities. Now let's look at the academic hubs on campus.

So much for the academic buildings on campus. What about the campus social scene?

In speaking, as in writing, transitions make the difference between keeping your audience with you and losing them at an important juncture.

[E] Exit Gracefully and Memorably Someone once commented that a speech is like a love affair: Any fool can start it, but to end it requires considerable skill. Most of the suggestions for introductions also apply to conclusions. Whatever else you do, go out with style, impact, and dignity. Don't leave your listeners asking, "So that's it?" Subtly signal that the end is in sight (without the overused "So in conclusion"), summarize your major points, and then conclude.

4. Choose Your Visual Aids

When visual aids are added to presentations, listeners can absorb 35 percent more information—and over time they can recall 55 percent more. Should you prepare a chart? Show a videotape clip? Write on the chalkboard? Distribute handouts? You can also make overhead transparencies on the computer, using large and legible typefaces. As you select and use your visual aids, consider these rules of thumb:

- Use readable lettering and don't crowd information.
- Introduce each visual before displaying and explaining it.
- Allow your listeners enough time for processing.
- Proofread carefully—misspelled words hurt your credibility as a speaker.
- Maintain eye contact with your listeners while you discuss visual aids.

5. Prepare Your Notes

Rather than read your presentation or attempt to memorize it, a better strategy is to memorize only the introduction and conclusion so that you can maintain eye contact and therefore build rapport with your listeners.

The best notes are a minimal outline from which you can speak extemporaneously. You will rehearse thoroughly in advance, but because you are speaking from brief notes, each time you give your presentation, your choice of words will be slightly different, causing you to sound prepared but natural. You may wish to use note cards, because they are unobtrusive. (Make sure you number them just in case you accidentally drop the stack on your way to the front of the room.)

After you become more experienced, you may want to let your visual aids serve as notes. A handout listing key points may also serve as your basic outline. Eventually, you may find you no longer need notes.

6. Practice Your Delivery

As you rehearse, form an image of success rather than failure. Practice your presentation aloud several times beforehand to harness that energy-producing anxiety.

Begin a few days before your target date and continue until you're about to go on stage. Rehearse aloud. Practice before an audience—your roommate, a friend, your dog, even the mirror. Ask for critiques so that you'll have some idea of what those changes should be. Consider audiotaping or videotaping yourself to pinpoint your own mistakes and to reinforce your strengths.

Using Your Voice and Body Language

Let your hands hang comfortably at your sides, reserving them for natural, spontaneous gestures. Don't lean over the lectern. Move comfortably about the room, without pacing nervously. Some experts suggest changing positions between major points in order to punctuate them. Face your audience and don't be afraid to move toward them while speaking.

Make eye contact with as many listeners as you can. This also helps you read their reactions and establish command. A smile helps warm up your listeners, although you should avoid smiling excessively or inappropriately. Smiling through a presentation on world hunger would send your listeners a contradictory message.

Project confidence and enthusiasm by varying your pitch. Speak at a rate that mirrors normal conversation—not too fast and not too slow. Consider varying your volume for the same reasons you vary pitch and rate—to engage your listeners and to emphasize important points.

Pronunciation and word choice are important, too. A poorly articulated word (such as "gonna" for "going to"), a mispronounced word (such as "nucular" for "nuclear"), or a misused word can quickly erode credibility. Fillers such as "uhm," "uh," "like," and "you know" are distracting, too.

Finally, consider your appearance. Convey a look of competence, preparedness, and success. As Lawrence J. Peter, author of *The Peter Principle,* says, "Competence, like truth, beauty, and a contact lens, is in the eye of the beholder."

A Final Word

Good listening, good note taking, good study habits, and good presentations add up to good grades. You need not study every waking hour of the day or night; that can be disastrous. At the same time, we hope you won't be tempted to party on the evening when studying matters most. The time to celebrate is after you know you've aced the exam or presentation. You've earned it.

Search Online! 《 ● 》

Internet Exercise 8.1 Examining Institutional Values

Many colleges and universities post campus rules and regulations on their Internet sites. One is Southern Methodist University, whose student code of conduct is at *http://www.smu.edu/~stulife/res_halls.html.*

A What policies and/or infractions does SMU provide for the following cases?
- Keeping bicycles in residence hall rooms
- Drinking alcohol in public
- Cheating

B Are these policies more or less strict than those at your college or university? How so?

C Compare SMU's regulations with the listing of "Student Rights and College Regulations of Brooklyn College of the City University of New York," at *http://www.brooklyn.cuny.edu/bc/info/right.htm.* How do they differ, and with which do you feel more comfortable?

D Now compare both codes of conduct with those on your campus. How do your rules differ, and with which of them do you feel more comfortable? (Go to *http://success.wadsworth.com* for the most up-to-date URLs.)

Internet Exercise 8.2 More Memory Devices

Use the Internet to improve your memory. Study the page "Memory Improvement Techniques" at *http://www.psy.flinders.edu.au/webpages/learning/lsmnln/page1.html.* Test your visual memory with the crime scene at the bottom of this Web page. (Go to *http://success.wadsworth.com* for the most up-to-date URLs.)

Internet Exercise 8.3 Discovering More About Making the Grade

Using *InfoTrac College Edition,* try these phrases and others for key-word and subject-guide searches: "mnemonics," "memory," "examinations," "cheating in college," "academic integrity," "truth," "honesty," and "public speaking."

ALSO LOOK UP:

Students are pulling off the big cheat. (college cheating rising) Carol Innerst. *Insight on the News,* Washington Times Corporation Mar 9, 1998 v14 n9 p41(1)

What we know about cheating in college. (includes resources for maintaining academic integrity) Donald L. McCabe, Linda Klebe Trevino. *Change* Jan-Feb 1996 v28 n1 p28(6)

Improve your memory. (includes memory quizzes and related articles on remembering names and humor) Kalia Doner, Ralph Schoenstein. *American Health* Mar 1994 v13 n2 p56(6)

Testing for truth: Joseph Conrad and the ideology of the examination. *CLIO* Spring 1994 v23 n3 p271(14)

Additional Exercises

These exercises will help you sharpen what we believe are the critical skills for college success: writing, critical thinking, learning in groups, planning, reflecting, and taking action. Also, check out the CD-ROM that came with your book—you will find these exercises and more.

Exercise 8.1 Designing an Exam Plan

Use the following guidelines to design an exam plan for one of your courses:

1. What are the characteristics of the exam?

   _____

   What material will be covered?

   _____

   What type of questions will it contain?

   _____

   How many questions will there be?

   _____

   What is the grading system?

   _____

2. Identify the approach you intend to use to study for this exam.

   _____

3. How much time and how many study sessions will you need?

   _____

4. Using your "To Do" list format, list all material to be covered.

   _____

   What still needs to be read?

   _____

5. Create a study schedule for the week prior to the exam, allowing as many 1-hour blocks for review as you need and specifically stating what you need to do.

Exercise 8.2 Forming a Study Group

Use the goal-setting process from Chapter 1 to form a study group for at least one of your courses. Think about your strengths and weaknesses in a learning or studying situation. For instance, do you excel at memorizing facts but find it difficult to comprehend theories? Do you learn best by repeatedly reading the information or by applying the knowledge to a real situation? Do you prefer to learn by processing information in your head or by participating in a hands-on demonstration? Make some notes about your learning and studying strengths and weaknesses here.

Strengths:

_____

_____

Weaknesses:

_____

_____

In a study group how will your strengths help others? What strengths will you look for in others that will help you?

How you can help others:

_____

_____

How others can help you:

_____

_____

In your first study group session, suggest that each person share his or her strengths and weaknesses and talk about how abilities might be shared for everyone's maximum benefit.

Exercise 8.3 Writing a Summary
Using underlining, highlighting, and margin notes for reference, write a summary of this chapter (or some other material), following the directions for summary writing. Exchange your summary with another student to discuss how well you summarized the material.

Exercise 8.4 Writing an Opening
Assume you've been assigned to give a speech at another college or university on the value of your first-year seminar class. Write an introductory paragraph, using one of the methods in this chapter. If time permits, present the opening to the class.

Your Personal Journal

1. Are you facing any issues related to academic honesty? What are they? What are you doing about them?
2. If you knew you could get away with cheating on an exam, would you do it? Explain your answer.
3. Assuming you have taken an exam, what strategies did you use to prepare? How did they work? If you haven't taken an exam, what strategies do you plan to use? Why?
4. It has been said that exams only measure how well you can memorize information and that, since some people have a natural-born talent for memorization, exams aren't fair. Can you punch any holes in this argument?
5. What else is on your mind this week? If you wish to share it with someone, add it to this journal entry.

Resources

Now that you've had time to think about academic integrity and organizing your study time, here are a few more things that will help you appreciate the value of studying well and doing well.

To learn more about cheating and values, find and read several articles on cheating from the Infotrac search bank. After reading them, condense their messages into a well-written paragraph.

....

....

....

....

....

....

....

....

Interview one or more of your teachers about cheating. Besides the obvious answer you will get about cheating being a dishonorable character trait, ask them to be more specific about what cheating can cause. Write those thoughts here.

....

....

....

....

....

....

....

....

Make a list of your exams, quizzes, and papers here. Add a way to celebrate when you've finished each one.

Class and Exam Date   **Reward**

....

....

....

....

....

....

Research

Your Campus Library and Computer Resources

dig in

**IN THIS CHAPTER,
YOU WILL LEARN**

- How to select a research topic and define your information needs

- How to work with librarians

- How to use library resources—from encyclopedias to the Internet

- How to get comfortable with computers

- How to use computers for word processing, spreadsheets, databases, graphics, and personal productivity

- How to use electronic mail (e-mail)

- How to be aware of ethical and legal issues regarding the use of information

"*Spreadsheets, databases, the World Wide Web, e-mail ... I never realized how many things you could do with computers. Even the campus library has computer stations for finding information, and the research librarians will help you use the many databases in their collection. Still, my instructors keep warning me that a computer is only as good as the person using it. Wonder what they mean by that?*"

What makes the information age exciting and potentially empowering for millions of people is the amount and diversity of information available through innumerable sources, the ease and speed with which you can obtain this information, and the incredible possibilities for applying it to everyday situations. Although the personal computer is but one tool, its impact on the way we live, work, and play cannot be denied. In the early part of the twentieth century, people who could not read found it almost impossible to earn a living wage; as we move into the twenty-first century, those who are not computer smart will face the same problem .

The growth of computer technology has had a tremendous impact on libraries. Most campus libraries now use computerized library catalogs or networks rather than the traditional card catalog. Many libraries also provide access to the Internet, online computer databases, and CD-ROMs, in addition to books, periodicals, and other printed sources.

The development of your critical thinking skills will depend a great deal on how much and how well you learn to use your campus library. The power of your arguments will depend on how well you can support them with facts and data. Reading numerous competing arguments about a question is a great way to begin creating sound arguments of your own.

SELF-ASSESSMENT: LIBRARY AND COMPUTER SKILLS

For those who aren't familiar with them, libraries and computers can be overwhelming. Checkmark those statements that best describe you. Circle the items with which you need help.

_____ Librarians will think I'm stupid if I ask them how to find information on a topic.

_____ Computers just make the library more complicated for me.

_____ I don't see any point in doing research and writing papers.

_____ I don't have to visit the library; I can get everything I need on the Internet.*

_____ I know how to do a search on the World Wide Web.

_____ I know how to use spreadsheet and database programs on the computer.

_____ I find it easy to type papers on the computer.

_____ I use e-mail frequently to communicate with friends, family, and teachers.

*You will not find all you need on the Internet. Many publications you may need are not on the Internet.

Get a Grip on the Library

Familiarize yourself with your library system before you have to use it. Is there more than one library on campus? If so, is one geared toward helping undergraduates? Your class may be able to schedule a tour to discover what your library offers you, such as an orientation via a computer system.

Does your library have handouts describing their various services, departments, and hours? Get them. Note the library departments that might interest you—for example, government documents, reserve collection, interlibrary loan, or a special collection devoted to one subject area.

Selecting and Surveying a Topic

Finding a topic is not always easy. You may wish to begin by focusing on something in which you are genuinely interested. Remember that defining and refining your topic is one of the objectives of research. When you visit the library, your goal should be to survey the topic and obtain ideas on how you might want to develop it.

While surveying the topic, ask "Does there seem to be enough information? Is there too much?" If there is not enough information, consider a broader approach. If there is too much, try zeroing in on one aspect. Instead of looking for information on crime, you might want to focus on a particular crime—relationship violence, for example—and examine how the police are responding to it.

Defining Your Need for Information

Begin to gather information by asking yourself several questions before you begin your information search. Although the following questions may be difficult to answer when you are starting out, don't worry. Try talking through your topic with a friend, a librarian, or your instructor.

1. **What do I already know about my topic?** Consider names, events, dates, places, terms, and relationships to other topics.
2. **Who would be writing about my topic?** For example, what scholars, researchers, professionals in specific fields, or other groups of people might be interested?
3. **What do I want to know about this topic?** Asking this question further focuses your research on your assignment. Sometimes your first question may be too general.
4. **What is the vocabulary of my topic?** What words describe it? Are there specialized terms for which I could search?
5. **What do I want to do with this information?** Am I writing a research paper, giving a speech, or preparing for a debate or an interview? (This will help you determine how much information you need and where to look.)
6. **What kinds of information do I need to find?**

   - **Introductory**   General information for an audience without prior knowledge of the topic
   - **In-depth**   Specialized and detailed information for those with prior or special knowledge
   - **Biographical**   About someone but by another person
   - **Autobiographical**   About someone and by that same person
   - **Current**   About an event or idea that just occurred
   - **Contemporary**   A perspective written at the time an event occurred
   - **Retrospective**   A reflection written about an event from the past

Libraries everywhere have been computerizing their catalogs. In many cases, however, not all resources are listed yet in the computer. Ask a librarian about sources that may not show up on the screen.

- **Summative** Providing an overview of a topic
- **Argumentative or persuasive** Expressing a strong point of view
- **Analytical** Breaking an idea into its components

Talking to Librarians

Librarians are usually more than willing to help you, and they can save you time and effort. When a librarian uses a term you do not know, ask for clarification.

Be prepared before you go to the library. Librarians expect you to know what your assignment is; to bring relevant assignment sheets, class notes, textbooks, and so on; to make decisions about the usefulness of sources; to ask questions; and to discuss what steps you have already taken.

Not all librarians are alike. Different librarians have different communication styles and areas of expertise. If you are not satisfied after talking to one librarian, seek another. Ask as many questions as you need to ask. Librarians generally welcome all questions.

Be as clear as possible about what you need. Don't worry if your topic is controversial or personal. Librarians have a professional responsibility to treat your request confidentially.

Finding Your Way

General Encyclopedias

Although general encyclopedias, such as *Encyclopaedia Britannica,* are useful tools for getting you started, instructors will not want you to rely on them as the major source for the papers you submit. Good encyclopedias have bibliographies that can lead you to more comprehensive sources. Your campus may have an electronic encyclopedia available on compact disc or via the World Wide Web.

Subject Encyclopedias

Subject encyclopedias are more specialized than general encyclopedias. Although they concentrate on a narrower field of knowledge and cover it in greater depth, the information they contain within their fields is still fairly general. The following subject encyclopedias do not constitute a comprehensive list. If you cannot find a title that fits your area of interest, ask a librarian. You can also try a key-word search of the library catalog, using your subject and the word "encyclopedias."

ARTS

The New Grove Dictionary of Music and Musicians

The Dictionary of Art

McGraw-Hill Encyclopedia of World Drama

Current Events and Social Issues

CQ Researcher

HUMANITIES

Dictionary of Literary Biography

Encyclopedia of Philosophy

Encyclopedia of Bioethics

Encyclopedia of Religion

Handbook of American Popular Culture

HISTORY

Encyclopedia of American Social History

Encyclopedia of African American Culture and History

Dictionary of American History

SOCIAL SCIENCES

International Encyclopedia of the Social Sciences

Encyclopedia of Educational Research

International Encyclopedia of Communications

Encyclopedia of American Economic History

Encyclopedia of American Foreign Policy

Encyclopedia of Psychology

Encyclopedia of Sociology

Guide to American Law

Encyclopedia of Human Behavior

NATURAL SCIENCES

McGraw-Hill Encyclopedia of Science and Technology

Encyclopedia of Computer Sciences

In its quiet way, having explored the "stacks" of the library may become one of your fondest memories of college. But you'll get the most out of your exploration if you've prepared well beforehand by exploring catalogs and indexes.

Catalogs

A catalog lists what a library owns. Your library's catalog may be a traditional card catalog; it may be computerized; it could be a combination of cards and computers; or it could even be available on microform (microfiche or microfilm) or in another format. You also may be able to log on to your catalog without even going to the library.

Indexes

Indexes identify articles in periodicals. The most common periodicals you will use are newspapers, magazines, and journals. Because articles are published more frequently and more quickly than books, they often contain more current information. An index does not contain the article itself but a citation listing the author(s), title of the article, title of the magazine or journal, date of the issue, and volume and page numbers. Some indexes, called abstracts, also provide a short summary of the article's content, which can tell you if the article is relevant.

Your library may also have a computerized version of a particular index, and some of these indexes, such as *InfoTrac,* may contain the full text of the articles.

Magazines and Newspaper Indexes If you want to find articles written for the general public or a popular audience, use an index for magazines or newspapers. Some computerized indexes may cover a wide range of articles from magazines, newspapers, and journals. Depending on the time period, your index might not be available on the computer. The index for the *New York Times* begins in 1851, and *Readers' Guide to Periodical Literature* goes back to 1900.

Library of Congress Subject Headings If you have trouble finding the right subject headings, you may want to consult an official list, such as that found in the *Library of Congress Subject Heading,* or LCSH. If your term is not a preferred subject heading, LCSH will refer you to appropriate terms. For instance, if you look up the term "college life," LCSH will tell you to use the term "college students." LCSH will also offer related terms and even subheadings or subject divisions once you have located the preferred subject heading. Ask a librarian for help using the LCSH.

Subject or Specialized Indexes Your instructors probably expect you to use scholarly sources for most of your library assignments. If you're not certain, be sure to ask. To find articles written by researchers or scholars in journals, you need only use a source that indexes these types of materials. If you aren't certain which subject index to use, ask a librarian to recommend one. The librarian will also show you how to use it to find the information you need.

Information Databases

Library catalogs and indexes are examples of databases. A database is a collection of records that is organized so that people can search it to find information. A cookbook could be called a database of recipes. When using a computer to find information, two little words are crucial in constructing key-word searches:

and   searches for both terms: "love and interpersonal"
or   searches for either term: "love or intimacy"

Some search programs require that these words be capitalized (AND and OR).

Because both terms must be present, *and* narrows a search. Use *and* to target your search when your initial search finds too much. *Or* is useful when you aren't finding much on your topic or when you want to simultaneously search for synonyms of your topic.

If you use both *and* and *or* when entering a search, enclose the terms you are joining with *or* in parentheses—for example, "(love or intimacy) and interpersonal." By using the parentheses, you are commanding the computer to look for either the word *love* or *intimacy* and to combine either word with the term *interpersonal.* In some computer systems, if you didn't nest the terms, the computer would retrieve all occurrences of the word *love,* whether *interpersonal* was included or not.   SEE EXERCISE 9.1

Periodicals

The most frequently asked questions in an academic library are about periodicals. Some libraries list their periodicals in the library catalog, whereas others keep a separate list. Even if you discover that your library owns a particular periodical, it isn't always obvious where it will be. For a variety of reasons, some libraries shelve periodicals with books. Other libraries have a separate section for periodicals. Magazines and journals might be shelved by their call number or by title. Perhaps some years are available on microfilm, whereas current issues are shelved in a different place. Ask.   SEE EXERCISE 9.2

World Wide Web Information Resources

The World Wide Web is an exciting and powerful way to communicate information through pictures, sounds, and text. What makes the Web so engrossing are links, which usually appear as buttons, underlined words, and/or in color. When you click on a link, the Web does the work of taking you to that section of a home page or connecting you to a different website altogether.

On the other hand, the Web is a little like a library with all the books piled all over the place in no order. The information may be there, but it can be difficult to sort through. No one is in charge of the Web, which is both an advantage and a disadvantage. The Web is changing all the time, and you can't be sure that what you find today will be in the same place or even on the Web tomorrow. Also, a great deal of published print information is *not* on the Web. A student who told his teacher he could not find any information on the Web pertaining to his topic was told to check periodicals in the library, where he found a treasure trove of data.

To be an effective Web searcher, you need to know strategies for efficient searching and evaluation of the information, and sometimes misinformation, you will find. Here are several key strategies for finding information on the Web. Which one works best will depend upon your situation—what you are looking for and what you already know.

Going Directly to a Website

If you already know the address, called a URL (uniform resource locator), you can enter it into the location box of your browser. A URL has three main parts:

protocol   domain name   directory path
http://www.yahoo.com/Entertainment

Common endings for domain names include:

.com   commercial sites
.edu   sites made available by educational institutions
.gov   government sites
.org   sites created by organizations

Using a Subject Directory

A Web directory leads you to Web resources by organizing sites into various categories. Yahoo was one of the first Web subject directories, and it is still a good way to browse the Internet. Use a directory when

- You aren't really certain what might be on the Web.
- Your topic is broad, or you can't be specific because you don't know much about the subject.
- The words you would use in your search are very general.

You can browse using the links provided by the directory or search for a word or phrase within the directory or section of the directory.

Using a Search Engine

A search engine is basically a large database of websites previously found by a computer search. The problem with search engines is that you can easily be overwhelmed by the sheer amount of the search results.

No single search engine can find everything on the Web, and they all work a little differently. It's a good idea to become proficient at first with one or two search engines. Some search engines will allow you to use *and* and *or* in constructing a search, whereas others might use the presence or absence of commas to distinguish between these options. The following additional searching conventions are also used by a variety of search engines.

- **Capital letters force an exact match, so usually it is a good idea to avoid using them.**
- **To search for a phrase, enter your words in quotation marks.** Search "census bureau" instead of census bureau, or the search engine may only find references to "bureau" or "census."
- **You can require that a term be present by typing a plus sign before the word.** To quickly find Lincoln's Gettysburg Address, a good search would be to enter +"Lincoln"+"Gettysburg Address"; a better example might be to use +"recipe"+"dessert" "chocolate" "lemon" to find recipes for desserts with either chocolate or lemon.

Critical Thinking

Evaluating Sources

Once you have located enough sources, you will need to critically evaluate each article, book, and other materials. As the volume of available information increases daily, never settle for the first sources you locate, for they may not be as relevant as others; they may be dated or inaccurate. To evaluate a source, ask the following questions:

- **Is the source relevant to my information needs?** Skim the contents of the source and ask if it's what you really are seeking.
- **Is the information in the source accurate?** If your topic is controversial, if you are relying on just a few sources, or if you are using a questionable fact, you might want to find some reviews or additional commentary to check on the accuracy of the information.

- **Does the author or the source show bias?** Consider why material was written or for whom it was written. You might need to seek a different opinion for the sake of objectivity.
- **What are the author's credentials?** If you can't answer, see a reference librarian.
- **Is the information timely?** Using up-to-date information and statistics is important, especially in a field constantly undergoing change (for example: computer science, medicine, economics).

Additional guidelines for assessing Web pages can be found at "Evaluating Web Resources," at *http://www2.widener.edu/Wolfgram-Memorial-Library/webeval.htm*

- **You can also exclude words in the results by typing a minus sign before the word.** You want to find information on the country New Guinea, but your initial search finds lots of items of interest to guinea pig owners. Try the search "New Guinea − pigs."

To become a good searcher, it is wise to read the Help screens for a search engine. You'll also find some good advice at these two sites:

"Internet Searching Strategies":
  http://riceinfo.rice.edu/Fondren/Netguides/strategies.html
"Searching the Internet":
  http://www.hamline.edu/library/bush/handouts/search.html

SEE SEARCH ONLINE!
INTERNET EXERCISE 9.1

Some of the widely used search engines are the following:

Excite   *http://www.excite.com*
Alta Vista   *http://www.altavista.digital.com/*
Infoseek   *http://www.infoseek.com/*
HotBot   *http://www.hotbot.com/*

(Go to *http://success.wadsworth.com* for the most up-to-date URLs.)

Computing for College Success

By the time you graduate from college, there will be new ways to use information technology that are difficult to imagine today. The Web already provides electronic access to books, newspapers, and magazines, scientific and commercial data, pictures, audio and video recordings, and other text and graphics. Soon, more will enter our homes, schools, and offices through this medium. This could provide tremendous benefits (or distractions!) for students.

As you become more knowledgeable about the tools available today, you will be better prepared to take advantage of future options and new technologies.

What You Need to Know

For most people, using a computer is like driving a car: You don't really need to know what's under the hood. Rather, you need a general sense of how it works—and how to make it work well for you. You also must know what to do if the computer won't do what you need it to do.

In normal use, it is almost impossible for you to damage a computer—unless, of course, you spill a drink on the keyboard or hit the machine angrily because it ate or destroyed some of your work. Yet a computer can do major damage to your work: It can quickly (and completely) erase the term paper you labored on late at night and through several weekends unless you get into the habit of saving your files frequently.

When you need help, ask. Good helpers show you how rather than doing it themselves. That's how you learn. They also know how to explain things clearly to you. If they don't, ask questions. If they start messing with your computer in an attempt to save you trouble, look for a different helper.

SEE EXERCISE 9.3

What if You Don't Feel Comfortable with Computers?

Face the facts: Technology skills will play a significant role in the job market of the twenty-first century. So meet this issue head on. You might begin with a book or workshop for beginners, or make a pact with a friend who shares your attitude about computers. Help each other by attending the same training session and reviewing class assignments that require you to use computers. Push (and pull) each other along.

Ask for help. Good helpers will show you how rather than doing it themselves. They will also know how to explain things to you in a way that you can understand.

Your college may incorporate computer instruction into some first-year courses to help you learn the basics. Many residence halls, libraries, or computer labs are staffed with troubleshooters who can help you learn.

Computer Basics

Keyboarding

Keyboarding remains the core skill for using a computer. If you can type, you're in good shape. If you can't, you need to learn. Find a keyboarding course that fits into your schedule or learn on your own with an inexpensive "typing tutor" software package. (To find the right one, look at ads in a computer magazine or ask someone in a computer store or your campus bookstore for suggestions.)

Accessing Computers

Does your college sell computers through the bookstore? Will you have to pay a lab fee for computer time and access for some of your classes? Will you be charged printing fees? The answers to these questions may depend on your major or your courses.

A small number of schools require (or strongly encourage) all students to own computers. These institutions have committed themselves to bringing information technology into nearly every aspect of academic life—from wiring residence halls into a campus network to including the cost of a computer as part of total college costs.

Campuses encourage computer use in many ways: selling computers in the bookstore, providing campus labs for student use, offering e-mail accounts to students, establishing a campus home page on the Web, allowing students to set up their own home pages, and offering various support services such as training classes and computer consultants.

Finding the Right Kind of Help

As you learn routine computing tasks, you'll have occasional problems or questions. Most often, you'll ask questions such as "Now that I'm doing X, how can I get the computer to do Y?" Here are some sources of help:

- **FAQs**   When you're getting started, most of the help you will need is what insiders call frequently asked questions, or FAQs. Your campus may have a source of FAQs and answers online. (*Online* means that you can locate answers via the computer itself.)
- **Support for academic computing**   Many campuses have a center or department responsible for academic computing—the use of computing and information technology for instruction and research. This unit often includes a user support service that can help you. Ask.
- **A few good souls**   Find a few people with whom you feel comfortable asking questions about computing. Also, try to find at least one librarian to answer questions about computer-related information resources in the library and through your campus network (if you have one) and World Wide Web.
- **A few good notes**   Don't assume that you will automatically remember the magic words and motions next time. Write down the steps. Keep handouts or notes where the information will be handy when you need it again.
- **A few good books**   Most bookstores will have dozens of books about computing, information technology, and computer software.

Examining Values

Here's a tough one. One of the secretaries in your college office, who is a friend of yours, tells you that she will be taking the afternoon off, so you can use her computer to write an assignment that is due the next day. "Do you have any questions about using the computer?" she asks. You shake your head. You've worked on computers before, and this one should be no different. "Well," she says, "just don't do anything with my folder. It's got everything I've *ever* done in it."

During the afternoon, you've combined a number of earlier files into a new file that will be the basis for your final draft, so you decide to trash the older files. As soon as you empty the trash, you look for the prominent folder on the screen with your friend's name on it. It isn't there. Knowing you've done something horrible, you scoop up your things, turn off the computer, and leave.

Days go by and you haven't received a call from the secretary. What should you do? What should you have done earlier? What about your friend? Is there anything she could have done to help you avoid this situation? Relate your decisions to some of the values you hold.

Preventing Disaster

SEE EXERCISE 9.4

Whether you're using your own computer or another one, take precautions to avoid the most serious catastrophes.

1. **Don't do anything silly to a computer.** Don't spill things on it. Don't drop it. Don't hit it.
2. **Learn how to start, stop, and restart the computer you are using.** Two common problems are (a) a computer gets hung up so that, no matter what you do, nothing happens and (b) you get lost in an application program, don't know what you're doing, and can't figure out how to move back to something that was making sense. When these things happen, ask for help. In both cases, the last (and very desperate) option is to turn off the computer and then restart (reboot) it. Although you'll probably lose whatever work you had done since the last time you saved or filed your work, at least you will be back in operation.
3. **Learn how to make backups.** Learn what diskettes, hard disks, portable memory drives, and network server shared storage are and which are available. Learn how to use them, especially a standard diskette that can hold about 1.3 megabytes or one of the larger disks that hold 100 or more megabytes. For most projects, you should probably do the following:
   a. *Save the document at least every 5 or 10 minutes (or every paragraph) while you work on it.* Give the file or document a name that you can easily recognize and remember. Use numbers to help identify the version number of the document. (Is it your first draft or your fourth rewrite?)
   b. *Virtually all computers allow you to copy documents (files) from the computer to a diskette (and vice versa).* Be sure you save your work on the document frequently and at the end of a work session. If what you're working on is extremely important, keep the diskette in a different room or building than the computer or purchase a portable drive that allows you to copy files from your hard drive and connect it to your computer.
   c. *If it makes you feel safer, print a hard (paper) copy of the most up-to-date version at the end of each work session and keep it in a safe place.* Use it to make corrections for future revisions.

d. *If you have your own personal computer, organize your desktop into folders labeled by course or topic, into which you can drop individual files pertaining to the title.* That way, you'll find it easier to locate a specific document.

Computer Applications

Word Processing (Writing)

For most students, word processing, or writing, is by far the most frequent application of information technology. Learning to use word processing with a spelling checker is essential. It is equally important to learn the limitations of most word processing software: It cannot help you pick the right word, cannot supply the ideas, and cannot do the research for you. But if you learn to use a reasonably powerful word processor, your papers will look better and require less effort to write and revise. Some word processing packages can even automatically place and number footnotes for you.

SEE EXERCISE 9.5

Word processing involves some risks and costs. If you are careless, you can lose the results of your work just at the wrong time. You can find yourself getting too fancy with choosing type fonts (sizes and styles) instead of working on the content. Access to a good word processing program also may increase your tendency to procrastinate. If you can produce a nice-looking paper in a few hours and can make changes right up until you are ready to print, you may be inclined to put off starting, forgetting that what a paper says is more important than how good it looks.

When you use a spelling checker, keep in mind that such programs don't end the need for your own careful proofreading. For example, spelling checkers won't pick up errors such as typing "there" for "their" or "too" for "to." Thus you will need to continue to proof your own work.

The main advantage of word processing over other forms of writing is that you can revise with much less effort, and revision is the key to successful writing. With practice, you can find the most effective techniques for writing—but this will work only if you also learn how to plan your time so that you can do more than one draft before the final version.

Spreadsheets

A spreadsheet program divides the computer screen into cells arranged in rows and columns. In each cell you can type a number, a short bit of text, or a formula that performs some calculation on the content of other cells. Spreadsheets are most widely used for budgeting and financial analysis. They are also useful wherever you need to experiment and calculate with numerical data. A good spreadsheet program can also calculate statistics. One great advantage of a spreadsheet over old-fashioned pencil-and-paper methods is that, once you have typed in the data, the computer does all the calculations, such as finding the total of a column of numbers. Spreadsheets are better than most calculators in that the spreadsheet stores the data so that they never have to be retyped. One way to learn about spreadsheets is to use one to work out your personal budget.

Databases

A database can manage, sort, summarize, and print out large amounts of systematic alphabetic or numerical data. Businesses use databases to keep records of such things as inventory, customers, and transactions. The electronic catalog in your campus library is a database. Researchers use databases to record and manipulate

Computer graphics aren't only for art and video commercials. They are also revolutionizing how computers help us see, share, and analyze complex information.

research data, such as survey results. One way to get started with a database is to use it in place of an old-fashioned personal address book, setting up fields for first name, last name, address, city, state, ZIP, phone number, and e-mail address.

Graphics and Presentation Software

Graphics and presentation software let you capture, create, and display visual images, maps, and other graphic data on the computer monitor, on projection screens, and in printed form. Computer graphics are everywhere you look today in art and advertising. They also have many uses on campus. For example, medical schools are now creating and using graphics software to teach human anatomy and medical diagnosis.

Personal Productivity Software

Personal productivity software includes personal information managers (PIMs) such as electronic phone books, calendars, and other tools, which help you manage information about your activities and contacts. Sometimes these come as bonus products when you buy a computer.

Communication over the Internet

At its simplest level, the Internet is many thousands of computers connected by telephone lines used to exchange messages and to find or offer other forms of information. It has no recognized governing body—just widespread agreement among users on some standard ways of packaging and sending information.

Most colleges and universities have computer networks of their own that are connected to the Internet. The personal computer that you now own or may soon own can be hooked to the Internet through a direct connection to your campus network or through a modem, a small device that lets your computer communicate with other computers via telephone lines. If your institution has a website or other online information system, you may find information on a computer about course offerings, campus policies and regulations governing students and faculty (perhaps including an "acceptable use" policy or guidelines suggesting appropriate online behavior), phone numbers, faculty ratings, course schedules, other institutional publications, and the campus events calendar.

Electronic Mail–Some Basics

Like many business networks, your campus network may have a system of electronic mail (e-mail) that lets you send and receive messages via computer. If it does, be sure and find out how to get your own e-mail address as soon as possible. E-mail messages may be local—on your campus, to other students and to faculty—or they may be sent to people at other campuses and to off-campus addresses via the Internet.

Perhaps the main advantage of e-mail is that it is asynchronous—you and the other person do not have to be using it at the same time. You can send a message that will travel almost instantly to someone else and wait until he or she sits down, reads it, and sends an answer back.

SEE SEARCH ONLINE! INTERNET EXERCISE 9.2

Faculty members often use e-mail to communicate with students. It may be easier for you to get a faculty member to answer a question via e-mail than to wait in line after class to try to set up an appointment.

E-Mail Etiquette One nice feature of most e-mail systems is that you don't have to look up someone's e-mail address every time. Usually, it is easy to reply to an incoming message. Unfortunately, people often use the Reply feature too quickly or without thinking carefully.

One common mistake occurs when you reply to a message that came from a listserv—a kind of online information service that relays messages provided by one person to all others on the service. When you respond to a message forwarded from a listserv, it is easy to think you are replying to the original author. However, the local e-mail system may send your message to the address that sent it to you—which may be someone other than the author and may even be a list of hundreds of people. It's usually easy to find out how your Reply feature works and to check that your outgoing reply is going where you intend.

Flaming refers to sending highly emotional, highly critical messages via e-mail. Sometimes this is exactly what you want and need to do, but most "flames" result from someone having an immediate strong emotional reaction to a message just received, writing an almost stream-of-consciousness response, and sending it without thinking about the consequences. Once you have sent a message, you cannot unsend it, and an apology offered afterward rarely undoes the harm or takes away the hurt.

And if you type anything in all caps, IT HAS THE EFFECT OF MAKING IT SEEM LIKE YOU ARE YELLING AT THE RECIPIENT!

It is usually easy to forward e-mail—to send a copy of a message you receive to someone else or to a list of e-mail addresses. Technically, this process usually can be done without permission from the original author. The ease and speed with which a message or document can spread through the Internet is truly amazing. You should consider the following before hitting the Send button:

- **An e-mail message you send to one person may be seen by others.** Pause and think about that before you send it.
- **Be careful to avoid publicizing what was sent to you as a private message.** If you have any doubt about the author's wishes, check with the author or copyright holder before sending a copy to someone else.

SEE EXERCISE 9.6

Ethical and Legal Issues

Your campus may have materials or courses explaining local policy and relevant law. You are responsible for knowing enough to avoid breaking the law. The best advice is to maintain your ethical principles and to learn enough of the relevant law and to whom to go for advice about what is and is not permitted. The library and the computing center are good places to start.

SEE SEARCH ONLINE!
INTERNET EXERCISE 9.3

Search Online!   《●》

Internet Exercise 9.1 Finding Information on the World Wide Web

1. If you know how URLs are typically constructed, sometimes you can guess what they will be. What do you think is the URL for the Public Broadcasting Service—the network of public television stations? Check to see if this is correct.

   _____

   Try finding it by directly entering a URL into your Web browser's location box.

2. Using the subject directory Yahoo, at *http://www.yahoo.com/*, find the current exchange rate for foreign currencies. Describe the steps you took:

   _____

   _____

   _____

3. Still using Yahoo, find newspapers that have websites from your local area or within your state. How did you go about trying to find this information? (There isn't necessarily just one route.)

   _____

   _____

   _____

   What is the URL for at least one local newspaper?

   _____

4. Using a search engine like Alta Vista, at *http://www.altavista.digital.com/*, find statistics on violence in public schools. (Go to *http://success.wadsworth.com* for the most up-to-date URLs.) Either try to put in words directly related to that topic or to think about who—what organizations or agencies—might make such information available and search for them. What searches did you try?

   _____

   Compare your experience with others in your class. What searches worked the best?

   _____

5. Now search for guidelines on how to cite Web resources in a bibliography. List the URL for one good website.

   _____

Search Online! 《●》

Internet Exercise 9.2 Learning to Use E-Mail

If e-mail is available on your campus, find out how to get an account. Write your e-mail address here:

_____

Write your password, if any, somewhere else where you won't lose it.

A Write in the e-mail addresses for the person teaching this course and one or two other students. Then send messages to each other. Learn how to use the Reply and Forward features. Try exchanging e-mail messages with someone at another campus by securing that person's e-mail address.

Teacher's name _____

E-mail address _____

Student's name _____

E-mail address _____

Student's name _____

E-mail address _____

B Send an e-mail message to the publishers of this book. Tell them how you like the book and how you think it could be improved for future first-year students. Address your message to *elana.dolberg@wadsworth.com* or to *sherry.symington@wadsworth.com.*

C Use e-mail to speak out on an issue that is important to you. Send an e-mail to any of the following:

NBC's *Dateline* news program in response to a story: *dateline@nbc.news.com*

The White House: *president@whitehouse.gov*

Newsweek magazine in response to a recent article: *letters@Newsweek.com*

Internet Exercise 9.3 Discovering More About Libraries and Computers

Using *InfoTrac College Edition,* try these phrases and others for key-word and subject-guide searches: "library," "liberal arts," "college library," "computer," and "microcomputer." Use PowerTrac to see the index of encyclopedias available on *InfoTrac College Edition.*

ALSO LOOK UP:

Now at a desktop near you. David Ansen, Ray Sawhill. *Newsweek* Mar 15, 1999 p80(1)

Riding the information superhighway: the Internet is great for retrieving information, but can it help businesses drum up clients and boost sales? Patrick Henry Bass. *Black Enterprise* Mar 1996 v26 n8 p82(5)

Looking back at looking ahead, or "the catalogs of the future revisited" with additional speculation. Norman D. Stevens. *Information Technology and Libraries* Dec 1998 v17 i4 p188(1)

The knuckle-cracker's dilemma: a transaction log study of OPAC subject searching. (Online Public Access Catalog) Terry Ellen Ferl, Larry Millsap. *Information Technology and Libraries* June 1996 v15 n2 p81(18)

The First Amendment and the right to hear. (Case Note) Dana R. Wagner. *Yale Law Journal* Dec 1998 v108 i3 p669(1)

Additional Exercises

These exercises will help you sharpen what we believe are the critical skills for college success: writing, critical thinking, learning in groups, planning, reflecting, and taking action. Also, check out the CD-ROM that came with your book—you will find these exercises and more.

Exercise 9.1 Key-Word and Subject Searching

If your library has an online or computer catalog, see if you can search by key word and by subject.

A Using the word "love," enter a key-word search.

How many hits or items did you retrieve?_____

Look at the information given about some of the items. Did you ever find "love" as an

author? _____

How about as a subject but not the emotion of love? _____

Where else did you find the word?_____

_____

_____

_____

B Now using the same word, "love," enter a subject search.

What were your results? How many items did the search find? _____

_____

_____

_____

Did the catalog organize the results differently than it did for the key-word search? How?_____

_____

_____

_____

Exercise 9.2 Getting Oriented to Periodicals

Find out how your library arranges the periodicals. It probably isn't obvious, so don't be afraid to ask. Why do you think the periodicals are organized this way?

_____

_____

_____

_____

_____

_____

_____

Exercise 9.3 **Rating Your Computer Skills**

Check the technology skills that are important for students in your major. Which skills are important for people in the career field you intend to pursue? If you don't know, find out. Ask an academic advisor, a faculty member, or a career counselor about the key technology skills for your major and intended career. Match their answers about key skills against your self-assessment of your skills. Taken together, this will help you set priorities and map a strategy for developing and enhancing your technology skills.

MY CURRENT SKILLS	MY PLANNED MAJOR	MY INTENDED CAREER	
_____	_____	_____	Keyboarding or typing
_____	_____	_____	Word processing
_____	_____	_____	E-mail
_____	_____	_____	Internet/World Wide Web
_____	_____	_____	Computerized library resources
_____	_____	_____	Spreadsheets/budgeting software
_____	_____	_____	Presentation graphics
_____	_____	_____	Computer programming
_____	_____	_____	Database management
_____	_____	_____	Statistical analysis
_____	_____	_____	Other: _____
_____	_____	_____	Other: _____

How will you address any needs suggested by this exercise?

_____

_____

_____

_____

_____

Exercise 9.4 **Preventing Disaster**

For any of the following information that you don't already know, ask someone and record enough notes on a sheet of paper to remind yourself what to do.

1. How to start your computer.

2. How to turn off and restart your computer in a *safe* manner.

3. How to file or save a document. Check to see whether your computer can file or save automatically every 15 minutes. If so, do so.

4. How to save a document from the computer onto a diskette and how to format (initialize) a diskette. Only format/initialize a diskette if you want everything already on that diskette erased forever.

5. How to print a document from the computer.

Exercise 9.5 **Word Processing**

If you're not using word processing, choose a paper you are assigned to write in one of your courses. If your campus offers a word processing workshop, sign up and go. Or try a tutorial or video disk. Use the computer to write, save, revise, and print your paper. Try reading the manual. If it's confusing (many are), buy an easier book about your particular word processing package. Keep it simple and write it well.

If you are already using word processing, mark each of the following true (T) or false (F):

____ 1. I routinely use a spell-checking program for all course work.

____ 2. I then check spelling before printing and turning in my work.

____ 3. I know how to create headers, footers, and footnotes. I use them frequently.

____ 4. I save my work regularly and never lose long or important work.

____ 5. I back up all my work on a disk.

____ 6. I don't waste too much time getting fancy with fonts, paragraph formats, type sizes, and other stuff.

If your answers suggest a need for improvement, get some help.

Exercise 9.6 **Computer Ethics**

Find out if your college or university has adopted a policy or guidelines for ethical and legal use of computers and telecommunications. Ask people in the academic computing office, the computer science department, or the library. If such a policy exists, get a copy. Be sure you understand the policy. Are there any aspects of the policy that seem unclear or difficult to follow? Be prepared to discuss your thoughts in class.

Your Personal Journal

Here are several things to write about. Choose one or more or choose another topic related to this chapter.

1. Think of the last time you used a library, whether in college or in high school. How easy was it to navigate your way through the information highway of databases, catalog holdings, reader's guides, and World Wide Web search engines to find what you were looking for? If it wasn't easy, how can you make it easy?

2. A more philosophical question: You've heard about the information explosion until you're probably sick of the expression. But if information is growing that quickly, what good is it to try and find information on a topic or two, when we know it will be impossible to learn about everything during our lifetimes?

3. If you want a computer of your own but can't afford it, ask the campus bookstore if it offers many payment plans for computers. Check prices of various brands. Check websites for Apple, Compaq, IBM, Toshiba, Gateway, and other brands. Learn what each model offers and don't purchase more computer than you need. After you've done your computer search, write a reaction to it.

4. What behaviors are you willing to change after reading this chapter? How might you go about changing them?

5. What else is on your mind this week? If you wish to share it with your instructor, add it to your journal entry.

Resources

Searching a Topic

Select a topic to research. If you are working on a paper in one of your classes, use that topic. Briefly answer the following questions as you go through your search.

1. What did I find on my topic in a general encyclopedia? How useful was it?

    ....

2. What subject encyclopedias pertain to my topic?

    ....

3. What did I find in them, and how useful was it?

    ....

4. What did I find in the online library catalog that pertained to my topic?

    ....

5. How easy was it to find pertinent information in those sources?

    ....

6. What information did I find searching article databases' CD-ROMs? How useful was it?

    ....

7. How helpful were subject indexes in my search? What did I find there?

    ....

8. How helpful was a search on the Web? How did I judge the accuracy of the material I found there?

    ....

Bookmarking Useful Sources on the World Wide Web

If you have a computer of your own and are using it frequently to search the Web, you'll find it handy to use bookmarks that call up the page without your having to type in the correct address. Below is a suggested list of bookmarks for you. What others should you add? If you do not have your own computer, do a search anyway and jot down the http addresses here for future reference.

Some Initial Bookmarks

Some favorite search engines are *Yahoo, Infoseek, Lycos,* and *Hotbot.* You can search these indexes, using key words to find information. Find out how they work and how enclosing words in quotes, or inserting a + or − sign between words can change the results of your search.

Preferred search engine ....

Second choice ....

Home page for my campus ....

(continued)

Home page for my academic major ....

Course listing for each term ....

Airlines I use to fly home ....

Pages I read for entertainment ....

Newspapers (check *The New York Times, The Washington Post,* and *The Atlanta Journal and Constitution*) ....

Magazine/journal in my academic field ....

Other ....

Other ....

Other ....

Get Connected!

Strategies for Success

PLAN AHEAD!	TAKE CHARGE OF LEARNING!	HONE YOUR SKILLS!	GET CONNECTED!	KNOW YOURSELF!
• Show up for class • Have work done on time • Set up a daily schedule • If full-time, limit work week to 20 hours. Work on campus if possible • If stressed, enroll part time	• Choose instructors who favor active learning • Assess how you learn best • Improve your reading, note-taking, and study habits • Develop critical thinking skills • Improve your writing	• Participate in class • Practice giving presentations • Learn how to remember more from every class • Learn from criticism • Take workshops on how to study • Get to know your campus library and other information sources • Embrace new technologies	• Study with a group • Get to know one person on campus who cares about you • Get involved in campus activities • Learn about campus helping resources • Meet with your instructors • Find a great academic advisor or counselor • Visit your campus career center • Take advantage of minority support services • Enlist support of your spouse, partner, or family	• Take your health seriously • Have realistic expectations • Learn how to be assertive yet tactful • Be proud of your heritage

Courses and Careers

Utilizing Academic Advisors and Other Resources

IN THIS CHAPTER, YOU WILL LEARN

- How to choose a good academic advisor/ counselor
- How your college catalog can be a helpful reference
- How majors and careers are linked—but not always
- Factors in career planning and choosing a major
- How to prepare a résumé and cover letter

ask for directions

"*Got the results of my career inventory today. It said I might want to go into the funeral business! And I thought I was interested in computers. Think I'd better ask my advisor what it all means. Better check the catalog, too, for courses in mortuary science. I just got here, and I'm already confused!*"

For a number of new students, choosing a major can be a difficult decision. Most students entering college straight out of high school (and even some who've worked for a while) don't know which major to select or for which career they may be best suited. What's more, many students change their majors at least once before earning their degree.

There are many reasons for this: a broader selection of fields of study than in high school; pressure from parents or others; or the lure of majoring in one of the high-paying fields even when you have no interest in it, knowledge about it, or aptitude for it. One person you can look to for advice on majors and careers is your academic advisor or counselor, one of the most important individuals you will meet in college. This person can guide you through the complexities of choosing courses that follow your interests and meet the requirements of your major.

Learning from Your Academic Advisor/Counselor

A mounting body of evidence suggests that poor academic advising is a major reason students leave college in the first year. At most colleges, you will have to visit your advisor or counselor at least once a term to obtain approval for courses that you will take the following term. Be sure you do! This advising period is usually widely publicized on campus. Beyond that, your advisor or counselor is available whenever you need help—

SELF-ASSESSMENT: MAJORS AND CAREERS

Some students enter college knowing what they want to major in, but many others are at a loss to declare a major. Either way, it's okay. Checkmark the statements that best describe your present situation. Circle the items with which you need help.

_____ 1. I have made contact with my academic advisor.

_____ 2. I have found useful information in my college catalog.

_____ 3. I have declared a major, but I don't know how it will lead to a career.

_____ 4. I have declared a major, but now I'm not sure I made the right choice.

_____ 5. I'm not sure I have the necessary skills to pursue the major of my choice.

_____ 6. I know how to prepare a good résumé.

_____ 7. I know how to prepare an effective cover letter to accompany my résumé.

_____ 8. I chose my major primarily because of the potential to earn lots of money.

_____ 9. I chose my major primarily because I enjoy this subject.

when you're having trouble in a course, when a medical emergency forces you to miss classes beyond the drop date, when you're doubtful about the major you have chosen, or for other reasons—academic and personal—that affect your success in college.

At many colleges, academic advisors and counselors are full-time faculty. At some campuses, some may be professional educators. In many community colleges, academic advising is done by counselors in the counseling/advising center. These counselors are trained in and responsible for assisting students with both academic and personal issues. Your institution may not assign you to an advisor in your intended major until you are formally admitted to a program. In any event, your advisor should be familiar with the requirements of your program.

Preparing for Your Meeting

SEE EXERCISE 10.1

Your advising sessions will be more productive if you are familiar with your college catalog. Make a list of questions before your appointment and arrive with a tentative schedule of courses and alternate choices for the coming term.

Discuss any major decisions—adding or dropping a course, changing your major, or transferring or withdrawing from school—before making them. You may also wish to discuss personal problems with your advisor. If he or she can't help you, ask for referral to a professional on campus who can. Be sure to clarify whether your advisor will respect your request for confidentiality on such matters.

Is Your Advisor/Counselor Right for You?

Do you feel comfortable with your advisor/counselor? Does this individual seem to take a personal interest in you, listen actively, provide enough time for you to accomplish what needs to be done, and either make an effort to get you the information you request or tell you where you can find it yourself?

If not, find someone else. Ask one of your favorite instructors or check with your department. Never stay in an advising/counseling relationship that isn't working for you.

What Are You Looking For in Your Academic Advisor?

This graph from a study of students at Harvard shows that men and women tend to seek different qualities in advisors. When asked about advising, men want an advisor who "knows the facts." Or "If he doesn't know the data, he knows where to get it or to send me to get it." Or one who "makes concrete and directive suggestions, which I'm then free to accept or reject."

Women more often want an advisor who "will take time to get to know me personally." Or who "is a good listener and can read between the lines if I am hesitant to express a concern." Or who "shares my interests so that we will have something in common." The women's responses focus far more on a personal relationship.*

What do you plan to look for in an advisor? What can you do to ensure that you get the advisor who is best for you?

What Students Want from Academic Advisors (percentage indicating "very important")

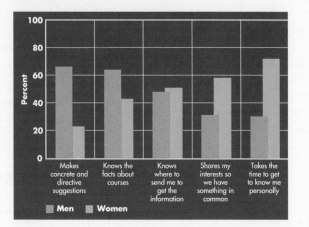

*Richard J. Light. *The Harvard Assessment Seminars, First Report.* Cambridge, MA: Harvard University Graduate School of Education and Kennedy School of Government, 1990.

Examining Values

The relationship between an academic advisor/counselor and a student is a vital one. In a short paper, describe the values you would seek in such a person. Then explain why those values are important to you. For example, would you prefer an advisor who valued helping you find the right academic program? Or one who valued a close relationship with students? Or one who valued his or her expertise on academic matters? Or what?

Your College Catalog

College can be less complex if you treat your college catalog as a user's manual. Learn what's in your catalog—it can be a valuable resource throughout your college years.

Much of the information in your college catalog may also be online. Campus computer bulletin boards and Internet home pages are especially useful for information that is in constant flux or that has changed recently. In addition to lists of classes and prerequisites, office hours, and student services, you can often search listings of job opportunities, scholarships, schedules, and departmental telephone numbers and e-mail addresses.

SEE EXERCISE 10.2

What's in the Catalog?

Publication Date and General Information Colleges and universities are constantly changing admissions standards, degree requirements, academic calendars, and so on. But the catalog in use at the time of your matriculation (the day you enrolled for the first time) will generally stand as your individual contract with the institution.

Most college catalogs include a current academic calendar, which states the beginning and ending dates of academic terms, holidays, and important deadlines. If you are not doing well in a particular class, you may want to drop the course rather than receive a failing grade, but you must do so before the deadline for withdrawal.

SEE EXERCISE 10.3

General Academic Regulations Don't rely on secondhand grapevine information. Become familiar with general academic regulations directly from the catalog. If you don't understand something in the catalog, seek clarification from an official source, such as your academic advisor.

Academic Programs By far the lengthiest part of most catalogs is the section on academic programs. It summarizes the various degrees offered, the majors within each department, and the requirements for each discipline. The academic program section also describes all courses offered at your institution: course number, course title, units of credit, prerequisites for taking the course, and a brief statement of the course content.

For more detailed academic information, check with individual departments.

Planning for Your Career

Majors = Careers? Not Always

The most common question college students ask is, What can I do with my major? Career planning helps you focus on a more important question: What do I want to do?

Obviously, if you want to be a nurse, you must major in nursing. Engineers major in engineering; pharmacists major in pharmacy. There's no other way to be certified as a nurse, engineer, or pharmacist.

However, most career fields don't require a specific major, and people with specific majors don't have to use them in usual ways. For example, if you major in nursing, history, engineering, or English, you might still choose to become a bank manager, sales representative, career counselor, production manager, or any number of other things.

What's more, if you're not certain about a major, it's perfectly okay to enter as an undeclared major. From 60 to 85 percent of entering students will change majors at least once, and it may be better to shop around during your first year before you make that important decision.

In most cases a college major alone may not be enough to land you a job. With the tremendous competition for good jobs, you'll need experience and skills related to your chosen field. Internships, part-time jobs, and cocurricular activities provide opportunities to gain experience and develop these competencies.

Table 10.1 is a college time line for exploring career ideas as you develop your qualifications. In the context of such a plan, your choice of an academic major takes on new meaning. Instead of being concerned with what the prescribed route of certain majors allows you to do, you'll use your career goals as a basis for academic decisions about your major, your minor, elective courses, internships, and cocurricular activities.

Consider these goals when you select part-time and summer jobs, too. Don't confine yourself to a short list of jobs directly related to your major; think more broadly.

Critical Thinking

Courses and Careers

Exercise 10.4 asks you to prioritize your life goals as a means to finding a career that matches those goals. After you complete the exercise, reflect on your top five goals. What influences (people, events, information, and so on) caused you to make those choices? What do they say about the kind of person you are? If, after writing a statement about your goals, you find you might like to change one or more of them, which would you choose, and which would you discard? What influenced you to make those changes?

TABLE 10.1 CAREER-PLANNING TIME LINE

FIRST YEAR: CHECK OUT CAREER POSSIBILITIES.

Meet with a career counselor to discuss your career goals.

Complete a career assessment or use computer resources at your career center.

Familiarize yourself with the career library. Note occupations of interest to you.

SECOND YEAR: FIND WAYS TO GET CAREER-RELATED EXPERIENCE.

Start building your résumé.

Seek a part-time or summer job related to your career goals.

Ask your academic advisor or career counselor about an internship in your field.

Shadow a professional on the job in your field of interest.

THIRD YEAR: KEEP GAINING EXPERIENCE AND LEARN HOW TO MARKET IT.

Attend résumé-writing workshops at your career center.

Complete an internship or co-op position in your field. An internship usually lasts one term and may offer academic credit. It may be paid or unpaid. A co-op is a two- to three-term commitment to an employer and almost always is paid. Or find a part-time job in your field for added experience.

FOURTH YEAR: DECIDE WHERE AND HOW TO MARKET YOURSELF.

Apply to graduate schools and take the appropriate qualifying exams.

Work with a career counselor to fine-tune your résumé.

Attend job-search and interviewing workshops.

Decide where you want to search and what you want to search for.

Use on-campus recruiting and placement services in addition to conducting your own job search.

Factors in Your Career Planning

Some people have a very definite self-image when they enter college, but most of us are still in the process of defining (or redefining) ourselves throughout life. We can look at ourselves in several useful ways with respect to possible careers:

- **Interests**   Interests develop from your experiences and beliefs and can continue to develop and change throughout life. You may be interested in writing for the college newspaper because you wrote for your high school paper. It's not

Biology . . . evolution . . . history . . . literature . . . ? Start your search for your major with some wide-ranging thought about your interests.

unusual to enter Psych 101 with a great interest in psychology and realize halfway through the course that psychology is not what you imagined.

- **Skills**   Skills are measured by past performance and usually can be improved with practice.

SEE EXERCISE 10.4

- **Aptitudes**   Aptitudes are inherent strengths, often part of your biological heritage or the result of early training. They are the foundation for skills. We each have aptitudes on which we can build. Build on your strengths.

- **Personality**   The personality you've developed over the years makes you the person you are and can't be ignored when you make career decisions. The quiet, orderly, calm, detail-oriented person probably will make a different work choice than the aggressive, outgoing, argumentative person.

- **Life goals and work values**   Each of us defines success and satisfaction in our own way. The process is complex and very personal. Two factors influence our conclusions about success and happiness: (1) knowing that we are achieving the life goals we've set for ourselves and (2) finding that we gain satisfaction from what we're receiving from our work.

Dr. John Holland, a psychologist at Johns Hopkins University, has developed a number of tools and concepts that can help you organize these various dimensions of yourself so that you can identify potential career choices.

Holland separates people into six general categories based on differences in their interests, skills, values, and personality characteristics—in short, their preferred approaches to life.*

- **R = Realistic**   These people describe themselves as concrete, down to earth, and practical—as doers. They exhibit competitive/assertive behavior and show interest in activities that require motor coordination, skill, and physical strength. They prefer situations involving action solutions rather than tasks involving verbal or interpersonal skills, and they like to take a concrete approach to problem solving rather than rely on abstract theory. They tend to be interested in scientific or mechanical areas rather than cultural and aesthetic fields.

*Adapted from John L. Holland, *Self-Directed Search Manual* (Psychological Assessment Resources, 1985). Copyright ©1985 by PAR, Inc. Reprinted with permission.

- **I = Investigative**   These people describe themselves as analytical, rational, and logical—as problem solvers. They value intellectual stimulation and intellectual achievement and prefer to think rather than to act, to organize and understand rather than to persuade. They usually have a strong interest in physical, biological, or social sciences. They are less apt to be people oriented.

- **A = Artistic**   These people describe themselves as creative, innovative, and independent. They value self-expression and relations with others through artistic expression and are also emotionally expressive. They dislike structure, preferring tasks involving personal or physical skills. They resemble investigative people but are more interested in the cultural-aesthetic than the scientific.

- **S = Social**   These people describe themselves as kind, caring, helpful, and understanding of others. They value helping and making a contribution. They satisfy their needs in one-to-one or small-group interaction, using strong verbal skills to teach, counsel, or advise. They are drawn to close interpersonal relationships and are less apt to engage in intellectual or extensive physical activity.

- **E = Enterprising**   These people describe themselves as assertive, risk taking, and persuasive. They value prestige, power, and status and are more inclined than other types to pursue it. They use verbal skills to supervise, lead, direct, and persuade rather than to support or guide. They are interested in people and in achieving organizational goals.

- **C = Conventional**   These people describe themselves as neat, orderly, detail oriented, and persistent. They value order, structure, prestige, and status and possess a high degree of self-control. They are not opposed to rules and regulations. They are skilled in organizing, planning, and scheduling and are interested in data and people.

SEE EXERCISE 10.5

Holland's system organizes career fields into the same six categories. Career fields are grouped according to what a particular career field requires of a person (skills and personality characteristics most commonly associated with success in those fields) and what rewards those fields provide for people (interests and values most commonly associated with satisfaction). Here are a few examples:

- **R = Realistic**   Agricultural engineer, electrical contractor, industrial arts teacher, naval officer, fitness director, package engineer, electronics technician, computer graphics technician

- **I = Investigative**   Urban planner, chemical engineer, bacteriologist, flight engineer, genealogist, laboratory technician, marine scientist, nuclear medical technologist, obstetrician, quality-control technician, computer programmer, environmentalist, physician, college professor

- **A = Artistic**   Architect, film editor/director, actor, cartoonist, interior decorator, fashion model, graphic communications specialist, journalist, editor, orchestra leader, public relations specialist, sculptor, media specialist, librarian, reporter

- **S = Social**   Nurse, teacher, social worker, genetic counselor, marriage counselor, rehabilitation counselor, school superintendent, geriatric specialist, insurance claims specialist, minister, travel agent, guidance counselor, convention planner

- **E = Enterprising**   Banker, city manager, FBI agent, health administrator, judge, labor arbitrator, salary and wage administrator, insurance salesperson, sales engineer, lawyer, sales representative, marketing specialist

- **C = Conventional**   Accountant, statistician, census enumerator, data processor, hospital administrator, insurance administrator, office manager, underwriter, auditor, personnel specialist, database manager, abstractor/indexer

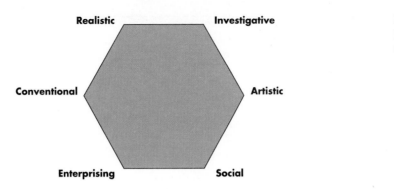

FIGURE 10.1
Holland's Hexagonal Model of Career Fields

Your career choices ultimately will involve a complex assessment of the factors that are most important to you. To display the relationship between career fields and the potential conflicts people face as they consider them, Holland's model is commonly presented in a hexagonal shape (Figure 10.1). The closer the types, the closer are the relationships among the career fields; the farther apart the types, the more conflict there is between the career fields.

Holland's model can help you address the problem of career choice in two ways. First, you can begin to identify many career fields that are consistent with what you know about yourself. Once you've identified potential fields, you can use the career library at your college to get more information about those fields, such as daily activities for specific jobs, interests and abilities required, preparation required for entry, working conditions, salary and benefits, and employment outlook.

SEE EXERCISE 10.6

Second, you can begin to identify the harmony or conflicts in your career choices. This will help you analyze the reasons for your career decisions and be more confident as you make choices.

SEE SEARCH ONLINE! INTERNET EXERCISE 10.1

College students often view the choice of a career as a monumental and irreversible decision. But, in its broadest sense, a career is the sum of the decisions you make over a lifetime. There is no "right occupation" just waiting to be discovered. Rather, you may find many career choices fulfilling and satisfying. The question to consider is, What is the best choice for me now?

Time for Action

Building a Résumé

Before you finish college, you'll need a résumé—whether it's for a part-time job, for an internship or co-op position, or for a teacher who agrees to write a letter of recommendation for you. Note the two résumés in Figure 10.2. One is written in chronological format, and the other is organized by skills. Generally, choose the chronological résumé if you have related job experience and choose the skills résumé if you can group skills from a number of jobs or projects under several meaningful categories. Try for one page, but if you have a number of outstanding things to say and they run over, add a second page. The following are other suggestions for good résumés:

- **Always put a contact block at the top.** This includes name, address, permanent address if applicable, e-mail address, and telephone number.
- **State an objective if appropriate.** If you're seeking a specific position, absolutely state an objective but be realistic. You're probably seeking an entry-level position at this stage. If you're applying for several different types of jobs, change your objective to fit each mailing.

CHRONOLOGICAL RÉSUMÉ

Rita Resume
3130 Appian Way
Columbia, SC 29229
(803) 989-000, rway@infi.com

OBJECTIVE
Seeking entry-level position in finance utilizing analytical, supervisory, and organizational skills.

EDUCATION
Bachelor of Science in Business Administration, May 2003
University of South Carolina, Columbia, SC
• Major: Finance
• GPA in major: 3.2/4.0
• Financed 60% of educational expenses

RELATED EXPERIENCE
Intern, Bank of Carolina, Summer 1998, Columbia, SC
• Developed procedures manual for tellers
• Performed financial analyses for loan packages
• Supervised summer student staff

OTHER EXPERIENCE
Assistant Manager, Pop's Deli, September 1998–present, Columbia, SC
• Supervised wait staff of ten
• Ordered $1,000 in supplies weekly
• Trained twelve new employees
• Increased sales by 10%

Manager's Assistant, Aiken Pool, Summer 1997, Aiken, SC
• Assisted with supervision of aquatic facility used daily by 300 people
• Organized concession stand with $300 daily sales

ACTIVITIES
President, Zeta, Zeta, Zeta Sorority
USC, Columbia, SC
• Organized and supervised work of ten committees
• Allocated annual budget of $15,000
• Interacted with university, city, and state officials
• Membership increased 10% during presidency

Chairman, Panhellenic Council
USC, Columbia, SC
• Convened and led weekly meetings
• Supervised work of all committees
• Organized fund-raising that raised $25,000
Delta Sigma Pi Business Fraternity
Water skiing Club
Equestrian Club

INTERESTS
Golf, tennis, English literature

REFERENCES
Available upon request

SKILLS RÉSUMÉ

Sammie S. Skillful
Sskillful@infi.com

Present Address
2424 Main Street
Columbia, SC 29211
(803) 999-9999

Permanent Address
39 Sherman Avenue
Lake George, SC 29999
(803) 267-8989

OBJECTIVE
Seeking hospitality related managerial position utilizing sales, organizational, and supervisory experience.

EDUCATION
Bachelor of Arts in English, December 2003
University of South Carolina, Columbia, SC
• GPA: 3.87/4.0
• Financed 100% of educational expenses

SKILLS

Initiative
• Developed and promoted summer pool parties
• Established and managed in-home dining service
• Developed marketing strategy and arranged promotions

Organization
• Organized parties for up to 500 area residents
• Hired and trained staff of six
• Ordered supplies on a monthly basis

Supervision
• Supervised staff of ten hired for New Year's Eve party
• Hired and trained staff of four for own dining business

Computer
• Designed promotional materials using desktop publishing
• Created and maintained customer database

EXPERIENCE
Self-Employed, June 1996–August 1998
Diner's Delight, Columbia, SC

Self-Employed, August 1994–May 1996
Parties Plus, Columbia, SC

Bagger, May–August 1993
Wee Pig Food Store, Charleston, SC
• Received six monthly awards for most courteous service

HONORS
Sigma Tau Delta English Honor Society, Golden Key National Honor Society, Dean's List, Phi Beta Kappa

INTERESTS
Jogging, skiing, reading

REFERENCES
Available upon request

FIGURE 10.2 Sample Résumés

- **List education to date.** As a first-year student, you can list under "Education" something like the following: "Enrolled in Bachelor of Arts, Psychology, University of Nebraska." When you're nearer to graduation and seeking full-time employment, state the degree and when you expect to receive it.
- **Give grade point average only if it's impressive.** What's important is that you demonstrate a balance between good grades and involvement in other areas of campus life.
- **Use action verbs in stating accomplishments.** "Developed bookkeeping system for company." "Organized special event that raised $5000 for charity." "Supervised editorial staff of twelve."
- **Separate the work experience related to your academic major from other work experience.** If you have no related work experience, simply list jobs under "Work Experience." Even though the job may not be related, it indicates someone thought enough of you to hire you and pay you.
- **Explain honors and awards thoroughly.** People will probably know what Phi Beta Kappa is, but how many will understand "Golden Dagger Award from Order of Service Supporters"?
- **Include interests.** These tell employers that you have interests in life beyond your work. Few prospective employers seek workaholics.
- **Be sure you have references if you state "references available upon request."** Let references know that a prospective employer may call. Nothing is more awkward—or harmful—than a reference getting a call and thinking, "Who in the heck is that?" when your name is mentioned.
- **Ask someone to review your résumé.** Ask your academic advisor, counselor, or someone else whose judgment you trust to look at your résumé before you put it into final form.

The Cover Letter

Sending a résumé without a cover letter is somewhat like forgetting to put on your clothes over your underwear: You can do it, but people will notice something important is missing. In writing a cover letter, heed the following suggestions:

SEE EXERCISE 10.7

- **Find out who should receive the letter.** It's not the same in all fields. If you are seeking a marketing position at an advertising agency, write to the director of account services. If you are writing General Motors regarding a position in their engineering department, either write to the director of human resources for the entire company or to the director in charge of engineering. Your academic advisor or career counselor can help you here, as can the Internet.
- **Get the most recent name and address.** Advisors or counselors can guide you to references in your campus or career library. *Never* write "To whom it may concern."
- **Use proper format for date, address, and salutation,** as shown in Figure 10.3.

More Things You Can Do

In this chapter you have done exercises aimed at gathering information about yourself and about the world of work and at clarifying the most important issues involved in your choice of career and academic major. Here are a few other activities that may help:

FIGURE 10.3
Cover Letter

Janet R. Mars
3130 Appian Way
Columbia, SC 29229

January 10, 2003

Mark B. Stoneridge
VP, Sales and Marketing
Ainsley Pharmaceuticals
3000 Appalachian Way
Pittsburgh, PA 49877

Dear Mr. Stoneridge:

(In your opening paragraph, tell why you are writing) When I receive my B.A. degree this spring, I would very much like to begin a career as a pharmaceutical salesperson.

(In the ensuing paragraphs, tell what makes you the right person for the job) I had no idea I would be interested in this field when I majored in speech. Then I chose a minor in marketing and discovered they fit together beautifully. The third part of the equation was knowing a friend of my mother who works for a pharmaceutical company in sales. I spent a good deal of time with her, shadowed her on calls, and decided this was the career I was meant for.

(In the last paragraph, tell what you will do next) I plan to visit Pittsburgh sometime around June 15 and would greatly appreciate a few moments of your time. If you have no openings at your company, perhaps you might refer me to other organizations. I will call you at least a week before I make my trip to see if you have time to visit with me.

(End with a proper closing)
Sincerely,

(signature) Janet R. Mars

Janet R. Mars

- **Career exploration**   Once you've selected possible career fields, talk with people working in those fields and try to spend a day observing them at work. Read what people in this field read. Visit local professional association meetings. Visit your campus career center and speak with a career counselor; ask about the resources available there. Many career centers have extensive libraries focusing on occupations, employers, and graduate programs. A counselor can direct you to Web links containing appropriate and current information about the job market. You may even find programs that allow you to preview positions, working environments, and others that make it possible for you to conduct a "virtual interview" on a computer.
- **Choice of major**   Talk with faculty members about the skills and areas of expertise you'll develop in studying the disciplines they're teaching. Ask if they're aware of careers or jobs in which the skills and knowledge they teach can be used.
- **Connection between major and career**   Ask employers if they look for graduates with certain majors or academic backgrounds for their entry-level positions.
- **Skill development**   Get involved in work experiences or campus activities that will allow you to develop skills and areas of expertise useful to your career plans. Find a summer job in that area or volunteer as an intern. Keep a record of skills you have demonstrated.

- **Understanding the marketplace**   What's popular today may not be so popular in 4 or 5 years. Never choose a major based on the "in" thing to do when you're a new student. For one thing, it may be all wrong for your skills, aptitudes, personality, and so forth. For another, by the time you graduate, it may be unimportant or even nonexistent.

Career planning isn't a quick and easy way to find out what you want to do with your life, but it can point you to potentially satisfying jobs and help you find your place in the world of work.

SEE SEARCH ONLINE!
INTERNET EXERCISE 10.2

Search Online!   《●》

Internet Exercise 10.1 Internet Career Resources

The Internet offers a variety of resources for choosing a career. These include Oakland University's "Definitive Guide to Internet Career Resources," at *http://phoenix.placement. oakland.edu/career/guide.htm*, an extensive listing of career sites; "The Catapult on Job Web," at *http://www.jobweb.org/catapult/catapult.htm*, a major guide with links to career and job-related sites; and "The Riley Guide to Employment Opportunities and Job Resources on the Internet," at *http://www.dbm.com/jobguide/*. Other Internet career resources include:

American Career InfoNet Career Resources Library:
   http://www.acinet.org/resource/misc/#diverse

Yahoo Business/Employment menu: *http://www.yahoo.com/Business /Employment/*

Career Resources Center: *http://www.careers.org/*

Advancing Women Career Center: *http://www.advancingwomen.com /awcareer.html*

Peterson's website: *http://www.petersons.com/*

What Color Is Your Parachute? The Net Guide: *http://www.washingtonpost.com/parachute*

(Go to *http://success.wadsworth.com* for the most up-to-date URLs.)

Describe the resources available at four or more sites.

_____

_____

_____

_____

Of the sites you visited, which is better for gathering information about a future job? Which is better for finding a job immediately?

_____

_____

Internet Exercise 10.2 Discovering More About Courses and Careers

Using *InfoTrac College Edition*, try these phrases and others for key-word and subject-guide searches: "career planning," "careers," "academic advisor," and "college majors."

ALSO LOOK UP:

The multiple roles of an undergraduate's academic advisor. Kenneth C. Petress. *Education* Fall 1996 v117 n1 p91(2)

Are you being held back by discrimination? Anne Fisher. *Fortune* Aug 16, 1999 v140 i4 p186

Making the transition from college to work. Calvin E. Bruce. *Black Collegian* Feb 1999 v29 i2 p80(3)

Your next job. (attitudes towards career changes) Daniel McGinn, John McCormick. *Newsweek* Feb 1, 1999 p42(1)

Additional Exercises

These exercises will help you sharpen what we believe are the critical skills for college success: writing, critical thinking, learning in groups, planning, reflecting, and taking action. Also, check out the CD-ROM that came with your book—you may find these exercises and more.

Exercise 10.1 Your Academic Advisor/Counselor

Fill in the following information about your academic advisor/counselor.

Name _____

Phone _____ E-mail _____

Office _____ Office Hours _____

Then prepare to meet this person by answering the following questions:

1. What is my major? What is my potential career? If I don't have a major, what would I like to major in?

   _____

   _____

   _____

2. What classes do I think I need to take next term?

   _____

   _____

   _____

3. Which classes must I take before I can take other classes?

   _____

   _____

   _____

4. What problems, if any, am I having this term? What should I do about them?

   _____

   _____

   _____

5. From which of my current teachers do I learn best? Least well? Why?

   _____

   _____

   _____

6. What do I need to know about services on campus, scholarships, internships, cooperative education, and so forth?

   _____

   _____

   _____

Exercise 10.2 Finding Your Catalog and Starting a File

A   Get a catalog. Make sure it's the one dated the year you began a program of study, not the year you applied for admission or were accepted. Ask your advisor/counselor where to find one.

B   Start a file for your catalog and other documents, including your grade reports, advisement forms, fee-payment receipts, schedule change forms, and other proof of financial and academic transactions with your campus. Keep all of these until your diploma is in your hands.

C   If you are thinking of transferring to another college, get a copy of the catalog for that school. It will help your advisor guide you in your choice of courses.

Exercise 10.3 Recording Key Dates

Use your college or university's Internet page to locate key dates for this term and the next. Or look in a current catalog or schedule of classes for this information.

_____ The love and admiration of friends

_____ Good health

_____ Lifetime financial security

_____ A lovely home

_____ International fame

_____ Freedom within my work setting

_____ A good love relationship

_____ A satisfying religious faith

_____ Recognition as the most attractive person in the world

_____ An understanding of the meaning of life

_____ Success in my profession

_____ A personal contribution to the elimination of poverty and sickness

_____ A chance to direct the destiny of a nation

_____ Freedom to do what I want

_____ A satisfying and fulfilling marriage

_____ A happy family relationship

_____ Complete self-confidence

_____ Other: _____

Record these dates in your calendar: first day of class, last day to add a class, last day to drop a class without penalty, midpoint in the term, last day of classes, final exam period (first day and last day), official end of term, and holidays from classes.

Exercise 10.4 What Are Your Life Goals?

The following list includes some life goals that people set for themselves. This list can help you begin to think about the kinds of goals you may want to set. Check the goals you would like to achieve in your life. Next, review the goals you have checked and circle the five you want most. Finally, review your list of five goals and rank them by priority—1 for most important, 5 for least important.

Note: Adapted from _Human Potential Seminar,_ by James D. McHolland, Evanston, IL., 1975. Used by permission of the author.

Exercise 10.5 Personality Mosaic

Circle the numbers of the statements that clearly feel like something you might say or do or think. When you have finished, circle the same numbers on the answer grid on page 170.

1. It's important to me to have a strong, agile body.

2. I need to understand things thoroughly.

3. Music, color, beauty of any kind can really affect my moods.

4. People enrich my life and give it meaning.

5. I have confidence in myself that I can make things happen.

6. I appreciate clear directions so I know exactly what I can do.

7. I can usually carry/build/fix things myself.

8. I can get absorbed for hours in thinking something out.

9. I appreciate beautiful surroundings; color and design mean a lot to me.

10. I love company.

11. I enjoy competing.

12. I need to get my surroundings in order before I start a project.

13. I enjoy making things with my hands.

14. It's satisfying to explore new ideas.

15. I always seem to be looking for new ways to express my creativity.

16. I value being able to share personal concerns with people.

17. Being a key person in a group is very satisfying to me.

18. I take pride in being careful about all the details of my work.

19. I don't mind getting my hands dirty.

20. I see education as lifelong process of developing and sharpening my mind.

21. I love to dress in unusual ways, to try new colors and styles.

22. I can often sense when a person needs to talk to someone.

23. I enjoy getting people organized and on the move.

24. A good routine helps me get the job done.

25. I like to buy sensible things that I can make or work on myself.

26. Sometimes I can sit for hours and work on puzzles or read or just think about life.

27. I have a great imagination.

28. It makes me feel good to take care of people.

29. I like to have people rely on me to get the job done.

30. I'm satisfied knowing that I've done an assignment carefully and completely.

31. I'd rather be on my own doing practical, hands-on activities.

32. I'm eager to read about any subject that arouses my curiosity.

33. I love to try creative new ideas.

34. If I have a problem with someone, I prefer to talk it out and resolve it.

35. To be successful, it's important to aim high.

36. I prefer being in a position where I don't have to take responsibility for decisions.

37. I don't enjoy spending a lot of time discussing things. What's right is right.

38. I need to analyze a problem pretty thoroughly before I act on it.

39. I like to rearrange my surroundings to make them unique and different.

40. When I feel down, I find a friend to talk to.

41. After I suggest a plan, I prefer to let others take care of the details.

42. I'm usually content where I am.

43. It's invigorating to do things outdoors.

44. I keep asking "why."

45. I like my work to be an expression of my moods and feelings.

46. I like to find ways to help people care more for each other.

47. It's exciting to take part in important decisions.

48. I'm always glad to have someone else to take charge.

49. I like my surroundings to be plain and practical.

50. I need to stay with a problem until I figure out an answer.

51. The beauty of nature touches something deep inside me.

52. Close relationships are important to me.

53. Promotion and advancement are important to me.

54. Efficiency, for me, means doing a set amount carefully each day.

55. A strong system of law and order is important to prevent chaos.

56. Thought-provoking books always broaden my perspective.

57. I look forward to seeing art shows, plays, and good films.

58. I haven't seen you for so long. I'd love to know what you're doing.

59. It's exciting to be able to influence people.

60. Good, hard physical work never hurt anyone.

61. When I say I'll do it, I follow through on every detail.

62. I'd like to learn all there is to know about subjects that interest me.

63. I don't like to be like everyone else. I like to do things differently.

64. Tell me how I can help you.

65. I'm willing to take some risks to get ahead.

66. I like exact directions and clear rules when I start something new.

67. The first thing I look for in a car is a well-built engine.

68. Those people are intellectually stimulating.

69. When I'm creating, I tend to let everything else go.

70. I feel concerned that so many people in our society need help.

71. It's fun to get ideas across to people.

72. I hate it when they keep changing the system just when I get it down.

73. I usually know how to take care of things in an emergency.

74. Just reading about new discoveries is exciting.

75. I like to create happenings.

76. I often go out of my way to pay attention to people who seem lonely and friendless.

77. I love to bargain.

78. I don't like to do things unless I'm sure they're approved.

79. Sports are important in building strong bodies.

80. I've always been curious about the way nature works.

81. It's fun to be in a mood to try to do something unusual.

82. I believe that people are basically good.

83. If I don't make it the first time, I usually bounce back with energy and enthusiasm.

84. I appreciate knowing exactly what people expect of me.

85. I like to take things apart to see if I can fix them.

86. Don't get excited. We can think it out and plan the next move logically.

87. It would be hard to imagine my life without beauty around me.

88. People often seem to tell me their problems.

89. I can usually connect with people who get me in touch with a network of resources.

90. I don't need much to be happy.

Now circle the same numbers below that you circled above.

R	I	A	S	E	C
1	2	3	4	5	6
7	8	9	10	11	12
13	14	15	16	17	18
19	20	21	22	23	24
25	26	27	28	29	30
31	32	33	34	35	36
37	38	39	40	41	42
43	44	45	46	47	48
49	50	51	52	53	54
55	56	57	58	59	60
61	62	63	64	65	66
67	68	69	70	71	72
73	74	75	76	77	78
79	80	81	82	83	84
85	86	87	88	89	90

Now add up the number of circles in each column.

R _____ **I** _____ **A** _____ **S** _____ **E** _____ **C** _____

Which are your three highest scores?

1st _____ **2nd** _____ **3rd** _____

Now go back and reread the descriptions of these three types and see how accurately they describe you.

Note: From Betty Neville Michelozzi, *Coming Alive from Nine to Five,* 4th ed. Mountain View, CA: Mayfield, © 1980, 1984, 1988, 1992. Used by permission of the publisher.

Exercise 10.6 The Holland Hexagon

A Go back to Exercise 10.5 and look at your three categories. Based on the list of careers for each category that appeared earlier in this chapter, how well do the three categories match your career interests?

B Now look at the Holland hexagon in Figure 10.1. Are your first three choices close together or far apart? If far apart, do you feel they reflect a conflict in your goals or interests? If so, write a brief statement about how the conflict has affected you so far. Or comment on the relationship among your three categories and how they reflect your career thoughts.

_____

_____

_____

_____

Exercise 10.7 Writing a Résumé and Cover Letter

A Following the models in this chapter, prepare two résumés of your accomplishments to date, using the chronological model for one and the skills model for the other. Then, using either model, write another résumé that projects what you would like your résumé to contain 5 years from now.

B Using your career or campus library, find a professional whose career path matches your major/career interests. Write this person a cover letter to go with your résumé and turn it in to your instructor.

Your Personal Journal

Here are several things to write about. Choose one or more or choose another topic related to this chapter.

1. If you've met your academic advisor/counselor, write how you feel when you meet with this person and how helpful he or she is with regard to answering your questions and commenting on your concerns. If you have not met your advisor/counselor, write about why you haven't and when you will.

2. If you have chosen a major, write about the people or events in your life that led you to make this choice. If you haven't chosen a major, write about several majors you are thinking about and why. If you don't know what your major will be, explain why it has been difficult for you to make that choice.

3. What interests, skills, and aptitudes do you possess that might lead you to a specific career/major choice? What factors in your personality might also affect this decision?

4. What behaviors are you willing to change after reading this chapter?

5. What else is on your mind this week? If you wish to share it with your instructor, add it to your journal entry.

Resources

Thinking about what you want for a career may feel overwhelming, you may have a clear idea even now, or you may fall somewhere in-between. Career interest information, academic program information, and major and course descriptions can sometimes seem abstract. One thing that can help you find the best fit for your talents and strengths is to talk to people who are taking the courses, following the majors, and pursuing the careers that you are interested in. Use this Resources page to find people whom you could interview for information about courses, majors, and careers. Be creative. Over the years, this list could grow into a major networking tool.

STUDENTS WHO COULD BE RESOURCES FOR MAJORS AND COURSES

Name:	Major:	Course(s):	Phone number:

OTHER PEOPLE WHO COULD BE RESOURCEFUL FOR CAREER AREAS

Don't forget your advisor, instructors, relatives, family, and friends. Also include people you may have met volunteering.

Name:	Career/job title:	Phone number:

Relationships

Friends, Family, and Campus Involvement

get support

**IN THIS CHAPTER,
YOU WILL LEARN**

- What to consider in dating and mating

- The stages of a relationship

- When intimacy should occur—and when it shouldn't

- That multiple dating can be good for you, but not multiple sex partners

- How to handle marriage and school

- To appreciate why your parents are concerned about you

- Why choosing the right friends can have a marked effect on your life

- How to deal with roommates

- How to get involved on campus

- The benefits of service learning

*"*o many different kinds of people here. It's not like my high school class.
Should I stick with people who are more like me, or should I try to make friends
with a bunch of different kinds of people? Might learn something from them.
Then again, what I learn might not be so great, either."

Once in a while, a class is so good or so bad that you may write about it in your journal. Much of the time, however, you'll write about relationships: with dates, lovers, or lifelong partners; with friends and enemies; with parents and family; with roommates and classmates; and with new people and new groups.

Relationships are more than just aspects of your social life; they can also strongly influence your survival and success in college. Distracted by bad relationships, you can find it difficult to concentrate on your studies. Supported by good relationships, you will be better able to get through the rough times, reach your full potential, remain in college—and enjoy it.

Dating and Mating

Loving an Idealized Image

Carl Gustav Jung, the Swiss psychiatrist, identified a key aspect of love: the idealized image we have of the perfect partner, which we project onto potential partners we meet.

The first task of any romantic relationship, then, is to see that the person you are in love with really exists. You need to see beyond attraction to the person who is really there. Face it: Sex drives can be very powerful. Anything that can make your

SELF-ASSESSMENT: RELATIONSHIPS

Checkmark those statements that are true. Leave the others blank. After reading this chapter, come back to this inventory and place an X beside any item about which you now think differently.

_____ 1. It's okay to avoid gay people if you're not comfortable being around them.

_____ 2. It's true that the best relationship is with someone you could call your best friend.

_____ 3. Good sex is essential to a good relationship.

_____ 4. Having sex when one partner really doesn't want to is okay if it brings two people emotionally closer to one another.

_____ 5. If someone has a partner back home, they shouldn't consider dating anyone on campus.

_____ 6. If your parents get on your nerves, perhaps it's simply that they worry about you.

_____ 7. If a roommate is stubborn about living arrangements, there's little you can do—even if the behavior bothers you.

_____ 8. Joining campus organizations can help a student make new friends who share the same interests.

knees go weak and your mouth go dry at a single glance can affect your perceptions as well as your body. Are you in love, or are you in lust? People in lust often sincerely believe they are in love, and more than a few will say almost anything to get what they want. But would you still want that person if sex were out of the question? Would that person still want you? A no answer bodes poorly for a relationship.

Folklore says love is blind. Believe it. Check out your perceptions with trusted friends; if they see a lot of problems that you do not, at least listen to them. Another good reality check is to observe the friends of someone to whom you're attracted. Exceptional people rarely surround themselves with jerks and losers. If the person of your dreams tends to collect friends from your nightmares, watch out!

You should think carefully and repeatedly about what kind of person you really want in a relationship. If a prospective partner does not have the qualities you desire, don't pursue it.

Sexual Orientation

Although many people build intimate relationships with someone of the opposite sex, some people are attracted to, fall in love with, and make a long-term commitment to a person of the same sex. Your sexuality, and with whom you choose to form intimate relationships, is an important part of who you are.

An important component of understanding your own sexuality is listening closely to your own feelings, beliefs, and values. Your sexuality is your own; it isn't dictated by your family, by society, or by what the media present as normal. Although listening to your feelings is important, you will also find many resources if you are struggling with questions about your own sexuality. Talk about your feelings with someone you trust. Read some of the many books on the subject of sexuality and sexual orientation (some are listed in "Suggestions for Further Reading" at the end of this book). Whatever your sexual orientation, it is important to remember that relationships involving communication, trust, respect, and love are crucial to all people.

Developing a Relationship

Early in a relationship, you may be wildly "in love." You may find yourself preoccupied—if not obsessed—with the other person, with feelings of intense longing when you are apart. When you are together, you may feel thrilled and blissful, yet also insecure and demanding. You are likely to idealize the other person, yet you may overreact to faults or disappointments. If the relationship sours, your misery is likely to be intense, and the only apparent relief from your pain lies in the hands of the very person who rejected you. Social psychologist Elaine Walster calls this the stage of *passionate love.*

Most psychologists see the first stage as being unsustainable—and that may be a blessing! A successful relationship will move on to a calmer, more stable stage. At this next stage, your picture of your partner is much more realistic. You feel comfortable and secure with each other. Your mutual love and respect stem from predictably satisfying companionship. Walster calls this stage *companionate love.*

If a relationship is to last, it is vital to talk about it as you go along. What are you enjoying, and why? What is disappointing you, and what would make it better? Is there anything you need to know? Set aside a regular time and place to talk every week or two as the relationship first becomes serious. Never let more than a month or two go by without one of these talks—even if all you have to say is that things are going great.

Most relationships change significantly when they turn into long-distance romances. Many students arrive at college carrying a torch for someone back home or

Examining Values

It's nearly impossible to talk about relationships without getting into a discussion about values. Think about what you value most in a relationship, whether it's with a partner, a friend, your family, a teacher, or an advisor/counselor. Make a list of at least five values for two or more of the people in the previous sentence. Now prioritize the values for each person, with the most important value at the top of your list. Are the lists the same? If not, why do you value certain things in one person and different ones in another? If the lists are identical, what does this tell you about how you approach relationships?

at another school. College is an exciting scene with many social opportunities. If you restrict yourself to a single absent partner, you may miss out on a lot, and cheating or resentment can be the result.

We advise you to keep seeing each other as long as you want, but with the freedom to pursue other relationships, too. If the best person for you turns out to be the person from whom you are separated, this will become evident.

Becoming Intimate

Sexual intimacy inevitably adds a new and powerful dimension to a relationship. We suggest the following:

- **Don't hurry into it.**
- **If sexual activity would violate your morals or values, don't do it.** And don't expect others to violate theirs. It is important to explain your values so that your partner will understand your decision, but you do not owe anyone a justification, nor should you put up with attempts to argue you into submission.
- **If you have to ply your partner with alcohol or other drugs to get the ball rolling, you aren't engaging in sex—you are committing rape.**
- **A pregnancy will certainly curtail your youth and social life.** Conception can occur even when couples take precautions. Data based on real-life use indicate that students who are sexually active for 5 years of college and use condoms for birth control all 5 years have around a 20 to 50 percent chance of a pregnancy (depending on how carefully and consistently they use condoms).

Here are some warning signs that should concern you:

- **Having sex when you don't really want to** If desire and pleasure are missing, you are doing the wrong thing.
- **Guilt or anxiety afterward** This is a sign of a wrong decision—or at least a premature one.
- **Having sex because your partner expects or demands it**
- **Having sex with people to attract or keep them** This is generally shortsighted and unwise. It will almost surely lower your self-esteem.
- **Becoming physically intimate when what you really want is emotional intimacy**

When passions run high, physical intimacy can feel like emotional intimacy, but sex is an unsatisfying substitute for love or friendship. Genuine emotional intimacy is knowing, trusting, loving, and respecting each other at the deepest levels, day in and day out, independent of sex. Establishing emotional intimacy takes time—and, in many ways, more courage. If you build the emotional intimacy first, not only the relationship but also the sex will be better.

Believe it or not, a thorough review of the literature on happiness finds no evidence that becoming sexually active increases your general happiness. If you are expecting sex to make you happy or to make your partner happy, the fact is that it probably won't for long. Sex relieves horniness, but it doesn't make happiness. Loving relationships, on the other hand, are powerfully related to happiness.

If you want sexual activity but don't want all the medical risks of sex, consider the practice of "outercourse": mutual and loving stimulation between partners that allows sexual release but involves no exchange of bodily fluids. This will definitely require direct and effective communication, but it is an option that can be satisfying and fun in its own way.

Getting Serious

You may have a relationship that you feel is really working. Why make it exclusive just because being only with each other has become a habit? Instead, ask yourself why you want this relationship to be exclusive. For security? To prevent jealousy? To build depth and trust? As a prelude to permanent commitment? An exclusive relationship is a big commitment. Before you make the decision to see only each other, make sure it is the best thing for each of you. You may find that you treat each other best and appreciate each other most when you have other opportunities to date.

Although dating more than one person can help you clarify what you want, multiple sexual relationships can be dangerous. Besides the health risks involved, it's rare to find a good working relationship if the partners have had sex with others. Sexual jealousy is very powerful and can arouse insecurities, anger, and hurt.

Being exclusive provides the chance to get a taste of what marriage might be like. But consider this: Studies show that the younger you are, the lower are your odds of a successful marriage. It also may surprise you to learn that trial marriage, or living together, does not decrease your risk of later divorce.

Above all, beware of marrying before both you and your partner know who you are and what you want to do in life. Many 18- to 20-year-olds change their outlook and life goals drastically. The person who seems just right for you now may be terribly wrong for you within 5 or 10 years. Why not wait to make a permanent commitment until you feel secure by yourself?

SEE SEARCH ONLINE! INTERNET EXERCISE 11.1

If you want to marry, the person to marry is someone you could call your best friend—the one who knows you inside and out, the one with whom you don't have to play games, the one who prizes your company without physical rewards, the one who over a period of years has come to know, love, and respect who you are and what you want to be.

Breaking Up

When you break up, you lose not only what you had but also everything you thought you had, including a lot of hopes and dreams. No wonder it hurts. But remember that you are also opening up a world of new possibilities that you may not see right away.

If it is time to break up, do it cleanly and calmly. Don't be impulsive or angry. Explain your feelings and talk them out. If you don't get a mature reaction, take the high road; don't join someone else in the mud. If you decide to reunite after a trial separation, be sure enough time has passed for you to evaluate the situation effectively. If things fail a second time, you really may need to forget it.

If you are married or have children, take steps to involve your loved ones in your college life.

What about being "just friends"? You may want to remain friends with your partner, but you can't really be friends until you have both healed from the hurt and neither of you wants the old relationship back. That may take at least a year or two.

If you are having trouble getting out of a relationship or dealing with its end, get help. Expect some pain, anger, and depression. Your college counseling center has assisted many students through similar difficulties. It is also a good time to get moral support from friends and family. There are good books on the subject, including *How to Survive the Loss of a Love* (see "Suggestions for Further Reading" at the end of this book).

Married Life in College

Both marriage and college are challenges. With so many demands, it is critically important that you and your partner share the burdens equally. Academic and financial pressures are likely to put extra strain on any relationship, so you are going to have to work extra hard at attending to each other's needs.

If you are in college but your spouse is not, it is important to bring your partner into your college life. Share what you are learning in your courses. See if your partner can take a course, too—maybe just audit for the fun of it. Take your partner to cultural events—lectures, plays, concerts—on your campus. If your campus has social organizations for students' spouses, try them out.

Relationships with spouses and children can suffer when you are in college because you will be tempted to take time you would normally spend with your loved ones and put it into your studies instead. It's very important to schedule time for your partner and family just as you schedule your classes, and keep to the schedule just as carefully.

SEE EXERCISE 11.1

You and Your Parents

If you are on your own for the first time, your relationship with your parents is going to change. Home will never be as you left it, and you will not be who you were before. So how can you have good relationships with your parents during this period of major change?

A first step in establishing a good relationship with your parents is to be aware of their perceptions. The following are the most common ones:

- **You'll harm yourself.** You may take risks that make older people shudder. You may shudder, too, when you look back on some of your stunts. Sometimes your parents have reason to worry.
- **Their daughter is still a young innocent.** And yes, the old double standard (differing expectations for men than women, particularly regarding sex) is still alive and well.
- **Although you're 20, they picture you as 10.** Somehow, the parental clock always lags behind reality. Maybe it's because they loved you so much as a child.

Parents mean well. Most love their children, even if it doesn't come out right; very few are really indifferent or hateful. Yet not every family works. If your family is like the Brady Bunch, you are blessed, but some families are truly dysfunctional. If love, respect, enthusiasm, and encouragement just are not in the cards, look around you: Other people will give you these things, and you can create the family you need. With your emotional needs satisfied, your reactions to your real family can become much less painful.

SEE EXERCISE 11.2

SEE EXERCISE 11.3

The old have been young, but the young haven't been old. Parental memories of youth may be hazy, but at least they've been there. To paraphrase Mark Twain, when you are beginning college, you may think your parents rather foolish; but when you graduate, you'll be surprised how much they've learned in 4 years. Try setting aside regular times to update them on how college and your life in general are going. Ask for and consider their advice. You don't have to take it. Finally, realize that your parents are not here forever. Show them they matter to you whenever you can.

Friends

Studies show that the people who influence you the most are your friends. Choose them carefully.

If you want a friend, be a friend. Learn to be an attentive listener. Give your opinion when people ask for it. Keep your comments polite and positive. Never violate a confidence. Offer an encouraging word and a helping hand whenever you can. You'll be amazed how many people will respect your opinions and seek your friendship.

Your friends are usually people whose attitudes, goals, and experiences are similar to your own. But in your personal life, just as in the classroom, you have the most to learn from people who are different from you. To enrich your college experience, make a conscious effort to make friends who embody one or more of the following:

Of the opposite sex	Of another race
Of another nationality	Of a different sexual orientation
Have a physical disability	On an athletic scholarship
Of a very different age	From a very different religion
Have very different politics	Have very different interests

These friendships may take more time and effort, but you will have more than just new friends; you will have learned to appreciate and get along with a much wider variety of people.

Roommates

Adjusting to a roommate on or off campus can be difficult. Roommates range from the ridiculous to the sublime. You may make a lifetime friend or an exasperating acquaintance you wish you'd never known. A roommate doesn't have to be a best friend—just someone with whom you can share your living space comfortably. Your best friend may not make the best roommate; many students have lost friends by rooming together.

If you are rooming with a stranger, establish your mutual rights and responsibilities in writing. Many colleges provide contract forms that you and your roommate can use. If things go wrong later, you will have something to point to.

If you have problems, talk them out promptly. Talk politely but plainly. If problems persist or if you don't know how to talk them out, ask your residence hall counselor for help.

SEE EXERCISE 11.4

Normally, you can tolerate (and learn from) a less than ideal situation; but if things get serious, insist on a change—your residence counselor will know how to help you.

Campus Involvement

New students who become involved with at least one organization are more likely to survive their first year and remain in college. Almost every college has numerous organizations, and you usually can check them out through activity fairs, printed guides, open houses, Web pages, and so on. Organizations help you find friends with similar interests. Together you can accomplish things you've never done before.

Fraternities and sororities also can be a rich source of friends and support. Some students love them; others find them philosophically distasteful, too demanding of time and finances, or too constricting. Fraternities and sororities are powerful social influences, so you'll probably want to take a good look at the upper-class students in them. If what you see is what you want to be, consider joining. If not, steer clear.

Another good place to make friends is on the job. A special kind of job opportunity available at many schools is called co-op. These programs place you in temporary, paid positions with organizations that hire students in your major. Not only will you get excellent firsthand experience working in your field, but you also will make contacts and possibly obtain a reference that may help after graduation.

SEE EXERCISE 11.5

Critical Thinking

Relationships

Look back at the section on "You and Your Parents" on pages 178-179. Think about the things you do that may not seem to be "risks" to you but that would make your parents shudder. If your parents seem to be treating you like a 10-year-old, does it have anything to do with your behavior while you're away from them? Putting yourself in your parents' shoes, write some things they might be thinking or telling one another about why they're worried about you. Then look at all the reasons you've written and, pretending you're writing to your parents, justify your behaviors in a logical manner. Read it again. If it sounds defensive, rewrite your answers until you believe you could speak these words to your parents and not cause a scene.

Learning Through Service

More than a half million students served nearly 30 million hours last year to benefit their communities as they learned.

SIX REASONS TO SERVE

1. You can improve the quality of life for many living in your local community.
2. You can put your critical thinking skills to practical use. Service allows you to apply classroom knowledge to real-world problems.
3. You can develop leadership skills by developing a service project and encouraging other students to get involved.
4. You can discover a variety of potential careers.
5. You'll meet new friends who share your interest in service.
6. You'll expand your ability to empathize with people of different ages and ethnicities.

FINDING A SERVICE OPPORTUNITY

1. Check with your campus community service office or career center.
2. Join a student organization that performs community service.
3. Start a service organization yourself.
4. Contact community agencies such as United Way for a list of service opportunities. Also check with Rotary and Lions clubs, YMCAs, churches and synagogues, and local government.
5. Search the Web for service-learning opportunities.

DIFFERENT WAYS TO SERVE

1. Short term: Play with children at their homes; help build a house for the poor; spend time with the elderly.
2. Long term: Tutor a child once a week; teach literacy; mentor a mentally or physically challenged child; serve food in a shelter once a week.
3. Longer term: Check with the Peace Corps, VISTA (Volunteers in Service to America), or Americorp.

If your days are packed with classes, try volunteering in the evening and during fall and spring breaks. Find projects connected with your classes. You could help at a local shelter as the basis for an English essay or write about local environmental problems for a biology course. Building a house for a family might help you design your own house in an architecture class.

You may even qualify for pay. Check with your financial aid office to see what types of paid service projects are available. Even if you don't qualify for work-study, you still may be able to get a service scholarship.

–David Janes, University of South Carolina

A word of advice: Avoid starting romantic relationships on the job. Dating someone who works over or under you creates problems in a hurry. Even if you are on the same level, you may feel awkward or miserable if the relationship ends but the two of you must still work together.

Relationships are an integral part of your college experience and can consume up to two-thirds of your waking hours. Whether you're a traditional-age new student or a returning student with family responsibilities, be sure to approach your relationships with the same effort and planning as you would approach your course work. Take life as it happens, but try to make it happen the way you would like. Long after you have forgotten courses you took, you will remember relationships that began or continued in college.

SEE SEARCH ONLINE!
INTERNET EXERCISE 11.2

Search Online! 《●》

Internet Exercise 11.1 Relationships and the Web

A *Join a Mailing List.* Discussion on the Internet often includes stories of happy couples who met on the Internet, as well as stories of people who have created fake identities. From one extreme to the other, the Internet provides numerous opportunities for social interchange.

Using the LISZT index of mailing lists, at *http://www.liszt.com/*, locate a mailing list of interest to you.

Name of mailing list _____

Content _____

Address for joining _____

Join the mailing list. What kind of mail do you receive from the list? Is it helpful? What have you learned from it?

B *Visit a Chat Group.* Using the Yahoo index of chat groups, at *http://www.yahoo.com/ Computers_and_Internet/Internet/World_Wide_Web/Chat/*, locate a chat group of interest:

Interest area _____

Name of chat group _____

Address _____

Log on and see what is being discussed. Is this a chat group you would like to join? What would you gain from being part of it?

C *Find newsgroups.* Scan the list of newsgroups available from your Internet provider.

- With Netscape Navigator 4.0, click on Window/Netscape News/Options/Show All Newsgroups.
- With Internet Explorer 4.0, click on Mail/Read News/News/Newsgroups.

Both major browsers, in their enlarged versions, now allow you to read newsgroups with the same tool used for reading e-mail. Netscape Navigator 4.0 includes Netscape Messenger; Microsoft Internet Explorer includes Outlook Express.

- With Netscape Communicator, select Communicator/Collabra Discussion Group.
- With Outlook Express, select Go/News.

Locate a newsgroup of interest to you:

Area of interest _____

Name _____

Scan the recent postings and make a list of the major topics being discussed.

D *Connect with a Long-Distance Friend.* Using the address *http://www.qucis.queensu.ca/FAQs/email/college.html*, locate the e-mail address of a friend or relative on another campus:

Name _____

College _____

E-mail address _____

Exchange e-mail. (Go to *http://success.wadsworth.com* for the most up-to-date URLs.)

Search Online! 《 ● 》

Internet Exercise 11.2 Discovering More About Relationships

Using *InfoTrac College Edition,* try these phrases and others for key-word and subject-guide searches: "college students and love," "college students and parents," "extracurricular activities and college," and "service learning."

ALSO LOOK UP:

Living with a stranger: thrown together, roommates can become the best of friends–or enemies. (Colleges: Best Buys) Viva Hardigg.
   U.S. News & World Report, Sept 25, 1995 v119 n12 p90(2)

Inner-city youth test their wings in possible careers. Metta Winter. *Human Ecology Forum* Fall 1998 v26 i4 p21(3)

The other curriculum: out-of-class experiences associated with student learning and personal development. George D. Kuh.
   Journal of Higher Education, Mar-Apr 1995 v66 n2 (33)

The new generation speaks out; student leaders discuss racism, love, sex and the black male-black female thing.
   (includes student profiles) Nicole Walker. *Ebony* Nov 1997 v53 nl p158

Additional Exercises

These exercises will help you sharpen what we believe are the critical skills for college success: writing, critical thinking, learning in groups, planning, reflecting, and taking action. Also, check out the CD-ROM that came with your book—you will find these exercises and more.

Exercise 11.1 Balancing Relationships and College

A   If you are in a relationship, what are the greatest concerns you have about balancing your educational responsibilities with your responsibilities to your partner? What can you do to improve the situation? If the balance poses a serious problem for you, is there someone on campus you can seek for counseling? If you're not sure where to turn, ask your instructor to help you find that person. Write a paper expressing your thoughts and consider using it in a group discussion with other students who have completed similar papers.

B   If you are married and have children, write a letter to your spouse and another to your children, explaining why you must often devote time to your studies instead of to them. Don't deliver the letters; read them first and keep revising them until they sound realistic and convincing. Attempt to strike a sensible balance between your commitments to family and to your future academic and professional growth. If there are other married students in your class, share letters and get reactions. Then decide whether it's prudent to actually share these thoughts with spouse and children.

Exercise 11.2 Gripes

A   Student Gripes. In surveys, these are the most frequent student gripes about parents. Checkmark the ones that hit closest to home for you:

_____ Why are parents so overbearing and controlling, telling you everything from what to major in to whom to date?

_____ Why do parents treat you like a child? Why are they so overprotective?

____ Why do parents worry so much?

____ Why do parents complain so much about money?

____ Why are parents so hard to talk to?

____ Parents say they want to know what's going on in my life, but if I told them everything they'd go ballistic and I'd never hear the end of it!

Reflect on the gripes you checked. Why do you think your parents are like that? How do your thoughts affect your relations with them?

B   Parent Gripes. Looking at things from the other side, students report the following as the most common gripes that their parents have about them. Checkmark those that ring true for your parents:

____ Why don't you call and visit more?

____ Why don't you tell us more about what is going on?

____ When you are home, why do you ignore us and spend all your time with your friends?

____ (if dating seriously) Why do you spend so much time with your boyfriend or girlfriend?

____ Why do you need so much money?

____ Why aren't your grades better, and why don't you appreciate the importance of school?

____ Why don't you listen to us about getting into the right major and courses? You'll never get a good job if you don't.

____ What have you done to yourself? Where did you get that (haircut, tattoo, style of clothes, and so on)?

____ Why don't you listen to us and do what we tell you? You need a better attitude!

How do such thoughts affect your parents? What do you think that they are really trying to tell you?

Exercise 11.3 **Five over Age 30**
Select five adults over age 30 whom you respect. Ask each the following questions.

- What were the best decisions you made when you were 18 to 22?
- What were the biggest mistakes you made in those years?
- What advice would you give someone who is 18?

Are there common themes in what they say? How good is their advice? Write a summary, bring it to class, and be prepared to share it.

Exercise 11.4 **Common Roommate Gripes**
Housing authorities report that the most common areas of conflict between roommates are those listed below. Checkmark those that are true for you.

____ One roommate needs quiet to study; the other needs music or sound.

____ One roommate is neat; the other is messy.

____ One roommate smokes; the other resents smoke.

____ One roommate feels free to bring in lots of guests; the other finds them obnoxious.

____ One roommate brings in romantic bedmates and wants privacy—or goes at it right in front of the other; the other is uncomfortable with this and feels banished from the room that he or she paid for.

____ One roommate likes the room warm; the other likes it cool.

____ One roommate considers the room a place to have fun; the other considers it a place to get studying done.

____ One roommate likes to borrow; the other doesn't.

____ One roommate is a morning person; the other is a night owl.

____ One roommate wants silence while sleeping; the other feels free to make noise.

____ One roommate wants to follow all the residence hall rules; the other wants to break them.

If you are rooming with someone, review this checklist and write about what you and your roommate(s) can do to improve the situation. If you live alone, which of these gripes would be reason for you to not want to share? How might you overcome such situations if they arose?

Exercise 11.5 **Connecting with Campus Organizations**
Get a list of your campus organizations from your campus student center. Choose six in which you might enjoy participating. Find out more about each: Attend a meeting, talk to an officer, or obtain and read detailed information. Choose two with which you would like to get involved this term. Bring your list to class and be prepared to discuss what you found and your reasons for the selections you made.

Your Personal Journal

Here are several things to write about. Choose one or more or choose another topic related to this chapter.
1. If the person you were in a relationship with before you came to college is far, far away, how are you handling your feelings about this? What things are you doing to make the separation easier?
2. If you are in or have been in a relationship, how can you apply the discussion of passionate and companionate love to your relationship? At which stage did the relationship become more meaningful? Why do you think this was?
3. The chapter advises college students to give themselves a chance to date others before making a final commitment to an individual. What's your reaction to that?
4. If you are a married student, what do you see as your biggest problem in balancing family and education? What are you doing to cope with it?
5. If you have made friends with people who are different from you, write about those relationships and tell what you have learned from them.
6. If you have a roommate, name the best things and the worst things about living with this person. Then tell what you should be doing to eliminate the things that bother you.
7. What behaviors are you willing to change after reading this chapter? How might you go about changing them?
8. What else is on your mind this week? If you wish to share it with your instructor, add it to this journal entry.

Resources

Relationships are important throughout life, and the support you get from them can keep you going with confidence and strength, especially during times of transition—moving to a new place, starting college, changing jobs, changing life situations. During transition times you can feel all alone, with no one to really support you. You probably have more resources than you realize. Use this Resources page to create a map of the relationships in your life. (See the example. Add photos if you want to transfer your map to a larger sheet of paper and make a collage of the important people in your life.) When you are feeling down, stressed, or alone, take a minute to look at this page and see the connections you have with other people. Give someone a call, write a letter, drop by to visit, or simply remember the good feelings and times your relationships bring you.

Example:

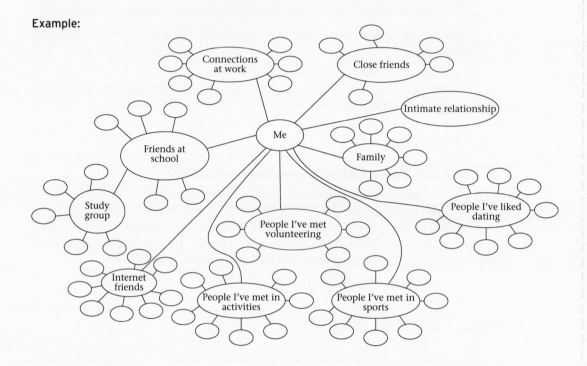

Create your map here:

Diversity

Celebrating Differences in Culture, Age, Gender, and Abilities

IN THIS CHAPTER, YOU WILL LEARN

- The difference between the "melting pot" and the "vegetable stew"

- That *diversity* means much more than cultural difference

- The value of sharing your uniqueness with others

- What colleges are doing to promote healthy diversity

- How to fight discrimination and prejudice on campus

- How the old minority is becoming "the new majority"

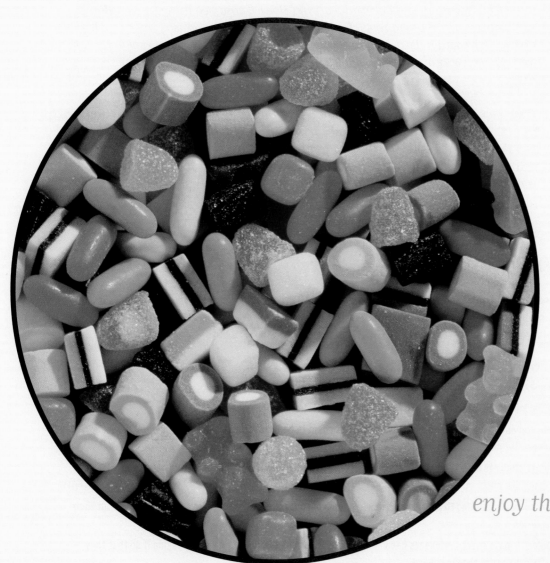

enjoy the variety

"I know diversity is in these days, but I'm not much into talking about it. I'm not even sure what it means. We had diversity celebration days in high school, but nobody took them very seriously. They seemed to separate us, not bring us together. I'm open to meeting other people, but I don't want to force anything. Live and let live."

Ask almost any person in this country about his or her background and you have the start of an interesting story:

My racial background is African American. The other thing I would add is that I see my background as Black and working class. Those two things go together for me; they are a part of my roots. I was born in California and was raised in Texas during segregation. Part of me grew up in a strongly segregated part of the South, and another part of me, as an adolescent, grew up in integrated California.

—Terrell

I'm American. I don't feel like I have a strong attachment to any particular group. My family is Italian, Polish, Irish, and French. On St. Patrick's Day, I say I'm Irish. If I go to an Italian restaurant, I pretend I'm Italian! I call one grandmother "Bapshee," and that's about how bilingual I am. Maybe I'm not anything.

—Eric

SELF-ASSESSMENT: DIVERSITY

Checkmark those statements that are true. Leave the others blank. After reading this chapter, come back to this inventory and place an X beside any item about which you now think differently.

_____ 1. Some of my good friends are people of other cultures and races.

_____ 2. I believe that "staying with your kind" puts less stress on friendships.

_____ 3. I'm not always comfortable with people of other cultures or races.

_____ 4. I'm uncomfortable when I know someone's sexual preference is different from mine.

_____ 5. Older students have their own agendas. They don't seem to be interested in making friends with younger students like me.

_____ 6. Younger students have their own agendas. They don't seem to be interested in making friends with older students like me.

_____ 7. I tend to avoid speaking to physically disabled people because it might make them self-conscious about their disabilities.

_____ 8. People who have special privileges because they are "learning disabled" are usually faking it so that they can have an easier time in college.

I am tired of pretending I am someone I'm not. I need the community of other gay people to help me deal with the homophobia on campus, and I want to celebrate a part of me that I have come to accept and love. Believe me, my life would be a lot easier if I could accept the "normal" heterosexual lifestyle that society keeps shoving down my throat. What do I want from life? I want what most people want—the chance to go to school, have friends, get a job, and find someone to love.

—Gary

I'm 42 and I've just started college. Guess that makes me part of a "different" group, too. I hate when 20-year-old students talk to me as if I were their mom. I share many of their interests . . . well, music's another thing! I was afraid I'd be challenged by all these bright, eager minds. But, you know what? I have a high B average and intend to keep it that way.

SEE EXERCISE 12.1

—Joanne

I jumped off a pier into shallow water when I was 14 and injured my spinal cord. So I'm confined to a wheelchair. But that hasn't stopped me from passing college courses. The college provides me with special housing, writers, and caretakers. I find that if I joke about my wheelchair in class that students are not as put off by it. One of the hardest things is to tell other students not to help me too much. It makes me feel like they're sorry for me. Besides, I need to do my own work.

—Dan

Expanding Our View of Diversity

Think of diversity and you probably think of cultural differences. He's White. She's Black. He's Italian. She's Lebanese. All well and good, but diversity on a campus and in life includes many more groups whose members share something in common.

If college is a place where you seek an education and develop values for life, appreciating and being tolerant of people who are different from you is one of its major lessons. Regardless of the group to which you belong, all college graduates share one thing in common: a degree that is the mark of an educated person. If you avoid the chance to know people from other groups, you'll be missing out on many of the benefits of your education.

Gays and Lesbians   To create a welcoming environment for gay and lesbian students, we must first unlearn stereotypical notions. For example, you can't tell someone's sexual orientation just by appearance. Just because a person is gay or lesbian doesn't mean he or she is attracted to all people of the same sex (are you attracted to all people of the opposite sex?). Also, being gay or lesbian is not always a choice. Each year, scientists find further evidence indicating that sexual orientation may be influenced by genetic as well as environmental factors.

SEE SEARCH ONLINE!
INTERNET EXERCISE 12.1

Returning Students   Adult students (those 25 and older) are enrolling in college courses in record numbers. Women may make this choice because children have grown up and it's a chance to learn skills for a new career. Other adults, men and women, may decide it's time to broaden their horizons or prepare themselves for a better job with a higher starting salary. Many returning students work full time and attend school part time. Their persistence is remarkable, given the stressors of family and work. One study found that older women in college were less stressed than younger students, partly because they had grown accustomed to wearing two or more hats while raising children, working, and living lives. Colleges have accom-

Examining Values

Make a list of negative stereotypical judgments you've heard about people of other races, cultures, and sexual preferences as well as older people and disabled people. Some of these—all incorrect—are: "All African Americans are angry at White students." "White students look down their noses at anyone who isn't White." "Gays and lesbians are always on the make for anyone they can catch." "Older students are too serious about college." "Handicapped students just want your sympathy all the time." When you've written your own list, reflect on what values instilled in you by family, friends, and experiences have caused you to either accept or reject such thoughts. Write it down.

modated the needs of adults with distance education courses, night courses, and other innovations.

Disabled Students   Learning disabled students are those who cannot learn some academic skills, such as listening, thinking, speaking, writing, spelling, or doing math calculations. The number of college students with learning disabilities continues to grow since learning disabled people tend to be as motivated as their nondisabled peers. Even though they lack the ability to learn some skill or skills, learning disabled students have normal or above normal intelligence and are motivated to learn coping strategies that aid them in facing different types of academic situations. Whereas learning disabled students are ordinary in appearance, physically disabled students are easy to spot. This means that not only do they require special care but they also must learn to defuse the perception among their student peers that they're unapproachable. Most campuses have a disabled students office where both types of disabilities are treated.

Race, Ethnic Groups, and Culture

The word *race* generally refers to a group of people who are distinct from other people in terms of certain inherited characteristics: skin color, hair color, hair texture, body build, and facial features. *Ethnic group* can refer to people of different races or to people of the same race who can be distinguished by language, national origin, religious tradition, and so on.

Culture refers to the material and nonmaterial products that people in a society create or acquire from other societies and pass on to future generations. Culture includes a society's beliefs, values, norms, and language. For example, many European societies believe children should learn how to be independent and self-sufficient at an early age, whereas Hispanic Americans tend to place a high value on strong family obligations. Culture may also include such tangible items as cellular phones, futons, basketballs, and college yearbooks.

As people from different ethnic groups marry one another and have children, the word *race* is slowly becoming insufficient as a descriptor of individuals with mixed heritages, and many such people are refusing to fill in the line asking for "race" on numerous government and business forms, especially when their only choices are White, Black, Asian, Hispanic, and the ubiquitous "Other."

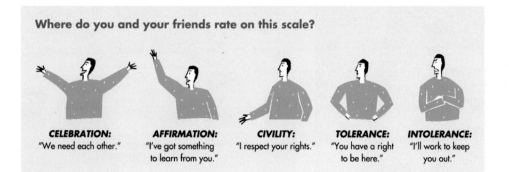

Where do you and your friends rate on this scale?

CELEBRATION:
"We need each other."

AFFIRMATION:
"I've got something to learn from you."

CIVILITY:
"I respect your rights."

TOLERANCE:
"You have a right to be here."

INTOLERANCE:
"I'll work to keep you out."

FIGURE 12.1 A Diversity Attitude Scale

Cultural Pluralism: Replacing the Melting Pot with Vegetable Stew

For years, students were taught that immigration created a melting pot—as diverse groups migrated to this land, their culture, religion, and customs mixed into this American pot to create a new society. The reality of what happened is more complex. Instead of melting into the pot, most immigrants were asked to adopt the culture of those already here, creating an Anglo-European soup.

In order to get ahead, immigrants had to change their names to more Anglo-American spellings. They had to make sure their children learned English, and they had to do business the American way. Some groups could accomplish this more easily, although not without experiencing some discrimination. Today, members of different cultural groups may be more likely to see themselves as Eric does—"just American." At the same time, many European Americans have retained strong ethnic ties, while many non-European groups (for example, Africans, Japanese, and Chinese) have found both laws and racial barriers impeding their integration into the culture at large.

SEE EXERCISE 12.2

As a result, many sociologists and educators have concluded that American society is less like a melting pot and more like a vegetable stew. Although all groups together create a common broth, each group has its own unique characteristics and flavor. The dominant culture gradually has begun to acknowledge and affirm the diversity of cultures within its borders. After years of stressing our ability to be assimilated into the American culture, we are now focusing on our differences, too.

Cultural pluralism has replaced the melting pot theory. Under cultural pluralism, each group celebrates and practices its customs and traditions, while also participating in the general mainstream culture. "Unity in diversity" is the new rallying cry.

Whoever you are, in some ways you are part of that mainstream culture. In other ways, however, you probably feel that you are part of a smaller group, a microculture within society.

Cultural pluralism doesn't mean groups must remain isolated. In fact, as you learn more about another ethnic group's heritage, you may discover customs and traditions in which you would like to participate. Particular values stressed in one culture may appeal to you. For example, you may prefer the punctuality emphasized in European American cultures or the more relaxed time schedule of Arab Americans. You may value the sense of duty and family obligation among Hispanic Americans or admire the sense of individual control and independence offered in the Anglo culture. Or your preferences may be directed toward the language, music, food, dress, dance, architecture, or religion of another culture.

Most colleges make an effort to help students feel welcome, respected, and supported in every way that the students themselves feel is important.

If you are going to accept and affirm the differences of other groups, each group needs to be ready to listen to the other without criticism, instead of simply assuming that a different perspective is misguided, wrong, or backward.

A Diverse Campus Culture

How diverse is your campus? Are you aware of the diversity that exists there? In what ways does your school encourage all students to feel welcome? How easy is it for students to express their culture and to learn about their culture or the cultures of others?

One way to answer these questions is by completing Exercise 12.3. For now, consider your campus diversity profile by answering the following questions based on your own observations in class, around campus, or elsewhere:

SEE EXERCISE 12.3

A. Diversity in Numbers
  1. In what ways are your student body, faculty, administrators, and staff diverse?
  2. What religious, linguistic, socioeconomic, gender, age, physical, and geographic differences have you observed among students?
B. Diversity in the Curriculum
  1. What are you learning about the contributions and concerns of people of color in your classes?
  2. What courses or workshops are available if you want to increase your racial awareness and understanding?
  3. Are courses offered that include the contributions and perspectives of gays and lesbians?
C. Diversity in Social and Residential Settings
  1. What individuals or groups are reflected in the artwork, sculpture, and names of buildings on your campus?
  2. What kinds of ethnic foods are served on a regular basis at the college dining facilities?
  3. If your school has campus residences, does the residential life staff schedule ongoing discussions regarding sexual orientation, disabilities, diversity, and tolerance? Who is in charge of these programs?
  4. Do students from different ethnic groups have organizations and hold social events? Give some examples. Does your campus support a variety of diverse activities brought to campus? Give some examples.
  5. Do gay and lesbian students have organizations and hold social events? Give some examples. Are there gay and lesbian support groups on campus? Who is in charge of these groups?

6. Do returning students (age 25 and older) have organizations and hold social events? Give examples. Are there special services for returning students on campus? What are they and what do they offer?

7. Where does cross-racial interaction exist on your campus? Is the atmosphere one of peaceful coexistence or resegregation? Where do students find opportunities to work, study, and socialize across racial/ethnic lines?

"I Know I Will Always Have a Cause I Am Fighting For"

Monita A. Johnson

It's been three years since I entered college. I was 18 and fresh out of high school when I journeyed to Hampton University.

I remember feeling scared and confused and thinking maybe this is not the right thing to do, then arriving at the beautiful campus and staring in awe at the old brick buildings. And the people, all the different Black faces. My apprehensions slowly fading.

I stayed at Hampton for two years and loved every day of it. However, the strain of tuition for a private university became too much. It was time for me to go back home.

I entered UC-Berkeley last fall. I felt I was really ready to battle and survive the competitiveness that I had heard so much about. I hung out in Berkeley when I was in high school. Yes, I was absolutely ready!

I knew I wanted to continue studying English, so I signed up for three classes: Shakespeare, American Literature, and an African American studies course. Shakespeare was great. I admit I was intimidated about taking the class with 300 students in a big auditorium. (At Hampton, my largest class was no more than 60 people.) Not to mention, I was one of about five African Americans in the class.

Shakespeare was a man before his time. He had a cause, I believe, to write about injustices he saw.

I was not as excited about my literature course. This was also a class of about 300 students, and again I was one of five. It's funny. When you're in a class that large, you begin to see how one can just fade away—our contributions, our struggle, our history. You almost forget you exist.

We read authors like T. S. Eliot, Virginia Woolf, and Henry James. I was not enthusiastic for this reason: Where are all the African American novelists? We did read Zora Neale Hurston's "Their Eyes Were Watching God," but that was all. This class focused on the modernist theme of "making it new"—authors from the late 1800s to the early 1960s. I can think of at least ten major African American writers who were pioneers then. We were "making it new" during the Harlem renaissance (the 1920s) with writers like Langston Hughes and Dorothy West. And we were around after that with Richard Wright, Ann Petry, and James Baldwin.

I asked my professor why we were only exploring European and American writers. She said African American writers of that time were mainly focused with writing the "protest novel," using literature to testify about the social and racial injustices African Americans endure. I struggled to understand why that was not as important and interesting as well.

I also took an African American studies course. I enjoyed it because I read authors from other ethnic cultures. I learned about Cesar Chavez and his efforts to organize Hispanic people to stand up for their rights. I learned about the migration of Korean families into America and the subhuman conditions they were forced to work under. Learning how similar all our struggles are sparked my interest and made me want to learn more.

At Berkeley I sometimes thought I was being watched and at any given moment one of the White students would come up and ask laughingly, "Do you really think you belong here?" I felt detached from social groups. Everything seemed different. It was hard to talk to my family about what I was going through.

I made it through the semester and—for whatever it is worth—academically, I did excellently. I also learned three valuable things. First, prestige has nothing to do with what a university can offer. Second, you are the only person responsible for making your educational experience all it can be. Third, grades don't mean a thing. It's what you learn and how you apply it that is important.

Recently I heard the writer and activist Amiri Braka say, "The conscious awareness of the need to struggle is priceless." I have not always understood why I have to constantly struggle. Becoming conscious of my struggle makes the issues much more personal! The challenge is understanding and fitting my people's fight within the greater circle.

My struggle has been to survive, just as those before me. And my mission is to pass on that courage to other young people like me, so that our spirit does not die.

San Francisco Examiner, May 3, 1998.
Used by permission.

D. Institutional Commitment to Diversity

1. How does your college mission statement address cultural pluralism? (Your college mission statement may be printed in the catalog.)

2. What policies and procedures does your school have with regard to the recruitment and retention of students of color? Contact your admissions office for information.

3. What policies and procedures does your school have with regard to the recruitment and hiring of faculty and staff of color? Contact your affirmative action/equal opportunity office for information.

4. Does your school administration feel responsible for educating students about diversity? Or does it assume that students and faculty will do this?

5. Does your school administration feel responsible for educating students about tolerance? Or does it assume that individual organizations will do this?

The New Majority

Why are institutions of higher learning so concerned about diversity on their campuses? By the year 2020 minorities will account for one-third of the population, and by the last quarter of the twenty-first century they will be a collective majority.*

As the general population has grown, so have the percentages of minority populations. Here are some of the groups currently considered minorities in the United States, although in some areas of the country they are actually in the majority.

African Americans

In 1990 African Americans made up about 12 percent (30 million) of the U.S. population.† For 1998 the projection was 34 million, or 12.7 percent. They come from diverse cultures and countries in Africa, the Caribbean, and Central and South America. Excluded from the mainstream White culture despite the end of slavery, they developed a system of historically Black colleges and universities dating from the mid-nineteenth century. These schools still award the majority of all bachelor's degrees received by African Americans.

Alaskan Native/American Indians

About 2 million (0.8 percent) Americans identified themselves as (non-Hispanic) Eskimo, Aleut, and American Indian in 1990, from more than 300 tribes. Their heritage includes more than 120 separate languages. By 1998 they were expected to reach 2.3 million, or 0.9 percent of the population.

Asian Americans

Since discriminatory immigration laws ended in 1965, Asians have become one of our fastest-growing groups. In 1990 they numbered 7.5 million, or 3 percent. By 1998 they were projected to grow to 10.2 million, or 3.8 percent of the population. The largest of the many groups are Chinese, Japanese, Korean, Asian Indian, Filipino, and Vietnamese.

Mexican Americans

All told, Hispanics in the United States were projected to reach 30 million, or 11.2 percent of the population, by 1998. Hispanics made up 9 percent of the U.S. population in 1990. The fastest-growing Hispanic group is Mexican Americans (almost 13 million). Mexican Americans have deep roots in the American Southwest from past centuries when that region belonged to Mexico and Spain. More than half of Mexican Americans live in Texas and California.

Puerto Ricans and Cuban Americans

Around 1990 Puerto Ricans living on the U.S. mainland numbered 2.3 million, and those living in Puerto Rico 3.3 million. All are U.S. citizens. There are more than 1 million Cuban Americans, mainly in Florida.

*Quality Education for Minorities Project, Education That Works (Cambridge: Massachusetts Institute of Technology, 1990.)

† This and other figures come from the U.S. Bureau of the Census.

Critical Thinking

Diversity

Do a search for an article or articles on discrimination. It might be something as simple as a private club that does not admit certain races or religions or as devastating as the Holocaust, which saw 6 million Jews go to their deaths at the hands of Germany's Nazi Party. Even though it may be difficult for you, try to be neutral so that you can seek the underlying causes for such discrimination and hate. What are the overriding ideas that lead to such situations? What do those ideas suggest? How can you organize your thoughts in a logical manner? Write a commentary on the situation you chose, attempting to provide a logical explanation for why some people choose to discriminate. Warning: Some of the logic may not make sense to you. Pursue it anyway to better understand what fuels prejudice and hate.

Discrimination and Prejudice on College Campuses

Unfortunately, incidences of discrimination and acts of prejudice are rising on college campuses. Although some schools may not be experiencing overt racial conflict, tension still exists; many students report having little contact with students from different racial or ethnic groups. Moreover, a national survey, "Taking America's Pulse," conducted for the National Conference of Christians and Jews, indicates that Blacks, Whites, Hispanics, and Asians hold many negative stereotypes about one another. The good news is that "nine out of 10 Americans nationwide claim they are willing to work with people of all races—even those they felt they had the least in common with—to advance race relations."*

Besides being morally and personally repugnant, you should know that discrimination is illegal. Most colleges and universities have established policies against all forms of racism, anti-Semitism, and ethnic and cultural intolerance. These policies prohibit racist actions or omissions, including verbal harassment or abuse that might deny anyone his or her rights to equity, dignity, culture, or religion.

SEE EXERCISE 12.4

SEE SEARCH ONLINE!
INTERNET EXERCISE 12.2

SEE EXERCISE 12.5

SEE EXERCISE 12.6

SEE SEARCH ONLINE!
INTERNET EXERCISE 12.3

Diversity is about more than racial or ethnic and religious backgrounds. It also encompasses gay, lesbian, bisexual, and transgender individuals who live in a world that is not always tolerant or accepting, much less affirming. All students grow when they learn to find pride in their own communities and to also accept the diverse groups around them.

*"Survey Finds Minorities Resent Whites and Each Other," *Jet*, 28 March 1994.

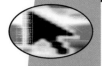

Internet Exercise 12.1 Questions About Homosexuality

The American Psychological Association's "Answers to Your Questions About Sexual Orientation and Homosexuality" page provides answers to the following questions. First, write your responses to the following questions and then look up the answers provided by the APA.

- Is sexual orientation a choice?
- Is homosexuality a mental illness or an emotional problem?
- Can lesbians and gay men be good parents?
- Can therapy change sexual orientation?

Now, compare your answers with the APA's answers, provided at *http://www.apa.org/pubinfo/orient.html.* (Go to *http://success.wadsworth.com* for the most up-to-date URLs.)

Internet Exercise 12.2 Diversity in the Population and on Campus

Estimate the percentage of each group listed both in the total U.S. population and in the U.S. undergraduate student population.

GENERAL POPULATION		UNDERGRADUATE POPULATION
American Indian	_____	_____
Asian	_____	_____
Black	_____	_____
White	_____	_____
Hispanic	_____	_____

Compare your estimates with the U.S. census national population projections, at *http://www.census.gov/population/projections/nation/nsrh/nprh9600.txt,* and *Digest of Education Statistics 1997,* at *http://nces.ed.gov/pubs/digest97/d97t207.html.* (Go to *http://success.wadsworth.com* for the most up-to-date URLs.)

- How far off were you in estimating the general population statistics?
- What conclusions can you draw about your perception of society?
- How far off were you in estimating the student population statistics?
- What conclusions can you draw about your perception of the student population?
- Locate statistics for your own institution on your institution's home page.

Internet Exercise 12.3 Discovering More About Diversity

Using *InfoTrac College Edition,* try these phrases and others for key-word and subject-guide searches: "diversity and campus," "ethnicity and campus," "hate crimes and campus," "disabilities and campus," and "gays and campus."

ALSO LOOK UP:

The adult learner challenge: instructionally and administratively. Randall Bowden, Richard Merritt, Jr. *Education* Spring 1995 v115 n3 p426(7)

Strength through cultural diversity. Barbara Heuberger, Diane Gerber, Reed Anderson. *College Teaching* Summer 1999 v47 i3 p107

Still a White man's world. (report on gender and race diversity of college athletic departments) (Brief Article) Richard Lapchick. *The Sporting News* Aug 23, 1999 v223 i34 p12

Teaching a simple lesson in fostering tolerance regarding personal choices. Joseph S. C. Simplicio. *Education* Fall 1995 v116 n1 p148(5)

Proposition 209 and the affirmative action debate on the University of California campuses. Ula Taylor. *Feminist Studies* Spring 1999 v25 i1 p95(1)

Additional Exercises

These exercises will help you sharpen what we believe are the critical skills for college success: writing, critical thinking, learning in groups, planning, reflecting, and taking action. Also, check out the CD-ROM that came with your book—you will find these exercises and more.

Exercise 12.1 Sharing Your Background

In the beginning of this chapter, a number of diverse students start to tell "their stories." Now it's your turn. Write a two-part essay. In the first part, describe the racial or ethnic groups to which you belong. Can you belong to more than one? Absolutely. Be sure to include some of the beliefs, values, and norms in your cultural background. How do you celebrate your background? What if you don't feel a strong attachment to any group? Write what you know about your family history and speculate on why your ethnic identity isn't very strong.

In the second part of your essay, discuss a time when you realized that your racial or ethnic background was not the same as someone else's. For example, young children imagine that their experiences are mirrored in the lives of others. If they are Jewish, then everyone else must be too. If their family eats okra for breakfast, then all families do the same. Yet at some point they begin to realize differences. When did you realize that you were African American or Hispanic American or European American or Korean American or whatever?

Share your essays with other members of the class. In what ways are your stories similar? In what ways are they different?

Exercise 12.2 Creating Common Ground

Examine the items in the following chart. For each item, decide whether you would describe your preferences, habits, and customs as reflecting the mainstream (macroculture) or a specific ethnic microculture. Enter specific examples of your own preferences in the appropriate column (two examples are given). For a given item, you may enter examples under both macroculture and microculture, or you may leave one or the other blank. In filling out the chart, you may want to look back at the essay you wrote in Exercise 12.1.

Category	Macroculture	Microculture
Language		
Food	hamburgers	sushi
Music (for your peer group)		
Style of dress (for your peer group)		
Religion		
Holidays celebrated		
Heroes/role models		
Key values	competition	cooperation (Native American)
Lifestyle		
Personal goals		

Compare answers in a small group. Do most people agree on what should be considered an example of the macroculture and what is an example of a microculture? Does anyone identify completely with the macroculture? Does anyone feel completely disconnected from the macroculture? What do you and others in your class regard as significant differences among you? In what areas do you share common ground?

Exercise 12.3 Getting the Diversity Facts on Your Campus

Consider campus diversity in a broader context—among the student body, faculty, administrators, and staff; in the curriculum; in social and residential settings; and at the institutional level (that is, the overall policies and procedures followed by the college). In groups of three to five, investigate one of the areas in the list on pages 192–194. Use the questions under each heading to help guide your research. Your instructor may be able to offer suggestions on where to locate relevant materials or appropriate people to interview. Each group should focus on two questions: (1) How easy is it for students to express their culture and to learn about their backgrounds or the backgrounds of others on this campus? (2) In what ways does our school try to make all students feel welcome? Groups should report their findings to the class.

Exercise 12.4 Checking Your Understanding

How clear is your understanding of discrimination and prejudice? Check your knowledge by circling T (true) or F (false) for each of the following:

T F   1. Positive stereotypes aren't harmful.

T F   2. Prejudice is personal preference usually based on inaccurate or insufficient information.

T F   3. The American Psychiatric Association lists homosexuality as a mental disorder.

T F   4. Racism combines prejudice with power.

T F   5. The problem of racism was solved years ago.

T F   6. Racism hurts everyone.

(See page 199 for the answers.)

Exercise 12.5 Combating Discrimination and Prejudice on Campus

What experiences have you had dealing with discrimination or prejudice on campus? Write briefly about the incident. Describe what happened and how you felt about it. Did you or anyone you know do anything about it? Did any administrator or faculty member do anything about it? Describe what was done. Do you think this was an effective way to deal with the incident? Explain.

If you have not experienced such problems, find out how your college would deal with acts of discrimination and prejudice. You may want to contact the campus affirmative action/equal opportunity office for information. Find out what steps students would need to take if they wished to follow up on an incident. Share your answers and information with other class members.

Exercise 12.6 Is Hate Speech Permitted on Your Campus?

In a small group, evaluate your campus policy on hate speech. Develop an argument for or against complete freedom of expression on Internet newsgroups accessible on campus computers. What values and what ideas about the nature of college or society does your argument reflect?

Answers to Exercise 12.4

1. *False.* Stereotypes, even if positive, assume that all members of a group are the same.

2. *True.* Racism reflects attitudes and actions rooted in ignorance.

3. *False.* The American Psychiatric Association removed homosexuality from its list of disorders in 1973.

4. *True.* Racism occurs when individuals use their prejudice to deny others their civil rights.

5. *False.* Check current newspapers, periodicals, and television reports for the latest incidents of racism.

6. *True.* Everyone benefits when all individuals are allowed to reach their full potential. A victim of racism might just be the person who could find a cure for AIDS.

Your Personal Journal

Here are several things to write about. Choose one or more or choose another topic related to this chapter.
1. Many people today are "pushing" for diversity. Others say, "Whatever will be will be. I don't think it's right to go out of my way to make friends with someone from another culture." What do you think?
2. When someone walks into the room and you know that person is gay, what is your normal reaction? Explain.
3. An older student arrives at class 10 minutes late each day and explains that she has to feed her child breakfast and drop him off at day care. How do you think the teacher should handle this?
4. A student in a wheelchair is taking notes, but it's a slow process. Should you offer to help or not? If you offer help, what might be the result? What is the best way to handle this situation?
5. How can you profit from having a diverse set of friends? How can they profit?
6. What else is on your mind this week? If you wish to share it with your instructor, add it to your journal entry.

Resources

How many connections with diverse communities do you already have in your life? Look back at the relationships map that you made for the Resources page in Chapter 11. Now copy part or all of your relationship map from Chapter 11 below. Using different color markers, highlight all the people (including yourself) by gender, age, racial/ethnic background, sexual orientation, religious background, and so on. Make a key at the bottom of the map to show which color represents which group. (Keep in mind that most people will fall into several groups.)

The next step is to educate yourself about communities you don't know as much about. For example, you may know a great deal about the contributions of Native Americans in U.S. history but know little about the role Asian Americans have played. You may know a lot about African-American artists but little about classical music. Consider some specific activities that would further your knowledge and understanding. For example, you could plan to attend a lecture that challenges your present thinking, interview a fellow student about his or her campus experience, switch the dial on your radio, or make a meal!

List at least three activities that you plan to do this semester to expand your understanding of and appreciation for diversity.

....

....

....

Part 6

Know Yourself!

Strategies for Success

PLAN AHEAD!

- Show up for class
- Have work done on time
- Set up a daily schedule
- If full-time, limit work week to 20 hours. Work on campus if possible
- If stressed, enroll part time

TAKE CHARGE OF LEARNING!

- Choose instructors who favor active learning
- Assess how you learn best
- Improve your reading, note-taking, and study habits
- Develop critical thinking skills
- Improve your writing

HONE YOUR SKILLS!

- Participate in class
- Practice giving presentations
- Learn how to remember more from every class
- Learn from criticism
- Take workshops on how to study
- Get to know your campus library and other information sources
- Embrace new technologies

GET CONNECTED!

- Study with a group
- Get to know one person on campus who cares about you
- Get involved in campus activities
- Learn about campus helping resources
- Meet with your instructors
- Find a great academic advisor or counselor
- Visit your campus career center
- Take advantage of minority support services
- Enlist support of your spouse, partner, or family

KNOW YOURSELF!

- Take your health seriously
- Have realistic expectations
- Learn how to be assertive yet tactful
- Be proud of your heritage

Stress
Management
Coping with Tension, Campus Safety, and Money Issues

**IN THIS CHAPTER,
YOU WILL LEARN**

- That stress is natural, but some proven ways can control it

- That rest, exercise, and a healthy diet can help combat stress

- How to protect personal property

- How to move safely around campus

- How to talk yourself into a relaxed mood

- How to manage your money

- How to avoid the "perils of plastic"

- How to seek financial aid for your education

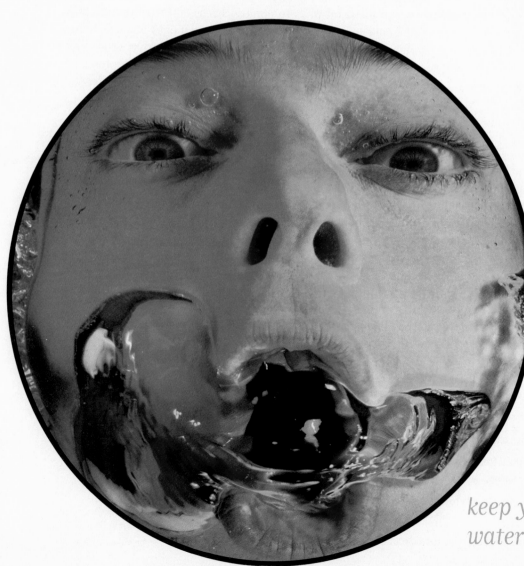

keep your head above water

"*ey you! Yeah, I said you! Watch where you're going. I mean, move and let me get by. I've gotta get to class, and I don't have time to hassle with you. What? Who are you tellin' to slow down? Hey, I was up till four studying . . . so maybe I'm a little edgy today. So chill!*"

Stress is natural. To the extent it is a sign of vitality, stress is good. Yet unless we learn how to cope effectively with stress-producing situations, stress can overwhelm us and undermine our ability to perform.

Stress seems to be with us a good bit of the time: studying for exams, writing a paper, hoping Friday's date turns out well, being pressured by family to earn higher grades or to finish college in exactly four years. We can't address all causes of stress in this chapter, but we will focus on ways to combat stress and then discuss two major causes of stress for college students: campus safety and money management.

Did you realize you have actually learned to be tense in most stress-producing situations? Now you can learn how to identify the warning signs or symptoms of stress. Once you are aware of the warning signs, you can choose how you will react.

A Healthy Lifestyle

The best starting point for handling stress is to be in good shape physically and mentally. If you are uncertain about what constitutes a healthy diet or whether yours is healthy, ask your campus health or counseling office for information, consult the library, or take a brief wellness course. Also, use the box on page 206 to determine how much caffeine you may be consuming on a regular basis.

SELF-ASSESSMENT: STRESS, CAMPUS SAFETY, AND MONEY ISSUES

Checkmark those statements that are true. Leave the others blank. After reading this chapter, come back to this inventory and place an X beside any item about which you now think differently.

_____ 1. Being stressed out is a sign of weakness.

_____ 2. When you're faced with papers and exams due all in 1 week, there's not much you can do to relieve your stress.

_____ 3. Although some would tell you differently, drinking a few beers can be an effective way to manage stress.

_____ 4. Meditation and prayer can help you reduce the amount of stress you're feeling.

_____ 5. It's too much trouble to lock my room if I'm just going down the hall. Chances are nobody will come in and take something.

_____ 6. Other than being able to park legally, there's no advantage in registering my vehicle with the college or university.

_____ 7. What's the point of trying to work out a budget? I'll still be in the hole financially.

_____ 8. All credit cards are more or less alike.

In moderate amounts (50–200 milligrams per day), caffeine increases alertness and reduces feelings of fatigue, but even at this low dosage it may make you perkier during part of the day and more tired later and may give you headaches when you cut down. Consumed in larger quantities, it may cause nervousness, headaches, irritability, stomach irritation, and insomnia.

If starting college means you're sleeping less than before, know that being rested makes you more efficient when you are awake. It also helps to make a lot of other activities more enjoyable and cuts down the likelihood that you'll succumb to annoying diseases, such as infectious mononucleosis.

Exercise regularly. The box "Start Healthy" suggests how. You may feel that you have no time for regular exercise, but even a daily regimen of stretches each morning can help lower stress, keep you looking and feeling trim, and enhance your energy.

Although competitive sports are fun and a great way to meet friends and although weight training may be appealing, it's more beneficial to find an aerobic activity—swimming, jogging, brisk walking, cycling, or vigorous racquet sports. People who undertake aerobic exercise report more energy, less stress, better sleep, weight loss, and an improved self-image.

When You Are Tense

Signs of stress are easy to recognize and differ little from person to person. Basically, your breathing rate becomes faster and shallower; your heart rate begins to race; and the muscles in your shoulders and forehead, the back of your neck, and perhaps even across your chest begin to tighten. Your hands and perhaps your feet probably become cold and sweaty. There are likely to be disturbances in your gastrointestinal system, such as a "butterfly" stomach, diarrhea, or vomiting; you may experience frequent urination. Your mouth may become parched, your lips may dry out, and your hands and knees may begin to shake or tremble. Your voice may quiver or even go up an octave.

A number of psychological changes also occur when you are under stress. As a result, you're more easily confused, your memory becomes blocked, and your thinking becomes less flexible. If the situation persists, you may also find it difficult to concentrate, and you may experience a general sense of fear or anxiety, insomnia, early waking, changes in eating habits, excessive worrying, fatigue, and an urge to run away.

Hardly the stuff good grades are made of.

The urges to stand and fight or to run away are two of the human body's basic responses to stress. But many times both urges must be suppressed because they would be inappropriate. For instance, a person taking an exam may want to bolt from the exam room, but it probably would not help the grade to do so, and it's pointless to fight with a piece of paper. So we often find we must cope with a situation in a way that allows us to face it. This is where learning to manage stress can make a difference.

Identifying Your Stress

Stress has many sources, but there are two prevailing theories about its origin. The first is the life events theory, which attributes health risks and life span reduction to an accumulation of effects from events that have occurred in the previous 12 months of a person's life.

SEE EXERCISE 13.1   Turn to page 219 and complete the College Readjustment Rating Scale (Exercise 13.1). If you find that your score is 150 or higher, think about why you experienced each of the scored events. In addition, you might consider what skills you need to learn either to repair the damage that these events caused or to prevent their recurrence.

Start Healthy

GET ENOUGH REST

Aim for 8 hours of sleep each night. Listen to your body and rest more when you need to.

GET ENOUGH EXERCISE

1. **Mode**   Pick something you enjoy and will stick with. You can cross-train doing different exercises. Find exercise partners to help you keep going.
2. **Frequency**   Exercise at least three times weekly. For greater improvement build gradually to four to six times weekly. Give yourself at least 1 day a week free of exercise so that your body can recover.
3. **Duration**   Exercise for at least 20–30 minutes at a time, even at the beginning.
4. **Intensity**   Monitor the intensity of your workout. To get aerobic benefits, your heart must be beating at a target rate. To determine this rate, subtract your age from 220 and multiply by .60. Then subtract your age again from 220 and multiply this time by .75. These two answers are the high and low limits of what your heart rate (pulse) should be during exercise.

EAT FOR HEALTH

1. **Eat a balanced diet each day.**
2. **Watch your caffeine content.**

Item	Caffeine (milligrams)
1 cup brewed coffee	85
1 cup instant coffee	60
1 cup tea	30–50
12-ounce cola drinks	35–65
Many aspirin compounds	30–60
Various cold preparations	30
1 cup cocoa	2–10
1 cup decaffeinated coffee	3

3. **Eat when you are hungry.** Don't eat for comfort or distraction. Use food to fuel your body with energy. For emotional support or cheering up, try connecting with a good friend or exercising instead of eating.

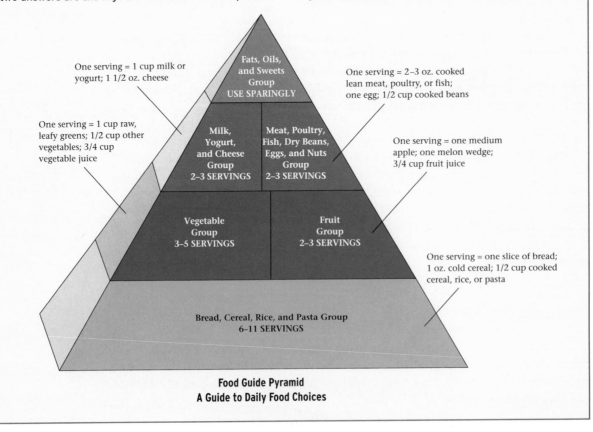

One serving = 1 cup milk or yogurt; 1 1/2 oz. cheese

One serving = 2–3 oz. cooked lean meat, poultry, or fish; one egg; 1/2 cup cooked beans

One serving = 1 cup raw, leafy greens; 1/2 cup other vegetables; 3/4 cup vegetable juice

One serving = one medium apple; one melon wedge; 3/4 cup fruit juice

Fats, Oils, and Sweets Group
USE SPARINGLY

Milk, Yogurt, and Cheese Group
2–3 SERVINGS

Meat, Poultry, Fish, Dry Beans, Eggs, and Nuts Group
2–3 SERVINGS

Vegetable Group
3–5 SERVINGS

Fruit Group
2–3 SERVINGS

One serving = one slice of bread; 1 oz. cold cereal; 1/2 cup cooked cereal, rice, or pasta

Bread, Cereal, Rice, and Pasta Group
6–11 SERVINGS

Food Guide Pyramid
A Guide to Daily Food Choices

The other major theory attributes our general level of stress to an overload of personal hassles and a deficit of uplifts or reliefs. This theory encourages us to evaluate our immediate problems while focusing on what's good about our lives and striving to notice positive events instead of taking them for granted.

We can't always control life's setbacks—an annoying roommate, being closed out of a course, not finding a parking space—but what we can control is our *reaction* to life's hassles. If we can adopt the attitude that we will do what we can do, seek help when appropriate, and not sweat the small stuff, we won't be as negatively affected by frustrations. It also helps to keep a mental tally of the positive things in our lives.   SEE EXERCISE 13.2

A Stress-Relief Smorgasbord

To provide yourself with a sense of relief, you need to do those things that help you let go of stress or invigorate your mind and body. However, many of the traditional things that people do with the intention of relieving stress—such as drinking alcohol, taking drugs, oversleeping, or overeating—don't relieve stress and may actually increase it! Many other ways of handling stress actually work.

Get Physical

- **Relax your neck and shoulders.** Slowly drop your head forward, roll it gently to the center of your right shoulder, and pause; gently roll it backward to the center of your shoulders and pause; gently roll it to the center of your left shoulder and pause; gently roll it forward to the center of your chest and pause. Then reverse direction and go back around your shoulders from left to right.
- **Take a stretch.** In any situation, if you pause to stretch your body you will feel it loosen up and become more relaxed, so stand up and reach for the sky!
- **Get a massage.** Physical touch can feel wonderful when you are tense, and having someone help you relax can feel supportive.
- **Exercise.** Physical exercise strengthens both mind and body. Aerobic exercise is the most effective type for stress relief.

Road Warrior

A student who commuted 23 miles to school was tailgated just before arriving on campus one day. The accident was minor, but unfortunately she had been sipping coffee at the time of the collision, and it splashed all over her dress. She was so embarrassed that she didn't go to class. Unfortunately, that was a particularly important class, and her absence eventually cost her a full letter grade.

If you commute a long distance, carry a store of supplies. Leave your survival kit in your car if you drive or in a locker at school if possible. Here are some things you should have in your kit. Talk with other students about other items that might be useful and add them to the list.

- Emergency medical supplies
- Flashlight
- One dollar in change
- Some pencils and paper
- Jumper cables
- Local bus schedule
- Rag or towel
- Spare set of clothes
- _____
- _____
- _____
- _____

Get Mental

- **Count to 10.** Many people discount this method because it sounds too simple. To give yourself time to gain that new outlook or to come up with a "better" way to handle the situation, count slowly while asking yourself, "How can I best handle this situation?"
- **Control your thoughts.** To gain control of negative thoughts or worries, imagine yelling "Stop!" as loudly as you can in your mind. You may have to repeat this process quite a few times, but gradually it will help you shut out angry or frightening thoughts.
- **Fantasize.** Give yourself a few moments to take a minivacation. Remember the pleasure of an experience you enjoy, listen to a child laugh, or just let your mind be creative. Make a list of some places or activities that make you feel relaxed and good about yourself. Next time you need to get away, refer to the list, close your eyes, and take a minibreak.
- **Congratulate yourself.** Give yourself pats on the back. No one knows how difficult a situation may have been for you to handle or even how well you may have handled it, so tell yourself, "Good going."
- **Ignore the problem.** This may sound strange at first, but many problems just don't need to be dealt with or can't be solved right now. Forget about the problem at hand and do something more important or something nice for yourself.
- **Perform self-maintenance.** Stress is a daily issue, so the more you plan for its reduction, the more likely it will be reduced.

Get Spiritual

- **Meditate.** All that meditation requires is slow breathing and concentration. Look at something in front of you or make a mental picture while you gradually breathe slower and slower and feel the relief spread through your body and mind.
- **Pray.** You don't need to go through life feeling alone. Prayer can be a great source of comfort and strength.
- **Remember your purpose.** Sometimes it is very valuable to remind ourselves why we are in a particular situation. Even though it may be a difficult situation, you may need to remind yourself that you have to be there and to realize that the situation's importance outweighs its difficulty.

Use Mind and Body Together

- **Take a break.** If possible, get up from what you are doing and walk away for a while. Don't let yourself think about the source of the problem until after a short walk.
- **Get hug therapy.** We need at least four hugs a day to survive, eight hugs to feel okay, and twelve hugs to tackle the world. "Hugs" can come from many different sources, and they can take many different forms. They can be bear hugs, smiles, compliments, or kind words or thoughts. If you have forgotten how to hug, ask a small child you know to teach you. Young children know that every time you give a hug, you get one back as a fringe benefit!
- **Try progressive relaxation.** Perform a mental massage of each muscle in your body from your feet up to your head. Take the time to allow each muscle to relax and unwind. Imagine that the muscles that were all knotted and tense are now long, smooth, and relaxed.

- **Laugh.** Nothing is so important that we must suffer self-damage. The ability to laugh at your own mistakes lightens your load and gives you the energy to return to a difficult task.
- **Find a pet.** Countless studies have demonstrated that caring for, talking to, holding, and stroking pets can help reduce stress.

Develop New Skills

- **Learn something.** Sometimes your problem is that you lack information or skills in a certain area. The sooner you remedy your deficiency, the sooner your distress will end.
- **Practice a hobby.** If you have one, use it; if you don't currently have one, then it's time that you did. A hobby can immerse you in an activity of your choice that provides you with a sense of accomplishment and pleasure.

SEE SEARCH ONLINE! INTERNET EXERCISE 13.1

Your present stress management habits are likely to serve you for the rest of your life. Learning to handle stress in a healthy fashion is important not only to survive and do well in your first year but also to cope with the demands and opportunities of adulthood. A healthy adult is one who treats his or her body and mind in a respectful manner. When you do that, you communicate to all other adults that you are handling yourself well and don't need them to baby you or to tell you how to live your life.

A Relaxation Process

Settle back and get comfortable. Take a few moments to allow yourself to listen to your thoughts and to your body. If your thoughts get in the way of relaxing, imagine a blackboard in your mind and visualize yourself writing down all your thoughts on the blackboard. Now put those thoughts aside for a while and know that you will be able to retrieve them later.

Now that you are ready to relax, begin by closing your eyes. Allow your breathing to become a little slower and a little deeper. Let your mind drift back into a tranquil, safe place that you have been in before. Try to recall everything that you could see, hear, and feel back there. Let those pleasant memories wash away any tension or discomfort.

To help yourself relax even further, take a brief journey through your body, allowing all your muscles to become as comfortable and as relaxed as possible.

Begin by focusing on your feet up to your ankles, wiggling your feet or toes to help them to relax, then allowing that growing wave of relaxation to continue up into the muscles of the calves. As muscles relax, they stretch out and allow more blood to flow into them; therefore, they gradually feel warmer and heavier.

Continue the process into the muscles of the thighs; gradually, your legs should feel more and more comfortable and relaxed.

Then concentrate on all the muscles up and down your spine and feel the relaxation moving into your abdomen; as you do so, you might also feel a pleasant sense of warmth moving out to every part of your body. Next focus on the muscles of the chest. Each time you exhale, your chest muscles will relax just a little more. Let the feeling flow up into the muscles of the shoulders, washing away any tightness or tension, allowing the shoulder muscles to become loose and limp. And now the relaxation can seep out into the muscles of the arms and hands as they become heavy, limp, and warm.

Now move on to the muscles of the neck—front, sides, and back—imagining that your neck muscles are as floppy as a handful of rubber bands. And now relax the muscles of the face, letting the jaw, cheeks, and sides of the face hang loose and limp.

Now relax the eyes and the nose and next the forehead and the scalp. Let any wrinkles just melt away. And now, by taking a long, slow, deep breath, cleanse yourself of any remaining tension.

Stress and Campus Crime

With all the stress you may be experiencing from relationships and your studies, one thing you certainly want to avoid is becoming a victim of crime.

College and university campuses are not sanctuaries. Criminal activity occurs on campus on a regular basis. It is important to take proactive measures to reduce criminal activity on your campus.

The first step is to learn how you can protect yourself as well as your personal property. Most campus crime involves theft. As students bring more valuable items to campus, such as computers, the opportunity for theft grows.

Personal Property Safety

Books can be stolen and sold at bookstores and if not properly marked will never be recovered. Computers and other expensive items are stolen and traded for cash. To reduce the chances of such occurrences, follow these basic rules:

- Record serial numbers of electronic equipment and keep the numbers in a safe place.
- Mark your books on a preselected page with your name and an additional identifying characteristic such as your Social Security number or driver's license number. Remember on which page you entered this information.
- Never leave books or bookbags unattended.
- Lock your room even if you are only going out for a minute.
- Do not leave your key above the door for a friend or roommate.
- Report lost or stolen property to the proper authority, such as the campus police.
- Don't tell people you don't know well about your valuable possessions.
- Keep your credit or bank debit card as safe as you would your cash.

Automobile Safety

- Keep your vehicle locked at all times.
- Do not leave valuables in your vehicle where they can be easily seen.
- Park in well-lighted areas.
- Maintain your vehicle properly so that it isn't likely to die on you.
- Register your vehicle with the proper authorities if you park on campus. This identifies your vehicle as one that belongs on campus and assists police when they patrol campus for unregistered vehicles belonging to potentially dangerous intruders.

Personal Safety

Each day we read about new tragedies: airplane crashes, accidental drownings, and violent crimes. Yet we still fly, swim, and go out at night, often finding ourselves alone with individuals we do not know or being involved in other risky situations. We can't always avoid potentially dangerous situations, but we can do something to make them less dangerous for us.

Here are some ways to increase your personal safety on campus:

- Find out if your campus has an escort service that provides transportation during the evening hours. Use this important service if you must travel alone during evening hours.

If you must travel on campus alone after dark, use the campus transportation system or a campus escort service.

- Write down the telephone number for your campus police. Find out if campus police have received special training in preventing crime on campus and are commissioned officers with the power to arrest. If your campus has emergency call boxes, find out where they are and how to operate them.
- Be aware of dark areas on campus and avoid them.
- Travel with at least one other person when going to the library or other locations on or near campus during evening hours.
- Let someone know where you will be and a phone number where you can be reached, particularly if you go away for the weekend. Sometimes parents call and become concerned when they can't reach you. An informed roommate can minimize parental concern.
- While jogging during the early evening and early morning, wear reflective clothing. Find a jogging partner so that you are not alone in situations where help is not readily available.

Your behavior both on and off campus should be proactive in terms of reducing opportunity. The fear that occurs after a critical incident is short lived. Concern, on the other hand, allows us to make safety measures a part of our everyday routine. Be concerned.

Examining Values

This part of the chapter reminds us that the world isn't as safe as we would like it to be. Should you give up things in life that make it interesting—dining out, attending a ball game, visiting a park, driving at night, and so forth—or should you find ways to do the things you want without putting yourself at high risk? Whether you choose security over adventure or vice versa, what values governed your choice? If you choose not to avoid places where things could go wrong, what steps would you take to reduce your risk?

Alcohol and Crime

The majority of violent crimes on or near college and university campuses have involved alcohol or drug use. Friends watch out for friends. Accordingly, pay attention to the "friends" with whom you socialize. Look out for one another.

A Word About Victims

You may not always use the best judgment, yet no one has the right to make you a victim. If you or a friend become the victim of a crime, report it to the authorities immediately. Never blame yourself! Reporting the crime quickly enables law enforcement officials to deal with it more effectively. If property is stolen, a quick report may help police recover and return the items.

Most institutions of higher learning are engaged in active crime prevention programs. If you live on campus, your resident advisor probably will sponsor crime prevention speakers as part of your residence hall programming.

Stress and Money

If you are putting yourself through school, you may have more expenses and less income than you had in the past. If your parents are helping you pay for college, you are probably responsible for making and spending more money now than you ever were before.

Our aim is to help you take control of your money so that you can worry less about it and focus more on your education. Money management boils down to three primary activities: analysis, planning, and budgeting.

Analysis

Analyze your finances by identifying and comparing your expenses to your resources. Unless you know what your costs are and how much you have available, you are not going to be in control of anything. Think in terms of your academic year (August or September through May or June).

Expenses Start by making a list of all the expenses you can think of, under two main categories of costs: educational and noneducational. Educational expenses are those you incur because you are a student, including tuition, fees, books, supplies, lab equipment, and so on. Noneducational expenses include all your other costs: housing, food, transportation, and miscellaneous and personal needs.

Be careful as you identify noneducational expenses because these costs are often hard to estimate. For example, it is easy to determine how much your tuition and fees are going to be, but it is not so easy to estimate utility bills or food and transportation costs.

Table 13.1 shows most of the types of costs you will face. If you have other expenses, add them to the list.

Resources Next, identify your resources. Again, list your sources of financial support by category (savings, employment, financial aid, parents, spouse, and so on). Be realistic about your resources. Table 13.2 lists some common types of monetary support. List any additional sources.

Comparing Expenses to Resources Once you have identified your expenses and resources, compare the totals. Remember that this is a tentative tally, not a final evaluation.

TABLE 13.1 TYPICAL EXPENSES (ACADEMIC YEAR)

EDUCATIONAL EXPENSES

Tuition and fees	$ 3,100
Books and supplies	635
Subtotal educational expenses	$ 3,735

NONEDUCATIONAL EXPENSES

Housing and food	$4,400
Personal	900
Phone	200
Transportation	400
Clothing	600
Social/entertainment	500
Savings	400
Subtotal noneducational expenses	$7,400
Total educational and noneducational expenses	$11,135

TABLE 13.2 TYPICAL RESOURCES (ACADEMIC YEAR)

A. Parents/Spouse

Cash	$2,000
Credit union loan	2,500

B. Work

Summer (savings after expenses)	1,500
Part time during year	2,000

C. Savings

Parents	0
Your own	500

D. Financial Aid

Grants	900
Loans	1,500
Scholarships	0

E. Benefits

Veterans	0
Other	0

F. Other

ROTC	900
Relatives	0
Trusts	0
Total	$11,800

TABLE 13.3 TYPICAL EXPENSE PRIORITIES (ACADEMIC YEAR)

FIXED EXPENSES

Tuition and fees	$3,100
Books and supplies	635
Housing	2,000
Subtotal fixed expenses	$5,735

FLEXIBLE EXPENSES

Food	$2,400
Transportation	400
Clothing	600
Personal	900
Phone	200
Social/entertainment	500
Savings	400
Subtotal flexible expenses	$5,400
Total fixed and flexible expenses	$11,135

TABLE 13.4 SAMPLE MONTHLY BUDGET (SEPTEMBER)

RESOURCES

Summer savings	$1,500
Parents/spouse	1,850
Financial aid	500
ROTC	100
Part-time job	400
Total	$4,350

FIXED EXPENSES

Tuition and fees	$1,550
Books and supplies	300
Residence hall room	2,000
Total	$3,850

FLEXIBLE EXPENSES

Food (meal cash card)	$200
Supplies	50
Personal	50
Phone	22
Transportation	50
Social	60
Total	$ 432

SUMMARY

Total resources	$4,350
Less total expenses	4,282
Balance	$ 68*

*Carried forward to October. Note that room is paid for entire term and will not be an item in October budget.

Next, classify your expenses as fixed or flexible. Fixed expenses are those over which you have no control; flexible expenses are those you can modify. Tuition, fees, and residence hall costs are generally fixed. Food may be fixed or flexible, depending on whether you are paying for a residential board plan or cooking on your own.

Table 13.3 shows some typical new-student costs divided into fixed and flexible expenses. The flexible expenses are listed in order of importance. If the total of your costs exceeds your resources, start revising your flexible costs, such as telephone, clothing, and entertainment. Although cutting wardrobe and entertainment costs may be less than enjoyable, good money management means being realistic.

SEE EXERCISE 13.3

Critical Thinking

Managing Money

Money! Although it isn't the root of all evil, it sure can cause havoc in our lives if we don't manage it properly. Do some digging at the library and on the Internet to find out what others are saying about college students and money. After you have at least five sources, synthesize the information and organize it into a meaningful paper. Where you disagree with a point, explain why. Where you agree, provide evidence (from your sources, your personal experiences, or from friends) that shows why you agree.

Planning

Next you need to plan how you will manage your money. Focus on timing, identifying when you will have to pay for various things and when your resources will provide income.

For planning, you will need an academic schedule and a calendar, preferably organized on an academic schedule, too. First, determine your school's registration and payment schedules. When is the latest you can pay your housing deposit if you live on campus? What is the deadline for tuition and fees? What is the school's refund policy and schedule? Enter these critical dates on your own planning calendar for the entire year. Find out if your school accepts credit cards for tuition payments.

Then turn your attention to other important dates that are not institutionally related. For example, if you pay auto insurance semiannually, when is your next big premium due?

After you have recorded the important dates of your major expenditures, do the same thing for your revenue. This knowledge is essential for planning because you can't very well plan how you're going to pay for things if you don't know when you'll have the money. For example, financial aid is typically disbursed in one lump sum at the beginning of each academic term, whereas paychecks come in smaller, more frequent installments.

If you will be a bit strapped paying all your tuition and fees at the start of the term, see if your school has an installment plan that will let you stretch out the payments or if you can reschedule semiannual payments (such as car insurance premiums) as monthly payments. Many schools also allow payment by credit card, but be careful about overloading your cards. This is a major reason students drop out of college.

Once you have determined the critical dates of income and expenses, planning becomes very simple. But keep in mind that if something can go wrong, it will—and at the worst moment. For example, you might leave the cap off your car's radiator and accidentally crack the engine block. Or a roommate might suddenly split for Bali, leaving you with higher expenses.

Although you can't avoid such surprises, you can prepare to some extent by being emotionally ready to deal with such things when they happen, by building up an emergency fund (even a small one), and by not departing from your money management plan.

Budgeting

Budgeting takes self-discipline. A monthly budget is a specific plan for each month's income and outgo—the final details necessary to make things work. It eliminates any confusion about what you must do in the near future, within a manageable block of time. It is also your method for maintaining continual control over your finances. Because it coincides with the cycle of your checking account, it also facilitates monthly balancing and scheduling.

To develop your monthly budget, put your expenses and income together on one sheet, as shown in Table 13.4 on page 213. After listing your fixed expenses, your flexible expenses, and your resources, subtract expenses from resources to create a summary for the month. Settle your fixed outlays and revise the flexible ones as necessary to achieve a reasonable balance. The September budget shown in the table happens to include the major start-up costs for tuition, fees, and so on. Make sure your budget is comprehensive and keeps track of how you spend what you spend.

You may want to consider investing in a financial program for your computer, one that will allow you to keep an on-screen checkbook and show you your assets and liabilities at a glance.

SEE EXERCISE 13.4

The Perils of Plastic

Consumer groups point out that most students use credit responsibly. VISA USA says about 60 percent of card-carrying college students pay their balances in full each month, compared with an industry average of about 40 percent.

But what about the 40 percent of students who don't pay in full? Currently, about two-thirds of college students carry at least one credit card. And credit card debt by entering students has caused many of them to drop out. It's gotten so bad that Catawba College in Salisbury, North Carolina, has banned credit card solicitations on campus and other schools are considering similar bans.

Students who work long hours to pay off debt can hurt their academic standing, college officials say. Credit card debt also makes it more difficult to repay student loans, which now average $11,400 for undergraduates.

VISA USA says its research shows that most college students "are carrying manageable balances of less than $1000." However, statistics don't always reveal that many times parents pay student debts to keep their credit records clean, consumer advocates say.

Before choosing a card, consider this advice:

1. **Limit yourself to one credit card.** Getting more than one to extend your line of credit can be disastrous.

2. **Shop around.** Interest rates can vary from less than 9 percent to more than 19 percent.

3. **Avoid cards that charge annual or monthly fees.**

4. **Look for a card that gives you an interest-free grace period** (the time between making a purchase and paying off the charge), usually around 25 days.

5. **Try not to use your card for cash advances.** They're costly.

6. **If you get a card, sign it right away.** Keep a record of the card number and expiration date and the number to call if it is lost or stolen.

7. **Save your charge slips to be certain your bill is correct.**

8. **Never lend your card or tell its number to anyone else,** unless it's absolutely necessary.

9. **Report lost cards immediately by phone.** You will probably have to pay no more than $50 of charges made with the stolen card.

10. **Instead of a credit card, consider a debit card,** which draws money from your checking account, or have one of each.

Increasing Resources

Once you're doing everything to manage your current finances well, you may still need more money. How you acquire more aid has both immediate and long-term implications.

Only by knowing how much your education is going to cost can you go about planning how to pay for it. If it is clear that you or your family cannot handle all the costs, you should certainly apply for financial aid.

Financial Aid

Financial aid refers to any type of funding you receive to assist yourself in paying for college. Most financial aid money is given according to *demonstrated financial need.* Demonstrated financial need is eligibility determined by some specific financial scale, most commonly the federal needs analysis system called the *congressional methodology.* Other types of financial aid awards may not depend on this type of eligibility.

Financial aid may be either gift or self-help assistance. Gift assistance does not have to be repaid. Self-help assistance requires you to do something in return, such as work or repay the money. An academic scholarship is gift assistance; a student loan is self-help assistance. Financial aid can be further categorized into two types of gift assistance—grants and scholarships—and two types of self-help assistance—loans and work opportunities.

The basis upon which financial aid is awarded varies, but typical criteria are academic merit, financial need, or some combination of the two.

Grants Most institutions offer numerous grant programs, the largest funded by federal and state governments. Generally, grants are aimed at students with the greatest financial need. Students can often receive more than one type of grant simultaneously, but institutions do place limits on the total amount of grant assistance awarded to any one individual.

Scholarships Scholarships are awarded on the basis of superior academic achievement or merit, although financial need may also be a criterion. Most colleges and universities have scholarships for new students as well as for continuing students. Thousands of scholarships are also available from hundreds of national foundations, organizations, state and federal agencies, businesses, corporations, churches, and civic clubs.

SEE SEARCH ONLINE!
INTERNET EXERCISE 13.2

To find out about scholarships, begin by checking groups and organizations in your home region. Review information from the primary education agency or organization in your state. Go to the library or financial aid office at your school to ask for assistance and to review publications listing scholarships. Ask, ask, ask.

Loans For more than 15 years, long-term, low-interest educational loans have become the major means for financing college. The large federal student loan programs are based primarily on need. In addition to student loans, there are also federally sponsored loans that do not require demonstrated need. The interest rate for this program can be as high as 12 percent, and repayment generally begins shortly after the loan is made.

Student loans are an extremely valuable component of the total financial aid picture, but it is important to remember that they are exactly what they are called: loans. *They must be repaid.* Failure to repay a student loan can have negative consequences, including damaged credit, garnishment of wages, confiscation of income tax refunds, and litigation. Be very careful in assuming loan indebtedness during college because a sizable monthly loan repayment can become a heavy burden. Take out student loans only to the extent that they are absolutely necessary for you to stay in school.

Work Opportunities

Part-time work is a valuable type of self-help aid. The College Work–Study Program, a federal student aid program based on need, lets you earn some of the aid for which you may be eligible through employment, generally on campus. Many schools also have their own programs through which students earn money or in-kind support such as board.

This type of assistance has two advantages. First, you are not indebted after graduation. Second, you may be able to work in areas related to your major.

Cooperative (co-op) education programs provide employment off campus in public and private agencies, business, and industry. Work may parallel education (part-time course load, part-time work) or alternate with it (full-time study one term, full-time work the next). This type of experience can also be invaluable when you look for that first job after graduation. Many graduates are offered permanent full-time positions as a result of co-op experience.

Applying for Financial Aid

Since procedures vary, you should contact your financial aid office to find out how to apply for financial aid. For information about federal loans, go to *http://www.ed. gov/prog_info/SFA/StudentGuide/1999-0/index.html.* (Go to *http://success. wads-worth.com* for the most up-to-date URLs.)

When you apply for financial aid, remember the following:

1. **Plan ahead.** Find out what is available at your institution, how to go about applying, and when you must apply. You need to determine what information will be required, and you need to allow enough time to gather it.
2. **Allow sufficient time for the process to work.** The financial aid application process is often slow. (Summer is the peak season, so allow extra time in the summer.) After you have submitted your initial application, you may be asked to provide additional information to support or clarify it. Be prepared to do this promptly.
3. **Keep copies of everything.** Maintain a file with copies of everything you complete or send, including the date it was completed or sent. This will help you avoid confusion or costly delays due to miscommunication or things getting lost in the mail.

A Final Word

SEE SEARCH ONLINE!
INTERNET EXERCISE 13.3

Sometimes our problems are either too overwhelming or too complex for us to resolve by ourselves. If that is the case, you might benefit from checking out the services provided by your college counseling center. Counseling centers often offer individual or group sessions on handling difficult times or situations. The support and skills of a trained professional can help make difficult issues a lot more manageable.

Internet Exercise 13.1 Stress, Anxiety, and Relaxation

When you prepare for and take tests or give speeches,

Do your hands get cold? _____

Does your breathing speed up? _____

Does your mouth go dry? _____

Do your muscles tense? _____

Do you sweat? _____

If you said yes to any of these questions, you are probably experiencing performance-related stress. Read "How to Master Stress" at *http://www.mindtools.com/smpage.html.* What did you find there that you will be able to use to help manage your stress? (Go to *http://success.wadsworth.com* for the most up-to-date URLs.)

Internet Exercise 13.2 Pell Grants and Scholarships

A Many students who cannot afford college tuition may be eligible for federal Pell grants, which in some instances do not have to be paid back. Using the information you prepared according to Tables 13.1-13.4, calculate your financial need for federal aid. For other federal aid options, check *http://www.ed.gov/prog_info/SFA/StudentGuide/1999-0/index.html.* (Go to *http://success.wadsworth.com* for the most up-to-date URLs.)

B Which of these procedures should you trust for obtaining a scholarship?

Send money for a list of proven scholarship opportunities unavailable anywhere else.

Send a "redemption" fee for a college scholarship worth thousands of dollars that you have been selected to receive.

Prepay the taxes to receive a college scholarship worth thousands of dollars for which you have been selected as a candidate.

Check your answers at the Common Scholarship Scams page of FinAid, "The Smart Student Guide to Financial Aid," at *http://www.finaid.org/scholarships/common.phtml.*

Internet Activity 13.3 Discovering More About Stress, Campus Safety, and Money Management

Using *InfoTrac College Edition,* try these phrases and others for key-word and subject-guide searches: "stress," "college and stress," "healthy diet," "how to relax," "campus crime," "managing money," and "credit cards."

ALSO LOOK UP:

Managing stress through outdoor recreation. (Cover Story) Paul Finnicum, Jeffrey B. Zeiger. *Parks & Recreation* Aug 1998
    v33 n8 p46(6)

Humor helps. (managing stress and anger) (Psychology) Carolyn J. Gard. *Current Health 2* April-May 1998 v24 n8 p22(2)

Securing safety on campus: a case study. (Canada) Jennifer Wood, Clifford Shearing. *Canadian Journal of Criminology* Jan 1998
    v40 n1 p81-95

Covering all the bases. Judy Sutton. *American School & University* May 1997 v69 n9 p42B(4)

Making cash king on campus. Janet Bodnar. *Kiplinger's Personal Finance Magazine* Sept 1999 v53 i9 p116

Good financial health begins in college. (Magazine) *USA Today* Sept 1997 v126 n2628 p8(2)

Credit-smart college students. Robert Frick. *Kiplinger's Personal Finance Magazine* Mar 1997 v51 n3 p121(3)

Additional Exercises

These exercises will help you sharpen what we believe are the critical skills for college success: writing, critical thinking, learning in groups, planning, reflecting, and taking action. Also, check out the CD-ROM that came with your book—you will find these exercises and more.

Exercise 13.1 **The College Readjustment Rating Scale**

The College Readjustment Rating Scale is an adaptation of Holmes and Rahe's Life Events Scale. It has been modified for college-age adults and should be considered as a rough indication of stress levels and possible health consequences.

In this scale, each event, such as one's first term in college, is assigned a value that represents the amount of readjustment a person has to make in life as a result of change. In some studies, people with serious illnesses have been found to have high scores on similar scales. Persons with scores of 300 and higher have a high health risk. Persons scoring between 150 and 300 points have about a 50–50 chance of serious health change within 2 years. Subjects scoring 150 and below have a 1 in 3 chance of a serious health change.

To determine your stress score, circle the number of points corresponding to the events you have experienced in the past 6 months or are likely to experience in the next 6 months. Then add up the circled numbers.

Event	Points
Death of spouse	100
Female unwed pregnancy	92
Death of parent	80
Male partner in unwed pregnancy	77
Divorce	73
Death of a close family member	70
Death of a close friend	65
Divorce between parents	63
Jail term	61
Major personal injury or illness	60
Flunk out of college	58
Marriage	55
Fired from job	50
Loss of financial support for college (scholarship)	48
Failing grade in important or required course	47
Sexual difficulties	45
Serious argument with significant other	40
Academic probation	39
Change in major	37
New love interest	36
Increased workload in college	31
Outstanding personal achievement	29
First term in college	28
Serious conflict with instructor	27
Lower grades than expected	25
Change in colleges (transfer)	24
Change in social activities	22
Change in sleeping habits	21
Change in eating habits	19
Minor violations of the law (for example, traffic ticket)	15

If your score indicates potential health problems, it would be to your benefit to seriously review "A Stress-Relief Smorgasbord" (pages 207–209) and select and implement some strategies to reduce your stress.

Note: Adapted with permission from T. H. Holmes and R. H. Rahe, "The Social Readjustment Scale," in Carol L. Otis and Roger Goldingay, *Campus Health Guide* (New York: CEEB, 1989).

Exercise 13.2 Protection from Stress

A   Feeling good about yourself can be an effective buffer against stress. Begin by identifying some of your personal strengths. Expand this into a longer list of what you like about yourself and keep the list in a private place. Every day, whether you feel the need or not, review your list and try to add a new positive thought about yourself.

B   Most of our worries are either passed on to us by other people or conjured up in our imaginations. List some of your current worries and then write what you can do to eliminate some or all of them.

Exercise 13.3 Setting Priorities

Note: If your expenses exceed your resources, try this exercise.

1. Using Tables 13.1 and 13.2, list your expenses and resources. Then, using Table 13.3 as a model, create a list that separates your costs into fixed versus flexible expenses. Focus on the flexible costs; which of them can be reduced? Change your figures to improve the balance of costs and resources but be realistic. Don't lower expenses that cannot be lowered.

2. If your expenses are still greater than your resources, review the chapter to see how you might add more to the resource side. Then come back and rework your figures to achieve a balance.

Exercise 13.4 Monitoring the Media

For a week or so, keep track of advertisements you see on television, hear on radio, or read in newspapers or magazines that not only hype credit cards but also suggest you need to own certain material things in order to be successful and happy. Subject these to a critical analysis. How do the positive outcomes depicted square with the impact of credit cards on your life? What essential facts, truths, and realities do these ads fail to portray? How would your life be different if credit cards or some other forms of borrowing money did not exist?

Your Personal Journal

Here are several things to write about. Choose one or more or choose another topic related to this chapter.

1. If you have been stressed lately, write about it. What do you think is causing it, and what options do you have for reducing it?

2. Try one or more of the relaxation processes described in "A Stress-Relief Smorgasbord" (pages 207–209). Then relax for a few minutes and write about what it felt like to go through the processes.

3. It's been said that anticipating a potentially stressful event can produce more stress than the actual event. Is that true for you? What were your biggest concerns before you came to college? Was your stress justified or not? Explain.

4. If you were a college senior and a first-year student asked you how to stay out of harm's way on campus, what advice would you offer?

5. What should you be doing now to improve your financial situation in the near future?

6. If you use a credit card, what rules do you impose upon yourself about how you may use it?

7. What behaviors are you willing to change after reading this chapter? How might you go about changing them?

8. What else is on your mind this week? If you wish to share it with your instructor, add it to this journal entry.

Resources

Use the charts below for 1 week to keep track of troublesome experiences and your reactions and responses to them. Pay attention to times when you suddenly feel fatigued, tense, angry, upset, frightened, and so on.

Event	Physical Signals	Emotional Signals
1.		
2.		
3.		
4.		
5.		
6.		

At the end of the week, analyze the chart. What were your responses to each situation? What would you do differently next time?

One key in managing your finances is finding sources of income. Go to your campus financial aid office or ask your academic advisor where to go for information on scholarships and grants. List the scholarships for which you are eligible:

List the grants for which you are eligible:

List work-study jobs for which you are eligible:

If your finances get out of control, consider the following resources:

The National Foundation for Consumer Credit (for debt management): 800-388-2227

Experian (for a copy of your credit report): 800-682-7654

Chapter 14

Alcohol, Other Drugs, and Sexuality

Making Healthy Choices

watch the chemistry

IN THIS CHAPTER, YOU WILL LEARN

- That all the things you hear about sex and drinking are not true
- The dangers of binge drinking
- How to reduce the risks of drinking too much
- Why students feel pressured to have sex when they arrive at college
- What sexually transmitted diseases can cause
- The relative safety of various birth control methods
- That it's important to make your own decisions about sex and alcohol
- To be aware of relationship violence and how to avoid it

A
"t the party I made a pass at a girl. She was drinking vodka, so I joined her for a while. But I'm not feeling very good this morning. A few of my friends are always bragging about who they were with last night. I'm not into that. Some women around here turn me on, but I just don't want a sexual relationship right now. Down the road a little, if I find the right person, who knows?"

The messages you hear about alcohol and sex are innumerable and confusing. Not all first-year students are sexually active. Nor do all students drink. However, college seems to be a time when recent high school graduates begin at least to think more seriously about sex and alcohol. Perhaps this has to do with peer pressure or a sense of one's newfound independence, or maybe it's just hormones. Regardless of the reasons, it can be helpful to explore your values and to consider which choices are right for you at this time.

Alcohol Ups and Downs

You are repeatedly tantalized by advertisements, movies, and television shows that tend to normalize, glamorize, and romanticize alcohol. Yet you hear about tragedies on college campuses, and you may hear official messages about how dangerous alcohol can be. It's no surprise that you pay little attention to most of these messages, particularly when the allure of a great party confronts you each weekend.

SELF-ASSESSMENT: ALCOHOL, OTHER DRUGS, AND SEXUALITY

Checkmark those statements that are true. Leave the others blank. After reading this chapter, come back to this inventory and place an X beside any item about which you now think differently.

_____ 1. Drinking is just part of the college scene, so enjoy it while you can.

_____ 2. The majority of college students have more than four drinks in one sitting.

_____ 3. If someone else wants to binge drink and pass out, I don't think it's any of my business.

_____ 4. If colleges would simply outlaw alcohol and other drugs, college students would be better off almost immediately.

_____ 5. Drinking slowly and choosing a soft drink between each alcoholic drink are good ways to avoid getting drunk.

_____ 6. All college students have already engaged in sexual intercourse at least once.

_____ 7. If you want a relationship to last, the only recourse is to have sexual intercourse with your partner.

_____ 8. As long as you stick to one partner, you won't be in danger of catching a sexually transmitted disease.

_____ 9. Most birth control methods also protect against sexually transmitted diseases.

In fact, many students remain angered by intrusions on their right to have fun and socialize. Colleges are torn between curbing abusive drinking on campuses and listening to protests from students who want to preserve their right to drink.

Why Do College Students Drink?

1. **Experiences prior to college**   Many students have grown up in a family environment that regularly includes alcohol consumption as a part of social celebrations. Some students may be children of alcoholics or chronic substance abusers.
2. **Normal human development**   Maturing from adolescence to adulthood may include experimentation and a quest for independence. Drinking is one of many expressions of breaking away from the family and establishing your self-identity.
3. **Desire for pleasure and escape from the stresses of daily living**   The pleasure afforded by alcohol contributes to its use—even though alcohol is a risky means of temporarily checking out of reality.
4. **Desire to develop personal relationships and to belong to peer groups** We tend to engage in activities that feel normal and place us in the mainstream with others. Because alcohol has become a dominant feature of the social scene, people find themselves in settings where alcohol consumption is expected.
5. **Influence of mass media**   Music, advertising, television, and social events bombard you daily with messages that drinking is sexy. Ads in your student newspaper may advertise happy hours. Alcoholic beverage companies may sponsor athletic events and concerts. Glossy, alluring beer ads associate the product with sun, fun, and sex. Such messages may make it impossible for you to understand the reality of alcohol use among your peers.
6. **The campus culture**   Social clubs, Greek organizations, alumni bashes, and campus events focused around the consumption of alcohol (including drinking rituals and games) can contribute significantly to your perception of normal and acceptable behavior.

Truths, Not Perceptions

Look at things realistically: Underage drinking is punishable by law. Although drinking is widespread on campus, a sizable minority of students choose not to drink. But, of course, the truth is that many people do drink. If they are of legal age, if they don't depend on alcohol to get them through the day, if they avoid drinking and driving, and if they drink in moderation, most likely they are in little danger of harming themselves, their friends, and their families.

The majority of students use alcohol responsibly or do not use it at all. Yet many students may think that the frequency and intensity of drinking is much higher than it actually is. According to research, college students who choose to drink consume an average of five drinks in a week, whereas if you ask college students what they think their peers consume, it may be one-and-a-half to two times that amount.

You shouldn't choose to do something just because you believe everybody's doing it. It could be—as we will soon discover—that everybody's not.

Binge Drinking

Light to moderate drinking may carry few risks, but abusive, high-risk, or binge drinking is an important public health and safety issue on campus.

For males, binge drinking, as recently redefined, occurs when an individual consumes five drinks at one social occasion. For females, whose lower body weight makes them more susceptible to the effects of alcohol, consuming four drinks is considered bingeing in some studies, while others use the same number used for males.

Binge drinking is a pattern that not only places people at a particular risk of injury, illness, and even death but also has a negative impact on academic and social situations. Because binge drinking has resulted in numerous college student deaths in recent years, it has received massive media attention.

The academic, medical, and social consequences of binge drinking can seriously endanger one's quality of life. Research based on surveys conducted between 1992 and 1994 by the Core Institute at Southern Illinois University provides substantial evidence that binge drinkers have significantly greater risk of adverse outcomes, as listed in Table 14.1.

SEE EXERCISE 14.1

Among other problems, the data identify increased risk of poor test performance, missed classes, unlawful behavior, violence, memory loss, drunk driving, regretful behavior, and vandalism among binge drinkers, compared with all drinkers

"The Police Got Me Drunk. Honest."

Michelle Sutherlin

Recently I went on a ride-along with Master Police Officer Kyle Harris of the Norman Police Department. He's a drug recognition expert who patrols a special RID (removing intoxicated drivers) unit. Officer Harris had invited me, a college student, to participate in officer alcohol training. I would be one of eight people volunteering to become intoxicated so the officers could practice field sobriety tests on me. I reluctantly agreed.

Because I'm not much of a drinker and terrified of losing control, it was hard to show up for training that day. I was a little worried what my peers and future employers might think. But it was for training purposes, and I would be in a controlled environment, so I decided to go.

I showed up early and sat in on the classroom training. I even practiced the tests, still sober, during breaks. The rest of the drinkers showed up just before 5 P.M. I didn't know any of them. I was shy and nervous. We took a breathalyzer before we had anything to drink, just to make sure we were clean.

We had to fill out an agreement that promised we wouldn't drive for 12 hours after drinking. We also had to give our names, addresses, body weights, and booze of choice. After the officers asked about our drinking history, it became clear that I was one of the most inexperienced drinkers there.

I started with a rum and Coke. About halfway through, I was everybody's friend. After I finished the drink, I had a buzz. Most of the other drinkers were finishing their second drink about the time I started mine.

A drink-and-a-half later, my neck and face were bright red. I was encouraged to drink more, but the last thing I wanted was to get out of control or sick. I nursed a third drink for about 45 minutes to maintain my level of intoxication. I was drunk. I was definitely one of the most impaired people there. Besides being talkative and flushed, I

was wobbly. I had to watch the chair to make sure it didn't move on me before I could sit down. I had to keep my feet apart and my knees bent so that I wouldn't fall on my face. My attention level was zero. If I'd have been driving, I'd have been all over the road.

We stopped drinking and took another breathalyzer test. The officers wouldn't let us see what our blood alcohol content was. I knew mine was high. I thought I was probably over .10, the legal limit to be driving under the influence. If I would have blown a .06 to .09, I would have been charged with driving while impaired and could be sent to jail.

I failed all three field sobriety tests with all seven groups of officers. I had practiced and knew what they were looking for, but I couldn't fake it. Every group would have booked me in jail. If I'd have been driving, I'd have a criminal record right now.

The last thing the officers did was reveal how many ounces of liquor we had and what our blood alcohol content was. Not only did I have the least to drink, my blood alcohol content was the lowest. I only blew a .03. Legally, I could have driven a car, but I was too drunk to shift gears or buckle my seat belt.

I don't think people realize that everyone is affected differently when they drink. Depending on several things, you could feel blitzed, as I did, at .03 or feel okay at .15. I know you'd fail the test if you had a blood alcohol content that high, even if you felt okay to drive. People who feel okay are the most deadly drivers on the road.

I believe it only takes a second to change a life forever. Don't drink and drive, no matter how much you've had to drink. That changed life could be your own.

The Oklahoma Daily, October 30, 1997.
Reprinted by permission.

TABLE 14.1 ANNUAL CONSEQUENCES OF ALCOHOL AND OTHER DRUG USE
(ALL STUDENTS = 44,319; ALL DRINKERS = 26,247: ALL BINGERS = 16,908)

CONSEQUENCES	% EXPERIENCING CONSEQUENCE		
	All Students	All Drinkers	All Bingers
Had a hangover	59.7	81.1	89.5
Performed poorly on a test	21.8	31.4	40.8
Trouble with police, etc.	11.7	17.4	23.7
Property damage, fire alarm	7.8	11.8	16.5
Argument or fight	29.5	42.0	52.2
Nauseated or vomited	47.1	63.9	73.5
Drove while intoxicated	32.6	47.0	57.3
Missed a class	27.9	40.9	52.9
Been criticized	27.1	37.2	45.3
Thought I had a problem	12.3	16.4	21.6
Had a memory loss	25.8	37.3	48.0
Later regretted action	35.7	49.8	60.4
Arrested for DWI, DUI	1.7	2.4	3.3
Tried, failed to stop	5.8	8.1	10.6
Been hurt, injured	12.9	18.8	25.2
Taken advantage of sexually	11.4	15.9	19.9
Took sexual advantage of someone	6.1	9.0	11.9
Tried to commit suicide	1.6	1.9	2.6
Thought about suicide	5.1	6.7	8.2

SOURCE: Adapted from C. A. Presley, P. W. Meilman, J. R. Cashin, and R. Lyerla. *Alcohol and Drugs on American College Campuses: Use, Consequences, and Perceptions of the Campus Environment*, Volume IV: 1992-94. Carbondale: The Core Institute, Southern Illinois University.

TABLE 14.2 CORRELATION OF DRINKS CONSUMED IN 1 WEEK WITH GPA

NUMBER OF DRINKS PER WEEK	GRADE POINT AVERAGE
3.4	A
4.5	B
6.1	C
9.8	D and F

SOURCE: Adapted from C. A. Presley, P. W. Meilman, J. R. Cashin, and R. Lyerla. *Alcohol and Drugs on American College Campuses: Use, Consequences, and Perceptions of the Campus Environment*, Volume IV: 1992-94. Carbondale: The Core Institute, Southern Illinois University.

and all other students. At the same time, college health centers nationwide are reporting increasing trends in the serious medical conditions associated with alcohol use: alcohol poisoning causing coma and shock, respiratory depression, choking, and respiratory arrest, head trauma and brain injury, lacerations, fractures, unwanted or unsafe sexual activity causing sexually transmitted diseases and pregnancies, bleeding intestines, anxiety attacks and other psychological crises, and worsening of underlying psychiatric conditions such as depression.

Although binge drinking has been associated with adverse consequences, even those students who drink without bingeing are likely to see an inverse effect on their grades, depending on the number of drinks they consume weekly. In fact, all Core Institute surveys conducted since the early 1990s consistently have shown a negative correlation between grades and the number of drinks per week. Findings are similar for both 2-year and 4-year institutions, as shown in Table 14.2.

TABLE 14.3 CORE ALCOHOL AND DRUG SURVEY

Used alcohol at least once in the preceding year	82.8%
Average number of drinks per week*	5.1
Binged at least once in the 2 weeks prior to completing the survey	41.7%
Students under the age of 21 using alcohol at least once in the preceding 12 months	82.4%
Students under 21 using alcohol within the preceding 30 days	68.8%
Students not engaging in binge drinking in preceding 2 weeks	58.3%

*For all students. A drink is defined as a bottle of beer, a glass of wine, a wine cooler, a shot glass of liquor, or a mixed drink.

SOURCE: C. A. Presley and J. S. Leichliter. *Recent Statistics on Alcohol and Other Drug Use on American College Campuses: 1995-96.* Carbondale: The Core Institute, Southern Illinois University.

Secondary Effects of Binge Drinking Students who binge drink harm not only themselves but also others around them. Statistics from the 1995–1996 survey from the Core Institute demonstrate the percentage of students who experience adverse effects as a result of others' drinking:

Study interrupted	29%
Space messed up	25%
Felt unsafe	22%
Unable to enjoy events	19%
Interfered with in other ways	32%

***Not* Everybody's Doing It** A majority of college students do not drink excessively on a regular basis. The Core Institute, which has been conducting nationwide surveys of drinking behaviors of college students since the early 1990s, provides important insights about drinking and its consequences. The most recent information was collected during 1995 and 1996.

SEE SEARCH ONLINE!
INTERNET EXERCISE 14.1

Researchers surveyed 89,874 randomly selected college students from 171 2- and 4-year colleges in the United States. Table 14.3 lists some of the key findings of the survey.

In a 1998 update of its 1993 data, the Harvard School of Public Health College Alcohol Study indicates a sharp rise in the percentage of those who "drink to get drunk," offset somewhat by a slight rise in the number of nondrinkers (Table 14.4).

Not all college students drink frequently and in excess or even at all. There are many enjoyable activities and events that do not need alcohol to make them fun.

TABLE 14.4 HARVARD SCHOOL OF PUBLIC HEALTH COLLEGE ALCOHOL STUDY (1998)

	1993	1997
Drink to get drunk	39%	52%
Binge drinkers	44.1%	42.7%
Frequent binge drinkers	19.5%	20.7%
Don't drink	15.6%	19%

SOURCE: H. Wechsler, G. W. Dowdall, G. Maenner, J. Gledhill-Hoyt, and H. Lee. "Changes in Binge Drinking and Related Problems Among American College Students Between 1993 and 1997." Results of the Harvard School of Public Health College Alcohol Study. *Journal of American College Health 47* (1998): 57–68.

The study also revealed that 19.8 percent of students surveyed had experienced five or more different alcohol-related problems (driving after drinking, damaging property, getting injured, missing classes, and getting behind in school work), an increase of 22 percent since 1993. And 35.8 percent of those surveyed reported drinking after driving, a 13 percent increase since the 1993 study.

Four out of five students who were not binge drinkers and who lived on campus experienced at least one secondhand effect of binge drinking, such as being the victim of an assault or an unwanted sexual advance, having property vandalized, or having sleep or study interrupted.

What Should *You* Do?

You can choose to abstain, but if you choose to consume know the difference between high-risk or abusive drinking and safe and responsible drinking. It can make a major difference in your life.

Chronic alcoholism or addiction is a commonly cited consequence of abusive drinking. Evidence indicates that teens who engage in heavy alcohol use before they reach 17 years of age are at increased risk of alcoholism.* Our advice? Reconcile the obvious moral and ethical conflicts before choosing to consume alcohol when it remains illegal or in violation of campus policy.

Reducing the Risks The following suggestions probably won't cut down on your fun (in fact, you may have more fun because you're still awake) but can make a big difference in making your fun safer:

- **If you drink, drink slowly.** Avoid drinking more than one or two drinks in less than an hour.
- **Combine your alcohol consumption with food.** Food tends to absorb alcohol in the stomach and slows its absorption into the bloodstream.
- **Consider alternating nonalcoholic drinks with alcoholic beverages.** Simply having alcohol every other drink will fill the time while reducing the total number of alcohol beverages consumed.
- **Assign designated drivers and use them.** Never drive when you're drunk, and never ride with a driver who has been drinking.
- **Avoid participating in drinking games.** Chugging contests and other ritualistic drinking games encourage rapid consumption of large amounts of alcohol and are highly associated with significant risk of illness or injury.
- **Familiarize yourself with information about the actual level of drinking among your peers.** You'll probably be surprised to find that most students drink much less frequently and imbibe fewer drinks than you expected.

*See B. F. Grant and D. A. Dawson. "Age of Drinking Onset Predicts Future Alcohol Abuse and Dependence," *Journal of Substance Abuse, 9* (1998): 103–110.

Choosing Not to Drink You certainly have the choice not to consume alcohol. By doing so, you become part of a group of students who value this course of action.

Undoubtedly, you already know of other ways to experience pleasure and reduce stress. A game of basketball, shooting pool, a movie, a walk in the woods, or a stroll through a museum can do a lot to reduce stress without putting you at significant risk of injury or illness. Pursuing healthy escapes from life's stresses through outdoor recreation, intellectual pursuits, music, or the creative arts will benefit you for years to come. What's more, alcohol and other drugs are only temporary stress relievers and offer no other compensations. When you wake up, your problems are still going to be there and may seem all the worse because of your consumption the night before.

SEE EXERCISE 14.2

Your Rights You have a right to a safe, clean, and secure academic and living environment. If drunk students are depriving you of this, consider rallying the support of others to prevent the secondary effects of abusive use of alcohol in your campus environment. Use your student government, student organizations, residence hall staff, or student life administration to influence policy development and to enforce the rights of other students.

Finally, insist that campus leaders apply the same standards of conduct for faculty, staff, campus visitors, and students. A campus demanding that students comply with existing drinking laws has difficulty gaining credibility if alumni, faculty, and athletic ticketholders repeatedly ignore state and local laws regarding consumption of alcohol.

Other Drugs

Compared with alcohol, illegal recreational drugs—such as marijuana, cocaine, ecstasy, LSD, and heroin—are used by a much smaller number of college students and far less frequently. These drugs are significant public health issues for college students, however, and we hope that the comparative statistics shown in Table 14.5 and the brief additional information that follows will provoke further reading and discussion.

All drugs listed in Table 14.5, with the exception of alcohol, are illegal, and the penalties associated with their possession or use tend to be much more severe than those associated with underage alcohol use. None of these drugs is considered safe or innocuous by the medical community. In contrast to earlier recommendations regarding the potential for moderate and lower-risk consumption of alcohol, we cannot offer similar advice for illicit drugs (except to *never* share drug needles). Side effects include the potential for long-term abuse, addiction, and severe health problems.

Additionally, athletic departments, potential employers, and government agencies do routine screenings for many of these drugs. Future employability, athletic scholarships, and insurability may be compromised if you have a positive drug test for any of these substances. A brief summary of the most prevalent drugs follows.

Marijuana

A single puff of marijuana has a half-life in the body of between 3 and 7 days, depending on the potency and the smoker. Consider how a number of these potential effects could affect your academic performance: chronically slowed reaction time, impaired hand–eye coordination, altered perception of time (slow motion), impairment of depth perception and recent memory, apathy, loss of drive, and unwillingness or inability to complete tasks.

TABLE 14.5 USAGE OF ALCOHOL AND OTHER DRUGS ON COLLEGE CAMPUSES

DRUG	PERCENTAGE USING AT LEAST ONCE IN PRECEDING YEAR	PERCENTAGE USING DURING PREVIOUS **30** DAYS
Alcohol	83.0	70.0
Marijuana	31.0	19.0
Cocaine	3.9	1.6
Amphetamines	6.9	3.1
Designer drugs (ecstasy)	3.6	1.3

SOURCE: C. A. Presley and J. S. Leichliter. *Recent Statistics on Alcohol and Other Drug Use on American College Campuses: 1995-96.* Carbondale: The Core Institute, Southern Illinois University. Used by permission.

Long-term use carries the same risks of lung infections and cancer that are associated with smoking tobacco. Some experts believe that marijuana may be a gateway to more potent and dangerous drugs.

Cocaine

Cocaine, whether snorted, injected, or smoked as crack, produces an intense experience that heightens senses. A crack high lasts only a few minutes; then the good feelings are gone. During the crash, the user may feel tired and unmotivated and find it impossible to sleep. Cocaine in any form can lead to a staggering number of physical, mental, and emotional problems, both short- and long-term. Sudden death has resulted from cardiac arrest.

Methamphetamine

Methamphetamine has caused special concern because it is relatively cheap, readily available, and can be lethal. A central nervous system stimulant, methamphetamine has a high potential for abuse and dependence. The drug's euphoric effects are similar to but longer lasting than those of cocaine. Methamphetamine takes the form of a white, odorless, and bitter-tasting crystalline powder, readily soluble in water or alcohol.

Street methamphetamine is referred to by many names including "meth," "speed," "zip," "go-fast," "cristy," "chalk," and "crank." Pure methamphetamine hydrochloride, the smokable form of the drug, is called "L.A.," or, because of its clear, chunky crystals, "ice," "crystal," "glass," or "quartz."

Even small amounts of methamphetamine can produce euphoria, enhanced wakefulness, increased physical activity, decreased appetite, and increased respiration. Hyperthermia (artificially induced very high temperatures) and convulsions sometimes can result in death.

Cardiovascular side effects include chest pain and hypertension and can result in cardiovascular collapse and death. In addition, methamphetamine causes increased heart rate and blood pressure and sometimes can produce strokes by causing irreversible damage to blood vessels in the brain.

Tobacco—The Other Legal Drug

Tobacco use is clearly the cause of many important and serious medical conditions, including heart disease, cancer, and lung ailments. Over the years, tobacco has led to the deaths of hundreds of thousands of individuals.

Unfortunately, cigarette smoking is on the rise among college students, jumping 28 percent in 4 years. "The rise in this group is really an alarming sign," said Henry Wechsler of Harvard University. Wechsler compared surveys of more than 14,000 students at 116 colleges in 1993 and again in 1997 and found a 28 percent increase over those 4 years.

Despite the fact that tobacco use causes many serious medical conditions and leads to the deaths of hundreds of thousands of people, cigarette smoking is on the rise among college students.

Because more women than men now smoke, the rate of cancer in women is rapidly approaching or surpassing rates in men.

Chemicals in tobacco are highly addictive, making discontinuation of smoking difficult. Although young people may not worry about long-term side effects, increased numbers of respiratory infections, worsening of asthma, bad breath, and stained teeth should be motivations to not start smoking at all.

Making Decisions and Finding Help

If you need to talk with someone or already have an alcohol or drug problem, one thing you might do is contact your campus counseling or health center, personal physician, or clergy. Unless your behavior is considered dangerous to yourself or to others, most counselors and physicians are required by their professional codes to respect the confidentiality of your visit and to try to help you with your problems. Before taking such a step, it's wise to check state and local laws on confidentiality because they vary widely across the country.

SEE EXERCISE 14.3

If you are a responsible drinker, we hope you won't be goaded into becoming a problem drinker. If you don't drink at all, we hope we have assured you that it's okay not to drink. And if you do have an alcohol or drug problem, seek appropriate professional care before things get worse. College is a time for growing up, for discovering your talents, for preparing to succeed in life. Why let something as potentially damaging as alcohol or other drugs put a kink in those plans?

Sex and the College Student

We know from numerous studies that about 75 percent of traditional-age college students have engaged in sexual intercourse at least once. Without being judgmental, we will encourage you to know your options and to recognize that you have the right to choose what's comfortable—and safe—for you.

TABLE 14.6   METHODS OF CONTRACEPTION (CONTINUED)

DIAPHRAGM (80-95%)

What It Is

Dome-shaped rubber cap that gets inserted into the vagina and covers the cervix.

Advantages

Safe method of birth control with virtually no side effects. May be inserted up to 2 hours prior to intercourse, making it somewhat spontaneous. May provide a small measure of protection against STDs.

Disadvantages

Wide variance of effectiveness based on consistent use, the fit of the diaphragm, and frequency of intercourse. Multiple acts of intercourse require use of additional spermicide.

Comments

Must be prescribed by a physician. Must always be used with a spermicidal jelly and left in for 6-8 hours after intercourse.

FEMALE CONDOM (80-95%)

What It Is

A polyurethane sheath that completely lines the vagina and acts as a barrier between the genitals. Two rings hold it in place, one inside and one outside the vagina.

Advantages

Highly safe medically; does not require any spermicide. Theoretically provides excellent protection against STDs–almost perfectly leakproof and better than the male condom in this regard.

Disadvantages

Has not gained wide acceptance. Visible outer ring has been aesthetically displeasing to some potential users.

Comments

Although the effectiveness is not as high as for the male condom, this method has the advantage of offering good STD protection that is in the control of the woman.

CERVICAL CAP (80-90%)

What It Is

A cup-shaped device that fits over the cervix.

Advantages

Similar to diaphragm but may be worn longer–up to 48 hours.

Disadvantages

Not widely available due to lack of practitioners trained in fitting them.

Comments

Longer wearing time increases risk of vaginal infections.

SPERMICIDAL FOAMS, CREAMS, AND JELLIES (80-90%)

What They Are

Sperm-killing chemicals inserted into the vagina.

Advantages

Easy to purchase and use. Provides some protection against STDs, including HIV.

Disadvantages

Lower effectiveness than many methods. Can be messy. May increase likelihood of birth defects should pregnancy occur.

Comments

As with condoms, it is suspected that failure is due to lack of consistent use. However, spermicides seem to work better in combination with other methods, such as the diaphragm.

NATURAL FAMILY PLANNING (80%)

What It Is

Periodic abstinence based on when ovulation is predicted.

Advantages

Requires no devices or chemicals.

Disadvantages

Requires a period of abstinence each month, when ovulation is expected. Also, requires diligent record keeping.

Comments

For maximum effectiveness, consult a trained practitioner for guidance in using this method.

COITUS INTERRUPTUS (80%)

What It Is

Withdrawal.

Advantages

Requires no devices or chemicals and can be used at any time, at no cost.

Disadvantages

Relies heavily on the man having enough control and knowing when ejaculation will occur to remove himself from the vagina in time. Also may diminish pleasure for the couple.

Comments

Ejaculation must be far enough away from partner's genitals so that no semen can enter the vagina. Provides no protection against STDs.

*Percentages in parentheses refer to approximate effectiveness rates based on 1 year of using the method. Where two numbers are given, the lower percentage refers to the *typical* effectiveness, and the higher number refers to a *possible* effectiveness if used correctly and consistently.

Sexually Transmitted Diseases (STDs)

The problem of STDs on college campuses has been receiving growing attention in recent years as an epidemic number of students have become infected. The idea that nice young men and women don't catch these sorts of diseases is dangerous and inaccurate. If you choose to be sexually active, exposure to an STD is a real possibility.

Approximately 5 to 10 percent of visits to college health services nationally are for the diagnosis and treatment of STDs. For more information, contact your student health center, your local health department, or the National STD Hotline (1-800-227-8922).

Chlamydia

- This is the most common STD in the United States. Over 4 million new cases are diagnosed each year.
- Symptoms usually appear 1 to 3 weeks after exposure. Even if symptoms are not apparent, an individual is still contagious and may transmit the disease to subsequent sexual partners.
- Chlamydia may cause pelvic inflammatory disease (PID) now thought to be the leading cause of infertility in women.
- In women, symptoms may include mild abdominal pain, change in vaginal discharge, and pain and burning with urination.
- In men, symptoms may include pain and burning with urination and discharge from penis.
- Men who go without treatment may become infertile.
- Chlamydia is treatable with antibiotics.

Gonorrhea

- Gonorrhea is a bacterial infection that produces symptoms similar to chlamydia.
- Gonorrhea is treatable with antibiotics.
- Men usually show symptoms, but women often do not.
- If untreated, it can lead to more severe infections in men and women.

Herpes

- Herpes is on the increase, with 45 million people infected—the majority of whom show no symptoms.
- Symptoms include blisters on genitals or mouth that appear 2 days to 2 weeks after exposure. Both oral and genital herpes can be transmitted by oral sex.
- Fifty percent of those infected may have outbreaks several times a year.
- There is no cure. Valtrex and Zovirax seem to reduce the length and severity of herpes outbreaks. People are most contagious after or right before lesions erupt.
- Asymptomatic people can transmit herpes because the virus continues to live in the body indefinitely.

Human Papillomavirus (HPV)

- HPV is the leading STD affecting college students. Recent studies show that as many as 40 to 50 percent of sexually active college students may be infected.
- HPV causes venereal warts, which affect both men and women on outer genitals and in the rectum of those who practice anal-receptive intercourse.
- The typical incubation period is at least 3 months, although symptoms may not appear for many months or years after exposure.
- The warts may be small, flat, pink growths, or larger, with a cauliflower-like appearance.
- There is no cure, but treatment is available in the form of burning, freezing, chemical destruction, and, in severe cases, laser surgery.
- The virus remains in the body and may cause recurrences. A person infected with HPV remains contagious to sexual partners indefinitely.
- HPV may cause cervical cancer in women.

Hepatitis B

- Transmitted through unprotected sex and contact with infected blood, hepatitis B is 100 times more infectious than HIV.
- When present, symptoms may include upset stomach and yellowing of skin and eyes.
- Most people recover completely, but some remain carriers for life.
- There is no cure and no treatment other than rest and a healthy diet.
- A preventive vaccine is available and recommended by the Centers for Disease Control and the American Academy of Pediatrics for all young adults.

HIV/AIDS HIV/AIDS is difficult to discuss briefly. The main thing for you to know is that the number of people with AIDS and the virus that causes it—HIV—continues to increase. During 1997, in the sixteenth year of the epidemic, the number of cases of AIDS had grown to over 600,000 in the United States. The Centers for Disease Control estimate that at least 1 to $1\frac{1}{2}$ million people are infected with HIV. The routes of transmission for HIV are through blood, semen, vaginal fluids, and breast milk or by being born to an HIV-infected mother.

In the late 1990s, those experiencing the greatest increases in new HIV infections and cases of AIDS were women, teens, heterosexuals, Hispanic Americans, and African Americans (who continue to be disproportionately represented among those with AIDS). It's important to keep in mind, however, that it's not *who* you are but *what* you do that puts you at risk for contracting HIV.

By the mid-1990s, AIDS had become the number-one killer of men and women ages 25 to 44 in United States cities with 100,000 people or more. Considering the long incubation period, it is likely that those dying in their late twenties and early thirties contracted HIV during their college years.

Statistics suggest that many students obviously are engaging in the behaviors that put them at risk for all STDs, including HIV. In addition, having other STDs may predispose people to contract HIV more readily if they are exposed to the virus.

As with other STDs, abstinence, monogamy, and condoms (in that order) are the best ways to prevent the sexual spread of HIV. Get as much information as you can through your student health service, your local health department, or the National AIDS Hotline (1-800-342-AIDS).

Preventing Sexually Transmitted Diseases

Abstinence Even if three-quarters of college students are having sex, that still leaves a solid one-quarter who are not. It can be difficult when you're in the minority, but the latter group are reaping benefits. One thing that can make the decision to abstain easier is realizing that abstinence doesn't have to mean a lack of intimacy or even of sexual pleasure, for that matter. For couples abstinence can encompass a wide variety of behaviors from holding hands to more sexually intimate actions short of intercourse.

SEE SEARCH ONLINE!
INTERNET EXERCISE 14.2

Monogamy Another safe behavior, in terms of disease prevention, is having sex exclusively with one partner who is uninfected. However, having a long-term monogamous relationship is not always practical because many college students want to date and either aren't interested in becoming serious or just don't find the right person. A second reason is that it is hard to know for sure that your partner was not infected to begin with.

Condoms As we enter the new century, the condom needs to be a given to those who are sexually active. Other than providing very good pregnancy protection, it can help prevent the spread of STDs, including HIV/AIDS. The condom's effectiveness

Critical Thinking

Alcohol, Drugs, and Sex

What should come across in this chapter is that entering college students tend to believe there's more drinking and more sex on campus than reality confirms. How do you think such beliefs got started? What is the best way to dispel such false notions among entering students before they "get hooked"? Brainstorm ways to educate new students and choose the way you think works best. Write it down and turn it in or share it with the class.

against disease holds true for anal, vaginal, and oral intercourse. The most current research indicates that the rate of protection provided by condoms against STDs is similar to its rate of protection against pregnancy (90 to 99 percent).

Unfortunately, the condom has long had a reputation of being a less spontaneous method and of diminishing pleasurable sensations. It may take some discussion to convince your partner that using condoms is the right thing to do. If he or she responds negatively to the suggestion, here are some comments that may help:

Your partner: Condoms aren't spontaneous. They ruin the moment.

You: If you think they're not spontaneous, maybe we're not being creative enough. If you let me put it on you, I bet you won't think it's interrupting anything!

Your partner: Condoms aren't natural.

You: What's not natural is to be uptight during sex. If we know we're protected, we'll both be more relaxed.

Your partner: I won't have sex with a condom on.

You: Well, we can't have sex without one. There are other things we can do without having intercourse. Why don't we stick to "outercourse" until we can agree on using condoms for intercourse?

SEE EXERCISE 14.5

Almost no one finds it easy to talk about sex with a potential partner. That's no excuse. Express your needs and concerns. Be sure you understand the other person's feelings and concerns as well.

Condoms

When selecting a condom, always consider the following:

1. **Use condoms made of latex rubber.** Latex serves as a barrier to bacteria and viruses, even those as small as HIV. "Lambskin" or "natural membrane" condoms are not as good for disease prevention because of the pores in the material. Look for "latex" on the package. For those allergic to rubber, there is a polyurethane condom on the market that also offers significant disease protection. Ask your pharmacist.

2. **Try different condoms until you find one that's comfortable and suits you.** Some men and women believe that condoms don't feel good. You have many options from which to choose. Different brands and features have their own unique feel. If the first condom you select isn't totally desirable, don't give up on condoms altogether. Try another brand.

3. **Use a lubricant with a condom.** One of the main reasons condoms break is lack of lubrication. Check the list of ingredients on the back of the lubricant package to make sure the lubricant is water based. Do not use petroleum-based jelly, cold cream, baby oil, or cooking shortening. These can weaken the condom and cause it to break.

SOURCE: Adapted from *Understanding AIDS: A Message from the Surgeon General.* HHA Publication No. (CDC) HHS-88-8404. Washington, DC: Government Printing Office.

Perilous Relationships

Abusive Relationships

How to Tell if Your Relationship Is Abusive You're frightened by your partner's temper and afraid to disagree. You apologize to others for your partner's behavior when you are treated badly. You avoid family and friends because of your partner's jealousy. You're afraid to say no to sex, even if you don't want it. You're forced to justify everything you do, every place you go, and every person you see. You're the object of ongoing verbal insults. You've been hit, kicked, shoved, or had things thrown at you.

What to Do if Your Relationship Is Abusive Tell your abuser the violence must stop. Say no firmly if you don't want sex. Have a safety plan handy: Call the police at 911, consult campus resources (women's student services, the sexual assault office, and so forth), call a community domestic violence center or rape crisis center, or call someone else on campus whom you can trust. Find a counselor or support group on campus or in the community. You can even obtain a restraining order through your local magistrate or county court. If the abuser is a student at the same institution, schedule an appointment with your campus judicial officer to explore campus disciplinary action.

Evidence indicates that violence tends to escalate once a person decides to make a break. Should you reach that point, it's wise to remove yourself from the other person's physical presence. This may include changing your daily patterns.

For further advice, go to your counseling center to find out about restraining orders, listing the abuser's name at the front desk, changing your locks, securing windows, and other precautions.

How to Support a Friend Whose Relationship Is Abusive Be there. Listen. Help your friend recognize the abuse. Be nonjudgmental. Help your friend contact campus and community resources for help. If you become frustrated or frightened, seek help for yourself as well.

Avoiding Sexual Assault

By the time they graduate, an estimated one out of four college women will be the victim of attempted rape, and one out of six will be raped. Most will be raped by someone they know, a date or acquaintance, and most will not report the crime. Alcohol is a factor in nearly three-quarters of the incidents. Whether raped by a date or a stranger, the victim can suffer long-term trauma.

Tricia Phaup of the University of South Carolina offers this advice on avoiding sexual assault:

- **Know what you want and do not want sexually.** Communicate it loudly and clearly to a partner.
- **Go to parties or social gatherings with friends and leave with them.** Sexual assaults happen when people get isolated.
- **Avoid being alone with people you don't know very well.** Do not accept a ride home with someone you just met or study alone in your room with a classmate you don't know well.
- **Trust your gut.** If a situation feels uncomfortable in some way, don't take chances. Get out of it.
- **Be alert to unconscious messages that you may be sending.** Although it in no way justifies someone taking advantage of you, be aware that if you dress in a sexy manner, spend the evening drinking together, and then go back to your friend's room, that person may think you want something.
- **Be conscious of how much alcohol you drink, if any.** It is easier to make decisions and communicate them when you are sober and also easier to sense a dangerous situation.

If you are ever tempted to force another person to have sex:

- **Realize that it is never okay to force yourself sexually on someone.**
- **Don't assume you know what your date wants.** He or she may want a different degree of intimacy than you do.
- **If you're getting mixed messages, ask.** You have nothing to lose by stopping. If someone really wants you, he or she will let you know. And if he or she doesn't, then it's right to stop.
- **Be aware of the effects of alcohol.** It makes it more difficult to understand the other person and is more likely to instigate violent behavior.
- **Remember that rape is legally and morally wrong.** If you have the slightest doubt about whether what you're doing is right, it's probably not.

The following people or offices may be available on or near your campus to deal with a sexual assault: campus sexual assault coordinator, local rape crisis center, campus police department, counseling center, student health services, student affairs professionals, women's student services office, residence life staff, local hospital emergency rooms, and campus chaplains.

Relationships with Teachers

Entering into a romantic relationship with one of your teachers can swiftly lead to major problems. On most campuses, faculty and staff are prohibited from having such relationships with students. It is tempting fate to enter into a personal, romantic relationship with someone who has power or authority over you—as you may learn when the relationship goes bad and you receive a low grade in the course. For this reason, it is imperative to avoid such entanglements and report problems to the proper campus authorities.

A Final Word

When sex happens in ignorance, in haste, or without regard for the other party involved, it may leave emotional scars that are difficult to erase. When individuals who have genuine feelings for each other can agree on the degree of intimacy and involvement, be honest and candid with each other, take proper precautions, and show respect for each other's needs and feelings, that's a different matter entirely.

SEE SEARCH ONLINE! INTERNET EXERCISE 14.3

Search Online!

Internet Exercise 14.1 The Core Alcohol and Drug Survey

Estimate the percentage of students who reported using each of the following drugs during the year prior to the Core survey.

Tobacco_____Alcohol_____Marijuana_____Cocaine_____Amphetamines_____

Go to *http://www.siu.edu/departments/coreinst/public_html/recent.html* and compare your estimates to the results in *Recent Statistics on Alcohol and Other Drug Use on American College Campuses: 1995–96* (statistics drawn from a sample of 89,874 college students from 171 2- and 4-year U.S. colleges by the Core Institute). (Go to *http://success.wadsworth.com* for the most up-to-date URLs.)

Internet Exercise 14.2 Speak of the Devil

The Internet can be a major source of information on topics that you are too embarrassed to ask about in person. Not all the information on the Internet, however, is either timely or accurate. One of the best sources for information on such topics as sex, abstinence, rape and sexual assault, sexual orientation, sexual dysfunction, and "101 Ways to Please Your Lover Without Doing It" is the Duke University "Healthy Devil" Online at *http://h-devil-www.mc.duke.edu/ h-devil/sex/101ways.htm.* See also the resources on pregnancy testing, options, and suggested resources at *http://h-devil-www.mc.duke.edu/h-devil/preg/preg.htm.* (Go to *http://success.wadsworth.com* for the most up-to-date URLs.)

Internet Exercise 14.3 Discovering More About Alcohol, Drugs, and Sex

Using *InfoTrac College Edition,* try these phrases and others for key-word and subject-guide searches: "binge drinking," "illegal drugs in college," "alcohol and health," "sexual activity in college," "birth control," and "abusive relationships." Also try the names of drugs about which you want more information (such as "methamphetamines").

ALSO LOOK UP:
Drinking, binge drinking, and other drug use among southwestern undergraduates: three-year trends. Melanie E. Bennett, Joseph H. Miller, W. Gill Woodall. *American Journal of Drug and Alcohol Abuse* May 1999 v25 i2 p331
Dying for a drink. (investigation of death of college student caused by binge drinking) John McCormick, Claudia Kalb. *Newsweek* June 15, 1998 v131 n24 p30(1)
Sexually aggressive men's responses to a date rape analogue: alcohol as a disinhibiting cue. Jeffrey A. Bernat, Karen S. Calhoun, Stephanie Stolp. *Journal of Sex Research* Nov 1998 v35 i4 p341(1)
Combating sexual offenses on the college campus: keys to success. Craig J. Vickio, Barbara Arps Hoffman, Elizabeth Yarris. *Journal of American College Health* May 1999 v47 i6 p283

Additional Exercises

These exercises will help you sharpen what we believe are the critical skills for college success: writing, critical thinking, learning in groups, planning, reflecting, and taking action. Also, check out the CD-ROM that came with your book—you will find the exercises and more.

Exercise 14.1 **Why Students Binge**

List the three most important reasons why you think students binge drink. Explain why each reason is important. If you had the task of modifying drinking behaviors at your institution, what would you do?

Exercise 14.2 **A Safe Stress Antidote**

In groups of three to five, make a list of activities that can be used by students at your institution as an antidote for stress. In other words, brainstorm activities that can be extremely pleasurable and can relieve the stress of daily living. The only caveat is that those activities should be safe and fun. Share your list with other groups in the class.

Exercise 14.3 **Advice to a Friend**

If you could make only three recommendations to a friend about partying safer, what would they be? Explain how each would help your friend enjoy the party without putting himself or herself at risk.

Exercise 14.4 **Which Birth Control Method Is Best?**

If you're choosing to be sexually active and don't desire children at this time, it's time to choose a method of birth control. Both partners should be involved in this decision. Consider various factors to decide what's right for you, your partner, and your relationship. You can answer these questions on your own and then have your partner complete the exercise, with both of you keeping in mind a particular method you're considering. Or you can complete it together, discussing the issue as you go.

	ME	MY PARTNER
1. Has a pregnancy ever occurred despite using this preferred method of birth control?	_____	_____
2. Will I have difficulty using this method?	_____	_____
3. If this method interrupts love making, will I be less likely to use it?	_____	_____
4. Is there anything about my behavior or habits that could lead me to use this method incorrectly?	_____	_____
5. Am I at risk of being exposed to HIV or other STDs if I use this method?	_____	_____
6. Am I concerned about potential side effects associated with this method?	_____	_____
7. Does this method cost more than I can afford?	_____	_____
8. Would I really rather not use this method?	_____	_____

Exercise 14.5 **What's Your Decision?**

Although you might know about the strategies to keep yourself from contracting an STD, knowledge doesn't always translate into behavior. Use the following chart to brainstorm all the reasons you can think of that people wouldn't practice each of the prevention strategies: abstinence, monogamy, or condom use. In other words, think about the barriers to safer sex. Then go back over your list and consider whether the barrier would apply to you (yes, no, or maybe). In this way you can better evaluate where you stand on the issue of safer sex and determine what areas you may need to work on to ensure that you protect yourself—always!

BARRIERS   **DOES THIS APPLY?**

_____   _____

_____   _____

_____   _____

_____   _____

_____   _____

Your Personal Journal

Here are several things to write about. Choose one or more or choose another topic related to this chapter.

1. Before reading this chapter, what were your attitudes about using alcohol and other drugs and about engaging in sex? How has this chapter affected those attitudes?

2. If you know of someone who regularly binges or have read or heard about someone who binges, write how you feel about that.

3. If you knew of someone who was guilty of sexual assault or was a victim of sexual assault, what would you do?

4. If a roommate told you he or she wanted to use your room for a sexual encounter one night, how would you answer that?

5. What behaviors are you willing to change after reading this chapter? How might you go about changing them?

6. What else is on your mind this week? If you wish to share it with your instructor, add it to this journal entry.

Resources

List some of the resources that will help you make sensible decisions about sex, by filling in the names, addresses, and phone numbers for any of the following people or places you might use:

Personal physician ....

Student health
center ....

Name of physician
at health center ....

Planned Parenthood
chapter ....

Local AIDS groups ....

Local gay/lesbian
resources ....

Counseling center ....

Spiritual advisor/
pastor/rabbi ....

Friends, relatives ....

Campus sexual
assault coordinator ....

Local rape crisis
center ....

Campus police ....

Women's student
services office ....

Find copies of current or recent magazines that are targeted to a young audience (ages 18-25). Go through them and note the ads for alcohol products and cigarettes. Explain what you believe are the tactics the advertiser is using to make the reader drink or smoke. Look at these and other ads in the magazines for examples of sexual appeals. Comment on them.

....

....

....

....

....

....

Suggestions for Further Reading

Chapter 1

Gordon, Virginia. *Foundations: A Reader for New College Students.* Belmont, CA: Wadsworth, 1995.

Newman, Richard. *The Complete Guide to College Success: What Every Student Needs to Know.* New York: New York University Press, 1995.

Pathways to Success. Washington, DC: Howard University Press, 1997.

Siebert, Al, & Bernadine Gilpin. *The Adult Student's Guide to Survival and Success.* Portland, OR: Practical Psychology Press, 1997.

Tufariello, Ann Hunt. *Up Your Grades: Proven Strategies for Academic Success.* Lincolnwood, IL: VGM Career Horizons, 1997.

Chapter 2

Campbell, William E. *The Power to Learn: Helping Yourself to College Success,* "Managing Your Time" (Chapter 2). Belmont, CA: Wadsworth, 1997.

Smith, Laurence N., & Timothy Walter. *The Adult Learner's Guide to College Success,* rev. ed., "Five Strategies for Time Management" (Chapter 3). Belmont, CA: Wadsworth, 1995.

Sotiriou, Peter Elias. *Integrating College Study Skills: Reasoning in Reading, Listening, and Writing,* 4th ed., "Your Learning Inventory: Your Learning Style, Study Time, and Study Area" (Chapter 2). Belmont, CA: Wadsworth, 1996.

Chapter 3

Bender, Eileen, Millard Dunn, Bonnie Kendall, Peggy Wilkes, & Catherine Larson. *Quick Hits: Successful Strategies for Award Winning Teachers.* Bloomington: Indiana University Press, 1994.

Brown, M. Neil, & Stuart M. Keeley. *Striving for Excellence in College: Tips for Active Learning.* Englewood Cliffs, NJ: Prentice Hall, 1996.

Halberstam, Joshua. *Acing College: A Professor Tells Students How to Beat the System.* Penguin USA, 1991.

Jalango, Mary R., Meghan Mahoney Twiest, & Gail J. Gerlach. *The College Learner: How to Survive and Thrive in an Academic Environment.* Englewood Cliffs, NJ: Prentice Hall, 1996.

Mears, Peter. *Team Building: A Structured Learning Approach.* Delray Beach, FL: Saint Lucie, 1994.

Midura, Daniel W., & Donald R. Glover. *More Team Building Challenges.* Champaign, IL: Human Kinetics, 1995.

Silberman, Mel. *Active Learning: 101 Strategies to Teach Any Subject.* Boston: Allyn & Bacon, 1996.

Sykes, Charles J. *Profscam: Professors and the Demise of Higher Education.* New York: St. Martin's Press, 1990.

Watson, Richard A. *Good Teaching: A Guide for Students.* Carbondale: Southern Illinois University Press, 1997.

Woodhull, Angela. *Coping with Difficult Teachers.* Rochester, VT: Schenkman, 1996.

Chapter 4

Lawrence, Gordon. *People Types and Tiger Stripes.* Gainesville, FL: Center for the Application of Psychological Types, 1982.

Malone, John C., Jr. *Theories of Learning: A Historical Approach.* Belmont, CA: Wadsworth, 1991.

Perry, William. *Forms of Intellectual and Ethical Development in the College Years: A Scheme.* New York: Holt, Rinehart & Winston, 1970.

Chapter 5

Browne, M. Neil. *Asking the Right Questions: A Guide to Critical Thinking.* Englewood Cliffs, NJ: Prentice Hall, 1997.

Daly, William. "Thinking as an Unnatural Act." *Journal of Developmental Education,* 18(2) Winter 1994.

Daly, William. *Teaching Independent Thinking.* Columbia, SC: National Resource Center for the First Year Experience and Students in Transition, 1995.

Elbow, Peter. *Writing Without Teachers.* New York: Oxford University Press, 1973.

Elbow, Peter. *Writing with Power.* New York: Oxford University Press, 1981.

Goldberg, Natalie, & Samuel Bercholz. *Writing Down the Bones: Freeing the Writer Within.* Boston: Shambhala Publications, 1986.

Lannon, John M. *The Writing Process: A Concise Rhetoric.* New York: Longman Publishing Group, 1997.

Maker, Janet, & Minette Lenier. *Academic Reading with Active Critical Thinking.* Belmont, CA: Wadsworth, 1995.

Murray, Donald. *Learning by Teaching.* Montclair, NJ: Boynton/Cook, 1982.

Murray, Donald M. *Read to Write: A Writing Process Reader.* Fort Worth, TX: Dryden Press/Harcourt Brace Jovanovich, 1993.

Smith, Donald E. P., Glenn M. Knudsvig, & Tim Walter. *Critical Thinking: Building the Basics.* Belmont, CA: Wadsworth, 1997.

Zinsser, William. *Writing to Learn.* New York: Harper & Row, 1988.

Zinsser, William. *On Writing Well.* New York: HarperPerennial, 1990.

Whitehead, Alfred North. *The Aims of Education.* New York: Mentor, 1949 (originally published in 1929).

Chapter 6

Allen, Sheila. *Making Connections.* "The Student's Role as Learner" (Unit 4). Fort Worth, TX: Harcourt Brace College, 1998.

Chaffee, John. *The Thinker's Guide to College Success,* "Reading Critically" (Chapter 6). Boston: Houghton Mifflin, 1995.

Laskey, Marcia L., & Paula W. Gibson. *College Study Strategies: Thinking and Learning,* "Questioning Strategies That Lead to Critical Thinking" (Chapter 11). Boston: Allyn & Bacon, 1997.

Pauk, Walter. *How to Study in College,* 6th ed., "Learning from Your Textbook" (Chapter 11), "Noting What Is Important" (Chapter 12), "Thinking Visually" (Chapter 13). Boston: Houghton Mifflin, 1997.

Seyler, Dorothy U. *Steps to College Reading,* "Developing a Reading Strategy" (Chapter 2). Needham Heights, MA: Allyn & Bacon, 1998.

Van Blerkom, Dianna L. *College Study Skills: Becoming a Strategic Learner,* 2nd ed., "Reading Your Textbook" (Chapter 6), "Marking Your Textbook" (Chapter 7). Belmont, CA: Wadsworth, 1997.

Chapter 7

Allen, Sheila. *Making Connections.* "The Student's Role as Learner" (Unit 4). Fort Worth, TX: Harcourt Brace College, 1998.

Chaffee, John. *The Thinker's Guide to College Success,* "Reading Critically" (Chapter 6). Boston: Houghton Mifflin, 1995.

Laskey, Marcia L., & Paula W. Gibson. *College Study Strategies: Thinking and Learning,* "Questioning Strategies That Lead to Critical Thinking" (Chapter 11). Boston: Allyn & Bacon, 1997.

Pauk, Walter. *How to Study in College,* 6th ed., "Learning from Your Textbook" (Chapter 11), "Noting What Is Important" (Chapter 12), "Thinking Visually" (Chapter 13). Boston: Houghton Mifflin, 1997.

Seyler, Dorothy U. *Steps to College Reading,* "Developing a Reading Strategy" (Chapter 2). Needham Heights, MA: Allyn & Bacon, 1998.

Van Blerkom, Dianna L. *College Study Skills: Becoming a Strategic Learner,* 2nd ed., "Reading Your Textbook" (Chapter 6), "Marking Your Textbook" (Chapter 7). Belmont, CA: Wadsworth, 1997.

Chapter 8

Campbell, William E. *The Power to Learn: Helping Yourself to College Success,* "Remembering and Reproducing What You Learn" (Chapter 6). Belmont, CA: Wadsworth, 1997.

Galica, Gregory S. *The Blue Book: A Student's Guide to Essay Exams.* Troy, MO: Harcourt Brace Jovanovich, 1991.

Longman, Debbie Guice, & Rhonda Holt Atkinson. *College Learning and Study Skills,* 3rd ed., "Tests: Preparing for and Taking Them" (Chapter 7). Minneapolis/St. Paul: West, 1993.

McKowen, Clark. *Get Your A Out of College: Mastering the Hidden Rules of the Game,* rev. ed., "The Art of Remembering" (Chapter 2), "Raising Test Scores" (Chapter 3). Menlo Park, CA: Crisp Publications, 1996.

Pauk, Walter. *How to Study in College,* 8th ed., "Mastering Objective Tests" (Chapter 15). Boston: Houghton Mifflin, 1997.

Chapter 9

Kurland, Daniel J. *The Net, the Web, and You: All You Really Need to Know About the Internet and a Little Bit More.* Belmont, CA: Wadsworth, 1996.

Lubar, Steven D. *InfoCulture: The Smithsonian Book of Information Age Inventions.* Boston: Houghton Mifflin, 1993.

Roszak, Theodore. *The Cult of Information: The Folklore of Computers and the True Art of Thinking.* New York: Pantheon, 1986.

Wurman, Richard Saul. *Information Anxiety Is Produced by the Ever-Widening Gap.* New York: Doubleday, 1989.

Chapter 10

Berg, A. *Finding the Work You Love: A Woman's Career Guide.* San Jose, CA: Resource Publications, 1993.

Birsner, E. P. *Mid-Career Job Hunting: Official Handbook of the Forty Plus Club.* New York: Prentice Hall, 1991.

Bolles, Richard N. *What Color Is Your Parachute? A Practical Manual for Job Hunters and Career Changers.* Berkeley, CA: Ten Speed Press, 1996.

Criscito, P. *Resumes in Cyberspace: Your Complete Guide to a Computerized Job Search.* Hauppauge, NY: Barron's Educational Services, 1997.

Dictionary of Occupational Titles (DOT). Washington, DC: Bureau of Labor Statistics. Published annually.

Directory of Directories. Detroit: Gale Research. Published annually.

Encyclopedia of Associations. Detroit: Gale Research. Published annually.

Field, S. *100 Best Careers for the 21st Century.* New York: Macmillan, 1996.

Gelberg, S., & Chojnacki. *Career and Life Planning with Gay, Lesbian, and Bisexual Persons.* Alexandria, VA: American Counseling Association, 1996.

Harbin, Carey E. *Your Transfer Planner: Strategic Goals and Guerrilla Tactics.* Belmont, CA: Wadsworth, 1995.

Holland, John. *The Self-Directed Search Professional Manual.* Gainesville, FL: Psychological Assessment Resources, 1985.

Jackson, Tom, & E. Jackson. *The New Perfect Resume.* New York: Doubleday, 1996.

Kennedy, J. L. *Hook Up, Get Hired! The Internet Job Search Revolution.* New York: Wiley, 1995.

Kissane, S. F. *Career Success for People with Physical Disabilities.* Lincolnwood, IL: VMG Career Horizons, 1997.

Kocher, E. *International Jobs: Where They Are and How to Get Them.* Reading, MA: Addison-Wesley, 1993.

Lauber, D. *Professional's Job Finder.* River Forest, IL: Planning/Communications, 1997.

Michelozzi, B. N. *Coming Alive from Nine to Five.* Mountain View, CA: Mayfield, 1996.

Occupational Outlook Handbook. Washington, DC: Government Publishing Office. Published annually.

Riley, M., F. Roehm, & S. Oserman. *The Guide to Internet Job Searching.* Lincolnwood, IL: NTC Publishing Group, 1996.

Rivera, M. *The Minority Career.* Holbrook, MA: Bob Adams, 1991.

Stair, Lila B. *Careers in Business: Selecting and Planning Your Career Path.* Homewood, IL: Irwin, 1986.

Tieger, P. D., & B. Barron-Tieger. *Do What You Are: Discover the Perfect Career for You.* Boston: Little, Brown, 1992.

Whitaker, Urban G. *Career Success Workbook: Five Essential Steps to Career and Job Satisfaction.* San Francisco: San Francisco Learning Center, 1992.

Chapter 11

Bass, Ellen, & Kate Kaufman. *Free Your Mind: The Book for Gay, Lesbian, and Bisexual Youth—And Their Allies.* New York: HarperCollins, 1996.

Bellah, Robert, et al. *Habits of the Heart: Individualism and Commitment in American Life.* New York: Harper & Row, 1985.

Cosgrove, Melba, Harold Bloomfield, & Peter McWilliams. *How to Survive the Loss of a Love.* New York: Bantam Books, 1976.

Daloz, Laurent A. Parks, et al. *Common Fire: Lives of Commitment in a Complex World.* Boston: Beacon Press, 1996.

Gaines, Stanley O. *Culture, Ethnicity, and Personal Relationship Processes.* New York: Routledge, 1997.

Hendricks, Gay, & Kathlyn Hendricks. *Conscious Loving: The Journey to Co-Commitment—A Way to Be Fully Together Without Giving Up Yourself.* New York: Bantam Books, 1990.

Hirsh, Sandra, & Jean Kummerow. *Life Types.* New York: Warner Books, 1989.

Kobrin, Michael, & Joanna Mareth. *Service Matters: A Sourcebook for Community Service in Higher Education.* Providence, RI: Campus Compact, 1996.

Myers, David G. *The Pursuit of Happiness: Who Is Happy and Why.* New York: Morrow, 1992.

Chapter 12

Bell, D. *Faces at the Bottom of the Well: The Permanence of Racism.* New York: Basic Books, 1992.

Boswell, J. *Same Sex Unions in Pre-Modern Europe.* New York: Villard, 1994.

DeVita, P. R., & J. D. Armstrong. *Distant Mirrors: America as a Foreign Culture,* 2nd ed. Belmont, CA: Wadsworth, 1998.

Divoky, D. "The Model Minority Goes to School." *Phi Delta Kappan* (November 1988): 219–222.

Fisk, E. B. "The Undergraduate Hispanic Experience." *Change* (May/June 1988): 29–33.

Giovanni, N. "Campus Racism 101." *Essence* (August 1991): 71–72.

Halpern, J. M., & L. Nguyen-Hong-Nhiem, eds. *The Far East Comes Near: Autobiographical Accounts of Southeast Asian Students in America.* Amherst: University of Massachusetts Press, 1989.

Mathews, J. Escalante. *The Best Teacher in America.* New York: Holt, Rinehart & Winston, 1988.

Paley, V. G. *White Teacher.* Cambridge, MA: Harvard University Press, 1989.

Smith, S. G. *Gender Thinking.* Philadelphia: Temple University Press, 1992.

Stalvey, L. M. *The Education of a WASP.* Madison: University of Wisconsin Press, 1989.

Chapter 13

Adams, Janelle P., ed. *The A's and B's of Academic Scholarships.* Alexandria, VA: Octameron Associates. Published annually.

Benson, H., & M. Z. Klipper. *The Relaxation Response.* New York: Morrow, 1976.

Chany, Kalman A., & Geoff Martz. *The Student Access Guide to Paying for College.* New York: Villard. Published annually.

College Check Mate: Innovative Tuitions Plans That Make You a Winner. Alexandria, VA: Octameron Associates. Published annually.

The College Costs and Financial Aid Book. Princeton, NJ: College Board Publications. Published annually.

Directory of Special Programs for Minority Group Members, 4th ed. Garrett Park, MD: Garrett Park, 1986.

Earn and Learn: Cooperative Education Opportunities with the Federal Government. Alexandria, VA: Octameron Associates. Published annually.

Financial Aid Fin-Ancer: Expert Answers to College Financing Questions. Alexandria, VA: Octameron Associates. Published annually.

Fisher, B. S., & J. J. Sloan. *Campus Crime, Legal, Social and Policy Perspectives.* Springfield, IL: Thomas, 1995.

Hyatt, C., & L. Gottlieg. *When Smart People Fail.* New York: Simon & Schuster, 1987.

Kennedy, Joyce, & Herm Davis. *The College Financial Aid Emergency Kit.* Cardiff, CA: Sun Features. Published annually.

Kinser, N. S. *Stress and the American Woman.* New York: Ballantine Books, 1980.

Leyden, L. A. *The Stress Management Handbook.* New Canaan, CT: Keats, 1998.

Luks, A., & P. Payne. *The Healing Power of Doing Good.* New York: Ballantine Books, 1992.

Miller, L. H., A. D. Smith, & L. Rothstein. *The Stress Solution.* New York: Pocket Books, 1993.

Paying Less for College. Princeton, NJ: Peterson's. Published annually.

Sapolsky, R. M. *Why Zebras Don't Get Ulcers.* New York: Freeman, 1994.

Schlacter, Gail A. *Directory of Financial Aid for Women.* Santa Barbara, CA: Reference Service Press. Published biannually.

Schlacter, Gail A., & David R. Weber. *Directory of Financial Aid for Minorities.* Santa Barbara, CA: Reference Service Press. Published biannually.

Seligman, M. *Learned Optimism.* New York: Knopf, 1991.

Student Consumer Guide. Washington, DC: Government Printing Office. Published annually.

Vorst, J. *Necessary Losses.* New York: Fawcett, 1986.

Chapter 14

Elliott, Leland, Cynthia Brantley, & Cynthia Johnson. *Sex on Campus: The Naked Truth About the Real Sex Lives of College Students.* New York: Random House, 1997.

Lear, Dana. *Sex and Sexuality: Risk and Relationship in the Age of AIDS.* Newbury Park, CA: Sage, 1997.

Nevid, Jeffrey S. *Choices: Sex in the Age of STDs.* Boston: Allyn & Bacon, 1995.

Powell, Elizabeth. *Sex on Your Terms.* Boston: Allyn & Bacon, 1996.

Sanday, Peggy Reeves. *Fraternity Gang Rape: Sex, Brotherhood, and Privilege on Campus.* New York: New York University Press, 1992.

Tannen, Deborah. *You Just Don't Understand: Women and Men in Conversation.* New York: Ballantine Books, 1990.

Warshaw, Robin. *I Never Called It Rape.* New York: HarperPerennial, 1988, 1994.

Index

A

Abstinence, 234, 237, 243
Abstract thinking, 68
Abusive relationships, 239
Academic advisement center, 14
Academic advisors:
  evaluation of, 155, 156
  goals and, 111
  learning from, 154–156
  as mentors, 45
  preparation for meeting with, 155, 166
  relationship with, 7, 39
  support services and, 14
  tutoring and, 113
Academic freedom, 45
Academic honesty, 109–111, 125, 127
Academic misconduct:
  reducing problems with, 110–111
  types of, 109–110, 125
Academic programs, 157
Academic regulations, 157
Academic skills center, 6, 14, 113
Academic support center, 113
Active learning:
  advantages of, 38–41, 88–90
  class participation and, 38, 39, 43, 44, 89
  collaboration and, 41–43
  high school/college differences and, 38, 48
  instructors and, 6, 39, 43–46, 89
  Internet and, 47
  journal and, 49
  listening and, 39, 80, 82, 83
  mapping and, 95
  note taking and, 80, 82, 84–85
Active listening, 82
Adult reentry center, 14
Adult students:
  diversity of, 189–190, 193
  enrollment figures for, 10
  families and, 8, 189
  responsibilities of, 12
  study skills and, 6
  transition and, 9

Aerobic exercise, 205, 207
AIDS, 237
Alcohol consumption (*See also* Drug abuse)
  binge drinking and, 225–229, 242
  choices regarding, 229–230, 232
  consequences of, 227
  crime and, 212, 225, 226, 230
  health issues and, 8, 225, 227
  Internet and, 241
  journal and, 243
  reasons for, 225
  risk reduction and, 229
  sexual assault and, 240
  sexuality and, 224, 227, 233, 238
  stress and, 207, 225, 230
Analytical learning style, 53, 58
Assertiveness training, 8
Attendance:
  alcohol consumption and, 226, 229
  collaborative learning and, 41
  exams and, 112
  grades and, 43
  stress and, 207
  student-teacher relationships and, 44, 113
  success strategies and, 5
Auditory learning style, 52, 53, 58
Automobile safety, 210

B

Bigotry, 8
Binge drinking, 225–229, 242
Birth control, 233–235, 242
Block scheduling, 26
Blume, Steven, 58
Branching mapping, 95
Budgeting, 141, 213, 215, 220 (*See also* Money management)

C

Caffeine, 204–205, 206
Campus activities, 7

Campus culture:
  academic misconduct and, 110
  alcohol consumption and, 225
  diversity and, 192–194, 198, 199
Campus resources:
  abusive relationships and, 239
  personal support services, 7
  student activities office and, 7
  student organizations, 180–181, 185
  study skills and, 6
  tutoring and, 113
  types of, 14
Career planning:
  choices in, 12
  factors in, 158–161, 164–165
  journal and, 171
  majors and, 7, 157–158, 159, 164
  personality mosaic and, 167–170
  résumés and, 161–164, 170
Career planning and placement center, 7, 14, 164
Carnegie Commission on Higher Education, 12
Catalog, college:
  information in, 155, 156–157
  student use of, 166–167
Catalog, library, 134, 141, 146
Centers for Disease Control, 237
Cervical caps, 235
Chaplains, 14, 240
Cheating, 109–110, 111
Chlamydia, 236
Class participation:
  active learning and, 38, 39, 43, 44, 89
  collaborative learning and, 41
  comprehension and, 86
  critical thinking and, 69
  grades and, 6
  learning and, 88–90
  learning style and, 53
  listening and, 83
  note taking and, 80, 84
  preparation for, 82
  student-teacher relationship and, 44
Cocaine, 231
Coitus interruptus, 235

Collaborative learning, 13, 41–43, 48
College education:
    benefits of, 11, 12–13, 16–17
    critical thinking and, 67
    dropout rate, 4, 8, 10, 154
College Readjustment Rating Scale, 206,
    219–220
Communication (*See also* E-mail;
    Presentations; Writing)
    collaborative learning and, 41
    critical thinking and, 67, 69
    Internet and, 142–144
    sexuality and, 177, 238
    student-teacher relationships and, 44,
    112
    writing and, 69–70
Commuter students:
    services for, 14
    stress and, 207
    time management and, 26, 29
Computer center, 14
Computer graphics, 142
Computers:
    access to, 139
    budgeting and, 215
    computer applications, 141–142
    developing skills with, 147
    ethical and legal issues of, 140, 144,
    148
    keyboarding and, 139
    libraries and, 130, 132, 134, 139, 145
    note taking and, 86
    personal property safety and, 210
    precautions in using, 140–141, 147
    research and, 130
    sources of help with, 139
    student use of, 6, 137–139
    time management and, 25, 33
    tutoring and, 25, 113
    writing and, 71, 141
Condoms, 176, 234, 237–238, 239, 243
Contraception, 233–235, 242
Cooperative (co-op) jobs, 158, 180–181,
    217
Core Institute, 226, 227, 228
Counseling center:
    abusive relationships and, 239
    alcohol consumption and, 232
    assertiveness training and, 8
    goals and, 111
    relationship breakups and, 178
    services of, 7, 8, 14
    sexual assault and, 240
    stress management and, 14, 217
Cover letter, 162, 164, 170
Cramming, 96
Creative thinking, 68
Credit cards, 210, 214, 215, 220, 221
Crime:
    alcohol consumption and, 212, 225,
    226, 230

drug abuse and, 212, 230
Internet and, 218
sexual assault and, 240
stress and, 210–212
Crime prevention, 212
Critical thinking:
    active learning and, 39, 41
    aspects of, 68–69
    career planning and, 158
    college and, 67
    developing skills in, 6, 72–74
    diversity and, 195
    essay exams and, 116
    examples of, 66–67
    information sources and, 137
    instructors and, 43, 45, 67, 69, 74
    journal and, 75
    key task words and, 117
    learning style and, 55
    libraries and, 130
    listening and, 83
    main ideas and, 87
    money management and, 214
    relationships and, 180
    sexuality and, 238
    study reading and, 96
    success and, 9
    time management and, 27
    as "unnatural acts," 68
    values and, 67
    writing and, 66, 69–70, 74
Criticism, 6
Cultural pluralism, 191–192, 194
Culture, 190
Cuseo, Joseph, 41

D

Daily plan, 23, 25, 32–33
Daly, William, 68
Databases:
    as computer application, 141–142
    as information resource, 6, 15, 135
Date rape, 176, 240
Dating, 174–177 (*See also* Relationships)
Definitional notes, 85
Depo-Provera, 234
Depression, 227
Designated drivers, 229
Diaphragm, 235
Digest of Education Statistics, 15
Disabled student services, 14
Discrimination, 195, 197, 198
Distractions, 26, 27
Diversity:
    active learning and, 39, 40
    campus culture and, 192–194, 198, 199
    collaborative learning and, 42
    cultural pluralism and, 191–192, 194
    diversity attitude scale, 191

exams and, 110
expanded view of, 189–190
Internet and, 196
"new majority" and, 194
prejudice and, 195, 197, 198
race and ethnic groups, 190
in student population, 188–189,
    197–198
study groups and, 42
Dropout rate, 4, 8, 10, 154
Dropping courses, 26, 46, 111, 157
Drug abuse (*See also* Alcohol
    consumption)
    cocaine and, 231
    crime and, 212, 230
    health issues and, 8, 230, 231, 232
    Internet and, 241
    marijuana and, 230–231
    methamphetamine and, 231
    stress and, 207
    tobacco and, 231–232

E

E-mail:
    active learning and, 39
    etiquette for, 143–144
    finding addresses for, 47, 113
    student use of, 6, 139, 145
    student-teacher relationship and, 44,
    143
E/I (Extroversion/Introversion), 54
Emergencies, 5, 113, 211
Employment:
    adult students and, 189
    career planning and, 158
    co-op jobs, 158, 180–181, 217
    College Work-Study Program and, 217
    computer skills and, 6, 138
    drug abuse and, 230
    full-time students and, 5
    majors and, 157
    money management and, 214, 215
    writing skills and, 6
Encyclopedias, 132–133
Engel, Eliot, 46
Escort service, 210
Essay exams, 109, 112, 115–117
Ethnic groups, 190, 192
Exams:
    campus culture and, 110
    high school/college differences in, 43
    journal and, 127
    key task words in, 116–117
    learning style and, 58
    learning teams and, 42
    lecture material and, 43, 82
    mapping and, 95
    mental preparation for, 112
    note taking and, 84

physical preparation for, 112
preparation for, 108–109, 111–113, 126
recall columns and, 87
strategies for taking, 115–119
stress and, 205
study groups and, 112, 113, 126–127
study habits and, 112, 114–115
study reading and, 94
types of, 109, 112, 115–118
Exercise:
   as alternative to alcohol consumption, 230
   exam preparation and, 112
   health issues and, 205, 206
   personal safety and, 211
   stress and, 207
   time management and, 25
Expenses, 212, 213, 214, 215, 220
Extrovert, 54, 55

F

Fact notes, 85
Families:
   adult students and, 8, 189
   goals and, 111
   inclusion of, 178
   responsibility for, 9
   support of, 8, 12
Feeler, 54, 56
Female condoms, 235
Financial aid, 5, 26, 214, 216–217, 218
Financial aid office, 14
Flaming, 143
Focused observation, 74
Food Guide Pyramid, 206
Forgetting, 81–82
Four-year colleges, 10, 227, 228
Freewriting, 70
Friends, 40, 111, 175, 179, 239
Fussman, Cal, 118

G

Gay students, 189, 192, 195
Gift assistance, 216
Goals:
   career planning and, 158, 159, 167
   cheating and, 111
   long-term, 13
   relationships and, 177
   short-term, 13, 14, 17
   study reading and, 95, 96, 100, 103
   for success, 13–14
   textbook marking and, 97
   time management and, 23, 27, 30
Gonorrhea, 236
Grades:
   alcohol consumption and, 227
   cheating and, 110, 111

class participation and, 6
conflicts over, 46
goals and, 30
high school/college differences in, 43
late assignments and, 5
note taking and, 80
stress and, 205
study groups and, 7
study habits and, 124
Grants, 216, 218
Grasha, Tony, 53
Grasha-Riechmann instrument, 53
GUIDE checklist, 120–123

H

Harvard School of Public Health College
   Alcohol Study, 228, 229
Health center:
   alcohol consumption and, 227, 232
   birth control and, 233
   services of, 14
   sexual assault and, 240
   sexually transmitted diseases and, 236
Health issues:
   alcohol consumption and, 8, 225, 227
   college education and, 13
   drug abuse and, 8, 230, 231, 232
   exams and, 112
   exercise and, 205, 206
   sexuality and, 8, 177
   stress and, 8, 204–205, 209
Hepatitis B, 237
Herpes, 236
High school graduates' income, 12
HIV, 237, 239
Hobbies, 209
Hogan/Champagne Personal Style
   Inventory, 59
Holland, John, 159–161, 170
Holland hexagon, 161, 170
Homework, 86
Honesty:
   academic, 109–111
   computers and, 140, 144, 148
Housing office, 14
Hug therapy, 208
Human Papillomavirus (HPV), 236

I

Income, 12
Indexes, 134–135
Information sources:
   catalogs and, 134, 146
   college libraries and, 6, 130, 132–135
   critical thinking and, 137
   databases and, 6, 15, 135
   encyclopedias and, 132–133
   indexes and, 134–135

journal and, 148
periodicals and, 135, 146
World Wide Web and, 6, 135–137
InfoTrac College Edition, 15, 16, 134
Instructors (*See also* Student-teacher relationships)
   academic misconduct and, 111
   active learning and, 6, 39, 43–46, 89
   attendance and, 5
   critical thinking and, 43, 45, 67, 69, 74
   emergencies and, 5, 113
   exams and, 112, 113
   high school/college differences and, 9,
      38, 43, 44, 48
   learning style and, 53, 58–59, 62–63
   learning teams and, 42
   as mentors, 45
   note taking and, 84
   office hours of, 7, 84
   research and, 135
   responsibilities of, 47
   teaching style of, 44, 53, 58–59, 62–63,
      89
Internet (*See also* World Wide Web)
   active learning and, 47
   alcohol consumption and, 241
   assessing information on, 6, 11, 102
   career planning, 165
   college catalogs and, 156
   communication and, 142–144
   critical thinking and, 73
   diversity and, 196
   learning style and, 59
   libraries and, 130
   memory aids and, 125
   relationships and, 182–183
   sexuality and, 241
   stress and, 218
   study reading and, 102
   study skills guides, 89
   time management and, 28
   writing and, 73
Intrauterine device (IUD), 234
Introvert, 54, 55
Intuitor, 22, 54, 56, 57, 58

J

J/P (Judging/Perceiving), 54
Jobs (*See* Employment)
Journal:
   academic honesty and, 127
   active learning and, 49
   alcohol consumption and, 243
   career planning and, 171
   critical thinking and, 75
   diversity and, 199
   exams and, 127
   information sources and, 148
   learning style and, 63

Journal (*continued*):
  note taking and, 91
  relationships and, 185
  sexuality and, 243
  stress and, 220
  study reading and, 104
  time management and, 32
  use of, 17
Judger, 22, 54, 56
Jung, Carl, 54, 174

K

Kinesthetic learning style, 52, 53
Kolb Learning Style Inventory, 59

L

Lakein, Alan, 25
Laughter, 209
Learning (*See also* Active learning;
    Learning style)
  class participation and, 88–90
  collaborative learning, 13, 41–43, 48
  forgetting and, 81
  Internet and, 89
  liberal education and, 13
  passive learning, 38, 39–40
  recall column and, 87
  remember and respond technique,
    86–87
  success and, 6
Learning center (*See* Academic skills
    center)
Learning style:
  analytical, 53, 58
  assessment of, 6, 60–62
  auditory, 52, 53, 58
  classroom behavior and, 53
  collaborative learning and, 42
  improving less dominant style, 57
  informal measure of, 53
  instructors and, 53, 58–59, 62–63
  kinesthetic, 52, 53
  personality preferences and, 54–57,
    60–62
  study groups and, 52, 57
  time management and, 22
  visual, 52, 53, 58, 95
Learning teams, 41–43, 48, 81 (*See also*
    Study groups)
Legal services, 14
Lesbian students, 189, 192, 195
Levinson, Daniel J., 45
Liberal education, 12–13
Librarians, 132, 133
Libraries, college:
  active learning and, 40
  computers and, 130, 132, 134, 139, 145
  learning teams and, 42

  personal safety and, 211
  research and, 131–132, 134
  resources of, 6, 130, 132–135
  time management and, 25, 27
Listening:
  active learning and, 39, 80, 82, 83
  developing skills in, 6, 80–81, 90, 91
  for information, 83
  Internet and, 89
  memory and, 6, 90
  preparation for, 82
  short-term memory and, 81–82
Loans, 216–217
Long-term assignments, 23
Long-term memory, 114

M

Major, selection of:
  academic advisor and, 154–155
  career planning and, 7, 157–158, 159,
    164
  first-year students and, 8, 9
Mapping, 95, 102, 114, 115
Marijuana, 230–231
Marriage, 177, 178, 183
Mass media, 225, 226, 233
Massage, 207
Master plans, 23
Matalene, Carolyn, 69
Matching exams, 118
Math center, 14
Meditation, 208
Memorization, 116
Memory:
  aids to, 118–119, 125
  alcohol consumption and, 226
  listening and, 6, 90
  long-term memory, 114
  recall column and, 87, 90–91
  remember and respond technique,
    86–87
  short-term memory, 81–82
  stress and, 205
Mental health, 112, 205, 208, 220, 227
Mentors, 7, 45
Methamphetamine, 231
Mind maps, 95, 114, 115
Minority students:
  bigotry and, 8
  campus culture and, 192
  enrollment figures for, 10
  as "new majority," 194
  support services for, 7
  transition and, 9
Money management:
  analysis of resources, 212, 214
  budgeting and, 141, 213, 215, 220
  credit cards and, 210, 214, 215, 220,
    221

  critical thinking and, 214
  Internet and, 218
  monthly budget, 213
  planning and, 214–215
  stress and, 212–215
  typical college expenses, 213
  typical resources, 213
Monogamy, 237, 243
Mononucleosis, 205
Multiple-choice exams, 112, 117
Murray, Donald, 70, 72
Myers-Briggs Type Indicator, 54, 55, 58,
    59, 64

N

National STD Hotline, 236
Natural family planning, 235
Norplant, 234
Note taking:
  active learning and, 80–81, 82, 84–85
  comparing notes, 85, 90
  computers and, 86
  developing skills in, 6, 80–81, 84
  high school/college differences in, 43
  homework problems and, 86
  learning teams and, 42
  main ideas and, 84
  in nonlecture classes, 84–85
  recall column and, 84, 85, 87, 90–91
  review of, 87, 91
  study reading and, 100
  styles of, 85
Nutrition, 112, 204, 206, 207

O

Older students (*See* Adult students)
One-minute paper, 41, 44
Oral contraceptives, 234
Outline notes, 85

P

Paragraph notes, 85
Parallels, 75
Parents:
  changes in relationship with, 178–179
  credit cards and, 215
  critical thinking and, 180
  gripes about students, 184
  money and, 212
  student gripes about, 183
Passive learning, 38, 39–40
Peer groups, 225, 233
Pell grants, 218
Pelvic inflammatory disease (PID), 236
Perceiver, 22, 54, 56
Periodicals, 135, 146

Personal productivity software, 142
Personal property safety, 210
Personal safety, 210–211, 225, 239
Personality mosaic, 167–170
Peter, Lawrence J., 124
Pets, 209
Phaup, Tricia, 240
Physical education center, 14
Pirsig, Robert, 71, 74
Plagiarism, 109, 110
Positive self-talk, 112
Prayer, 208
Pregnancy, 176, 227, 233–235, 237–238, 242
Prejudice, 195, 197, 198
Presentations:
    audience for, 120, 121
    body language and, 124
    computer software for, 142
    developing skills for, 6, 127
    GUIDE checklist for, 120–123
    main ideas for, 122
    notes for, 123
    objective for, 120
    organizing ideas for, 122–123
    rehearsal for, 123, 124
    steps for success in, 120–124
    visual aids for, 123
Prewriting, 70–71, 72
Priority setting, 23, 27, 29–30, 220
Procrastination, 26–27, 28, 111, 141
Progressive relaxation, 208
Psychological inventories, 53–57, 59–62, 159–161, 167–170 (*See also* specific test names)
Public speaking (*See* Presentations)

R

Race, 190
Racism, 8, 199
Rape, 176, 240
Reading (*See also* Study reading)
    high school/college differences in, 43
    learning teams and, 42
    listening and, 82
    preparation for, 94
    success and, 6
Recall column, 84, 85, 87, 90–91
Recall sheets, 114
Relationships (*See also* Student-teacher relationships)
    abusive relationships, 239
    alcohol consumption and, 225
    balancing demands of, 181, 183
    breaking up and, 177–178
    campus involvement and, 180, 185
    critical thinking and, 180
    dating and, 174–177
    development of, 175–176

employment and, 181
friends and, 40, 111, 175, 179, 239
initiation of, 7–8
Internet and, 182–183
intimacy and, 176–177
long-distance, 175–176
marriage and, 177, 178, 183
with parents, 178–179, 183–184
roommates and, 180, 184–185
seriousness of, 177
sexual orientation and, 175
sexuality and, 233, 238
Relaxation, 112, 207, 208, 209, 218, 220
Research:
    computers and, 130
    information needs and, 131–132
    information sources and, 132–135
    librarians and, 132, 133
    time management and, 25, 27
    topics and, 131–132
Résumés:
    building of, 158, 161–162, 164, 170
    career planning and, 161–164, 170
    samples of, 163
Returning students (*See* Adult students)
Rewriting, 72
Riechmann, Sheryl, 53
Roommates, 9, 180, 184–185

S

S/N (Sensing/Intuitive), 54, 57
Sax, Linda J., 11
Scheduling, 5, 23–26, 30–33
Scholarship office, 14
Scholarships, 216, 218, 230
Search engines, 136–137
Self-discipline, 26
Self-fulfilling prophecies:
    negative, 13
    positive, 13, 112
Self-help assistance, 216
Senser, 22, 54, 56, 57, 58
Service learning, 181
Sexism, 46
Sexual assault, 176, 240
Sexual harassment, 46
Sexual orientation, 175, 189, 195
Sexuality:
    abusive relationships and, 239
    alcohol consumption and, 224, 227, 233, 238
    birth control and, 233–235, 242
    choices involving, 232
    health issues and, 8, 177
    Internet and, 241
    intimacy and, 176–177
    journal and, 243
Sexually transmitted diseases (STDs):
    alcohol consumption and, 227

prevention of, 237–238, 243
rate of, 233, 235–236
types of, 236–237
Short-term memory, 81–82
Sleep, 112, 206, 207
Special populations (*See* Adult students; Commuter students; Diversity; Minority students; Students with disabilities)
Spermicidal foams, creams, jellies, 235
Spirituality, 208
Spreadsheets, 141
SQ3R method, 101
STDs (*See* Sexually transmitted diseases (STDs))
Sterilization, 234
Stern, Isaac, 120
Stress:
    adult students and, 189–190
    alcohol consumption and, 207, 225, 230
    counseling center and, 14, 217
    crime and, 210–212
    health and, 8, 204–205, 209
    identification of, 205–207, 219–220
    Internet and, 218
    money and, 212–215
    part-time enrollment and, 5
    relief of, 207–209, 220, 242
    symptoms of, 204, 205
    transition and, 8
Student activities office, 7
Student-teacher relationships (*See also* Instructors)
    attendance and, 44, 113
    communication and, 44, 112
    e-mail and, 47, 143
    initiation of, 7, 48
    problems with, 46
    romantic relationships, 46, 240
Students (*See also* Adult students; Commuter students; Minority students; Students with disabilities)
    alcohol consumption of, 224–225, 227–228
    computer use of, 6, 137–139
    diversity of, 188–189, 197–198
    e-mail use of, 6, 139, 145
    employment of, 5, 158, 180–181, 217
    expectations of, 8
    first-year, 7, 8, 9, 10, 11, 12
    gripes about parents, 183
    as mentors, 45
    parent gripes about, 184
    student development theory, 40
    support services for, 14
    transition to college, 8–9
Students of color (*See* Diversity; Minority students)
Students with disabilities, 14, 189, 190

Study groups:
    active learning and, 39
    collaborative learning and, 41–43
    exams and, 112, 113, 126–127
    learning style and, 52, 57
    study reading and, 100
    use of, 7
Study habits:
    development of, 6
    exams and, 112, 114–115
    forgetting and, 82
    grades and, 124
    mind maps and, 114, 115
    recall sheets and, 114
    study groups and, 7
    summaries and, 114
    time management and, 26, 27
Study reading:
    concentration and, 95, 96
    mapping and, 95, 102
    monitoring comprehension and, 97, 100
    overviewing and, 94–95, 102
    reading style adjustment, 100–101
    reviewing and, 100
    SQ3R method and, 101
    textbook marking and, 96, 97–100, 102–103
    textbook reading and, 6, 94, 96–97, 102–103
    understanding and, 96
    vocabulary development and, 101, 103–104
Study skills guides, 89
Success:
    critical thinking and, 9
    goals for, 13–14
    strategies for, 4–8
Summaries, 114, 127
Syllabus, 32, 58, 82
Systematic thinking, 69

T

T/F (Thinking/Feeling), 54, 57
Teacher-student relationships (*See* Student-teacher relationships)
Teachers (*See* Instructors)
Teaching style, 44, 53, 58–59, 62–63, 89
Term assignment preview, 23, 24, 30
Tests (*See* Exams; Grades)
Textbooks:
    high school/college differences in, 43, 94
    marking in, 96, 97–100, 102–103
    note taking and, 81
    reading of, 6, 94, 96–97, 102–103
Thinker, 54, 56
Time management:
    active learning and, 39
    cheating and, 111
    daily schedule and, 23, 25, 32–33
    exams and, 112, 115, 116
    financial aid and, 217
    goals and, 23, 27, 30
    instructors and, 44
    Internet and, 28
    learning and, 6
    learning style and, 22
    master plan and, 23
    planning and, 5
    priority setting and, 23, 27, 29–30
    transition and, 8
    weekly schedule and, 23–25, 30–31
    working with, 26–27
    writing and, 72
Tobacco, 231–232
Topics:
    for research, 131–132
    for writing, 70–71
True/false exams, 112, 118
Tutoring, 25, 113
Two-year colleges, 10, 227, 228

V

Values:
    academic advisors and, 156
    active learning and, 40
    career planning and, 159
    cheating and, 111
    computers and, 140
    critical thinking and, 67
    defining, 9–10
    diversity and, 190
    Internet and, 125
    learning style and, 56
    listening and, 83
    personal safety and, 211
    relationships and, 176
    sexuality and, 176, 233
    study reading and, 97
    time management and, 26
Victims, 212
Visual learning style, 52, 53, 58, 95
Vocabulary development, 101, 103–104
Voice mail, 39

W

Walster, Elaine, 175
Website addresses:
    academic honesty and, 125
    alcohol consumption and, 241
    career planning and, 165
    critical thinking and, 73
    diversity and, 196
    financial aid and, 217, 218
    instructors and, 47
    learning style and, 59
    memory and, 125
    procrastination and, 28
    relationships and, 182
    stress and, 218
    student population statistics and, 15
    study reading and, 102
    study skill guides, 89
    URLs and, 136, 144
Wechsler, Henry, 231
Weekly schedule, 23–25, 30–32
Wheel mapping, 95
Women:
    academic advisors and, 155
    as adult students, 189
    binge drinking and, 225
    enrollment figures for, 10
    HIV and, 237
    income of, 12
    sexual assault and, 176, 240
    stress and, 189–190
    tobacco use and, 232
Word processing, 71, 141, 148
Work-Study Program, 217
Workplace (*See also* Employment)
    college training and, 11
    technology and, 6, 10
World Wide Web (*See also* Internet; Website addresses)
    as information resource, 6, 135–137
    search strategies for, 136–137, 144
Writing:
    active learning and, 39
    critical thinking and, 66, 69–70, 74
    developing skills in, 6, 70–74
    study reading and, 100, 101
    word processing and, 71, 141, 148
Writing center, 14

Z

Zinsser, William, 69

We'd Like to Hear from You

Thank you for using *Your College Experience*, 4th Concise Media Edition. We care a lot about how you liked this book and how useful you found it. Please let us know how we can improve the next edition by returning this page with your comments, using the postage-free label on the other side. Or send us an e-mail message to *csuccess@wadsworth.com*. Either way, we'd like to hear your thoughts.

Overall, how valuable was the book as part of the course? Why? _____

_____

_____

_____

Which parts or exercises were particularly helpful? Why? _____

_____

_____

_____

Which parts or exercises should be changed? Why? _____

_____

_____

_____

Are there any topics not covered in the book that you think should be added? _____

_____

_____

_____

How else can we improve *Your College Experience*, Concise Media Edition? _____

_____

_____

_____

Thanks and good luck!

John Gardner   Jerry Jewler

Your name _____ School _____

Your address _____

City/State _____ Zip _____

Your instructor's name _____

May Wadsworth quote you, either in promotion for *Your College Experience* or in future publishing ventures?

Yes _____   No_____

FOLD HERE

TEAR PAGE OUT

FOLD HERE

BUSINESS REPLY MAIL
FIRST CLASS   PERMIT NO. 34   BELMONT, CA

POSTAGE WILL BE PAID BY ADDRESSEE

John N. Gardner / A. Jerome Jewler
Your College Experience, 4th Concise Media Edition
C/o College Success Editor
Wadsworth Publishing Company
10 Davis Drive
Belmont, CA 94002-9801